CANADA:
THE CASE FOR STAYING OUT
OF OTHER PEOPLE'S WARS

CANADA:
THE CASE FOR STAYING OUT OF OTHER PEOPLE'S WARS

*For all the unrecognized
and unappreciated who strive for peace*

WILLIAM S. GEIMER

CANADA: THE CASE FOR STAYING
OUT OF OTHER PEOPLE'S WARS

iUniverse books may be ordered through booksellers or by contacting:

iUniverse
1663 Liberty Drive
Bloomington, IN 47403
www.iuniverse.com
1-800-Authors (1-800-288-4677)

ISBN: 978-1-5320-1057-6 (sc)
ISBN: 978-1-5320-1059-0 (hc)
ISBN: 978-1-5320-1058-3 (e)

Print information available on the last page.

iUniverse rev. date: 12/05/2016

Contents

Introduction

This book presents the case for staying out of other people's wars. By other people's wars, I mean those in which Canada's national security, by any reasonable definition, is not measurably at risk. We will examine all of Canada's wars, assess their costs and benefits and consider the vision of a better role for Canada in the world.

This is a particularly important time for a rational conversation about Canada and her wars. We are remembering the centennial years of the Great War (1914-1918). The recent change in government provides an opportunity for this conversation that has not been possible for a decade. The years of the Harper government featured rigid information control and a relentless propaganda campaign in support of Canada as a warrior nation. The only message was that we achieved our national identity on the battlefields of the Great War. If that were true, it follows that Canada should not shrink from invitations to join armed conflicts. Indeed, she should be alert to new opportunities.

The new government of Justin Trudeau has tentatively expressed a different vision. Within 24 hours of coming to power, Trudeau notified the U.S. that Canada would withdraw its planes from the war in the Middle East. He was immediately subjected to criticism for this move, as well as for the decision to fast-track acceptance of Syrian refugees. The government, however, remained committed to the war and pledged to explore new ways to assist the latest coalition assembled by the U.S. This is the time for Canadians to look critically at our war history and be heard.

I am a trial lawyer. I present my case, not the case of my learned friends who promote Canada's continued involvement in other people's wars. Their case is not difficult to access and it is put by those with far greater resources than I. Consult any works of David Bercuson or Jack Granatstein.

The outcome of this case will have important consequences for us as a people. For example, if military action really is good for our position in the world, we must accept that we will always lack the capacity to be a major military power in our own right. That means we must ally ourselves with a strong military patron. That patron was once Great Britain and is now the United States. Attaching ourselves militarily to a patron requires ceding some of our sovereignty and independence in decision-making, thus yielding control of an important part of how we are perceived in the world. It also includes being, and being seen as, complicit in the human rights abuses of the patron.

We do well to remember also that any call to join in military action will be made on the basis of what the patron sees as its national interest, not ours. Persuading the Canadian public to accept such subservience requires, in turn, accepting the notion that we need the protection of the patron, and dealing with what the patron requires in return.

Why do people continue to support war in general, in spite of its poor record of benefits? Why does Canada in particular involve herself in other people's wars? An examination of Canada's wars suggests that there are recurring factors, each with characteristics and themes that begin to inform the answers to these questions. We will see that most of them appear each time Canada goes off to fight someone else's fight. These factors, individually and in combination, provide compelling reasons to stay out of any particular war. For that to happen, however, the factors must first be recognized and evaluated. It really does not matter whether the evaluation is done in a personal emotional manner or as a cold cost-benefit analysis. The war loses. But in reality, war always wins. And Canada, never under any realistic threat of invasion, continues to fight. Why?

In our look at Canada's wars, all fought on behalf of western powers, three of the factors tend to encourage all wars and promote popular support for them. These war-promoting factors are (1) the marriage of capitalism and imperialism, (2) propaganda and the failure of journalism, and (3) organized religion. In addition, four factors recur that could ordinarily be expected to discourage wars as a means of resolving international disputes and undermine public support for them---provided they could overcome the power and influence of the first three. The antiwar factors are (1) horror and senseless military deaths, (2) human rights violations and civilian deaths, (3) racism, and (4) peace movements. The problem is that the controllers of the war-promoting factors, including governments, business, and churches, have to date constituted such a powerful bloc that they have managed to minimize or hide these factors sufficiently to keep them from becoming part of a rational public dialogue.

Finally, five more factors appear that seem uniquely Canadian. Why they appear is not completely clear, but they may have evolved as part of a developing national character. These recurring characteristics in the story reflect our ambivalence about other people's wars and confirm that we are now indeed at a crossroads. Three tend to draw us toward war: (1) Canadians have demonstrated remarkable military skill and bravery despite poor foreign leadership. (2) The understandable longing of a young nation. As Pierre Berton put it: "the modicum of international acclaim we have always craved".[1] Canadians fight well and want others to recognize that. (3) The flawed structure of our democracy, which generally tilts the balance toward war, against rational public debate, and minimizes the influence of a majority of Canadians. This factor is particularly vulnerable to manipulation by a prime minister bent on exploiting the flaws.

This is the factor, however, with the potential for change. The flaws are not fatal. Our story also reveals two factors that point away from war: (4) Canada's decision to participate in war has often been a reluctant one. That reluctance has been expressed by national leaders, or the public, or both. (5) Our participation has been accompanied by a persistent desire to minimize losses.

You will see in our story of Canada's wars a disproportionate emphasis on the Great War. This war originated or brought into maturity many of the war-promoting factors as well as means of suppressing antiwar factors.

Like its leftover unexploded shells that killed people decades later, the Great War also gave the world latent international relations explosives that virtually ensured the coming of World War II. Beyond that, it provided a legacy of problems for the world in the 21st century, particularly in Africa, the Middle East, and Central Europe. No nation should define itself through its participation in any war, but certainly not this one. Nevertheless, this is the war that governments of Canada have chosen to celebrate and glorify. Whether we examine the reality of that war critically will seriously impact our reaction when the next call to arms comes—and the next.

As you note the appearance of all these factors in our story, and the facts that bring them to light, I invite you to analyze and evaluate their effect on the prevailing warrior nation narrative in the way that a good trial lawyer would urge if you were a member of a jury deciding an important case. Carefully consider the factual context of the evidence presented. Give weight to some parts of it, less or none to other parts. Know why you have made these choices. Be prepared to discuss the matter with your fellow jurors when you retire to deliberate.

In her opening statement, a good trial lawyer would offer you a detailed preview of the factors that she considered important for you to recognize and consider from the evidence in support of her case. I think that is a good way for us to begin.

War-Promoting Factors

1. The Marriage of Capitalism and Imperialism

We will see that nationally sanctioned armed violence has been employed in service to the international commercial interests of every combatant in Canada's wars. Britain, the power for whom Canada fought in her first three wars, was quite open about the function of armed imperialism in support of her version of capitalism. Industrialist Cecil Rhodes, who at one time virtually owned huge swaths of Africa, said *I would annex the planets if I could.*[2] General Sir Douglas Haig, commander of British ground forces in the Great War, said *I am not ashamed of the wars that were fought to open the markets of the world to our traders.*[3]

The successful union of capitalism and imperialism does not always have to involve raw conquest. Conquerors, after all, are left with some responsibilities toward the conquered populace. That can be a real headache. Rhodes developed a better model for his dealings with indigenous Africans. On one occasion, for example, he simply tricked the native monarch into granting trade concessions that in practice forfeited sovereignty. He then secured a royal charter and when there was trouble later, just brought in troops with superior weaponry to mow down the dissidents.

Rhodes' template has been of great utility to Canada's patrons in all her wars. We will see the terminology change from open imperialism to more benign sounding "protectorates," "colonies," "mandates," "areas of vital national interest" and the like. Whatever the terminology, governments tend not to describe the purported necessity for conflicts in economic terms. Rather, they cloak every call to violence and death in the highest moral, even religious language. We will see all combatants in Canada's wars claim they were forced into it despite their wish for peace. But the economic influence is always present and formidable. For example, without capitalist demands for military backing in contests over European resources, as well as paranoia over the emergence of a competing economic system, Bolshevism, there may well have been no World War II for Canada to join. The economic contest later became the Cold War and drew Canada into perhaps her most senseless conflict, the Korean War on behalf of her new patron, the U.S. Finally, the new patron's call to join the eternally futile effort to control Afghanistan may well be motivated as much by the competition for Central Asian natural resources as by the prospect of preventing people whose usual mode of transport is oxcart from finding more ways to fly airplanes into symbols of capitalism and the military. Therese Delpech, French diplomat and scholar, writing from a European perspective, captures the true nature of the values that continue to dominate international relations: *Despite all the speeches about the values of Europe, whom do we see in the airplanes of heads of state when they travel abroad but the representatives of stock market values?*[4] In addition to being told that we live in a "post-9/11 world," we are advised that everyone is now part of a "global economy." When we consider whether to be resigned to one or both of those conditions, we should recognize the mandate for violence implicit in them.

What is accepted as capitalism in any era has plainly been a driver of imperialism by whatever name and in whatever form. Without that combination, the world would have experienced far fewer wars.

Noting the many names and descriptions of capitalism and imperialism over the years alerts us to the powerful imagery of words. "Capitalism" and "imperialism," along with "socialism," "communism," and especially "terrorism," have in modern discourse become buzzword substitutes for thought, analysis, and communication. They have become virtually meaningless. The absence of definition has not prevented governments from imprinting in the public mind the superficial notion that capitalism equals good, socialism equals bad. Still, it is only fair to essay a few working definitions. University of Victoria professor John Price captures the relationship between capitalism and imperialism by defining imperialism as *a world system that produced and reproduces unequal relations between capitalist centres and peoples on the peripheries. Its existence is predicated on projection and protection of state powers.*[5]

It will be helpful to keep in mind that when governments speak of promoting "democracy" or responding to threats to it, closer examination often reveals that what they mean is capitalism.

Part of this semantic problem is that people advocating progressive positions often fail to appreciate that they are currently losing the battle over the power of word imagery. They rail against "international capitalist hegemony" and the evils of "multinational corporations," rather than naming the real human wrongdoers who control these entities.

Whatever its current state, this may well be the most important of the recurring factors that are part of the story of Canada's wars. Socialism was not always a dirty word and the struggle between those who proudly bore that label in the face of opposition from government officials and capitalists who held power is an essential part of the narrative of every war.

So I invite you to put aside your first reaction to buzzwords and aversion to hyperbole on both sides and follow the evolution of the marriage of capitalism and imperialism and its place in the story of the wars that Canada has embraced. Whatever one's economic views, it is undeniable that none of Canada's wars could have happened without that union.

2. Propaganda and the Failure of Journalism

Along with the marriage of capitalism and imperialism, this is the factor most influential in perpetuating war. I will use the term propaganda broadly to include both dissemination and suppression of information. Its importance lies less in the affirmative promotion of wars, though it certainly serves that function, than in preventing reasonable consideration of the antiwar factors. Propaganda cannot prevent some of the horrible reality of wars from getting through to the public, but it can deploy an effective counterweight: the message that none of the horrible deaths were senseless. In the world of war propaganda, nobody dies in vain. Without that message, the notion that Canada's experience in Flanders was glorious would be very difficult to sell. Neutralizing concern for civilian deaths requires only a slight variation in this message: their deaths were unfortunate, but necessary to achievement of a greater good. You will see also that wartime propaganda not only downplays the racist aspects of war, it affirmatively displays a degree of racism that would be the cause of great debate and even shame in peacetime. Finally, propaganda that appeals to patriotism, fuels fears of adversaries, and promotes an ethic of *machismo* is a powerful weapon against the voices of peace. We will see propaganda play an essential role in all of Canada's wars on the matters of how they started, how they have been conducted, and what happens when they end.

Most of the functions of propaganda will be discernible in the stories of each of Canada's wars. In the Boer War and the Great War, look in particular for propaganda as an affirmative tool to boost recruitment numbers. Propaganda came of age in the Great War and the full panoply is on display there, including rigid control of information and creative use of emerging media forms. During and after that war, we will also see it employed as a weapon against conscientious objectors and peace activists. The art of demonizing enemies was refined in the Great War and perfected in World War II. The overt racist propaganda that characterized the imperial era and both global wars became only slightly subtler in Korea and Afghanistan.

But as you read accounts of some propaganda that is so crude as to be almost laughable, do not assume that modern sophistication has eliminated it or diminished its impact. There is as much or more propaganda today as there ever was. There are more outlets for it, and it is just as powerful. There is a direct line of lies, half truths, and distortions from the Great War stories of Germans bayoneting Belgian babies to the current jihadis executing innocent civilians. These features are characteristic of every nation. It is as necessary for your country to demonize your supposed enemies as it is for theirs to demonize you. The Tory campaign to rebrand Canada as a warrior nation was but one example.

An essential part of your evaluation of this factor will include the performance of the media. The fourth estate has traditionally been assigned the role of principal check on government misinformation. Particularly in the story of the Boer War and the Great War, you will see some journalists performing that role admirably, even having some effect. From the beginning of war correspondents in the mid 19th century, there were individuals who got the truth out. The general picture you will see, however, is one of governments and businesses coercing or co-opting media into cooperation or at least silence. That task has been made easier in the latest conflicts because news is now more often presented as entertainment. The editorial decision to run with the story of brave Canadian forces constructing schools for girls in Afghanistan instead of an analysis of the reasons for blowing apart five civilians in order to kill one "militant" is an easy call. It is even easier because there is no need to lie, only to edit. The brave Canadians really are building schools for girls.

3. Organized Religion

Organized religions of all types have played a part in promoting wars. Organized Christianity has been the most important to western powers. Christian Canada fought against the Christian descendants of the Dutch in the Boer War and Christian Germans again in the next two. Oddly, organized Christianity was somewhat less strident in the war against nominally Shinto Japan in World War II. Korea comprised an amalgam of eastern religious traditions. Afghanistan is nominally a Muslim country. To some degree, all sides see a need to put God, by whatever name, on their team.

The influence of organized Christianity in promoting and sustaining western participation is not what it once was. Only in the first two wars did the church play the role of vigorous cheerleader. After the Great War, what the Canadian government has needed and received from the church has essentially been passive benediction, though we will see that it did call on a group of religious leaders to whitewash Canadian atrocities in Korea. Yet it is difficult to imagine that war making could have achieved the level of acceptance it has enjoyed absent some sort of government/church alliance.

At the outset, it is important to get Jesus, Muhammad, and Abraham out of the discussion. Real "fundamental" Christianity, Islam, and Judaism speak messages of peace, not war. Fanatics of all persuasions have found ways around that truth. Christians, for example, developed requirements for waging a "just war". Unfortunately, the Christian hierarchy has never decided that a war conducted by its country is unjust.

You will see that organized Christianity acted as an affirmative promoter of war at a time when the church had real influence over the lives and attitudes of ordinary people. From World War II on, it has been more difficult to assess its strength. That is in part because of the perpetual divide between hierarchy and laity. For example, in the run up to World War II Canada's United Church and other denominations abandoned their antiwar pronouncements almost before the ink was dry. Some ministers went on to condemn pacifism as a sin. Today, mainstream churches mostly ignore the issue, leaving it to traditional peace churches and fringe sects like Quakers, Mennonites, and Doukhobors. That is just fine with government.

Whatever the continuing force of organized religion today, it remains a useful tool in the effort to keep everyday people onside and acting against their interests. It continues at the very least as a significant factor in the ethical perspective of millions who do not darken the doors of churches. If pastors no longer scream from the pulpit for the enemy's blood, as you will see them do during the Great War, their acquiescence remains a significant war-promoting factor.

While the continued force of organized religion in support of war may be difficult to measure, the current danger of its influence over international powers should not be overlooked. Muslims and Jews cite religion as an excuse for violence—internal and external. No office seeker in Canada or the U.S. dares neglect to pay homage to God, generally understood to be the Christian version. It is the faction known as the "Christian right" that calls most loudly for war.

As you note the record of organized religion in the story of Canada's wars, evaluate the motives and methods of those who sought to add a divine dimension to the question of her participation. Is it still God we implore to keep our land glorious and free?

Antiwar Factors

These factors should give pause to anyone contemplating war. I invite you to consider what the impact might be if they were clearly understood and part of contemporary public discourse about Canada's past and future wars. You will see why it is important to supporters of military adventures that such conversations not occur.

1. Horror and Senseless Military Deaths

Public support for wars is dependent upon the ability of governments to conceal or dilute the impact of this factor. It is difficult to believe that anyone, surely including Canadians, would continue to spill blood if millions of senseless deaths and how they came about were thoughtfully considered. All of the war-promoting factors must operate to ensure public acceptance that soldiers have "fallen". They are resting peacefully in the knowledge that they and their comrades fought to achieve the lofty purpose for which they had made the supreme sacrifice. This image dishonours the memory of those who died. We will see that most who went off to war did not go for King or Queen and Country. They joined up for far more mundane, human, and understandable reasons. Most did not fight for the lofty ideals trumpeted by political leaders.

Paradoxically, it is the Great War that most clearly gives lie to the fiction of the "fallen". Canadians, and millions of others, did not fall. Usually they died filthy and wet, watching rats eat the body parts of their closest friends. They died in similar fashion in Korea. They died of disease in South Africa. They were blown to bits at Dieppe and in Kandahar. Many died protecting one another. They did not die to protect liberty, democracy, justice, et cetera. This is a hard truth and a very painful one for families of the dead. I take no pleasure in stating it. But the lives and futures of young men and women depend on challenging the eloquent call to arms in the final verse of *In Flanders Field*.

The image of the fallen hero dying nobly for the greater good is the way all wars are sold, even when the number of deaths is comparatively low, as it was for Canada in South Africa, Korea, and Afghanistan. The official message was not that soldiers had fallen in support of a British struggle over someone else's gold, or in service of U.S. Cold War paranoia, or revenge for the 9/11 attacks. When Canadians suffered massive casualties in the Great War, the message was not that the casualties were incurred in an effort to influence the outcome of a petty imperial squabble that got horribly out of hand.

But even facing this painful reality is not enough. Awareness of the truth about how tens of thousands of Canadians have met death over the years in Canada's wars apparently does not itself give us pause to consider that perhaps we should have stayed out. Much of that truth is now easily accessible and has been for some time. We have become inured to the accounts of horror. We have honed our ability to ignore and compartmentalize.

I will try in these pages to capture some of the horror behind the statistics. I hope you will consider it, not only for its visceral impact but also in the context of how senseless and unnecessary it was.

2. Human Rights Violations and Civilian Deaths

I link these matters for two reasons. I consider all civilian deaths from war to be human rights violations. We will see particularly in Canada's wars not only complicity with the patron, especially in World War II, but also direct participation in these violations. Canadians have been guilty of exploiting the vulnerability of civilians and perpetrating abuses that sink to the level of crimes.[6]

Any honest evaluation of our past wars and decisions about future ones should involve consideration of this factor. I doubt that Canadians would come down on the side of killing people whose crime was being in the wrong place at the wrong time. Consequently, it is quite important that war supporters employ their resources to minimize the impact of this factor. We must not be allowed to picture our own children being destroyed from the air because of something someone decided, correctly or not, that their father had done. We must not be allowed to picture our own houses raided and family members murdered or turned over to torturers.

Respecting the killing of civilians from afar, the Great War brought a sea change in the manner of war making that has thereafter spelled death for the innocent on a previously unimagined scale. That war inaugurated the general acceptance of making war on civilians and it was the first to provide the technology that continues to enable such a war to be conducted with detached efficiency. Thérèse Delpech is one of many who point to the gap between ethics and ability. She puts the issue quite succinctly: *Another cause for the return of barbarism in the twentieth century has been the growing gap between the progress of science and technology and the absence of comparable progress in the ethical realm...Industrial methods revolutionized war in 1914, and as early as 1918 they made possible the most monstrous forms for the organization of societies and camps.*[7]

In spite of this insight, Delpech reflects the same myopia that generally inhibits rational public debate about this factor. She is concerned about it only because of the destruction of civilians by *the other side*. None of the events she uses to illustrate the harm wrought by the ethics/technology gap are actions of western allies. Her targets from the past are the Germans, Soviets, Chinese, and Japanese. Her forecast for this century targets the Chinese, North Koreans, Russians, and terrorists.[8] The past outrages are real, to be sure. But it is difficult to understand how an intellectual such as she can miss the greater ethical issue raised by the examples she omits. If *they* are doing all this, should *we* do likewise? If yes, is there any difference between *us* and *them* save that our cause is always "just" and theirs is not?

Should we ever get around to discussing this important factor, one of the first things we will note is a meticulous counting of military deaths so that all the fallen can be honoured and celebrated as heroes, whatever the circumstances of their death. In contrast, we will see that the number of deaths of those who had no weapons — deaths of children, mothers, and the elderly, are almost always only estimated, if they are mentioned at all. There is no effort to name them, much less call attention to any who may have accomplished heroic things. The wars that are said to mark Canada's emergence were the first to bless war on civilians, who in the earlier history of warfare had fared somewhat better.

This is the pattern for dealing with military and civilian deaths, even though by the most conservative estimates many more civilians than soldiers have died in Canada's wars. An honest discussion of the more complex ethical issues, the questions raised by consideration of our actions as well as those of our adversaries, would likely give this antiwar factor greater weight as a reason for Canada to stay out of other people's wars. That conversation would have to include, for example, not just the German murder of Belgians in the Great War, the German death camps, the Holocaust, and the bombing of Britain in World War II. It would include British concentration camps in the Boer War, the British naval blockade that starved Germans even after the signing of the Great War armistice, Allied bombing of Berlin, Dresden, Tokyo, and the ultimate horror of Hiroshima and Nagasaki. We would be required to debate our latest ground war in Afghanistan, where the generals assured us that every effort was made to minimize civilian casualties, but where there was much "collateral damage". We would have to demand more than the standard denial that Canadians in the ill-considered current air war in Iraq and Syria are killing civilians.[9] Finally, we might also have to direct some attention to drone strikes currently doing the sanitized job of extraterritorial and extrajudicial killing of suspected terrorists — and a few nearby unlucky civilians.

A national debate on this matter should include this position: No Killing Civilians. No Exceptions. If a planned military operation will result in civilian deaths, cancel the operation.

3. Racism

This important factor involves more than difference in skin colour. To be sure, that difference has been sufficient to produce overt violent action. But we will see the use of the difference as only a starting point for more nuanced varieties. There are several examples of paternal racism, actions and policies based on the assumption that the "other" are naïve and childlike, unable to make their own decisions. There are even examples of white versus white racism, based on some sort of perceived evolutionary gap.

Price again offers definitions that will be helpful as we trace the factor in Canada's wars: **Racism** *refers to an ideology that asserts a group's superiority or inferiority based on physical appearance, ethnicity, or culture. It usually involves the capacity to dominate.* **Race** *refers to social relations that have been defined by reference to it and have thereby become social constructions, reflections of power relations.* **Racialization** is the process of constructing race.[10]

The story of Canada's wars includes appallingly racist actions, by the military, and particularly by the federal government and the government of British Columbia, all ignored or enthusiastically supported by a majority of the public. Apologies came later, but there is no record of anyone in power owning up to racism at the time. There was always another explanation.

Neither does anyone want to admit that racial considerations make it easier to make war. That is part of why there has been little scrutiny of the reasons Canada's adversaries have so often been people of colour. The legacy of racism we have helped to create would likely put this factor squarely in the antiwar column. At the very least, we would want to know if race played any part in the next invitation from our patron. The factor is not difficult to identify. It was clearly a part of the Boer War, where Canada has the honour of having helped establish the system of apartheid which created untold misery that continued for 90 years. Even if we assume that the ethnic variety of racism was a less influential factor in the Great War and World War II, we should not ignore what we helped to bring about in the rest of Africa, the Middle East, and Asia in relation to those conflicts. Korea, Afghanistan, and the bombing campaigns in Libya, Iraq and Syria continue the pattern.

Unlike other antiwar factors, it has not been necessary for governments to work very hard at suppressing consideration of this one. Denial on this matter has long been deeply ingrained in our collective psyche. A further obstacle is the difficulty of determining the place of racism in wars among other motivations. Reaction to seeing comrades die horribly at the hands of an adversary, for example, may partially explain war crimes, maltreatment of civilians, and other human rights excesses. But what is it about the particular difference of race among us that seems to evoke an added measure of the worst within us? Why has racism been a continuing element of Canada's wars?

I do not lay the blame entirely at the door of the capitalism/imperialism union, though racism has been very helpful to economic conquest. It was not by accident that Africa was the site of the Boer War, other military rehearsals for the Great War, and of post-war "protectorates". Particular strains of racism lend themselves well to the human characteristic of self-deception. Many influential figures among the western powers either truly believed or talked themselves into believing that they were bringing a superior civilization to people of colour in Africa and Asia, in spite of overwhelming evidence that they were doing no such thing and often displacing arguably superior societies.

Whatever the connection to other factors, the evidence is overwhelming that the racism that resides in all of us is particularly manifested in time of war. The epithets "huns," "chinks," "japs," "gooks," "slopes," and "ragheads," spoken casually by otherwise decent soldiers are unbroken links in the chain of warfare we examine. The terms also reflect the attitudes of those who sent the troops.

Confronting the factor could help cast participation in some past wars as a mistake and work to caution us against future involvements, but mass denial makes addressing the role of racism a challenge.

4. Peace Movements

The success of peace movements would, of course, be the ultimate antiwar factor. A dedicated minority of Canadians has always opposed our participation in wars. Its members were particularly prominent and even somewhat effective in the period after the Great War and in the 1930s. In the story of these individuals and peace groups, we will see that the question is not just why their position did not prevail. Of equal importance is the story of how they were not afforded a fair opportunity to be heard.

To be sure, many of the wounds suffered by peace advocates were self-inflicted, though quite understandably so. A diverse group, with diverse goals and priorities and without access to the machinery of government, the movement encountered impediments common to all coalitions. Indeed, looking back at the Canadian peace movement and its British counterpart is at times like looking in on Parliament's question period on a particularly bad day.

Some opponents of our wars were religiously motivated pacifists, though there is scarcely enough consensus on the meaning of that term to determine accurately how many. In this group were people from fringe denominations as well as mainstream churches. The peace positions of many others had secular ethical roots, influenced by but not grounded in religion. From both groups came conscientious objectors. From both groups also came those who saw a link between peace and a diverse list of social justice issues, from women's suffrage to temperance to decent wages. Among them were those who saw this link in overall economic terms. As early as 1919, J.S. Woodsworth, a minister and Canada's most famous pacifist political figure, identified the capitalism/imperialism factor as war-promoting. He emphasized that the people's enemy was not just capitalism. It was capitalism in league with militarism and imperialism, producing a deadly mixture that caused war.[11] Picture all these people in a room trying to determine what actions to take, where, and in what order, and you have a glimpse of the collective difficulty of peace movements.

Government, business, and organized religion aggravated the difficulties inherent in peace coalitions. During Canada's wars, for no legitimate reason, governments destroyed free speech. At one point, the federal government specifically criminalized any statements that "could weaken the country's spirit." Conscientious objectors were imprisoned. The government shamefully manipulated the democratic process by disenfranchising conscientious objectors, "persons of German speech", and naturalized citizens. Corporate leaders happily employed police and military supplements to their own teams of thugs and violently put down labour demonstrations. Propaganda stirred people not only to shame those who declined to enlist, but also to condone and encourage brutal treatment of them. As noted, mainstream churches reversed their proclamations in support of peace, defrocked pacifist ministers, and railed from the pulpit against peace advocates. They preached that, as the government had the right to suppress peace propaganda, so the church had the right to prevent unpatriotic sermons and could not condone the "sin of unpatriotic speech."[12]

Although the story of World War II era peace activists and Canada includes many of the oppressive measures employed by government in earlier campaigns, the relationship between the two adversaries improved. We will see that there was in fact a good deal of constructive dialogue that could serve as a model for improving the current relationship. This is perhaps an indication that some progress might be made now. If non-involvement in wars becomes a real possibility, there is much that peace advocates would offer to help make an alternative course successful.

The greatest obstacle to the success of past peace movements, however, was created by the connection between peace and social justice issues that brought advocates of each into coalition. Their joint concern over poverty and working conditions handed the coercive element of capitalism and imperialism a potent weapon, one it would put to good use for a very long time. During the Great War, millions of working people and many peace activists saw the Russian revolution as a beacon of hope. It was at the time the only alternative with the authority of a government behind it to the prevailing Dickensian reality. From its very first day, the revolution panicked capitalist governments, including Great Britain and Canada. We will see that Canadian and British troops were sent immediately after the defeat of Germany in the Great War to intervene in the Russian Civil War that followed the revolution. As would be the case in Korea, the troops had no idea why they were fighting. Some Canadian units mutinied. Still fearful, the governments backed off and regrouped to fight another day in another way.

Their opportunity came in the mid 1920s, the high water mark of global peace movements. In light of the horror and stupidity of the Great War and the capitalist-induced Great Depression that brought on the "Dirty Thirties" in Canada, the peace/justice coalition might have had some prospect of success. That success did not come, in significant part because of two disastrous developments. The first was the accession to power of Joseph Stalin in1926. He hijacked the legitimate aspirations of workers and peasants and turned Russia into a police state dictatorship that was as brutal as that of the Tsars. Second, too many peace and justice people were too slow to appreciate the significance of these events.

Just at a time when economics driven imperialism was beginning to show some fraying edges, these developments enabled capitalists and colonialists to recover. In fact, they were able to associate efforts of those pursuing peace and basic labour rights with "godless, totalitarian communism" for more than sixty years. The ability of western governments to link peace efforts to oppressive communism served them magnificently right up to the recent past, when they replaced the communists with the "terrorists."

Government propaganda and oppression, along with the general messiness inherent in loose associations of well-meaning people provide some of the reasons the peace movement did not win out. But being stuck with the stigma of the Soviets, however unfairly, was the most massive blow.

We will see how the red scare wasted Canadian lives in the Korean War. Also, how it brought millions much closer to nuclear annihilation than most people realize.

As we examine these events, you may be tempted to conclude that all the overt oppression and stifling of voices of peace occurred in the past and we are free now to conduct openly that conversation about our future. Perhaps. Perhaps not. Consider, for example, how former defence minister Peter MacKay vilified anyone who criticized any course other than demonizing our purported enemies. More broadly, consider how the last government's actions in the latest war, the "global war on terror" deprived all Canadians, not just war opponents, of privacy and significantly damaged our sense of community. Have the obstacles to a fair debate disappeared, or simply been adapted? Will we be able to have a free and open conversation about our past wars and our proper place in the world community? That is up to us.

Uniquely Canadian Factors

The story of Canada's wars reveals factors that highlight the importance of engaging in a national conversation. These factors appear to be uniquely Canadian and putting them into the mix complicates considerably any explanation of why we go to war at all, as well as whether and how we will do so again.

Two of the factors that characterize our experience suggest that we are likely to continue on the current path. But two give hope that we can choose another role on the world stage. Where we go may ultimately be determined by a fifth factor.

Canadian War-Promoting Factors

1. Military Skill and Bravery Despite Poor Leadership

Canadian commanders have sometimes provided poor leadership, but its most deadly source has been commanders from our patron nations. Canadian forces have been subject to dreadful foreign command decisions including the Boer War in which the British had no idea of how to engage in unconventional warfare; the almost criminal leadership of General Douglas Haig and others in the Great War; the deadly experimental raid at Dieppe and the Hong Kong debacle in World War II; the arrogance of American General Douglas MacArthur and the ineptitude of American politicians in Korea. The pattern continued with a senseless trickle of deaths brought on by misguided American leadership in Afghanistan.

Yet Canadians in all of these conflicts, though often undertrained and underequipped, have distinguished themselves. Consider their performance, as well as examples of outstanding Canadian leadership such as that provided by General Arthur Currie in the Great War, and who would not be justifiably proud? That pride might simply be channeled into honouring those who suffered and died to fashion such a remarkable record, but it is too often co-opted and used as a tool in support of future wars.

2. Longing for Recognition

We are a new nation. That we appreciate public praise from nations that are older and more powerful is quite understandable. But the story of Canada's wars is a story of sacrificing far too much for that praise. More than once, when Canada had no important interest at stake, she has allowed herself to be led along by superficial accolades.

Particularly in World War II, when at a turning point on the issue of a truly independent identity, Canada deferred too often to the decisions of patrons. We will see times when Canada did assert herself, but the human cost of the times she did not has been staggering. That cost is not only measured in dead and wounded. Canada has also deferred to the questionable moral and ethical decisions of others.

These two Canadian war-promoting factors are, of course, related. After all, it was real skill and bravery that our patrons were praising. And as they strove to keep Canada onside they might have been motivated to be even more effusive by the knowledge that their commanders had often led poorly. Nevertheless, at difficult points in the transition of dominance from the British to the Americans, it was not the responsibility of these patrons to assess the proper role of Canada. It was and is solely a Canadian responsibility. The record on that is far from perfect. We will see Dieppe as but one example of a longing for recognition that prompted a campaign for Canada to be a player in any operation conceived by her patrons, at any cost.

The confluence of Canadian war-promoting factors is not the result of any dark conspiracy by Canada's leaders, patrons, or anyone else. It came about because of who and where we were in the world at the time of each of our wars. That is all the more reason they should be recognized and evaluated as we go forward.

Canadian Antiwar Factors

1. Reluctant Participation

Either we have simply learned some lessons from participating in other people's wars, or there really is something in the Canadian national character that is unenthusiastic about war. Whatever the reason, Canada has never been an eager war maker. This has been true even though the war-promoting factors, especially propaganda, have moved the public to support them enthusiastically at times, at least until things started to go badly.

If our reluctance to participate is a characteristic, it has been reflected over decades in the personalities of prime ministers. In the heyday of imperialism, Wilfrid Laurier would not spend public money for the Boer War. While the ties to Britain were still strong, he sought compromises to limit our involvement in the Great War. Even his Tory successor, Robert Borden, initially sought to provide only naval support. More importantly, Borden began to learn. Though he eventually led Canada into the war, after the slaughter at Passchendaele he is said to have warned the British not to count on us in the future. After the war, he worked for disarmament and in support of the League of Nations. William Lyon Mackenzie King was openly reluctant to take us into World War II. It was in no small measure due to the personalities of Lester Pearson, Pierre Trudeau, and Jean Chretien that Canada was spared the futile blood baths of Vietnam and Iraq.

Standing in contrast to these leaders at times of important decision making about war was only Stephen Harper, who made following the Americans into Afghanistan a priority. His alliance with the U.S. and the blind support of the two for Israel is a costly reminder of Canadian propensity to answer the call of her U.S. patron.

The attitude of most prime ministers does not entirely explain our usual reluctance. But the reluctance is real. In fact, we will see instances when outside events not directly connected to war were instrumental in overcoming our reluctance and drawing us in.

2. Desire to Minimize Casualties

As best exemplified by World War II, once drawn into a conflict Canadians have taken the approach that they may as well participate enthusiastically. At the same time, the course taken by both governments and individuals has made the desire to minimize casualties a distinctly Canadian characteristic.

Here again, lessons learned may be part of the explanation. In World War II, for example, most volunteers, knowing what they did about the Great War, chose to serve anywhere but in the infantry. At higher levels, even including the ego-driven world of military leadership, lessons were learned. It is true that some Canadian as well as British and American generals apparently valued career advancement more than protecting those in their charge. We will see, however, that Canadian leaders usually demonstrated more real concern that the lives of their people not be wasted. Finally, the record is clear that our political leaders have almost always sought a way to participate that, while sufficiently raising our international profile, would keep our casualty total comparatively low.

These two antiwar factors are also interrelated. Is there something in them that helps to explain why so many Canadians still see us as a nation of peacekeepers, even though we have not done peacekeeping for years? We will examine that subject in the final chapters.

The Deciding Factor?

The prime minister's announced that Canada would fight in Afghanistan before parliamentary debate began is but one example of perhaps the most important factor in Canada's future war decisions: flaws in the structure of her democracy.

A journalist wrote that Ottawa is a democracy theme park. If that is not entirely true, it is only a slight exaggeration. Canada elects her leaders through an inherited first past the post system. One scholar dates it from the 12th century.[13] In 19th century England it once produced a riding with a unique twist on the "one person one vote" theme. Year after year, a village with one voter sent one MP to Parliament.

Whatever the general demographic or democratic merits of a parliamentary system, Stephen Harper's government revealed its vulnerability to abuse. In the Harper years, Canadians were unable to put into effect their characteristic reluctance to make war. Government structure permitted imposition of what it is not too extreme to term a dictatorship.[14] There is no mechanism to prevent a manipulative prime minister from doing what he or she wishes.

The personalities and positions of a prime minister and his cabinet do and should have an appreciable impact in a fair debate. But the dictatorship of Stephen Harper was in part the result of a structural problem that badly needs to be addressed.

We will analyze the problem further in the final chapter, and review examples of government exploitation of the issue.

These flaws need not be fatal to an honest national debate about war and our position in the world, an exchange that could give us a new vision of our history and ourselves. In the near term, advocates of a new role can increase their numbers, amplify their voices, and offer alternatives. In the final chapter, we will examine some means of being heard and some alternatives in support of a new vision.

In the trial of the metaphorical case we are considering, the opening statement of counsel might conclude: *Members of the jury, what should your verdict be? Will an honest examination of the factors that have influenced Canada's involvement in other people's wars reveal important reasons that we should have stayed out of them? Will it show the costs outweighing the benefits? Will it refute the policy of joining others in violence as a guide for the future? In my respectful submission, it will do all those things. Let us proceed to the evidence.*

Chapter I

THE BOER WAR: FIRST AND FOOLISH

The factors we are examining appear in bold relief in the story of the Boer War. Their appearance in this poorly remembered South African adventure previews many aspects of the world conflagration that soon followed:

* It was the quintessential example of the union of capitalism and imperialism.

* Canada's participation allied her with gross human rights abuses and civilian deaths.

*As it was a white on white, Christian versus Christian war, it was necessary that churches and the government machinery of propaganda play a major supporting role. They did that.

* The racist assumptions underlying the conflict were deplorable. The actual treatment of Africans was far worse.

The common reaction to the Boer War by Canadians, if they recall it at all, is "Well, you have to understand that we were part of the British Empire". That is perhaps some explanation. But when the war ended, a realistic assessment of the costs and benefits to Canada might very well have kept her out of the global slaughter that would erupt little more than a decade later. Such an assessment might have identified the influence of the war-promoting factors in play.

Uniquely Canadian antiwar factors were also apparent in the story of Canada's participation in this little war. The imperial expedition to South Africa was the first war in which Canadians fought overseas

1

as Canadians. It was also arguably the most foolish. Perhaps an understanding of just how little Canada had at stake is at least part of the reason for the appearance of the Canadian antiwar factors. Our participation could have been more extensive and more costly absent the reluctance of the prime minister and the ruling party. The relatively small size of our expeditionary force reflected the desire to minimize casualties. Many of the troops were privately financed volunteers. In spite of poor British leadership, Canadian troops were far better at the kind of war they were called upon to fight than were the British. We were delighted when the British belatedly praised their performance.

Incidentally, we begin with the Boer War because the War of 1812 was not a Canadian war. That one was a bloody boundary adjustment between the British and their breakaway American colony. The half million "Canadians" were British, disaffected Americans, and original inhabitants caught between the two. Absolutely essential to what the British were able to gain in the adjustment was the participation of First Nation warriors led by Shawnee Chief, Tecumseh. The chief was certainly not fighting to establish Canada. He wanted a united native entity, free from white oppression and his earlier experiences had led him to believe that the British were a better choice than the Americans. As it turned out, his choice did not matter. For First Nations, both sides had rigged the game against them.[1]

The War of 1812 was as senseless as those that followed. The conflict also revealed some of the nascent Canadian antiwar factors. It settled nothing that could not have been settled without it, though it did adjust some borders in areas that were destined in any event to develop as separate countries. Canadians are fortunate that the war marked the point where the two big powers got tired of fighting one another. It was always up to them to make that decision.

Pre-War Canada and Britain: Parallel Political Struggles - Imperialism Prevails

Any understanding of the Boer War requires a bit of elementary reference to its background. Canada's mother country was at the height of her imperial glory in the years leading up to this war. Although Canada by 1897, the year of Queen Victoria's lavish Diamond Jubilee, was well along the road to autonomy, it is understandable that the two peoples shared a similar approach to world affairs. At least that was true of English Canadians. They eagerly bought the solemn pronouncements of their Protestant churches that every war fought by the British was a just war.[2]

Nevertheless, the leaders of the two countries would each find in the ranks of their governments some opposition to this war, and the more horrific one for which it served as a dress rehearsal.

In Britain, Benjamin Disraeli and William Gladstone alternated as prime minister in the late 19th century. The contest was between Queen Victoria and Disraeli on one side, and Gladstone and the memory of Victoria's beloved consort Prince Albert on the other.[3] In Canada, it was between Wilfred Laurier, elected the country's first French-Canadian prime minister in 1896, and a friend, Henri Bourassa from Quebec, whom he had recruited to run for a seat in Parliament and who became the voice of French speaking Canada.[4] For the public, the tension represented by the sides in Britain was between the intoxication of imperialism and the sobering truth that its material fruits were denied most of the population, who lived in appalling poverty and degradation.[5] In Canada it was between the imperialist loyalties of English Protestant Canadians, opposed by French Catholic Canadians whose aspirations for their country understandably did not include blind support of the British.[6]

Had Victoria not been queen and had not psychiatry been in its infancy in her time, she might have been in danger of involuntary commitment. In 1861, the 20th year of her reign, Prince Albert died. For the rest of her life, she wore mourning clothes and engaged in eccentric behavior, including having his wardrobe laid out daily and

3

otherwise pretending that he still lived. She had depended on him for everything, which may partially explain her need to keep him alive in some form.

Unfortunately, what Victoria was not able to preserve was Albert's worldview. His was a more enlightened imperialism, holding that might should serve right, and he had a vision of improving the lives and education of ordinary people around the world. After his death, the question of whether his more benign vision would be the main influence on Victoria or whether she would succumb to the call to raw power was played out in the contests between Disraeli and Gladstone. Disraeli was a Conservative Party imperialist. Gladstone a Liberal who shared Albert's vision and was determined to keep Britain out of pure conquest. The two would alternate as prime minister for over 15 years. Disraeli, and war, won out.

One strain of Canadian imperialism was a bit different. In a study of the years leading up to the Boer War and the Great War, [7] Carl Berger saw Canadian imperialism as a form of nationalism. In the view of its advocates, Canada supported the Empire in order to establish a more important, even dominant place within it. Independence was not a realistic option. It would mean living under the shadow of the powerful British. Even living under U.S. protection, as one writer put it, Canada would be like a kept woman, living "a harlot's independence."[8]

In Berger's portrait of Canadian imperialists are also interesting aspects of the factors we are examining. They include an ethnic variety of racism that assumes a special ability to govern inherent in the "Anglo-Saxon race". Apparently, climate as well as genetics produced this remarkable trait. It resided in those living in northern climes and their descendants. The view was, as Emerson wrote, "Wherever snow falls, there is usually civil freedom".[9]

Canada was also said to be blessed by her French/English mix with a harmonious blend in service of militarism. Grace and cheerfulness were inherent in the French; drive and will in the Anglo-Saxons. The two "races" shared a "birthright of military spirit derived from long lines of warlike ancestry".[10]

Regardless of these imperial nuances, the practical result was the same. Canada went to war when Britain called. But Berger's outline of the context in which Canadians sought to define their role at the time is valuable to understanding how the contest between Laurier and Bourassa differed from that between Disraeli and Gladstone.

Laurier and Bourassa were initially of one mind that British designs on the Boers were part of a petty tribal conflict in which Canada need have no part. Laurier, however, though sincerely and desperately trying to hold together a new country, eventually relented. He was a Canadian nationalist with respect for the mother country, yet he was perhaps the first of our leaders to see international matters from a Canadian perspective. Nevertheless, the combination of imperialist sympathy, propaganda, and religion captured the public imagination and overwhelmed his wise initial position. Laurier had also made a promise to the British that he probably came to regret. He had been feted at the Diamond Jubilee, given a knighthood and a carriage right behind that of the queen in the parade through London. At a reception, he made a florid promise that if England were ever in danger, the colonies would do whatever was required to help her.[11] Two years later, though England was certainly not in any danger, Victoria called in that pledge.

Since Canada's choice was, as it always is, not whether to lead but whether to follow, the deciding drama was the Disraeli/Gladstone contest. Victoria had lost interest in everything upon Albert's death. While Disraeli was prime minister, he revived her spirits with charming personal and affectionate letters as a substitute for the stiff formal reports he was required by protocol to make. The letters included flattery and a romanticized version of the Empire. When Gladstone was in and it was his turn to report, his liberal views did not sit well with Victoria. She was, well, Victorian—horrified, for example, by moves toward female equality.

Disraeli's flattery also included encouraging the queen to come out of her shell and take a greater role in public affairs. And the struggle between Disraeli and Gladstone was not simply a mismatch of charm skills. All Gladstone could offer was an appeal to justice and a comparatively enlightened view of empire, similar to that of her beloved Alfred. Disraeli managed concrete additions to the empire, the most significant of which was the Suez Canal—trade lifeline and passage to the Jewel in the Crown—India.

In 1875 when the canal's owners, the ruler of Egypt and French investors, got into difficultly they offered it for sale and a bidding war began. Britain was not in a financial position to compete but Disraeli, with Victoria's blessing, pledged the full faith and credit of the country as collateral and secured funding from Baron Rothschild. The queen was pleased. Securing the canal would prompt Victoria to opt for investiture as Empress of India in 1876 in a grand ceremony that stoked public support for aggressive imperialism. More importantly, British jitters in the future about the security of the canal would soon be the focal point for bloody involvement in Africa. The jitters would surface again in 1956, when the diplomacy of Canadian Lester Pearson averted significant bloodshed—a story we will later visit. In the late 19th century, however, the imperial vision of getting to the canal via a railway running the length of the continent would cost many lives, some of them Canadian.

The canal gave the British a great advantage, as all the European powers were competing for African territory and commercial dominance. One example illustrates not only another chapter in the Disraeli/Gladstone struggle but also the triumph of propaganda, even over religion. The Turks, whose aging Ottoman Empire still controlled much of North Africa, were massacring their Christian population. Disraeli, however, feared encroachment by Russia if the Turks were weakened. He took a position reminiscent of current western backing of Middle East dictators like the military rulers of Egypt and Saudi Arabia. Disraeli argued that Britain had to back the Turks in the name of "stability" no matter what they were doing to their people. Gladstone, a powerful orator, came out of retirement and for a time gained attention with accounts of Turkish atrocities. Disraeli, with the backing of the queen, countered by demonizing the Russians. The British already considered themselves superior to the Russians, having defeated them in the Crimean War of 1854-1855.

Disraeli even gained public support for another war. Fortunately, the Russians asked for negotiations and diplomacy won out. Victoria continued to back Disraeli and made him an Earl.

Gladstone did have a curtain call, but his reluctance to back aggressive imperialism in Africa finally did him in. After the British waged war on the Zulus and with superior weaponry and slaughtered 10,000 of them, his powerful appeals to justice swept the Liberals back into power. Victoria refused to see him. The final undoing of Gladstone came when his concern for fairness prompted him to back revolutionaries in Sudan instead of a stable but despotic government. A popular general got himself trapped in the war. Gladstone, like Laurier in the war to come, was hesitant to send troops and sought compromise. By the time he relented, the general had been killed by rebels and was glorified at home as an even greater hero. Gladstone lost the next election and the way was clear for unlimited imperialism in Africa.[12]

Final Warm Up

Consistent with the well known propensity of the British officer corps to view war as a sporting event[13], there would be one more practice session for the conflict that would a short time later include Canadians. Sudan would again be the practice field. This session introduced some of the major players in Canada's next *two* wars. Practice included use of an alarming new development in weapons technology—the machine gun.

In 1898, Sudan was still not behaving in a properly subservient manner. The British sent a large contingent of troops, along with some journalists. The entourage included two officers, Major General Sir Horatio Herbert Kitchener and Major Douglas Haig. In the Boer War, Kitchener would qualify in the eyes of many as a war criminal. In the Great War, Haig, a solid believer in the unity of imperialism and capitalism, would be an extravagant spender of lives. The journalists included Rudyard Kipling and future British wartime prime minister, Winston Churchill, who would all be valuable assets in the propaganda effort.[14]

The "battle" of Omdurman, burnished the reputations of Kitchener, Haig, and Churchill. Of the 50,000 Sudanese, armed with spears and obsolete rifles, the new British Maxim machine gun managed to kill almost 11,000 and severely wound 6,000 more. The British lost 48 men. The Germans, who had also wielded machine guns in their tardy efforts at African imperialism, watched this development, and later others in the Boer War, with interest. They also failed to appreciate the impact of the change heralded by the new weaponry. Many in British and German leadership anticipated a future war between the two countries. That they were blind to the devastation that modern weaponry would wreak in that war may be partly attributable to the racism that is inherent in imperialism. The sight of mowing down blacks apparently did not evoke an image of the same scene in a future white on white encounter. [15]

Rhodes and Milner: The War's Most Powerful Faces of Capitalism, Imperialism, and Racism

The persons most responsible for precipitating the Boer War were civilians who were not present at Omdurman. They were fortune seeker Cecil Rhodes, who would become arguably the most dangerous man in the Empire, and Sir Alfred Milner, appointed in 1897 to be High Commissioner to South Africa. While the views of the two conveniently overlapped, Milner was primarily the aggressive imperialist, impatient with any political delay in expanding the reach and rule of the Empire. His refusal to compromise on any matter that he saw as even a minor impediment to British supremacy during peace negotiations with the Boers prolonged the war and the dying. Rhodes was all for imperialism also, but primarily for economic reasons. By the time of the war, he had created two colonies of his own, named after himself. They were subsidiaries of his own Crown Company, complete with their own private army, police force, and armed paddleboat navy.[16] Rhodesia would become Zimbabwe in 1980. The legacy of imperialism there has provided the excuse for massive corruption and a campaign of white-hating racism employed by president Robert Mugabe. Rhodes was not averse to politics. He was even elected prime minister of the Cape Colony. But the primary use of imperial politics for Rhodes was to facilitate making money. The two men embodied the union of capitalism and imperialism.

Rhodes and Milner were in complete agreement that overt racism based on colour was an essential ingredient of each of the main interests they sought to further. In addition to his famous quote *I would annex the planets if I could,* Rhodes once said *I contend that we are the first race in the world, and that the more of the world we inhabit the better it is for the human race.*[17] Milner was every bit his equal and a little more blunt: *The white man must rule, because he is elevated by many steps above the black man; steps which it will take the latter centuries to climb.*[18] The pre-war Cape Colony was race-neutral. Blacks had the vote and even sat on juries judging whites. Milner and Rhodes sought to have that taken from them, and it was done.[19] Rhodes' and Milner's little war laid the foundation for Apartheid in South Africa. The continuation of institutionalized racial oppression until the 1990s was thus a significant part of what Canadians fought for in the Boer War.

The "Enemy" and the Stakes

One important aspect of fighting to assist in other people's wars is that the helper does not get to choose the adversary. Who were these Boers? Why was Canada called upon to help kill them? Here is an outline answer to these questions[20]:

- 1652 Dutch East India Company founds a shipping station at Cape of Good Hope. The colonists are religious dissidents. They call themselves Afrikaners and speak a variant of Dutch called Afrikaans. The poorest and most independent are farmers, the Boers.
- 1806 British take permanent possession of the colony.
- 1834-1837 Britain declares an end to slavery throughout the Empire. This prompts the Boers, who are even more

racist than the British, to flee the colony and form two new republics, Transvaal and the Orange Free State, to the north.

- 1843-1881 Relations between the British and the Boers blow hot and cold until 1877 when Britain annexes Transvaal. The annexation is partially reversed by force of arms in 1881 when Boers defeat the British at Majuba. Britain, in Gladstone's final term, negotiates continued control of foreign policy, but otherwise concedes autonomy to the Transvaal.
- 1886 A rich lode of gold is discovered in the Transvaal.

Canadians would fight Canada's first foreign war to settle a dispute between two white powers over a black resource. Our military history on the "world stage" began with a simple capitalist/imperialist conflict. Fortunately, thanks to British overconfidence and misjudgment, we would not be present for the worst of it.

Before the British could acquire the gold, there remained the task of provoking a war with Boers and selling it as something other than a fight against other God-fearing whites. There turned out to be a political hook: voting. Rhodes made a clumsy failed attempt to exploit this issue with an armed foray. His effort, however, ultimately provided Milner with enough propaganda value to bring off his war.

The discovery of gold drew a large number of British fortune seekers and a fair amount of British capital into the Transvaal. The former were referred to as Uitlanders and at one point may have outnumbered the Boers. Fearing for the future of their culture and independence, the Boers denied the Uitlanders the vote.[21] Rhodes, who had already amassed a fortune in African diamonds, was of course interested in the gold as well. In 1895, he decided to invade Transvaal with a small force of volunteers and armed charter company police from Rhodesia. This was supposed to cause the oppressed Uitlanders to revolt. Either someone forgot to inform the Uitlanders, or they were much more interested in wealth than violence. The raid was a disaster. The raiders were arrested and turned over to the British. Rhodes lost his premiership of Cape Colony.[22]

There was, however, some propaganda value to be mined from the voting issue. Anti-Boer sentiment in Britain even got a boost from Rhodes' blunder. It remained only for Milner to get a war underway in a more subtle and effective manner. Having been sent to deal with the recalcitrant Boers, he faced two tasks. The first was to condition public opinion at home and in the colonies to accept some sort of just war veneer. Everyone accepted the conquest of Africans but seizing land controlled by white people was something else again. Uitlanders served this purpose well and Milner handled the campaign brilliantly. Working with his ally, Colonial Secretary Joseph Chamberlain, he compared them to slaves in ancient Greece, and had them petition the queen directly. He eventually achieved enough support that Parliament pledged to take up the Uitlander cause. Milner was manoeuvred into negotiations with Boer President Paul Kruger but turned them to Britain's advantage. He deemed concessions made by Kruger to be insufficient and was able to saddle Kruger with the blame.[23]

The second task was to fashion an acceptable way to provoke the Boers into starting the war. Milner was aided in completing that work by two military realities of the day. First, a factor also in the beginning of the next war, it took time to move troops and supplies. Lightning strikes and responses were not possible. This was especially true in Britain's case, since her forces had to come by sea. Understandably, from the Boer perspective, it was not prudent to wait while your adversary massed forces at your border. The complementary reality was the overwhelming superiority of British numbers. Britain would eventually put almost a half million troops in the field. The Boers never had more than 70,000.[24] Milner and his allies worked tirelessly to get the largest force possible into South Africa quickly. In October 1899, he was able to manoeuvre the Transvaal into issuing an ultimatum demanding withdrawal of British troops from its borders and the return of troops that were on their way. The British rejected the ultimatum, the Orange Free State stood with Transvaal, and the foolish war was on.[25]

Propaganda Wins Canada?

Not only did Canada have no stake in this conflict, she had ample opportunity not to participate. The British request for assistance was couched more as a generous offer to share in imperial glory, even though the mother country could easily handle this little matter alone. As would be the case in the next war, the British assumed that this one, begun in October, would bring victory by Christmas. Canada, as she would do in future wars, responded by giving more than she was asked.[26] Why? Given Canada's growing sense of autonomy and her own internal struggles, this war was simply too preposterous a venture for unquestioning loyalty to Britain to be a complete explanation. The exploitation of Canadian imperialism by a government/church propaganda alliance may be the key.

Laurier was no fervent imperialist. Initially, he did not want to send a single Canadian to South Africa.[27] There was also the eloquently anti-imperialist voice of Henri Bourassa in French Canada, opposed to *all* empires. Bourassa once remarked acidly that the sun never set on the British Empire because not even God trusts the British in the dark.[28] There was also a segment of French Canadians who were understandably in sympathy with the Boers, as they themselves had been victims of imperial conquest.[29] What could change this climate into one where Laurier would claim that England had never fought a more just war than this one, and yet sweep French Canada in the election of 1900?[30] Propaganda was the answer in Pierre Berton's view,[31] and there is much evidence to support it. Canadians were sold a British campaign of distortions and lies, combined with rigorous censorship.

The campaign to convert greed for gold into a struggle for democracy marked the beginnings of a powerful system that major combatants would refine and employ to promote every future war. It would include both dissemination of lies and distortions, and the suppression of truth. Still, there was only so much mileage to be gained from the "oppressed Uitlanders" angle. Propaganda around that justification could not sustain all of Milner's aims and it would particularly lack strength in the colonies. He was already worried that erosion of Empire authority over its white colonies would impede the effort to turn the black colonies into sources of wealth and power.[32] The case for unquestioning colonial participation could not rest solely on saving the Uitlanders.

Milner may have been assisted in Canada by that interesting genre of ethnic racism that Price and Berger identified: "racialization". In propaganda, the Dutch-descended Boers were vilified as evolutionary throwbacks to a savage earlier time. In some illustrations they were drawn ape-like. Montreal Anglicans added a touch of divine manifest destiny to the racial profile: The Boers might be Christian but they were obstructing God's caretakers of freedom. Responsibility for the world had once been given to the Israelites, but now was Britain's charge.[33]. A Methodist publication spoke of Briton and Boer alike rejoicing when the black race was freed from Boer oppression to enjoy the blessings of the gospel. Academics also took up the God-race rhetoric. An article in McMaster University Magazine not only claimed that the war was an example of the "Anglo-Saxon race" scattering the seeds of civilization everywhere, it claimed that the spirit of the British fighting there embodied the teachings of Jesus *upon that sunny vine-clad slopes of Judea.*[34] Military chaplains may have provided the clearest outline of how racializing other white Christians worked. The chaplain of the Strathcona Horse intoned that God had given no small part of the duty of advancing civilization to the "English-speaking race". (Winston Churchill would select this phrase in 1946.) This divine mission meant that waging war against an "inferior race" or a "lower civilization" could not be morally wrong.[35]

Measured in terms of blood, the Boer war propaganda campaign did relatively minor damage. But it produced a draft that would be sharpened in the Great War with far more horrible consequences and imitated by combatants around the world, including Nazi Germany.

Then there was the problem of the Boers as white Christians. A staple of the Empire was carrying the Christian gospel to the heathen of the world. Some who carried it were sincere, others were not, but this theme obviously would not support this war. The war had to be sold as a noble struggle for freedom and democracy. The white Christian enemy had to be demonized.

That task fell into two parts. The public had to be convinced of the unspeakably bad things that the enemy *did*. That required taking really bad acts actually committed, and there are always plenty of those to go around on all sides, and reporting them in the most graphic terms. It also required distorting and exaggerating other enemy conduct. Sometimes the effective way to demonize was just to invent the outrages. The second part of the task was to convince the public that the enemy does these awful things because of *who they are*. They are not like us. They are "the other". These elements have been present as part of every Canadian war.

The Boers, every bit as greedy and racist as the British, courted European support, especially in Germany, with their own bizarre atrocity stories of what the British did and who they were.[36]

British newspapers had the Boers slaughtering civilians, including their own people who tried to surrender. Movies were new, and people flocked to theatres. A film shown as a newsreel depicted Boers firing on a Red Cross tent as British doctors and nurses tried to treat the wounded. The film was shot outside London with professional actors. The *Hamilton Spectator* reported that the Boers had dynamited a train carrying women and children refugees. The *Montreal Star* had a member of a pro-British organization in South Africa being kicked to death by a Boer gang.[37]

Rudyard Kipling materially aided the propaganda effort in the Boer War and later in the Great War. Already famous at the time of the Boer conflict, he admired Milner and Rhodes and made several visits to South Africa. Writing for an army newspaper, he penned a stronger version of his *White Man's Burden*, demanding "freedom or war". [38] If the petty South African war over someone else's resources had to be converted into some sort of crusade for freedom and justice, the British could have no greater ally than a celebrity who was a brilliant writer and, most importantly, one who was known genuinely to honour the common solider. [39] Indeed, some of Kipling's works exemplify a perpetual problem for supporters of peace. How does one oppose war and at the same time honour and respect warriors? Those who wish to marginalize peacemaking efforts are aware of this dilemma and exploit it. When the "Support the Troops" ribbons come out, the message is really "Support the War." This tactic is also a feature of all Canada's wars.

The other essential element in a propaganda campaign is concealment of several truths from the public. Among the most important of these are the reality of the ordinary soldier's experience, immoral misconduct by *both* sides, and poor leadership by those held up as heroic symbols. Of these three, concealment of the reality of war is probably the most important because if that truth were fully realized, the pool of volunteers would shrink dramatically. Recruiting offices in Canada were overwhelmed with eager volunteers in her first two wars. A few recruits joined because they bought the "freedom and democracy" message. A general feeling of patriotism motivated some. Most, however, were simply seeking excitement and adventure. [40] Had they known what they were getting into, their eagerness would have waned quickly. It was the job of government and military commanders to ensure that they did not know.

It is the job of journalists, particularly those who are present in a war zone, to report the truth even if the government and military commanders do not like it. Failures of journalism help to explain failures of the public. Phillip Knightley's valuable work, *The First Casualty* [41] examines this issue in 20th century wars with a clear eye. He praises war correspondents who overcame obstacles and damage to their reputation and livelihood to report the truth. He criticizes in equal measure those who did not. He provides examples of three levels of reporting. Some correspondents actively promote the propaganda line, even helping to invent favourable stories. Others are simply lazy. They do no investigation and simply pass on what officials tell them. Some writers, however, find ways to defeat censorship, do their own investigation, and report the reality of a war.

At Omdurman and in the Boer War, Winston Churchill was an example of the first two types. Young Churchill could not decide whether he wanted to be in the war zone as a soldier or a reporter. With his family connections, he managed both. He secured a commission as a cavalry officer in Kitchener's forces. This regrettable conflict of interest presaged much of modern war reporting where journalists are "embedded" with military units.[42] What reporter can be expected to file a story that in effect says to the decent, honourable soldier he has been living with every day: "If you are killed here, it will be for nothing?" How can a journalist be expected to report about abuse of prisoners in such a situation? In those circumstances, truth is indeed the first casualty of war.

Censorship of the war in South Africa was rigorous. It was enforced by the government and military commanders, including two who would spend many Canadian lives in the next war, Haig and Kitchener. The few correspondents who wrote criticism faced ostracism at home and the censor often discarded their reports without reading them. The chief censor told one of them: *There is only one thing I will allow you to write today—a description of the new Union Jack that has just been run up over headquarters.* [43] The correspondent then had his article complaining about censorship censored.[44] The effect of censorship, denial of access, and even intimidation of correspondents into complying with government preferences in their reporting is difficult to measure. We do not know, for example, what prompted the correspondent who reported the bayoneting and decapitation of young boys by British troops after overrunning a Boer position, to then blame the deaths on their Boer fathers for bringing them there. Still, it is not surprising that the same correspondent who tried to complain of censorship later wrote pieces telling the world that,

Our indomitable soldiers walked erect and straight forward...to do their duty—glory or the grave.[45]

Knightley appreciated the massive effect on public support for wars that results from failure to report reality. He fully recognized the obstacles but did not excuse the members of his profession who were eager, passive, or resigned participants in sending propaganda home. His position was that determined correspondents can find a way to get the truth out. Indeed, to their credit, in every war some have.

But in evaluating the power of propaganda, it is important not to overlook the responsibilities of members of the public. Politicians dare not say it, but "the people" at the turn of the 20th century and in every war that followed have failed to examine propaganda critically. The cost of that failure has been immense.

Canadians Off to War: Realities and Previews of Realities

No British leader thought Canada would be essential to the war effort, but it was important to Milner that the white colonies be more closely bound to the Empire, even if only symbolically. The imperialist position in both countries was that Canada should send a small official contingent to the war. The solution from a reluctant Laurier was compromise. Canada's troops would go to South Africa but as individual volunteers. Upon arrival, they would be integrated into British units. In the interest of Canadian nationalism, Laurier declined the British offer to pay for their equipment and transportation.[46]

The experiences of those Canadian units in the Boer War reveal similarities great and small with what was to come in all her wars. The first contingent bound for South Africa, exactly like the ill-fated expedition to Hong Kong in 1941, was comprised of 1,000 undertrained volunteers, with the wrong clothing, crammed into a refitted vessel half the proper size. When the troops arrived they found, as would those who fought in the Great War and Korea, that they would be under the command of officers who had little or no understanding of the kind of war they were fighting.[47]

Three episodes in the war are particularly relevant to the factors we are examining. They illustrate Canadian skill despite poor foreign leadership, the brutal experience of ordinary soldiers, racism, human rights violations and civilian deaths. It is these stories and not the plentiful accounts of battles that are important to a fair evaluation of Canada's involvement in other people's wars.

At the outset in October 1899, the Boers were fully aware of the impossible imbalance they faced in arms and resources. Their strikes were designed to achieve early successes that they hoped would deflate British enthusiasm and lead to an early negotiated settlement. This was a perfectly reasonable strategy at the time. The civilized negotiated settlement that had ended their first conflict with the British was the usual practice in European wars.[48] Not until the next war would the world be introduced to the devastating consequences of demands for unconditional surrender and total victory.

As she did in World War II, Canada contributed more than was asked.[49] As would be the case in Korea, there were in effect two wars. Canada would be spared participation in the worst of the two.

In accordance with the agreed upon strategy, the Boers struck quickly, and laid siege to the towns of Ladysmith, Kimberly, and Mafeking. Ladysmith was the first to be relieved. Kimberly was next and following its relief the Royal Canadian Regiment played a part in the first British victory of the war.

Episode 1: Kimberly and the Foolish Charge at Paardeberg Drift

Freeing the 50,000 civilians and 600 British troops trapped in the Cape Colony town of Kimberly had been an understandable British priority. Kimberly produced 90 percent of the world's diamonds and Cecil Rhodes himself was one of those surrounded by the Boer forces. Boer sieges did not succeed in blocking contact with the outside. Rhodes complained to Britain and the world, loudly and often. He demanded immediate rescue, incessantly interfered with the conduct of the town's defence, and generally acted as the supremely important person he was sure he was.[50]

One ominous aspect of the siege of Kimberly did not bode well for civilians in future conflicts. Sieges, of course, had been a part of warfare for hundreds of years. They always caused civilian deaths. Starving the besieged was after all part of the strategy. The targeted town or castle, however, was often walled and the primary use of large siege weapons was to penetrate these fortifications and speed surrender. In the Boer war, as it would in all future conflicts, advances in weapons technology made the situation significantly grimmer for civilians. The Boers developed a huge cannon, the Long Tom, and directly bombarded not walls but living quarters in Ladysmith and Kimberly, killing women and children among others.[51]

The British retook Kimberly. Rhodes threw a champagne party. Boer commander Piers Cronje was left disheartened and in tactical trouble when the Canadians arrived to supplement the British force. The Boers were already beaten at that point and Cronje was contemplating the best direction for retreat. It was here, at a place called Paardeberg Drift that Canadians would first learn of the inability of British officers to get beyond the romance of the gallant charge and come to terms with the reality of modern warfare.

Unfortunately, it must be said that the first dangerously poor leader was Canadian. The regimental commander, Lieutenant Colonel William Otter, brought a distinctly undistinguished career to the post. Otter's ineptitude had been on display in defeats during the Fenian conflict of 1866 and in an 1885 unauthorized and unnecessary attack on a First Nations force. In that action, he apparently did not learned to respect the impact of sharpshooters. The Boers were justly famous as marksmen. From the Canadians, Otter apparently wanted a drill team rather than a fighting force. He insisted on spit and polish and saluting, to the exclusion of any realistic preparation for battle.[52]

The British leadership, with one exception, was no better. Like the American leaders who would later endanger Canadian lives in Korea and Afghanistan, the British commanders had no understanding of how to fight the unconventional war they were entering. They confidently assumed the solid red line with bayonets fixed that had served them well in the Crimean War would easily vanquish the ragged Dutch settlers, especially when topped up with a glorious cavalry charge. The British would soon have their hands full with highly mobile sharpshooters fighting in a most unsporting manner.

Not only did the Canadians have their own Colonel Otter to deal with, the only reasonable British commander was ill. General Sir Abraham Roberts, affectionately known as "Bobs", was a competent commander and seen as a hero on the order of Lord Wellington. Honouring him was the last official ceremony of Victoria's long reign.[53] More important to Canadians, he had regard for his men and was loath to spend lives recklessly. The fate of Canadians at Paardeberg was instead left to a man who would become justly infamous in this war and the next, Lord Kitchener.

The Canadians were eager to fight. They believed, with some justification that they were being held out because the British were contemptuous of them as inferior colonials. Otter got into an argument with, a LTC Aldworth, the commander of an adjacent British unit. Neither had made any attempt to gather intelligence about the strength and location of Boer positions. The words they exchanged displayed the British arrogance so resented by the Canadians and Otter brashly told Aldworth that his troops would lead a charge against the entrenched Boers and Aldworth should keep up if he could. Lord Kitchener ordered the charge, but it was the playground level dispute between Otter and Aldworth that wasted lives. The charging British and Canadians were mowed down and never got within 300 yards of the hidden Boer marksmen. That senseless charge killed 21 Canadians and wounded 63. British casualties numbered more than 1,000. In Canada's future wars, similar decisions that make this charge look brilliant by comparison would waste tens of thousands of lives.[54]

Roberts recovered in time to take over from Kitchener and save further loss of life by negotiating the surrender of Cronje's starving troops on reasonable terms. Although British losses at Paardeberg were the worst of any day in the war, Roberts himself, heaped praise upon our troops: *"Canadian" now stands for bravery, dash and courage. A gallant deed, worthy of our colonial comrades.* Another British commander added: *Their charge toward the Boer trenches really took our breath away...they sprang ahead like racehorses. Though beardless youths they fought like veterans.*[55] This was but the first example of the kind of praise that Canada would relish---at great cost.

Part of that cost was the daily reality of war in the life of the ordinary soldier. It was nothing like the adventure presented by the propaganda campaign. Its watchwords were heat, thirst, lice, and disease. Volunteers for the Royal Canadian Regiment had not been advised that forced marches in 46-degree heat would drive them to drink enthusiastically from swamp water filled with rotting corpses of animals and men. Nor would they know that their constant tormenting companions would be lice. Of the 7,368 Canadians who went to South Africa, "only" 89 of the 224 who died were killed in action. The remainder died of disease.[56]

These are just numbers, and numbers are numbing. The numbers, however, represent the lost lives and potential of real people. Hidden again from the eager volunteers of a decade later would be the true experiences of Hadley Adams and Francis Anderson, who enlisted at Calgary and died of fever; of Cecil Barry, killed in the foolish Paardeberg charge; of John Cameron, who enlisted at Halifax and died of dysentery.[57] Had these men lived, perhaps they would have benefited their families and communities. Perhaps what they experienced would render them a burden. When viewed in light of what they died for, however, their loss can only be seen as just that—loss.

Episode 2: Mafeking, Human Rights, and the Racist Boy Scout

Though Canadians were not involved in the defence or relief of the border town of Mafeking, its story provides a devastating commentary on the cause for which they fought. It is a story of denial

21

of a basic human right---food. It is a story of racism and cruelty. It is a story of eccentric incompetence transformed by propaganda into heroism. Behind all of these stories is colonel Robert Baden-Powell, founder of the scouting movement.

Powell raised two regiments in country and instead of carrying out the active mission he had been assigned, holed up in Mafeking on the border of Transvaal. There an incompetent Boer force besieged the equally incompetent Powell. Unlike the panicky Rhodes, Powell sent home reports that, while generally accurate, were couched in brave, "stiff upper lip" terms, suggesting that the siege was worse than the report disclosed. The public assumed that the heroic British must be enduring terrible hardship with typical English pluck. Across the Empire, Powell was hailed as a hero. During the siege, the queen sent him a message expressing admiration for the *patient and resolute defence which is so gallantly maintained under your ever resourceful command.*[58] News of the relief of Mafeking sparked a five-day celebration in London that exceeded those that followed the Great War and World War II. Powell became a figure revered on the order of Lord Nelson.[59]

It turns out that Baden-Powell's reports were only partly incorrect. The siege of Mafeking was not terribly onerous—for white people. Powell himself made it an ordeal for people of colour. A standard military history of the war echoes the praise of his brilliant defence and acknowledges his rise to iconic status. It describes him charitably as "on occasion ruthless", reporting that he meted out "stern (perhaps too stern) sentences in the interest of security".[60]

Knightley provides a more detailed and accurate account, as does Thomas Pakenham, whose exhaustive history nevertheless praises Baden-Powell's professionalism and will to win. Both show a very different situation than the one offered to the outside world.

The Boers launched desultory bombardments that mostly killed natives. Another matter presented the natives with a much greater threat. Mafeking was the last town to be relieved, raising the issue of food. Whites were never in want. Baden-Powell and his officers enjoyed an eight course Christmas dinner that included oysters and suckling pig. He managed the issue of food for the native population with a regimen of starvation, beatings, and executions. He set up a system of white rations and black rations. Whites without cash could purchase food on credit or by drawing on a special fund. Blacks had to pay cash, including cash for the purchase of food seized from their own stocks. In the early days, natives who could do so paid three pence for a bowl of horsemeat soup. Those who could not pay starved, or became living skeletons.

As the siege wore on, Baden-Powell figured out a way to sustain the white population's supply of flour of a quality "considered edible by white people", and still keep alive some of the blacks he had pressed into labour and defence. He cut the already minimal grain supply allocated to natives with horse feed. After reducing the allocation even further, he apparently decided to wash his hands of unproductive native families by stopping the sale of food to them altogether, hoping they would leave. Aside from the natives who were part of his defence scheme, blacks were given the option of leaving or starving. One result of this move was the spectacle of 2,000 outcast natives searching for scraps on rubbish heaps and digging up corpses of buried dogs.

In Baden-Powell's scheme, of course, there was also the matter of enforcement. His "occasional ruthlessness...in the interest of security" accomplished this task. He had firing squads execute some of the starving natives caught stealing food and had others flogged.[61]

None of this story of Mafeking concerned the white people who knew of it. Writing 77 years later, the author of the "occasional ruthlessness" phrase dismissed the food policy in one sentence, remarking that Baden-Powell's scheme simply emphasized "commonplace racial assumptions in southern Africa.[62] Milner did not hesitate to summarize Mafeking in accordance with those assumptions: *You have only to sacrifice 'the nigger' absolutely and the game is easy.*[63]

23

Why was the general public in England and Canada unaware of the reality of Mafeking? Would it have mattered if they had known? Why should Canadians be concerned about Baden-Powell and Mafeking since no Canadians were involved?

The answer to the first question is fairly simple. While the world at one end of the line of communication relished reports of Baden-Powell's plucky defence, alternative narratives were forbidden. Baden-Powell told all correspondents he would permit no criticism of the conduct of the siege. After someone suggested that natives should have a share of white food rations, he issued an order that anyone hearing that idea again should apply the toe of a boot to the speaker. Nevertheless, since all the hero stories got out, Knightley is convinced that a more professional corps of war correspondents should have been able to publish the truth.[64]

The answers to the remaining questions are a bit more complex. Perhaps the prevailing European and British Empire view of Africans as barely human savages, in need of imperial Christianity but otherwise expendable, would have meant that the truth of Mafeking and of the war itself would not have mattered. But Canadians at least had an opportunity for a racial ethic that imperial powers did not. With the notable exception of British Columbia and the Canadian Pacific Railway,[65] the new land of Canada was not at that time as heavily invested in racism generally or as an aid to plundering resources. There is at least a slight chance that awareness of the racist atrocities of the Empire's wars might have given some Canadians pause when it appeared as part of future wars to which Canada would be invited.

Perhaps that is too much to expect. But racism would indeed be a factor in of all of Canada's future wars. If it is unrealistic to expect that Canadians in 1902 would engage in any sort of national discussion evaluating their role in this little war, when might that discussion occur? When would a fact-based analysis of the dark side of joining a powerful patron happen? Has it happened yet?

Lord Kitchener's war on civilians, and an unlikely hero journalist

The Boer War featured another tragic preview of what was in store for civilians, even white ones. In the Great War, they would suffer on a massive scale even though the leaders of the principal combatants were not only white, but also members of the same family.

Soon after Kimberly, the Boers themselves were starving and began to flee toward the Transvaal capital of Pretoria, with the British and a newly arrived and better-equipped contingent of Canadians in pursuit. The British took Pretoria and assumed the war was over. It was not. They would find that the war had entered a second phase. In it they would be schooled in full-scale guerilla warfare. Civilians would pay the price for that schooling.

The British were at times dismissive of Canada's rough colonials. They would have done better to imitate them. A comparative disparity in discipline characterizes Canadian forces in all her wars. On balance, that disparity is probably a good thing. Young tamers of the prairie, removed from the strictures of the British class system, were more imaginative and less amenable to fighting as one of Colonel Otter's drill teams. They shared these characteristics with the Boers. The average British soldier was expected to obey orders mechanically and let his officers think for him. The British officer corps was drawn from the privileged class and taught to think of war as a glorious team sporting contest fought fairly, with themselves as the star athletes. The glorious cavalry charge was an extension of the splendid rugby try. This attitude would kill a greater percentage of junior officers than of the troops they led. Conversely, the Canadians and Boer forces were drawn largely from a single class. They were more independent and were encouraged to think for themselves.[66]

In part for this reason, Canadians were better than their British counterparts at responding to Boer tactics from the beginning. One of the men in the second Canadian contingent commented on how his comrades made use of cover, making it difficult for the Boers to locate them, noting that the British kept under cover only when being fired upon. He later spoke with a Boer prisoner who expressed admiration for the way the lines of British marched bravely to their death. He regretted having to kill such brave men, although it was quite easy to do.[67]

When the unexpected second phase of the war began, British regimentation became even more of a problem. They occupied all of the towns and cities, but mounted Boer guerillas raided outposts, destroyed rail lines, conducted ambushes, and then disappeared. Anyone familiar with the war in Vietnam or Afghanistan will have no difficulty picturing this situation and understanding the frustration of the British.

That frustration in the second phase of the war became the first phase of a disaster for Boer women and children, and for the families of native labourers who lived with them. The ordeal for civilians began with the burning of farms. Lord Roberts, before turning command over to Lord Kitchener, began the practice in the Orange Free State. There it was ostensibly instituted as a reprisal, directed at families of rebels and prisoners who had broken their pledge not to return to the fighting. Whatever the justification, in 1900 more than 600 farms were burned.[68] Kitchener, aided enthusiastically by Colonel Douglas Haig, later jettisoned the niceties of justification, and brought the war on civilians to the level of crime.

Burning out civilian families was not what ordinary soldiers had signed up for and it troubled many of them. Canadian artillery Lieutenant E.W.B. "Dinky" Morrison, who had observed the deadly difference in the Canadian and British use of cover was one: *We moved from valley to valley 'lifting' cattle and sheep, burning, looting and turning the women and children to sit and cry beside the ruins of their once beautiful farmsteads.* Some of Morrison's British allies experienced a similar distaste. An officer wrote: *The worst moment is when you first come to the house. The people thought we had called for refreshments, and one of them went to get milk. Then we had to tell them we had come to burn the place down…We rode away and left them, a forlorn little group, standing among their household goods—beds, furniture, and gimcracks strewn about the veldt; the crackling of the fire in their ears, and smoke and flame streaming overhead.*[69] Burning families out of their homes was not the entire exercise. Haig and other commanders ordered their troops to cut down fruit trees, destroy crops in the field, slash bags of grain, and slaughter animals. This was the fate of some 30,00 farms.[70]

Fortunately, the Canadian force left South Africa before the worst of the war on civilians. Unfortunately, Roberts, thinking the war was over, also left about the same time. This left Kitchener in charge, looking for an answer to the Boer refusal to "fight fair". He had already attempted to corral the elusive commandos by constructing 500 hundred miles of fortified blockhouses connected by barbed wire.[71]

Considering the thousands of families already made homeless by the farm burnings, Kitchener could scarcely adopt the modern counterinsurgency tactic of trying to win the hearts and minds of the Boer civilians. He did not try. Instead, he modified the rationale of the farm burning policy. He viewed the guerrilla fighters as fish sustained by a civilian pond. As many cruel and foolish future commanders would do, he decided to drain the pond. He decided to make war on women and children.

Kitchener herded 160,000 civilians into concentration camps. The prisoners were mostly women, children, the elderly, and African farm workers. Initially, *a la* Baden-Powell, there were two ration programs. Women and children whose men were known to be still fighting were denied meat. For everyone, rations were meagre— no vegetables; no fresh milk for children and babies. That diet, along with overcrowding, foul water, and appalling sanitation invited disease. The inmates died in droves from measles, typhoid, malaria, pneumonia, and a host of other maladies. In one camp the annual death rate reached 383 per 1,000 adults, 500 per 1,000 children. Almost 28,000 civilians died in Kitchener's camps, twice the number of Boers killed in combat, along with 12,000 people of colour.[72] For the Boers, it was safer to be a man riding around the veldt with a gun than to be a child in one of the camps.

In contrast to Knightley's view, Berton concluded that no journalist could risk his career by reporting the deaths in the camps. [73] One heroic woman did so, risking far more than a professional livelihood. It fell to an unlikely amateur journalist to expose the scandal, give a boost to parliamentary opponents of the war, and ultimately bring about improvements in the camps, saving thousands of lives.

News of the truth about the concentration camps would not have reached the British public but for the actions of this little known hero. The British called them voluntary refugee camps and Kitchener gave assurances that everyone was happy in them---looked after better than in their own homes. [74] Milner recognized the public relations danger posed by the camps and ordered censorship. But one day in 1901 there came upon the scene one of the great heroes of journalism and peace: Emily Hobhouse. Her remarkable courage in the face of misinformed public opinion would also be part of the story of the next war.

Emily Hobhouse was derisively described more than once as a dumpy middle-aged spinster. [75] Whatever her appearance, there was no questioning her persistence and sense of justice. She founded a group called the South African Women and Children's Distress Fund and went to South Africa with two carloads of supplies for Kitchener and Milner's internees. Through family connections, she arranged a meeting with Milner and persuaded him to let her tour the camps. That was Milner's mistake. What she saw made her become, among other things, the journalist that the many war correspondents present were not. She flooded English newspapers with her accounts. Some refused to print them but enough did to make the camps an international scandal. She spoke at public meetings. She wrote to family members. She was also a particularly dangerous journalist because through those same family connections she had the ear of prominent politicians. They included David Lloyd George, who would be prime minister during the Great War and who already opposed the South African venture. Thanks to her, people heard the truth about the camps.

Emily Hobhouse did not tell her story with statistics. She told the truth about individuals and families she had witnessed as she moved from tent to overcrowded tent: *a six month old baby gasping for life on its mother's knee…a girl of twenty one lay dying on a stretcher. The father… kneeling beside her while his wife was watching a child of six also dying.*[76]

On a second visit, she found that minor improvements had been wiped out by an influx of new inmates. She saw the death rate as the worst since the great plagues of Europe: *…the whole talk was of death—who died yesterday, who lay dying today, who would be dead tomorrow.*[77]

The cause Hobhouse led met with considerable opposition. One newspaper justified Kitchener with the same line that would be heard in similar conflicts in the future: *Women and children are frequently employed to carry messages. Of course they must be included in military measures and transported or despatched.*[78] Speaking at public meetings, she was heckled as a traitor and the target of missiles made of stone, chairs, and fruit.[79]

Milner saw the concentration camp uproar as his biggest obstacle to pursuing the war. He was forced to return to London to deal with what he called "pro-Boer ravings." To Kitchener, Emily Hobhouse was "that bloody woman", to Colonial Secretary Chamberlain, a "hysterical spinster".[80] She had already angered the powers that be with her opposition to the war itself. In 1900, she had convened a women only meeting of the Women's South African Conciliation Committee to pass antiwar resolutions based in part on what always drives war makers crazy---real patriotism.[81]

About the camp scandal Emily Hobhouse could not be silenced. After six months in England, she resolved to return to the camps. She found that Milner was on the same ship and learned that she, as would be so many responsible reporters in future wars, had been under surveillance. She did not reach the camps this time because Milner barred her from coming ashore and had her forcibly placed on a troopship returning to England. But the damage was done. A few months before the Boers finally surrendered, Kitchener ordered his commanders to stop bringing women and children to the camps and improved conditions. The death rate went down dramatically.[82] The courage and tenacity of Emily Hobhouse in the face of public opinion in time of war had saved lives.[83] Milner would hear from her again in the next war.

Some Canadians remember Haig and Kitchener, though not for their part in farm burnings and concentration camps. Few have ever heard of Emily Hobhouse. That is not the case in South Africa, where she is remembered and revered. When she died in 1926, her ashes were sent to be interred at the base of the women's memorial at Bloemfontein. Businesses closed. Flags were flown at half-staff. The mounted honour guard had been boys in the concentration camps. Two of the girls who carried the casket bore the name Emily Hobhouse. Two others were from spinning and weaving schools that Emily had returned to establish.[84]

One name among those who eulogized Emily Hobhouse is familiar to most. Mahatma Gandhi had not forgotten that she had intervened to help him get access to government leaders in South Africa on behalf of Indians there. He wrote: *She loved her country and because she loved it, she could not tolerate any injustice done by it.*[85]

Today, Canadian and world media could use a few more dumpy middle aged spinsters like Emily Hobhouse.

The conversation we did not have

Canada had no national conversation following the Boer War. The factors we are examining were not unearthed and discussed. Could our minor contribution to this war have been the subject of a national conversation about whether it was worth it? Could there have been an examination of lessons learned? National enterprises of smaller magnitude are the subject of such inquiries. That the times made such a thing impossible may be somewhat accurate, but it is a facile answer.

If Canadians had examined the Boer War from the perspective of the legitimate interests of an emerging nation, what might have been the effect on the question of whether to join future wars? What would the conversation have looked like?

A post-war pamphlet by Toronto historian and journalist, Goldwin Smith contained several likely agenda items for the conversation we did not have. On the issue of propaganda, he noted that the Boers had been demonized as barbarians and savages---until they were re-integrated into the Empire and praise as "gallant antagonists". On human rights and racism, Smith wrote that that the war showed that equal rights were reserved for white men, though five sixths of the population of the Empire was made up of people of colour. He saw through the Uitlander democracy issue for the pretext it was and condemned the war as a struggle to ensure cheap labour for the extraction of resources.[86] Smith wrote truth but he was no Emily Hobhouse. His opposition to the war stemmed in part from a desire for closer ties with the U.S. He also claimed that the Boer War was instigated on behalf of Jewish financiers.[87]

A broader conversation might have included virtually all of the factors we are examining. Why did we place our forces under the command of others? Should we ever do that again? In a racist world, shall we continue to play along? If so, what might be the impact on our future? If not, what steps should we begin to take? Is there anything we can do to hold propagandists more accountable to truth and to make our response to propaganda more intelligent? Because Canadian troops went home early, are we free of responsibility for the civilian deaths, especially in the concentration camps? Will we be asked to be part of morally questionable decisions by our allies in the future?

All of these matters and more would have produced a long list of costs. Internally, English Canadians saw the war as an opportunity to enhance Canada's place within the Empire as an ally rather than a colony.[88] That might be counted as a benefit. But even if true to some degree, we would have to consider as a major cost the deepening of a French/English divide that we have yet to bridge.

Even had we managed the conversation, however, we probably could not have seen that all of the costs would be magnified exponentially by one horrible development that no one appreciated. The Boer War was a rehearsal for a larger conflict that both Britain and Germany intended to have and in which it was assumed that Canadians would again join—the real "coming of age" war. Many assumed that it would be another tidy South Africa adventure, replayed on a slightly larger scale. They were unaware that advances in the technology of death would make it a horror show that has yet to be duplicated. As we examine the Great War tragedy, I invite you to look back occasionally into the mirror of it that was the Boer War.

Chapter II

Joining the Global Insanity: The Great War

"A lengthy period of insanity"
British Field Marshal, Lord Allenby, describing battle of Verdun

Opting out of the Great War?

All of the factors that influenced Canada's participation in the Boer War were present in this one. Their impact was magnified a thousand fold. Whether due to the comparatively small loss of life in South Africa, or continuing ties to the Empire, or the success of propaganda, or other reasons, between 1902 and 1914 Canadians did not have the conversation they should have had about what to do when the next call came. If that conversation had happened, it would have included compelling arguments for staying out of the Great War. The conversation would have had to include consideration of evidence that the Boer War was a mistake and that participating in the Great War would be a much greater one. We should now examine the question of whether it was a mistake, not because we can change history, but in order to be perhaps a bit wiser in the future.

The argument that Canada should have demurred is, of course, a radical proposition. That it is indeed radical is confirmed by the apparent consensus of historians that at least until 1919 and possibly until 1931 or later the choice was not open to us. The consensus is bluntly captured in *Canada, A People's History: As a colony, Canada was automatically at war when Britain was.*[1] With respect, I would like us to examine that assertion more closely.

Those who argue that Canada could have stayed out of Britain's wars would have to concede at the outset that the legalities say otherwise. The Supreme Court of Canada has pointed to Canada's separate signature on the 1919 Treaty of Versailles as well as the popular benchmark of the Statute of Westminster in 1931 in attempting to define the coming of our independence. In the judicial system, the word of the Privy Council of London was technically final until 1949. It is well understood that final patriation did not come until 1982, and even that event did not prevent serious discussion in 2008 about whether the Governor General could and should refuse the prime minister's request to prorogue Parliament. Further complicating matters, from 1867-1982 there were numerous statutes granting Canadian autonomy on one matter or another, short of but related to, international affairs. I will return to possible implications of this hodgepodge, but I do not contend that it alone means the historians are wrong about our status on paper. They are not. Yet Canada had no July 4th, 1776. So, in *practical* historical terms is it possible to call up earlier times and think outside the legal/imperial box? Let's try.

U.S. history is characterized by a "rights-oriented" approach. Written law is important. Essentially, governments may do what they wish in the absence of recognized statutory or constitutional bars. They also rely on specific texts to justify the exercise of powers.

Canada's legal heritage from Britain is quite different. There is much that is not written down. Many issues are simply finessed. Push does not usual come to shove over who has the "right" to do what. Canadians are consequently better at the responsible exercise of discretion than their U.S. counterparts. I see this contrasting dynamic as important to Canada's relationship with Britain at the time of the Great War.

While pre-1914 ambiguities are not the cornerstone of my argument that Canada might have opted out of the Great War, one Canadian historian appears to confirm the overall structure I have outlined. Professor Andrew Heard of Simon Fraser University set out all the legalities I have mentioned, and more. While I doubt he would agree with my conclusion, he wrote that in broad terms: *Canada's transition from a self-governing British colony into a fully independent state was an evolutionary process, which arose in such gradual fashion that it is impossible to ascribe independence to a particular date.* Referring to the fact that even after 1982 legal traces of our colonial past remain, he said: *The persistence of these vestiges of Canada's former status* ***illustrates how much Canada owes its independence from Britain to political developments, rather than legal changes in the formal constitution.*** (Emphasis added) Even more telling in my view: *The process by which Canada acquired a complete and international personality was characterized by the evolution of new* ***political arrangements rather than changes in positive law.***[2] (Emphasis added)

In the colonial period we are examining, given Canada's evolving formal authority over matters essentially domestic but linked to warfare; given the political arrangements of the time and the operational ethic that not every power that could be exercised would be exercised; and given the laudable tradition of exercising discretion responsibly rather than invoking rights based on legislation, I suggest that Canada could have plausibly maintained that decisions about the blood and treasure of her people were hers to make. As we will see, she sometimes acted as if this were so.

Further, it is practical reality, not formal legality that ultimately governs. Even clear formal obligations do not rigidly govern human conduct. Arrangements are re-negotiated in response to the ongoing needs of the parties. And what would Britain's options have been had Canada respectfully declined? Imposing political and economic consequences perhaps, but that would have risked moving us closer to the U.S.

Of course, all of this independence analysis was rendered moot. The issue never came to a head. In both the Boer War and this one, the overconfident British did not invoke their purported authority because they thought they could easily handle their adversaries but would offer us the chance to participate in the glory. Canada enthusiastically accepted. But if we have yet honestly to evaluate Canada's choices about participation in other people's wars, is it not worthwhile to suspend disbelief about formalities long enough to learn from this one? If so, let us look at what might have been, as well as what was.

Like the Boer War, national security by any practical definition was not involved. Other imperialist squabbles between the main European contestants had recently been settled through diplomacy or limited warfare without us. In practical terms, Canada's ties to the empire were loosening. In 1914, the world went insane. If Canada did not have to join the insanity, why did she?

Prologue Canada: Flirting With Freedom From Europe

There were developments between the Boer War and the Great War that raised the possibility of Canada's freedom from the intrigues of foreign patrons. One was the resolution of a long-standing Alaskan boundary dispute with the U.S. The matter was to be decided by an impartial tribunal with three American and three British members. U.S. President Theodore Roosevelt made no pretense of impartiality. He appointed his secretary of war to the tribunal and threatened to take the disputed territory by force if necessary. The British cast the deciding vote against Canada's claim. Whatever the merits, the vote stoked anger at both countries.[3]

The perfidy of Britain in the boundary dispute could not, of course, alone sustain a major shift away from the Empire. But the changing population base had the potential to do so. Canada's efforts during this period to fill its vast territory with immigrants did not in itself fuel national cohesion but it did serve to separate us further from the two greater powers. It was a racist policy, seeking only white immigrants, but those who came had had their fill of Europe and the U.S. As the Great War approached, Canadian imperialists were still over-represented in centres of power but the new demographics were working against them.[4]

Two matters reversed the budding nationalist trend---at least on the question of following Britain into the Great War. First, Germany in 1909 committed the unpardonable sin. She began a naval building program seeking to challenge British supremacy on the seas.[5] The Empire owed its existence to that supremacy. The British could hardly be expected to view a German naval buildup with anything less than panic.

To make matters worse, mother was short of cash. Her appeal to Canada for ships or money sparked a spirited controversy here. Laurier was still prime minister, still a nationalist at heart, still seeking compromise but just as he had been at the Diamond Jubilee, also unable to watch his words.

Pure Canadian imperialists were all for "One Flag, One Fleet, One Throne". Laurier, however, had to contend with the emerging provinces in the west, as well as his old nemeses, Henri Bourassa and French Canada. He proposed a compromise. Canada would have her own small navy that would be provided to the British in the event of an emergency. In a speech eerily similar to the rhetoric the Americans and the Canadian military lobby employ today to describe Canada's "free ride", he said:

Canada should no longer delay in assuming her proper share of the responsibility and financial burden incident to her exposed coastline and great seaports.[6]

Even though the small fleet he proposed was ridiculed as a "tin pot navy", it appeared for a time that the compromise would help Laurier navigate the tricky political waters. His gambit might have worked had he not once again made intemperate remarks when pressured by imperialists over the kind of emergency that would trigger the obligation to go to Britain's aid. Did a "real emergency" include all the petty little wars in which European countries, including Britain, were so wont to engage; or did a real emergency only include conflicts that affected Canada? In spite of earlier having strongly affirmed Canadian autonomy, Laurier responded:

War everywhere. When Britain is at war anywhere, Canada is at war; there is no distinction. If Great Britain, to which we are subject, is at war with any nation, Canada is exposed to invasion.[7]

Both of the proffered justifications found in Laurier's unfortunate choice of words are specious, though one is understandable. One can appreciate his position that notwithstanding their growing autonomy, Canadians remained British subjects and were duty bound to permit Great Britain to determine matters of war and peace. The assertion, however, that if Britain is at war anywhere Canada is exposed to invasion was absurd. Picturing Kaiser Wilhelm's General Staff plotting the invasion of Canada evokes images of Monty Python.

In the pre-Monty Python world of 1910, it was again left to Henri Bourassa to pick up on Laurier's foolish speeches and continue his campaign against all empires. In *Le Devoir*, he tried to remind Canadians of what he called the comedy of 1899 in South Africa. He failed. Further, his nationalist stance alienated those in Quebec who had tired of second-class status. And, of course, he alienated imperialists. His task was a difficult one and his wisdom was rejected. Berton wrote: *His hopes and expectations for a united country have never really been realized. That is his tragedy; it is also our own.*[8]

We do not know what direction Canada's path would have taken her had Bourassa's views prevailed. Would 60 years of effort to implement them after 1910 have avoided or at least mitigated the separatist turmoil of the 1970s? Clearly, Bourassa's hopes for a united country have yet to be realized. Quebec stands awkwardly today as a state within a state, the recipient of special favours from pandering politicians of all stripes, yet unsatisfied—perhaps yet misunderstood. To be sure, Quebeckers have done their part in all of Canada's wars. Nevertheless, part of their historical disenchantment includes resentment at federal fawning before British and U.S. patrons. Overall, the wars have been an ongoing negative influence on the effort to forge a single workable nation. The matter of what kind of emergency was needed to embroil Canada in Europe's wars was never debated and resolved. Laurier's junior navy bill failed and the country was for a time without either navy or naval policy.[9]

The next blow to the possibility of freedom from Europe was an economic dispute that brought down Laurier and bound us more closely to Great Britain—and her wars. That dispute had elements both prophetic and ironic. By 1911, the power and influence of farmers in the west was growing. Farmers were increasingly and understandably upset by a national policy that forced them to sell their wheat on an unprotected world market but required them to buy equipment and household items on the protected higher priced markets of Central Canada. They wanted to change to a reciprocal trade agreement, first with the U.S. and later Great Britain. As the dispute wore on, Laurier and the Liberals were poised to give it to them.

The eastern Tory opposition wanted none of this. Their initial argument predictably relied upon the damage that reciprocity with the U.S. would allegedly do to Canada's place in the Empire. Soon to be prime minister Robert Borden, who would later be a voice for Canadian independence, made this imperialist argument in a speech. Ironically, the speech condemned "entangling treaties or alliances" that would interfere" with Empire economics.[10] As every elementary school student knows, "entangling treaties and alliances" of a quite different kind were a major cause of the Great War.

There was also prophetic irony in the part played by the U.S. in this reciprocity battle. The clumsy comments of her politicians helped scuttle the deal and revealed their lingering imperialistic designs on Canada. The cruder aspects of those aspirations have been muted today, though economic and cultural dominance as well as pressure to join all U.S. wars continue to make Canadian sovereignty a topic of concern.

The Americans were considerably more blunt in 1911 as they helped the reciprocity debate take a turn that would ultimately give Conservative imperialists the ability to form a government without qualms about joining the Great War. The statement of the speaker of the house of representatives that he hoped to see the American flag flying over all of British North America is probably the most well known example. Full marks for candor, however, to one member who said: *Be not deceived. When we go into a country and get control of it, we take it.*[11]

Canada's debate over trade reciprocity was about more than trade. In many respects it was a surrogate for multi-faceted arguments over the problems presented by Canada's position between two powers. In the end, the combination of pure imperialists and those who saw the way forward as limited to seeking greater influence within the Empire prevailed. Canada opted for Britain.[12] Laurier lost the election, unable even to carry all of the western provinces whose concerns he had heeded. Robert Borden and the Conservatives took power. The imperialists were in charge.

Borden's parliament scuttled Laurier's modest naval bill and when British prime minister Herbert Asquith requested funds for the arms race, the government tabled a bill that would provide money to help pay for three battleships to be placed at the disposal of the British "for the common defence of the empire". That bill failed, but by 1913 it was clear that much more than money would be placed at the disposal of the British, whenever they asked and with no strings attached.

What would have been the result had the reciprocity controversy not arisen when it did? More importantly, what would have happened if Germany had picked some means other than sea power to challenge the British Empire? We have seen that demography and geography were slowly operating in favour of Canadian nationalism and against blind support of the British, even if that nationalism did not necessarily embody immediate independence. Might we have stood apart from the next European conflict—the one that this time would engulf much of the world? What would have been the result of a reasonable cost/benefit evaluation of our participation in the preliminary contest in South Africa? Might Canada at least have demanded control over her contribution to the Great War and insisted on making her own military decisions? Even those limited measures would have saved tens of thousands of Canadian lives.

Prologue Great Britain: Many Reasons Not To Go To War

Since Canada joined the coming conflagration at the behest of the Empire, it is worthwhile to examine how Great Britain might also have acted more wisely.

Notwithstanding that Germany had dared to embark on a spate of warship building and was competing as vigorously as she could manage for control of other people's lands in Africa, there were many reasons for the British to stay out of the conflict that arose in the summer of 1914. Among them were labour strife, trouble in Ireland, and an annoying women's rights movement often aligned with a small but significant antiwar faction.

Protestants in Ireland, fearing a Catholic majority in the northern provinces, formed militias to ensure that the entire island remained an exploited colony. Irish nationalists armed themselves and formed militias. The delighted Germans sold arms to both sides.[13]

Two of the Boer War imperialists, Milner and Kipling, were heavily involved in the effort to deal with the "Irish problem". Milner viewed the Irish with the same contempt he had heaped on the Boers. Kipling considered the Irish Catholics "the Orientals of the west." Milner made speeches opposing Irish home rule. Kipling supplied money to arm Protestant militias. The two vigorously stirred a pot that would boil for decades. Instead of devoting resources to finding a reasonable solution, on the eve of the Great War British troops fired on protesters in Dublin.[14]

During the same period there were signs that those at the bottom of the rigid British class system would be passive no more. They were no longer willing to abide the most egregious excesses of the industrial revolution. Labour union membership was growing and there were numerous strikes. The socialist movement gained strength. The government response to this was as ill advised as its Ireland policy. Thousands of troops were called up. Two warships were sent to Liverpool.[15]

The Boer War had also produced antiwar groups and opposition voices, including that of future Prime Minister David Lloyd George, then a Welsh MP, who had linked peace and social justice when he said that every shell fired at the Boers carried away with it an old age pension.[16] The most important coordinators of antiwar and economic justice dissent were found within the campaign to gain the vote for women. Two figures in this effort were sisters Emmeline and Sylvia Pankhurst. Their stories not only illustrate the common effort among members of the three movements, they also help to explain what became of those movements when the government propaganda effort turned the public against them. That government was hardly less rigid in its response to the suffragists than it was to union members and the Irish. Women were jailed. When they went on hunger strikes, they were brutally force-fed.[17]

Emmeline at one point characterized all wars as a byproduct of male stupidity. Kipling worried aloud that women were weakening the empire's martial spirit. Employing the old "aiding the enemy" theme used so effectively in propaganda today, he fretted about how the Germans would be helped by English feminists.[18]

There were many other reasons not to have this war. Apart from the pressing issues at home, there had been almost 59 years of relative calm within Europe while its powers competed for territory elsewhere. And of course, the ruling class royalty were pretty close. England's King George V, Russia's Tsar Nicholas II, and Germany's Kaiser Wilhelm were related and had known each other for years. Wilhelm was Victoria's grandson and was at her bedside when she died.[19]

In spite of all this, England would choose war, exacerbating her own problems and leaving a legacy of many more—to the detriment of all of us who would have to deal with them in later decades. Emmeline Pankhurst and Lloyd George would turn in favour of the war and in 1915 work together for it and against labour unions. This development is even more remarkable because she had once been imprisoned for inciting the firebombing of his house. The only apparent explanation for this strange alliance would seem to be his rise to political power and her willingness to sacrifice anything in the cause of women's suffrage. Peace and social justice would have to be considered later.[20]

Prologue Germany: Late to the Race

Virtually all of the war-fostering characteristics and factors attributable to Great Britain and her allies also influenced Germany. She drifted into the war by making most of the same mistakes. I do not examine these matters in comparable detail as they applied to Germany. It is events in England, Canada and the U.S. that are most relevant to the examination of Canada's involvement in other people's wars. It was the job of Canadians opposed to the Great War to speak to Ottawa, not Berlin.

Germany came late to the European race to acquire territory because she did not fully become a nation until January 1871. At that time Great Britain was near the height of her imperial power, ruling nearly one fifth of the people on the planet. Like Germany, the U.S. was something of a latecomer to imperialism. The process of wresting territory from Spain and Native Americans was interrupted by a bloody civil war. Canada, of course, had only achieved some sort of confederation of provinces by 1867 and had neither the means nor the inclination to become an imperial power.

Part of the story of Germany's unification is particularly relevant because it helps to explain the vindictiveness of the French following the Great War. That hostility would play a significant part in bringing about the war that followed.

The Franco-Prussian War completed the nationhood process for Germany. The war began with events that were even pettier than those that would later trigger the Great War. Chancellor Bismarck and Napoleon III had been dickering over boundaries and territories for a number of years. This competition had not produced a war even though the French Emperor usually got the worst of the exchanges. But a diplomatic insult in a disagreement over the successor to the throne of Spain resulted in Napoleon's foolish declaration of war on Prussia in July, 1870. From such trivial discourtesy was born a factor that would have significant influence on this little war and the larger one to come.

The heretofore loosely confederated German provinces united militarily under Prussia and the French were soundly defeated by September. France lost the territories of Alsace and Lorraine. The creation of the German Empire was proclaimed at Versailles on January 18th, 1871.[21] This date also marked the beginning of intensified French hatred for the Germans. French political and military decisions thereafter would be guided by the desire for revenge. That attitude would continue at the peace conference following the Great War. There, given that the war had been contested largely on French soil, it was difficult for the other two post-war powers, Britain and the United States, to control a French animosity that had been festering since 1870.

Germany, Great Britain, and France cannot be faulted for failing to foresee the scope of the devastation that imperialist competition would bring. Wars tend to get out of hand. None of the European contestants could have known what would be wrought by a war fought with 20th century weapons and 19th century tactics and leadership. Germany came fully into being at a time when military, diplomatic, and religious back and forth was the norm on the continent, as was the practice of financing expansion with the resources of subjugated countries. Germany's desire to catch up with the leader was understandable. But her battleship-building spree not only spooked the British and began to draw Canada into the contest, it also prompted Great Britain to put aside her historic antipathy toward France and enter one of many agreements that would turn out in 1914 to be dominoes of doom for millions.

Yet, was not sea power the natural starting point in this imperial catch-up game? And in any event, in the late 19th century, without foreseeing the scope of the devastation to come, the imperialist powers of Europe had nevertheless anticipated and intended that they would wage war with one another soon. If not the German naval buildup and French resentment over 1870, the trigger would probably have been something else. By 1914, the major contestants were "all in" to the territorial and imperial contest. An additional player was Russia, anxious to dislodge Austrian hegemony over fellow Slavs in the Balkans. Contrary to a cornerstone argument of some, Germany was no more or less to blame for the coming tragedy than were the other European powers.

Canada, of course, was not in---all or otherwise. To draw her into someone else's war, the British would have to overcome a reluctance that, thankfully, continues today.

The Tragi-Comic Beginning

The triggering event of this holocaust was somewhat more serious than the boorish behavior that started the Franco-Prussian war. This time an important figure was assassinated, along with his pregnant wife. Archduke Franz Ferdinand was heir to the throne of Austria-Hungary. Still, assassinations of central European princes up to that time had certainly not been seen as an international call to arms.

Nevertheless, when Serbian nationalist Gavrilo Princip fired two point blank pistol shots at Franz Ferdinand's open touring car in Sarajevo, the world was soon to experience the folly of the "entangling alliances" that the designs of the major powers had spawned. Because the military forces of the already shopworn Austria-Hungary Empire performed so badly in the coming war, we tend almost to forget about that empire's part. The Vienna rulers, like many rulers who would follow, paid insufficient attention to accommodating the numerous ethnic groups within the empire. There was a nation of Serbia, but there were also many ethnic Serbs in Austria-Hungary. Some of them, like Princip, had a vision of a greater Serbia. Vienna's way of dealing with the problem was to look for any chance to invade Serbia and form a greater Austria-Hungary—a chance Princip presented.

Germany was Austria-Hungary's biggest supporter and the two were long bound by military treaty. The Serbs were ethnic Slavs, backed by Russia. In spite of the potential for conflict that these affiliations represented, nothing much happened in the immediate aftermath of the June 28th, 1914 assassination. Europe's nobility and political elite were customarily on holiday in July. So it was four weeks after the assassination that Austria issued an ultimatum to Serbia containing terms that she knew could not be met. Germany had already given approval and encouragement to an invasion of Serbia. Austria-Hungary declared war on Serbia and fired the first shots of the Great War on the Serbian capital, Belgrade, on July 29th.[22]

The Serbs mobilized and appealed to Russia for support. Here the plot thickens. France was tied by treaty to Russia. Germany, with the strongest army on the continent, saw an opportunity to seize territory from both France and Russia. Note that at this point Great Britain, and certainly Canada, had no stake in this particular fracas. Germany was Great Britain's main trading partner. The British and French had been making war on one another for centuries.

Neither was Britain formally obligated by treaty to act militarily on behalf of France in the now looming contest between France and Russia on one side, and Germany and Austria-Hungary on the other. But in addition to the alliances noted here, there were many other treaties and agreements of lesser status lying around---too many, in fact, to restate here. A cursory examination suggests that their main purpose was more the diplomatic settlement of competing imperialistic claims than the establishment of military obligations. This was the nature of something called the Entente Cordiale, which Britain and France had signed in 1904. It settled some colonial disputes and committed the parties to closer diplomatic cooperation. Unfortunately, the agreement was also interpreted as placing a "moral obligation" on the parties to aid each other in time of war.[23] And so, Britain ultimately chose to enter the war on behalf of France. For Canadians, it would turn out to be a most unfortunate choice.

This diplomatic web that included the Entente Cordiale was probably not the principal force that moved the British. It is more likely that the choice to go to war was influenced by Great Britain's relationship with Belgium, a country that she had long watched over in a benign manner, mainly out of a desire for a friendly nearby continental shoreline. Germany planned to move through Belgium to attack France. Militarily, this was exactly the right thing to do.

Politically, it would turn out to be Germany's second great mistake. Germany asked Belgium to permit its troops to cross. Belgium refused, and to the surprise of the Germans began blowing up bridges and railways.

Re-enter the confusing stack of treaties and agreements. There was an almost forgotten 1839 document called the Treaty of London, that everyone read as a British commitment to guarantee the neutrality of Belgium militarily, though the text contains no such explicit guarantee. Germany asked Britain to ignore it. Britain instead asked Germany to guarantee Belgian neutrality. Germany did not answer but, having no indications otherwise, assumed that the British response would be confined to diplomatic protests. It was not. Though the British had themselves not hesitated to march through neutral countries in Africa and Asia, Great Britain went to war ostensibly to protect Belgium.[24] If that was really the aim, it failed badly. Thousands of Belgian civilians would be killed by the Germans and would not see the great day of victory in 1918.

All of the great national leaders of Europe had miscalculated badly. The Great War was on, a bizarre international team effort. After a warning from the British that they could not stand aside in general conflicts on the continent, the Kaiser tried without success to pull the Austrians back. It may have been Russia's Tsar Nicholas II who ultimately provoked the war when he mobilized his vast army. That forced the Germans to mobilize. The French were still smarting over Alsace-Lorraine. The British had an empire to look after. Off they all went into the abyss.[25]

In the struggle for Africa, the imperial powers had learned the value of early mobilization, as well as early attack even if based on pretext. While they were dividing up that continent, they were anticipating war with one another sometime. Why not now? They almost certainly believed that this new war was not a momentous matter. There would be winners and losers. Borders would be adjusted accordingly and new treaties signed before the next round began. The game would go on. Not this time.

Not surprisingly, all parties assumed they would soon be victorious. The same estimated time period for rapid and glorious victory appears in the story of most of Canada's wars. The victorious troops would be "home by Christmas".

The Home Fronts: Governments, God, and the Press Saddle Up

Once Germany invaded Belgium and Britain went to war in aid of France, governments faced the task of stirring up sufficient public support for expending the blood and resources that war would require. In Canada and Great Britain, the Boer War had served not only as a preview exercise for this one, but had also provided a rough preliminary template for a more extreme campaign of propaganda. Knightley contends that more deliberate lies were told during the Great War than in any other period of history. He observes that even though propaganda dates back 2,400 years, it was first used in an organized, scientific manner in the Great War.[26]

Propaganda more than any other factor may have prolonged this war long beyond the time when it would have ended under the old rules, and set the stage for a disastrous approach to constructing the peace that finally ended it. Predictably, the leaders of the warring nations pronounced solemnly and sadly that in spite of their desire for peace war had been thrust upon them. They then proceeded with the work of characterizing their imperialist squabbles as the final struggle between good and evil. The day after Britain declared war, British Prime Minister Herbert Asquith somehow managed with a straight face to tell the House of Commons that the country was not fighting for the advancement of its own interests, but for *principles whose maintenance is vital to the civilized world.*[27] In Canada, a clerical pronouncement was at least a bit more candid. Bishop Farthing of Montreal's Christ Church Cathedral feared that the empire was at stake and: *Our nation may go down if we should be defeated and **our***

power will be lost. *We shall be stripped of our power and of the future, no man can tell*. (Emphasis added)[28] Not overly spiritual, but at least honest about motive.

Asquith's speech embodied an essential first prong of pro-war propaganda: the importance of the struggle and the purity of the cause. The second is demonizing the enemy. The French press pithily captured both prongs, terming the conflict a holy war of civilization against barbarity. Everyone joined in. The Russians were going to fight against the "German yoke". The Germans pronounced that Russia wanted to crush the culture of all Western Europe and that the British, French, and Russians had conspired to annihilate them. When Turkey joined on the German side, her sultan pronounced the war a sacred struggle.[29] The imperial powers may have originally planned to have another comparatively polite war. If war is a cataclysmic battle for the preservation of all that is good, however and the enemy is less than human, that is not possible. The only option is total victory. When rivalry, dislike, and contempt are converted to pure hatred, the nature of warfare is fundamentally altered. It is no longer sufficient to defeat the enemy. He must be destroyed.

During the war, "brave little Belgium" would be a major propaganda asset. The politics around that theme would even have a direct and costly effect on war strategy, as we will see in an examination of the Canadian experience at Ypres. For these reasons, while in no way denigrating the loss of civilian life there, it should be remembered that brave little Belgium was herself a brutal imperial player in Africa. In 1885, the European powers ceded to Belgian King Leopold II a territory the size of Poland as his personal colony. What became the Belgian Congo did not get free of that yoke until 1960. In the interim, Belgium administered a colonial holocaust that slaughtered six to nine million people in the course of plundering ivory, rubber and minerals.[30]

At the outset, the "brave little Belgium" story fit particularly well into the extreme propaganda narrative. In their initial advance, the Germans killed some 5,000 civilians, some shot as guerilla fighters or hostages, some simply murdered. British and French propaganda spun this into amazing atrocity stories as part of a campaign to characterize the Germans as embarking on a deliberate campaign of terror, torture, sacrilege, and barbarism. The most creative one was a cooperative effort: the Belgian baby without hands. A *London Times* war correspondent passed on a hearsay account to a Catholic official of seeing German soldiers cut off the hands of a baby who was clinging to its mother. The French propaganda unit produced what purported to be a photograph of the handless baby. A French newspaper then republished the story along with a drawing showing German soldiers eating the hands. Post-war inquiries found no evidence to substantiate the story.[31] By then, of course, it did not matter.

In Britain, the *Financial News* reported that the Kaiser had ordered German airmen to make a special effort to kill King Albert's children, and that he had personally ordered the torture of three year olds, specifying the particular tortures.[32] Kipling chimed in that there were only two divisions in the world, human beings and Germans.[33]

Germany did the best it could to join in the demonization derby, but she would be no match for the Allies---until the next war. In the Great War, German newspapers cited reports of colonial troops sneaking across the lines at night to slit German throats and drink their blood. They told of hospitals filled with German soldiers whose eyes had been gouged out, bolstering this story with the purported account of a 10 year old boy who had seen a bucket full of soldiers' eyes.[34]

Throughout the period of the war there was no shortage of people who knew this was all hyperbolic nonsense. That they did not speak, or their voices were silenced or drowned out is testament of the power of propaganda, backed by the coercive power of government.

Public support for the war in Canada and Great Britain displayed a common pattern. It was enthusiastic---until, in spite of the effort of governments and a compliant press to suppress it, word began to get out that that things were not going well. In the Great War, it took about two years for the truth to begin to emerge. From 1916, we will see a dramatic change in the popular and political landscape. In

Canada, as the truth seeped through it produced a division that must be counted among the costs of the war—the fight over conscription.

At the beginning, however, we see the usual fervor. Why did men, especially working class men, flock to recruiting stations to enlist? The reasons remain something of a mystery although there are clues. The impact of the propaganda campaign is a significant reason but not the only explanation. The residue of support for the empire was a factor. Two-thirds of those who initially joined up had been born in Great Britain, though most had been settled here for 15-20 years. First Nations recruits sought recognition and respect for the their people. Some people actually feared a German attack. Also, the new country by its nature was not short of people who had an interest in the prospect of an adventure. Propaganda and secrecy about the Boer War, as well as its light casualty toll had given no indication that this one would be anything other than another lark. There were also economic factors. In Canada the war was preceded by a two-year depression. Much as their great grandchildren would do after the next economic disaster, many joined up because the food, shelter, even the meagre army wage was the best deal available to them. The popular term was "hungerscription".[35]

The propaganda effort was not just an exercise in soaring rhetoric appealing to patriotism. The message had a hard edge and encouraged division. As the war progressed, men who did not want to join the military were outed, ridiculed, and sometimes kidnapped and taken to recruiting offices. Governments also gave tacit approval, and sometimes more than that, to mob violence against dissenters.[36]

Whatever the mixture of reasons, the period of insanity began enthusiastically on all fronts.

Canada: Not Ready, But In Anyway

Canadians entered the Great War as they would enter the next one: ill trained, ill equipped, and with too many lives in the hands of poor leaders. Sustaining this war would test the limits of even the British/Canadian propaganda machine. In part that was because this was a war that went badly for Britain and her French and colonial

51

allies from the very beginning. While there was no Dunkirk, it soon became clear that this would be no Boer lark. Nobody would be home by Christmas—at least not alive. Very early on, it became essential to hide the truth.

In varying degrees, the Canadian experience reflects all of the factors we are examining. They are apparent in the story of four battles. These stories particularly highlight Propaganda and the Failure of Journalism, Horror and Senseless Military Deaths, Military Skill and Bravery in Spite of Poor Leadership and Longing for Recognition. The purpose of recounting these battles is not to construct a military history. There are plenty of good military histories, none better than those by Tim Cook. Rather, it is to call attention to matters that should already have been part of a national conversation about going to war. The four battles became the foundation of the narrative that fighting in other people's wars was Canada's path to international recognition. The four milestones are Ypres, the Somme, Vimy, and Passchendaele.

Some in the cast of characters for these events are by now familiar. You will recall Lord Herbert Kitchener, the commander of troops in 1898 who used machine guns to wipe out 10,000 Sudanese armed with spears in the "battle" of Omdurman. In the Great War, he was the secretary of state for war, the first military person to hold that office in 250 years.[37] In spite of the African experience he, like many in the military hierarchy, still failed to appreciate the impact on warfare of modern weaponry. The weapons included not only machine guns but also the artillery that Cook alleges was an even more devastating bringer of death.[38] He was also, of course, the architect of the Boer concentration camps exposed by Emily Hobhouse. Kitchener, however, showed that he had at least learned two lessons from the South Africa adventure. He was one of the few who knew this was not going to be a "home by Christmas" conflict, and he began to assemble a massive force. The concentration camp experience may also have taught him about the need to suppress independent war reporting. He hated war correspondents and did his best keep them out of the war zone throughout the conflict.[39]

Sir John French was the initial commander of British forces. He had served under Kitchener in the Boer War and had been responsible for herding civilians into the concentration camps. This was somewhat ironic, as he was the brother of peace activist Charlotte Despard. French did have some concern for the welfare of his troops, not a prevailing characteristic among his peers.

For the Canadians, the deadliest of all would turn out to be Sir Douglas Haig, who had friends in high places, including the monarchy and would eventually manoeuvre his way into replacing French. A distillery heir, Haig had been present as a young major at the Omdurman machine gun exercise. He had also failed to learn from that experience. He was in love with the glorious cavalry charge, as was French.[40] He would preside at the Somme over the greatest single day loss of soldiers' lives in the history of warfare. He would go on from there to develop and defend a strategy of attrition that counted as unsuccessful any day when a minimum number of the men under his command were not killed.

These were three of those into whose hands the lives of arriving Canadians were committed. Kitchener and French were true to form in the early days of the war. French's expeditionary force went to the aid of the French army, which at the highest levels of command also had no effective leadership. Clad in brightly coloured and easily visible uniforms, the French forces in effect re-enacted the role of the Sudanese at Omdurman. They charged the German machine guns with bayonets. In a few months, 300,000 of them would be casualties---losses that would not be reported by the British press. French's much smaller British force suffered similarly, blundering into a large German force at Mons. The French army retreated to reorganize. French, out of concern for his men, sought to do likewise. Kitchener ordered him not to move.[41]

Haig and Kitchener combined for another spectacular defeat at Loos, where they marched troops in parade ground formation into German machine guns. So many were killed that a German commander later reported his gunners were so filled with pity, remorse, and nausea that at one point they refused to continue firing. Haig blamed Loos on French.[42]

Four *"Coming of Age" Battles*

Ypres

In the fall of 1914, the first contingent of Canadians arrived in England where they received badly needed training. In March 1915, they took their places in what by then had become static trench warfare. In the training period, they demonstrated the exuberant lack of discipline that, for some would translate to creativity on the battlefield. While they were not revolutionary colonists like the Americans, neither were these volunteers beholden to the British class system. They had not left the effort to tame the prairies of Saskatchewan just to march unquestioningly to their deaths at the behest of some young aristocrat officer who had gained his commission through cash or connections. Like the Boers, Canadians were averse to rigid top-down discipline. It was an attitude that would ultimately save many lives.[43]

This rowdy, undertrained but confident bunch first saw major action at the Ypres salient in April 1915, though they had suffered some losses earlier at Armentieres. By definition, a salient exposes its defenders to fire from three sides. As one Canadian lieutenant confirmed, that often exposes the rear also: *The Ypres salient is the worst place one could imagine. We get shot at from three sides, and the support trenches come in for hotter fire than the front lines.*[44] Defending a salient is consequently quite difficult to justify for tactical or strategic reasons. The reasons for the defence of the Ypres salient were not primarily military considerations. Defence was largely a matter of propaganda. Though there was some strategic value in defending a gateway to channel ports, the important point was that the salient edged into Belgium.[45] It had to be defended so that the folks back home could be told the Germans had not completely overrun "brave little Belgium". For that, thousands of men would suffer and die before battling to a stalemate---three times.

In what was technically the second battle of Ypres, the Canadians faced a German thrust that was accompanied by a chlorine gas attack. Although gas attacks were not a major factor in the war, they added measurably to its already horrible reality. One soldier reported: *A man dies by gas in horrible torment. He turns perfectly black… he foams at the mouth as a dog in hydrophobia; he lingers five or six minutes then—goes West.* Another soldier: *Some of the men were clawing at their throats. Their bodies were swelled… Some of the Canadians were writhing on the ground, their tongues hanging out.*[46]

None of this reality could be permitted to get back to the families of the soldiers. The openly acknowledged purpose for censorship and the propaganda effort was to ensure that recruitment levels would remain high. Parents of the volunteers would have to be convinced that the deaths of their sons came about under heroic circumstances, all for a higher cause. Commitment to that version of death continues. One wonders what would have been the effect if British and Canadian mothers had received telegrams like this: *We regret to inform you that your son, Private Benson, choked to death in a spasm similar to hydrophobia, clawing at his throat, while gallantly defending a worthless piece of land called the Ypres salient.*

The use of poison gas at Ypres and elsewhere by both sides was but an early example of a drastic and tragic change in the conduct of warfare introduced in the Great War. Soldiers and innocent civilians have been paying a high price for that change ever since.

The Germans had no monopoly on this terrible weapon. Haig had ordered it for the first time at Loos but it blew back into the British trenches. A month before the soon to be famous Vimy battle, Canadians tried their own gas attack there, also a failure.[47] When the rapid strike to subdue France failed and the Germans found themselves fighting on two fronts, the high command elected gas warfare. Most of the generals argued against it but the commander of the army facing Ypres finally gave in.[48]

A future Nobel Prize winner developed chlorine gas. His wife was a brilliant chemist in her own right. After a party celebrating a German attack at Ypres, she committed suicide.[49] Apparently none of the combatants had similar reservations about gas warfare on humanitarian grounds, though The Hague Conventions of 1899 and 1907 had outlawed it. The U.S. would not sign, and to this day, the major western military powers have refused to destroy their stockpiles of chemical weapons.

The German attack at Ypres initially succeeded in breaking through the salient and endangering 50,000 Allied troops. One reason they did not follow up was apparently fear of the gas lingering in shell holes. The limiting factor on this weapon, and indeed on any weapon in the Great War, seemed to be whether it would work reliably rather than any moral or ethical concern. The establishment of efficacy over morality as the dominant factor in the use of weapons technology is one of the most tragic legacies of the Great War.

The use of gas not only damaged the already frayed notion of waging war in something of a civilized manner, it also marked fundamental changes in the way future wars would be conducted. Military leaders on both sides could be forgiven for failing to grasp them but they became exponentially significant in every later war.

Advanced weaponry virtually cancels the importance of valour, bravery, and individual soldiering skill. Daring and fearlessness no longer matter much.[50] The victims of that first major gas attack died at the hand of an enemy they could not see, much less engage in combat. In that manner also have died millions of others as warfare today has come to resemble a deadly video game.

The disappearance of moral considerations and the unquestioning use of advanced weaponry begun in the Great War are linked to an even greater tragedy: the general acceptance of killing civilians. For the most part, armies on battlefields fought earlier European wars. In this one, German Zeppelins killed civilians. France bombed villages in Morocco. In the latter stages of the war, giant German guns bombarded Paris from a distance of 70 miles.[51] In the next war, atomic bombs and fire bombings would kill more than half a million civilians in a day. Today, bombs and "targeted" drone aircraft strikes kill thousands of civilians.

Killing with advanced weaponry has sent the powers employing the most advanced weapons on a quest for a moral fig leaf. One principal justification the Americans offer for drones is the same as the best they could do for Hiroshima: The lives of a lot of soldiers would be lost if conventional tactics were employed, so the loss of civilian lives is OK. Sacrificing innocent lives to save those of professional soldiers turns moral reasoning on its head.

There is an additional and apparently unappreciated consequence of letting technology mandate use, with justifications composed later. It is that what one does to one's adversary, one implicitly authorizes to be done to one's self—as and if the ability to do so becomes available. Canada has no control of the weaponry decisions of her patrons, and has no guarantee of immunity from the consequences of those decisions.

The German breakthrough at Ypres was achieved only with huge losses because German commanders also did not understand the power of modern weaponry or fully appreciate the advantage of defenders in static warfare. Canadian units saved the day with counterattacks and successful defence of the salient. As they had done in South Africa, our British patrons kept us on the string with effusive praise. One general simply recycled and rephrased his accolades from the Boer War: "...*the whole army realized that it was only the gallant actions of the Canadians that saved Ypres; otherwise one of the great disasters in the history of the British Army might have occurred. The Canadians had many casualties, but their gallantry and determination undoubtedly saved the situation.*[52] Sweet music to the ears of a fledgling nation longing for recognition. And the only price of this praise for the defence of a piece of propaganda value real estate was 6,000 Canadians dead, wounded or missing to be replaced by enthusiastic new recruits. [53] Yea Ypres.

It is not, however, the prowess of Canadian troops in their first major engagement, or the praise from the patron nation that marks Ypres most significantly in our national mythology and our story of lessons unlearned. It is the tragic eloquence of a 41-year-old artillery officer in the First Canadian Division, John McCrae. His story almost has the texture of fiction, which adds to the enduring impact of his short masterpiece. As Canadians who know little else about the war are aware, he is the author of *In Flanders Fields*.

McCrae had recently graduated at the top of his class in medicine at the University of Toronto when the Boer War began. He was a member of the military reserve and may have been influenced to volunteer for South Africa by his admiration for the works of Rudyard Kipling. Oddly, the reality of that war did not escape him. He wrote: *Every day there are from 15 to 30 Tommies dying from fever and dysentery. Every one who dies is sewn up in a blanket, and four shillings are taken out of the pay for the blanket. The soldier's game is not what it's cracked up to be.*[54] In spite of this intelligent understanding, he volunteered for the Great War, though he told a friend that he knew it would be a terrible one.

At Ypres, McCrae was an artillery gunner and unit medical officer tasked with the grisly work of dealing with Canadian casualties. The generally accepted account of the birth of the iconic poem is that after the gas attack artillery exchanges resumed and McRae's friend, Lieutenant Alexis Helmer, 22, was killed. McCrae presided over the committal ceremony, remembering the words as best he could.[55] The next day, in about 15 minutes he wrote the poem that has been memorized by generations of Canadian students and, along with the flowers he described, has become a symbol of how we remember this war. Tragically, it has also become a symbol of how we and many other nations view our option to get out of ill-advised wars. McCrae wrote:

In Flanders fields the poppies blow
Between the crosses, row on row,
That mark our place; and in the sky
The larks, still bravely singing, fly

Scarce heard amid the guns below.
We are the Dead. Short days ago
We lived, felt dawn, felt sunset glow,
Loved and were loved, and now we lie
In Flanders fields.
Take up our quarrel with the foe:
To you from failing hands we throw
The torch; be yours to hold it high.
If ye break faith with those of us who die
We shall not sleep, though poppies grow
In Flanders fields.[56]

Consider the remarkable elegance and pathos of the first two verses. The first speaks of a still beautiful and ongoing world of flowers and birds amidst the chaos. The second richly describes what the dead have lost. Would that the third verse had been a call from the dead to ensure that ignorant and perverse leaders never again be permitted to add to their number. But that was not to be the third verse.

The third verse, equally eloquent, has been used to perpetuate the tragic lie that somehow if 10,000 are slaughtered, they will have died for nothing unless another 10,000 are sent to follow. What Berton saw as the message was that anything short of a total victory is a betrayal of those who fought and bled for it.[57] Without mentioning the poem, Hochschild also recognized its message: *Men had been maimed and killed in such unimaginable numbers that any talk of compromise peace risked seeming to dishonor them and render their sacrifices meaningless.*[58]

One can and should fault the Haigs and Kitcheners of the world. One does not fault the line soldier who has experienced the reality of war and seen his friends die. One does not fault John McCrae. I doubt that in his grief he could have foreseen that his writing would foster vacuous pronouncements from politicians in future wars that to "cut and run" is unthinkable. I doubt he would have anticipated that his poppies would gradually become symbols to some of the noble nature of war rather than a remembrance of the pain of families like that of Lt. Helmer. Would it have been better for the family to learn that their son was probably not asleep in Flanders fields? More likely, the artillery shell that killed him scattered his body parts across the churned earth. Would it have saved another family such pain?

McCrae had little time to be questioned or explain his work, even in the unlikely event that he could have recognized its potential significance. It was first published in December, 1915. He died of pneumonia three years later.[59]

Skill and bravery, and praise for it, as well as a tragically magnificent poem defined the first of the battles we remember. The obliteration of one tiny unit in a massive campaign was important to its next chapter. That annihilation is symbolic of a campaign would tell us much about what is wrong with using this war to define much of anything positive, much less a nation.

The Somme

Mercifully, Canadians escaped the worst of the Somme campaign, which included war's bloodiest day---July 1st, 1916. The story of the Somme is usually included as part of our remembrance primarily because of the 801 men who were the Newfoundland Regiment, part of the British 29th Division. The next day only 68 answered roll call.[60] Since becoming the last province to join Canada in 1949, many Newfoundlanders observe July 1st not as a Canada Day celebration but more as a day of painful remembrance. The Newfoundlanders were part of the Empire's 57,000 dead or wounded on that day in 1916.[61]

Canadian forces entered the Somme line in September. The Somme battles continued for months. It was long after the July 1st day of slaughter that the 4th Division took the bulk of Canada's 25,000 campaign casualties capturing a ditch called the Regina Trench. It was as unimportant as any other piece of real estate in the area but had been designated as a face-saving objective after the disastrous earlier attacks.[62] Ypres revisited.

The battle for the Regina Trench was also a microcosm of the greater tragedy that was soon to unfold. The German trench system ran some 3000 metres in front of the Canadian lines. British General Julian Byng, of whom much more will be said later, had taken over command. Byng was far ahead of his superiors in creative tactics, but he had little room to manoeuvre here. Byng had high regard for his Canadian units and agreed with Canadian commanders who saw a frontal assault as folly. Unfortunately, his superior, General Hubert Gough, overrode his objections. Byng was ordered to take the trench "at all costs". The attack failed. Depleted and undersized units suffered massive casualties.[63]

As they had done in the aftermath of earlier failures, the higher commanders blamed the troops, particularly the Canadians. Of them, General Douglas Haig said: *I think the case was that in the hope of saving lives they attacked in too weak numbers...They [the Canadians] have been very extravagant in expending ammunition.*[64] Haig's concern about Canadian ineptitude did not keep him from writing a self-congratulatory report to the king while the battle for the trench was in progress.[65]

The Regina Trench story is but one example of the importance of considering the Somme campaign in some detail. At the Somme, the factors we are examining played out on such a huge scale that their impact was felt in both Britain and Canada. The campaign was a British disaster of such magnitude that its aftermath presented the propaganda campaign with its greatest challenge. Public enthusiasm waned as the truth about the Somme slipped through the censors. Soldiers began to have even less concern for killing and more for surviving. 1916 should have begun the process of ending the war in some semblance of the way European conflicts had historically been settled.

The story is significant also as an example of the poor leadership to which Canadians were subjected. If Regina Trench was a microcosm of the Somme, the Somme campaign itself provided a snapshot of everything that was wrong with this war.

An important part of the story, illuminating those factors, is the conduct of General Douglas Haig and what it tells us about the kind of leadership forced on Canadians by their integration into the British army. Characterizing Haig with any charity at all is a challenge. Whatever other qualities he may have had, he was absolutely the wrong person at the wrong time to be in command of anything. Canadians would endure bad foreign generals in future wars, but Haig is the clearest example of Canadians acquitting themselves well in spite of poor leadership. Tens of thousands of young people lost their lives needlessly because of him. When the Somme campaign began, he had manoeuvred Sir John French out of command. He had the ear of the king. Kitchener had been killed. In current parlance, "this was all on him".

Haig did initially resist the idea of his French counterpart Joseph Jacques Joffre for a massive assault on the strongest point in the entire German line. Though Joffre had earlier authored a battlefield disaster at Verdun, Haig eventually acquiesced; again not for military reasons but to ease tension between the British and French over which country was pulling its weight in the war.[66]

Subordinates of Haig and Joffre were left to implement the *strategically* mistaken choice of the Somme using outdated and mistaken *tactics.* Modern tactics for infantry attacks include one part of a unit laying down a base of fire while the other advances, sometimes in a flanking move. All keep heads down and the manouevre element moves quickly. Before the Somme, Canadian units had been experimenting with similar tactics.[67] In contrast, the Somme attackers were trained and ordered to proceed directly forward, fully upright, weapons at the port position, at a slow steady pace, each man carrying 66 pounds of equipment. One historian described the effect of German machine guns on the first day: *the lines...began to melt away. Men simply rolled forward slowly to lie on their faces, their knees bent under them in a posture of prayer...The bobbing line of helmets thinned away to nothing.*[68] British artillery observers in a position to see the advance at first thought the troops were simply lying down to avoid the fire and would get up. *To their horror, it began to dawn on them that all the khaki figures sprawled in rows before the German lines were dead.*[69] Haig continued to order attacks in this manner. Eventually, the 25,000 Canadian casualties would be only part of an allied total of nearly a million, including 200,000 French. It is impossible to communicate such numbers in human terms. The entire campaign netted the Allies seven miles of ground.[70]

Haig's strategic choice of a massive frontal attack was in furtherance of his notion of a "Big Push" that would break the trench war stalemate. The greatest artillery barrage the world had ever known preceded it. The 3,000,000 shells were supposed to destroy the German barbed wire so Allied troops could walk through virtually unmolested. That did not happen, and because Haig had no effective intelligence capability the first to learn that truth were attacking troops who died by the thousands on the wire.[71]

The Germans suffered massive losses at the Somme as well, but as defenders the resulting stalemate operated in their favour. In the old game of warfare, time was on their side. In the 19th century mindset and especially after Verdun and the Somme it was reasonable for Germany to assume that eventually this war would end in the manner of earlier ones.

The temptation of a Big Push strategy was understandable. The war was going nowhere. What is not understandable is the means of implementing the strategy that Haig would come to favour, both as a way to put a better face on the Somme carnage and as a way forward. It was not simply a strategic error. The moral issue was Haig's pursuit of a war of attrition and his apparent lack of concern for the lives of his troops at the Somme and throughout the war. He accorded priority to "body count". In fact, Haig may have been hedging his bets toward attrition even as the Somme attack kicked off. On June 30th, one of his senior staff officers wrote: *We do not expect any great advance...We are fighting primarily to wear down the German armies and nation.*[72]

Haig's own writings revealed his attrition approach as well as its hallmark---disdain for human lives. On July 2, as he continued to order attack after futile attack, he was given a report that casualties had to that point totaled 40,000. He wrote in his diary: *This cannot be considered severe, in view of the numbers engaged, and the length of front attacked.*[73] He began to use language to justify both the "breakthrough" and attrition strategies. He wrote of reason to believe that enemy morale was deteriorating, that the British army was confident in its proven superiority, and that German civilians were demoralized. Attrition was working, he said. He called the Somme a success because it was costing the Germans more in dead and wounded.[74]

Haig was wrong on all counts. He had really not pushed the Germans significantly at all. And Allied casualties at the Somme, eventually put at over 623,000, exceeded German losses of 465,000. Not that any of this mattered to a compliant British and Canadian press. Berton provides a sample of Somme headlines in Canada: BRITISH SCYTHE OF DEATH CUTS NEW SWATH... BRITISH SMASH FOES ON SOMME.[75]

There is more evidence that Haig's approach to implementing his war of attrition made it not just wrong but immoral. He decided that the German body count was bound to be inadequate if his own casualties were too low. He was prone to angry outbursts when too few of his own people had died, once deploring in his diary that one of his divisions had only lost 1,000 men that day. The death of 5,000 of his own soldiers each day was an acceptable indicator that the Germans must be losing more. His generals began to refer to the figure as "normal wastage".[76] British prime minister Lloyd George deplored Haig's strategy. He wrote: *We could certainly beat the Germans if we could only get Haig to join them.*[77] Haig's political connections, however, rendered Lloyd George powerless to replace him.[78]

Haig bears responsibility for numerous other factors that ensured defeat and waste of life in the Somme campaign. He surrounded himself with sycophants as staff officers. They told him only what he wished to hear in the critical fields of intelligence gathering and communications. Worse, they were incompetent. Before the attack, intelligence patrols and front line officers reported that the wire had not been breached and the attack could not possibly succeed. Haig and his generals derided the messengers as insufficiently aggressive. During the attack, when reports of the carnage finally trickled back to his headquarters Haig continued to order frontal assaults.

Haig's was but an extreme example of the British leadership model to which Canadians were subjected. The Canadian model, at times comparatively short on discipline and ceremony, was a better one. As we will see, the presence of independent-minded and well informed troops familiar with the battle plan helps to explain the much celebrated victory at Vimy.

The tactical command structure to which the Canadians were subjected before Vimy was a three-tiered system. At the bottom, of course, were the ordinary soldiers and N.C.O.'s. Their living conditions were abominable and their lives were freely spent. When it came to exposure to danger, there was a very definite division within the British officer corps. Though they came from a privileged class, junior officers were trained to see war as a team game, where they were to lead by heroically exposing themselves to fire to encourage the team. Though their everyday living conditions were a little better, the consequences of this ethic were deadly. Like their troops, the subalterns and lieutenants died by the tens of thousands, learning too late that courage counted for very little in the face of modern weaponry.

Generals and other senior staff officers lived a very different life and Haig was a prime example. He and his commanders fought the Somme campaign from a chateau in Montreuil, 50 miles behind the line. He never visited the front. His son wrote that Haig felt he should not visit the casualty clearing stations because doing so made him physically ill.[79] Instead, he and his staff and frequent high placed guests dined on lamb, fresh fish, and *foie gras.* [80] Ordinary soldiers were not ignorant of the three-tiered system. They were especially resentful of headquarters staff officers, the ones who were entertained with light music during dinners served by female corps members with the GHQ colours in their hair ribbons.[81] Knightley reports that when staff officers made their infrequent visits to the front their identifying red tabs evoked an intense desire for their death among ordinary soldiers and tactical officers alike.[82]

Religion in service of war may also have played some part. Another voice Haig heard was that of God. He prayed daily and wrote that every step of his plan was taken with divine help; that he could not stand the strain if a "Great Unseen Power" was not sustaining him. Tim Cook writes: *His belief in divine providence guiding his hand helped him deal with the terrible losses, but acting on such blind faith was without a doubt a disservice to his troops.*[83] Amen. Haig's chosen pastor complained: *we lament too much over death.* Haig agreed, writing that the nation must be taught to bear losses for the divine cause and the loss of one-tenth of the manhood of the nation was not too great a price to pay.[84]

It is not known whether God spoke to Haig about military courtesy and dress, but he and his generals remained quite concerned about these matters. Incredibly, soon after the Somme debacle, Haig recalled in his diary that he had called the attention of some of his senior commanders to *the lack of smartness and slackness of one of its battalions in the matter of saluting.* Even Lord Edmund Allenby, who not only saw the insanity of the war but also many of the errors Haig was making in the Somme preparation, was a prisoner of spit and polish. He once loudly berated a soldier in a trench for wearing an incorrect uniform. The soldier gave no answer. He was dead. [85] This fetish was not just stupid. It was deadly. Private William A. Tucker's memoir refers to the compulsory polishing of brass buttons on uniforms as "criminally idiotic iniquities", noting that all who operated in No Man's Land between the trenches had vivid memories of presenting clear outlines in the form of the polished buttons, and German machine gunners did not overlook these gifts.[86]

Haig's massive frontal assault on the most fortified and most geographically challenging portion of the German line was a *strategic* mistake.

Separating senior commanders from manoeuvring units was, of course, a deadly *tactical* mistake.

It is difficult to find the proper word for Haig's his lack of concern for the lives and well being of his men. "Mistake" is clearly inadequate.[87]

In 1916, war makers on both sides were in trouble. Would public awareness of the scale of the slaughter, the stalemate, and the reality of the war as ordinary soldiers experienced it have hastened its end? Lloyd George thought so. The following year, after listening to an account by one of the few returning war correspondents willing to report the truth, he opined to the editor of the *Manchester Guardian*: *If people really knew, the war would be stopped tomorrow.*[88] He immediately acknowledged that they would not know because: *The correspondents don't write and the censorship would not pass the truth.*[89]

1916 should have marked a negotiated end to the war. Instead of more big pushes spending hundreds of thousands of lives, people would have been better served if governments had taken seriously the peace mission that year of Boer War hero Emily Hobhouse. She made her way to Berlin and managed talks with German foreign minister Gottlieb Von Jagow. She had three objectives. First, to get peace talks moving to avoid further bloodshed. Second, to obtain release of civilian internees on foreign soil. Why, for example, could not Britain and Germany at least exchange all civilian prisoners not of military age? Third, to get relief to the people of Belgium. She had ideas about how to partially lift the British naval blockade to accomplish this. Von Jagow was cautiously receptive and willing to use her as a conduit for talks. Other officials raised at least the possibility of the return of Alsace-Lorraine in exchange for peace.

She returned from Berlin and, again relying on family connections, expected that Von Jagow's counterpart Sir Edward Grey would be interested in her report. Instead she was summoned to Scotland Yard for interrogation, her passport was revoked and officials undertook a determined but fruitless effort to find an offence with which to charge her. Hochschild wrote: *But however hopeless her lone-wolf diplomacy…in the course of the deadliest conflict the world had ever seen, she was the sole person from any of the warring countries who actually journeyed to the other side in search of peace.*[90]

It is difficult in hindsight to know whether full public knowledge about the reality of what their sons were enduring would have produced a demand that the war be settled and ended. Governments made every effort to ensure that as little of that reality as possible reached Britain or Canada: *But if you ever had to write home about a particular mate, you'd always say he got it cleanly and quickly with a bullet and didn't know what happened.*[91] Battlefield censors ensured that only that kind of letter reached the homeland. Similar watch was kept over truthful descriptions of life at the front. The suppression arm of propaganda was pervasive on both sides. The Germans in 1916 began to fake their casualty figures and the process became so muddled that the true figures will probably never be known.[92]

Most accounts by ordinary soldiers were published only after the war. An Australian lieutenant, who had watched two of his fellow officers go insane, wrote: *I have one man's puttee, a dead man's helmet, another dead man's gas protector, a dead man's bayonet. My tunic is rotten with other men's blood, and partly spattered with a comrade's brains.*[93] Before he was killed, he wrote that his friends were being murdered by the "incompetence, callousness, and personal vanity of those in high authority". Another Australian's plea was: *For Christ's sake, write a book on the life of an infantryman, and by so doing you will prevent these shocking tragedies.*[94]

Another enlisted man wrote of an earlier battle that had yielded two miles of territory at the cost of 61,000 casualties: *It was impossible to bury them all… You'd go along the trenches and you'd see a boot and puttee sticking out, or an arm or a hand, sometimes faces.*[95]

Lice and rats were constant companions of the trench soldiers. The troops could hear as rats started on the corpses of their comrades, beginning with the eyes and working onward until the only remnant of what was once a human being they had known consisted of a skeleton and ragged fragments of uniform.[96]

During the war, these were the kinds of accounts that required censorship if the flow of recruits was to continue. The press helped all it could. The *London Times* management for example, openly acknowledged that the mission of the paper was to was to increase the flow of recruits and the truth would not serve that mission. [97]

After the Somme, there was trouble at home. Battlefield censorship was not completely successful. Leaders in Britain and Canada knew that the disasters of 1916 presented a significant public relations problem as the ongoing war of attrition continued to chew up lives in frightening numbers. An estimate of casualties reported that one serviceman of British birth or speech was killed every 45 seconds of that calendar year.[98] Dealing with the problem required not only lies and misinformation, but also enlisting religion and silencing dissent. Haig wrote that the press was the best means of handling "ill-informed" public opinion.[99] So the press was told in threatening terms what it could and could not print. The government also secured the support of many prominent authors. Foremost among the dissenters was distinguished scientist, Bertrand Russell. Lloyd George warned Russell the he would not hesitate to prosecute someone for publishing the Sermon on the Mount if it interfered with the war effort.[100] Russell was later jailed for speaking out.

The British government organized a War Propaganda Bureau, which produced books, films, and posters but distributed them under the names of legitimate well-known publishing houses. Not satisfied with the truth of what the Germans were doing in Belgium, which was brutal enough, the office conjured up and distributed stories of German troops bayoneting babies and crucifying peasants… and a Canadian Sergeant! How a Canadian was chosen for this honour we do not know but the fiction played widely and well in Canada, where gruesome details of the atrocity were invented and disseminated. The stories were sometimes illustrated with a cartoon of a giant German soldier with children speared on his bayonet. It was a military version of the handless Belgian Baby.[101]

The office also had films made, including one that rewrote the Somme battles and made them into victories. Nineteen million people saw *Battle of the Somme* in its first six weeks. The film was highly successful in shoring up public support. Minister of information and major propagandist John Buchan made sure Canada got a similar film, *Canadians on the Western Front.* These efforts were so successful that the Germans rushed out their own film, *With Our Heroes at the Somme.*[102]

Religion willingly played its part. At a time when church attendance was high, clergy were urged to redouble their efforts to make sure parishioners knew whom God favoured. How the Church of England could have done more, however, is not clear. Before the campaign, the Anglican Bishop of London intoned from the pulpit: *Kill Germans! Kill them! Not for the sake of killing, but to save the world...Kill the good as well as the bad...Kill the young men as well as the old...Kill those who have shown kindness to our wounded as well as those fiends who crucified the Canadian sergeant...I look upon it as a war for purity, I look on everybody who dies in it as a martyr.*[103] The service would have ended, *BISHOP: Go in peace, to love and serve the Lord. CONGREGATION: Thanks be to God.*

In Canada, there was comparatively less zeal from a divided Roman Catholic Church, populated extensively by French Canadians. The Protestants, however, did their best to make up the difference. One observer's concluded that the Methodist Church became the most radical religious organization in Canada in support of this "just" war. The general superintendent of the church claimed that pacifism, which the church had once supported, could now not be tolerated, "no matter who teaches it."[104] Methodists were urged to enlist in the army and *go to the front as bravely as one who hears the call of God.*[105] This "just war" was marketed as a Christian Crusade against the German antichrist.[106]

Canadian newspapers were so helpful that censorship did not have to be quite as heavy handed as it was in Britain. Our compliant press even banned stories that had been cleared by British censors. The editor of the *Moncton Times* apologized abjectly to the chief censor for publishing an account of shrapnel wounds that took off a piece of the ear of a local Somme volunteer.[107]

Still, Canada was blessed with an occasional journalist in the mold of Emily Hobhouse. One was Robert Service. The chief censor cracked down hard on his editor after this battlefield account: *I cannot turn the car in that narrow road with the wounded lying under my very wheels. Two mangled heaps are lifted in. One has been wounded by a bursting gun. There seems to be no part of him that his not burned… The skin of his breast is of a bluish color and cracked open in ridges.*[108] The censor did not hesitate to explain that the reason for his reprimand was the effect of such writing on recruiting in Canada.[109] He went on to require that all stories and images depict cheerful soldiers, spotless trenches, and peaceful deaths.

The effort to keep the war going also had an ugly side that would have a tragic consequence for the post-war world. The British and Canadian information managers, aided by many well-known authors stoked the essential element of propaganda—hatred. They acknowledged that promoting hate against Germans as it had never existed before was a war goal. They succeeded to an extent that would delay the end of the Great War, seriously sabotage the post-war world and contribute significantly to the arrival of the next war.

In Britain, the shaming campaign against those who did not volunteer included women handing out white feathers symbolic of cowardice and employing other forms of derision. Peace rallies were violently disrupted. People of German origin, or even with German sounding names fared much worse. In London, mobs smashed their windows and looted their shops. Fueled by news headlines like "The Enemy in Our Midst", the riots differed from the "Krystal Nacht" to come in 1930's Germany only in degree, not in kind.[110]

The same situation prevailed in Canada, which by the end of 1916 was running out of volunteers. The rules for enlistment were changed, standards were lowered, and a full scale shaming campaign was conducted. The white feathers were handed out by the Women's Home Guard, in their own uniforms. A popular song was "Why Aren't You in Khaki?" When shaming did not work, members of some military units in Berlin, Ontario (before it became Kitchener) simply dragged men off the street to the recruiting station. Members of another unit in St. Thomas stopped men and threatened them with violence if they did not enlist.[111]

Even all of this was not enough. The extravagant expenditure of life typified by the Somme produced another serious blow to Canada's effort to forge a nation at all, never mind one that could come of age on the world stage. Conscription became an issue. The Somme and 1916 spawned the deeper divisions and the greater violence and oppression that are the companions of conscription. Compelling a young man against his will to kill and be killed is not a small matter. The damage the issue caused Canada was mitigated only marginally by the fact that the controversy arose very late in the war. It would reappear in the next war.

As noted, the Somme and 1916 also marked a turning point for ordinary soldiers. Harris writes: *The enthusiastic volunteers were enthusiastic no longer. They had lost faith in their cause and in their leaders, in everything except the loyalty of their comrades. The war had ceased to have a purpose and was now merely a contest of endurance.*[112] Instead of telling the heroic stories their indoctrinated friends wanted to hear, returning Canadian troops often fell silent. The seeds of Post Traumatic Stress Disorder (PTSD) had been planted, to be reaped by their children and grandchildren in the decades ahead. Dead fathers, husbands, brothers, and uncles could be lionized by adopting the mythology of the noble struggle. But how were the family members of survivors to understand the stony silence or periodic violent lashing out of survivors, who had been such different people when they left for the war?

The story of the Somme battles, and the Canadian part in them, provides a more accurate portrait than more celebrated encounters of what Canada bought into by joining the Great War---and the price she paid. It is an ugly picture. In the face of the Somme truth, the underpinning of such a glorious coming of age story would require a victory by Canadians, led by Canadians, free from the oppressive British class system, free from the deadly strategic and tactical errors that system produced. With judicious downplaying of just a few facts, Vimy would provide all that.

Vimy: Bending the Truth

Most myths contain a component of truth. What we should be cautious about are exaggerated claims, alleging additional truths and marketing them as flowing naturally from the basic truth. It is that embellishment that can make the original myth dangerous.

The historical truth is that on Easter Monday, 1917, well led Canadian units, fighting together for the first time captured a piece of terrain that allied forces had been unable to secure for months. The victory did not change the strategic situation. In fact, it was part of a larger offensive that failed badly.[113] The extent of the truth that should flow from this event is that Canadian troops and Canadians at home felt great pride in this accomplishment. The victory did promote a sense of national identity, in Canada and among the soldiers who had won it, strengthening the unique bond common to all troops in combat. That is no small matter. In that limited sense, it can be said that Canada came of age at Vimy. The question is whether that moment has any value in determining the role of the country in the 21st century.

The temptation to embellish and mold the basic truth by ignoring some aspects of it and inventing others is understandable. The Canadians who took Vimy Ridge, some of whom were children, were fighting under abominable conditions, in a senseless war that should have ended earlier.[114] They were not fighting for freedom, justice, democracy, or to end wars. By this time, most were fighting to improve the chances that they and their friends would survive. In that context, was Vimy anything more than a military victory gained under circumstances that gave a boost to Canadian nationalism?

The contrast with the deadly leadership of so many British commanders enhanced Canadian pride in Vimy. The human and military failings of Haig and the like stand out in contrast to the leadership of Julian Byng, an atypical British general, and Canadian Arthur Currie, who succeeded him as commander of the Canadian Corps of 100,000 troops. The strengths of these two match almost exactly Haig's moral and military weaknesses.

In contrast to the disdain of Haig and his staff for the lives and well being of their ordinary soldiers, Byng and Currie stayed in contact with their men. They cared about their comfort and their lives. Both approved or disapproved of particular operations with a view toward conserving lives rather than wasting them.

The challenges faced by the two generals were formidable. Because of Big Push slaughters exemplified by the Somme, Byng's Canadian Corps was heavy on raw recruits. This may have been something of a positive factor. Many of the war weary veterans of Haig's assaults were no longer enthusiastic. With their typical Canadian rowdiness and enthusiasm, the new troops were likely open to the superior preparation for the attack that they would receive. They had not been trained in the fatal frontal assault tactics of their predecessors.

One characteristic of Canadian troops was independent thinking. Historian Ted Barris saw this as one of the main reasons Byng's plan to take Vimy Ridge worked.[115] It is to the credit of Byng and Currie that they recognized the value of this trait and made it part of the preparation for the assault. Unlike the British generals, they sought to ensure that the details of the plan were known up and down the ranks of the Corps.[116]

In the recollection of a 16-year-old Private after the battle one can see how good tactics blended with national pride. Robert Henley wrote: *At Vimy, it was the first time that we did what the Brits couldn't do, what the French couldn't do…If the officer was killed, the senior N.C.O. took over. If he was killed, the private carried on. In most armies, if the officer is gone, well, what are we going to do now. We were a proud group. We were Canadian…I think Canada was born at Vimy.*[117]

The attack plan to which the entire Canadian force was privy was far more sophisticated and intelligent than the one the British had employed. Byng, before turning over command of the Canadian Corps to Currie, sent him to the Somme and Verdun to analyze and report back on lessons learned. As a result, enemy gun positions were better identified in advance of the attack.[118] This time, artillery pieces fired shells that destroyed barbed wire.

Ordinary soldiers not only knew the plan, they practiced their individual parts in it. For six weeks, troops practiced walking over replicas of the craters, wires and trenches they would have to negotiate during the attack. They practiced advancing by fire and manoeuvre instead of a straight line. They practiced staying just behind a creeping artillery barrage.[119] The recollection of another enlisted man reflects the pride these preparations produced: *You could brief the lowest soldier, any private, and from memory he could say just where he was going. He could point to the map and he could tell you where he was going and what he was supposed to do.*[120]

It was not possible to surprise the Germans. Their position on a wide ridge gave them a panoramic view of the region below that stretched toward Paris, only 150 kilometres away. Protected trenches, shelters, and tunnels lined the slopes of the ridge.

Yet the Canadians took Vimy ridge. In a difficult but minor engagement, the inconclusive battle of Arras near Vimy, a legend was born. Militarily, the sacrifice of 10,000 Canadian dead or wounded settled nothing. The British largely ignored the battle. Hochschild's exhaustive account of the war does not mention it. But newspapers rhapsodized: *It put Canadians on the map. It showed we actually do stuff. We became important.*[121] As Berton put it, *Vimy provided the shining vision that still illuminates our folk memory. We carry it with us, for it has been drilled into our minds by constant repetition, a tale retold like a looped movie.*[122]

It is unfortunate that the real importance of Vimy, together with *In Flanders Fields,* has come to be its leading role as part of a message that would obscure reality and help to ensure many times 10,000 casualties in the future.

Consider this analogy. Suppose four drunk drivers crashed their vehicles, horribly killing and maiming many of the passengers in those vehicles and a school bus full of children as well. Suppose further that a passenger in one of the vehicles, who had failed to appreciate the condition of the driver when he boarded, bravely administered medical assistance and saved many lives on the scene. Does the heroism of the passenger re-characterize the nature of the event? What lessons should the passenger take away? The surviving drunk drivers? Is it possible to honour the Canadians at Vimy and understand the national pride the victory produced and leave it at that?

After Vimy came another opportunity to learn of the reality of this absurd war. The dying was not over for the victors of Vimy. The misguided Field Marshall Haig looped Canadians back into the Ypres salient.

No legends would be born at Passchendaele, no epic poems, no heroic victories, only senseless death on a scale that would provoke such outrage and disgust that it reportedly led Canadian prime minister Borden to seize British prime minister Lloyd George by the lapels and warn him that if the disaster were repeated, not a Canadian soldier would leave the shores of Canada again.[123] Did Borden not know about colonial legalities?

Passchendaele

By late summer of 1917, the Germans had made their third fatal mistake. They had increased unrestricted submarine warfare, which brought in the Americans. From the outset, the U.S. had been only quasi-neutral, allowing its citizens to travel on British ships that were in danger of being torpedoed while ignoring the deadly effect of the British naval blockade on German civilians.[124] Whether the German effort to starve Britain was a reciprocal effort, it was a geopolitical mistake. The pivotal propaganda opportunity for U.S. hawks had come two years earlier when a German submarine sank the *Lusitania,* killing 128 Americans. Neither the fact that the vessel was loaded with American made war materiel, nor the repeated public warnings Germany gave to the passengers dampened the growing war fever.[125]

Haig, still justifying his actions as a war of attrition or the prospect of big breakthrough, whichever seemed best at the moment, did not wait for the Americans to arrive. Seeking further glory, he launched an offensive near the Ypres salient on July 31st.

Although this time his intelligence staff correctly informed him about the coming rains, he ignored the warning. The monsoon came to the lowlands. The drainage system of the battlefield had long since been destroyed by the big guns of earlier battles. He added to the devastation with a massive opening two-week barrage, all of which ensured that battles would be fought in an ocean of mud. A lightly wounded soldier who fell, or even one who just stumbled would often drown. He would drown not only in mud, but in a foul smelling gumbo spiced with the bloated corpses and body parts of his comrades. Charles Miles of the Royal Fusiliers wrote of the experience of manoeuvring over this terrain: *In a way it was worse when the mud didn't suck you down…you knew it was a body you were treading on…You would tread on one on the stomach, perhaps, and it would grunt all the air out…The smell would make you vomit.*[126] It was into this morass the Canadians were welcomed.

With his usual mindless straight ahead strategy, Haig churned through most of his available British units in fruitless attacks against recently reinforced German positions. His units suffered 26,000 casualties in the first days of the offensive. In October, he sent for the Canadian Corps, now commanded by Arthur Currie. Haig had a new ridge he wanted the Canadians to take, named Passchendaele Ridge, not Vimy. Apparently he was in "breakthrough" mode that day. Currie was Haig's subordinate but he did his best to talk some life saving common sense to the "Ego in Chief": *Passchendaele! What's the good of it? Let the Germans have it—keep it—rot in the mud! It isn't worth a drop of blood.*[127] He argued that Canadian casualties would reach 16,000—to what end? Haig insisted and Currie obeyed, but not before Haig dressed him down several times for insubordination. Nevertheless, Currie no doubt saved lives by stubbornly insisting that, contrary to Haig's practice of patching units together willy-nilly, the Canadians must be permitted to fight as one unit under Canadian command.

Two weeks later, the Canadians began a series of assaults on the ridge that nearly wiped out three of their units. One, the 49th Battalion of the Canadian Mounted Rifles, had a casualty rate of 75 percent.

It is interesting to read in contemporary media accounts of modern wars that this unit or that one was "decimated". It is a reminder of just how vicious wars have become over the centuries. The term comes from Roman days when losses of 10 percent were considered horrific. Units in the third battle of Ypres were not decimated; they were virtually annihilated.

When the Canadians finally took Passchendaele Ridge on November 6th, Currie's prediction turned out to be not far off. The casualty total was 15,654. The battle also provided an answer to Currie's insubordinate questioning about the worth of the objective. Six months later, the British gave it back to the Germans without firing a shot.[128]

No breakthrough and no attrition success either. From the end of July until he finally called off the campaign in November, Haig spent 300,000 lives.[129]

With such staggering numbers it is almost impossible to picture real people, their children, their grandchildren, their lives, had they not ended in war. Thanks to the son of William Walter Ruddy, a survivor of Passchendaele, we can try.[130] Dick Ruddy, is a sprightly octogenarian, still so obviously in love with his wife of 64 years, Doreen, that friends often refer to them as "the honeymooners". Contrasting his father's account of survival and his later life with the absence of any such story for those who were killed may provide at least an idea of Canada's generational losses.[131]

William Ruddy enlisted on December 29th, 1915 and survived to be discharged on July 1st, 1918. He was posted to Passchendaele with the 91st Overseas Battalion. He was severely wounded by a cluster bomb. Dick writes of the triage decision: *He was sent to the death tent to see if he would live any amount of time. His five kids are glad he lived long enough to be operated on.*

Five children and their families. In contrast, thousands of empty frames instead of the vibrant presence of people like Dick and Doreen. The gift of their lives is part of the legacy of one who survived; a gift denied to tens of thousands of never-to-be children and grandchildren.

Thus ended the last of the four battles that are popularly perceived to have brought about Canada's coming of age on the world stage. The Canadian Corps continued to perform well under Currie and in spite of Haig and the entry of the Americans eventually turned the tide to break the ghastly stalemate. It could not end too soon for the newly acceptable category of casualties---the civilian population. The very effective Royal Navy blockade was starving Germans. U-Boats were intercepting supplies and starving Britons.[132] It was not a naval contest in the best maritime tradition.

With Germany eventually worn down, the Armistice was signed on November 11th, 1918. That event provides an appropriately insane coda to an insane war. The document was signed at 5 a.m., but to go into effect six hours later. In those six hours, the allies continued to attack and nearly 3,000 men from both sides lost their lives.[133] The last Canadian death at Mons may well have been the final one of the Great War. Everyone was lying low in the last hours, but Private George Lawrence Price, 25, from Moose Jaw, Saskatchewan rose to respond to a wave from a young Belgian woman. A few minutes before 11, a sniper shot him dead. Price was a conscript.[134] Fortunately, his family was probably not informed that he died for absolutely nothing.

For Canadians, would that the ridge most prominently remembered and taught to generations of school children had been Passchendaele instead of Vimy. Many of the factors and themes we are examining have operated to ensure that this did not happen. Both ridges are in Flanders, but it is the first verse of McRae's poem that yet can be found on our ten dollar bill.

An important part of the conversation Canadians should have before going into combat at the behest of any future patron is how the proposed action would likely compare to the disaster that was this war. A review of some of the factors we are examining in the context of the Great War legacy can provide a guide to some of the questions that should be raised.

Civilian Deaths and Weapons of Mass Destruction

The most destructive legacy of the Great War may be the general acceptance of killing civilians without reservation, to be accomplished with whatever advanced weaponry technology can provide. A desire to minimize *military* casualties has continued to characterize Canada's participation in other people's wars. If anything, the Great War appears to have strengthened that factor. More than 60,000 Canadian dead, one young man killed for every eleven who enlisted, brought the lesson home.[135] Civilian deaths in the Great War were only estimated but they clearly exceeded military deaths. Hochschild puts the number at 10-13 million and notes that the Great War marked the end of long standing distinctions between civilians and soldiers. His casualty estimate does not include the significant number of former soldiers who committed suicide after the war. Nor does it include the deaths of forced African labourers and their families.[136] Questions about the fate of civilians in any future conflict are the most important questions Canada should ask of any patron. Such question should have been asked before Canada joined the war in Afghanistan, Libya, and Syria.

Propaganda and Journalism

The legacy of propaganda and failure of journalism is also high on the list. This issue permeates the entire story of Canada's wars and affects every factor we are examining. Just as the Boer War was a military dress rehearsal for the Great War, the Great War was propaganda practice for the next one. All participants controlled information, lied and dissembled to their people, wrecked basic civil liberties, and persecuted dissenters. The British model was followed in many instances even more enthusiastically in Canada. The world's first government War Propaganda Bureau was not set up by Joseph Goebbels on orders from chancellor Hitler, but by Charles

Masterman on orders from prime minister Asquith.[137] The scope of its multi-media activities was impressive. As noted, they included the new medium of film, something that did not escape the notice of the later employers of famous Nazi filmmaker, Leni Riefenstahl.

The Propaganda Bureau enlisted literary figures known around the English-speaking world. Most, including Thomas Hardy, Arthur Conan Doyle, and H.G. Wells joined in willingly. Particularly enthusiastic participants included Rudyard Kipling and novelist John Buchan, another former governor general, whose imaginative propaganda romanticizing the war would be found in the most widely read books written while the war was in progress.[138]

The presence of propaganda machines in all wars is a well-known reality. Yet its practical power to influence events has never been adequately understood or appreciated. Propaganda fuels the start of wars, keeps them going when enthusiasm flags, and poisons the peace. Hatred is its most pernicious feature. The hyperbole in an open letter from 52 literary figures and the stories of the bayoneted Belgian babies stoked public hatred of Germans in the very early days of the war. The letter called on the English speaking "race" to fight for the "ideals of Western Europe" against the rule of "Blood and Iron". Kipling's writings banished Germans from humanity and recounted with joy the story of a wounded German burned to death when shells hit a dressing station.[139] British and Canadian "white feather" shaming campaigns helped to swell the number of volunteers.[140] The power of propaganda fosters getting into wars.

The power of propaganda also prolongs wars, even muting the opposing voices of powerful people. One of those voices was that of a respected figure, well known to Canadians. There is scarcely a better example of the futility of facing down propaganda than the 1917 effort of Sir Henry Charles Keith Petty-Fitzmaurice, Lord Lansdowne, who had been a popular governor general from 1883-1888.[141]

Lansdowne had impressive imperialist credentials. He had been Viceroy of India and secretary of war. In fact, he had been instrumental in negotiating that non-binding understanding with France that was so important in drawing Great Britain into the war.

But the reality of the Somme gave him pause about the war and the slaughter at Passchendaele caused him to express his misgivings publicly. His call for peace negotiations was prescient and prophetic. He wrote in an open letter to a London newspaper that, while the Allies would not lose the war, prolonging it would spell ruin for the civilized world. *Just as this war has been more dreadful than any war in history, so, we may be sure, would the next war be even more dreadful than this.* ***The prostitution of science for purposes of pure destruction is not likely to stop short.*** (Emphasis added)[142]

In the letter, he proposed a peace framework that included a kind of forerunner of the League of Nations and the United Nations--- the compulsory arbitration of international disputes. As a senior government official, he was aware of intelligence reports that many highly placed Germans and Austrians favoured negotiations. He advised that the Allies could strengthen their hand by assurances that they did not wish "the annihilation of Germany as a Great Power".[143]

Perhaps Lansdowne had experienced a fundamental change of heart about war. But its is more likely that his was simply a last call from an old imperialist for wars to be conducted and ended in the comparatively more civilized fashion that he had known. At the time of his letter, Germany had already sought to negotiate peace on that basis and U.S. President Wilson had called for "peace without victory". Whatever Landsdowne's motivation, the result was failure. Britain would have none of it.[144] He was praised by many soldiers, but vilified by former associates. The press dutifully attacked him. One of the most articulate critics was Kipling, who managed concisely to impugn his patriotism and mental health while adding a dollop of sexism. He said that Lansdowne was an old imbecile who must have taken such a cowardly position because some woman worked on him.[145]

The British and French governments issued hardline statements after the letter, thus undermining German peace parties and ensuring another year of civilian and military dying. No matter how insane, the war must continue and only total victory and subjugation of the enemy would be acceptable. Death must beget death or death is meaningless. What a tragic message. Lansdowne never had a chance. Propaganda prolongs wars.

The power of propaganda also poisons the peace. Lloyd George for Britain and Georges Clemenceau for France were arguably more important figures in the shaping of the post-war treaty than was U.S. President Woodrow Wilson. Hochschild observed that the greatest propaganda barrage in history had yielded a public that demanded after the war no other course than severe punishment for Germany.[146] How any conflict to which Canada is called is to end should be a part of the conversation before she commits.

We have seen that the Great War also featured government control and suppression of information about the reality of the war. Especially now that news has almost completely morphed into entertainment and government efforts to control it continue, it will also be important to talk about the rules on that front. The last Canadian government's model of control over information on many subjects is not dissimilar to the one Britain and Canada relied upon to spin the Great War.

Damage to Democracy

The Great War featured grossly unjustified impositions on civil liberties, motivated by fear and hate propaganda. In recent years, the advent of volunteer forces and the reduction in scale of military operations has resulted in less overt interference, though ugly examples continue. Knee- jerk xenophobic terrorism legislation and massive government intrusions into privacy are reminders. How will any future action affect the democracy and freedom touted by the government as the cause for which the Canadian Expeditionary Force fought?

An equally damaging legacy of the Great War was the conscription crisis. It came about because, especially once fragments of truth began to filter back from places like the Somme and Passchendaele, men would not volunteer in numbers sufficient to feed Haig's death machine. In the first five months of the year that included the great Vimy victory Canadian troops suffered 56,000 casualties. In that period, 36,000 signed up to replace them. The simple mathematics of that ratio would continue and prompted prime minister Borden to backtrack on his earlier pledges that there would be no conscription. The Military Service Bill was enacted in the summer of 1917, sparking violent division in the country and introducing us to the issue of Quebec separation. A member of the Quebec assembly tabled the first separatist motion a few months after the enactment of conscription. A Manitoba legislator urged a Winnipeg crowd to burn down the recruitment office. There was a general strike in Vancouver to protest the police shooting of a man who had been called up after earlier being excused because he had tuberculosis.[147]

The conscription issue damaged democracy as well as personal relationships. It is difficult to imagine a more divisive activity than forcing a person to die for someone else's country. Vast numbers of French Canadians did not wish to do that, though much of the war was being fought on French soil. Less well remembered, vast numbers of English Canadians did not either. Berton did not exaggerate when he termed the conscription crisis that began in December 1917 the greatest in Canadian history, sowing the seeds of Quebec separatism and affecting Canadian participation in the next war.[148]

The structure of democracy was also damaged. Borden planned an election for December and knew that he would have a problem with new immigrants from outside Quebec who also had no allegiance to the Empire and were opposed to the draft. The solution chosen was simply to rig the election. The Wartime Elections Act gave the vote to every soldier, whether present in Canada or not. In a generous gesture to women, it also enfranchised wives, mothers, sisters, and daughters—of anyone in uniform. Disenfranchised by the act were conscientious objectors and all naturalized citizens from enemy countries who came to Canada after 1902.[149]

Along with every conflict over conscription rides a nasty sidekick, one that brings out the very worst in those trying to establish compulsory service: Militant misguided patriotism. The Wartime Elections Act permitted Borden's Conservatives, aided by a handful of Liberals, to stay in power. The campaign included a vicious personal attack on Liberal leader Laurier. In the attacks Laurier was portrayed as, you guessed it, an unpatriotic quitter and dupe of the Kaiser. It also included claims by Borden that if the Germans won they would invade Canada.[150] Monty Python *redux*.

The conscription crisis of 1917 must be counted as a major cost of Canada's participation in this absurd war. Opposition to conscription considerably intimidated the government. It also turned out that by this time young men across the country not only did not wish to storm recruiting offices as they had done at the beginning of the war, they did not care to be drafted either. More than 90 percent of the men eligible for conscription sought one of the many exemptions in the act. Interestingly, more of them were from Ontario than Quebec. Many whose exemption claims were denied simply refused to serve, sometimes resulting in deaths and injuries when troops sought to arrest them.[151]

This divisive controversy, to be repeated in the next war, took a toll on the Canadian nation building effort. Fortunately, the toll did not include wholesale loss of life among the unwilling warriors. By the summer of 1918, only a few months from the end of the war, only 25,000 draftees had made it France.[152]

Canada is unlikely to resort to conscription again. The complicating factor is that making war with an exclusively volunteer force engenders public indifference about where, how and for what the war is conducted as well as its costs. It will be important to sort out this conundrum in any conversation about future actions.

A Lethal Adjustment in the Capitalism/Imperialism Relationship

The fundamental change in the conduct of imperial wars necessarily required a difficult adjustment in the marriage of imperialism and capitalism. That marriage has its ups and downs, but the two never divorce. The change from "defeat" to "destroy" altered the relationship.

Philosopher and historian Hannah Arendt writes that power had before been thought to be synonymous with economic and industrial capacity resulting from exchange. The two partners in the marriage were in agreement that the state's means of violence was to be used exclusively for protection of business interests and national property. Proper exercise of power, however, depended on the game being played the old way, on the assumption that competition automatically sets up limits before one competitor has liquidated all the others. The Great War was the first conflict to upset that relationship. Arendt observed: *How a competition between fully armed business concerns— "empires"---could end in anything but victory for one and death for the other is difficult to understand.*[153] The development of nation states into industrial entities during the 19th century made it difficult if not impossible to play the game in the usual manner. To the deadly detriment of civilians, the Great War combatants demonstrated a mutual inability to understand what full-scale conflict among fully armed business concerns would entail. Only after the next world war would capitalism and imperialism make an adjustment, continuing to wage all out destructive war, but with the victors choosing to rebuild rather than destroy the losers, primarily to preserve old markets and open new ones.

A constant in the relationship is the time-honoured practice of war profiteering. In 1915 for example, the British were experiencing a significant shortage of precision optical equipment for camera lenses, rangefinders, periscopes, and particularly binoculars. In Germany, the British naval blockade, in addition to starving civilians, had produced an acute shortage of rubber. Agents of the two governments met in Switzerland and made a deal. The Germans supplied the binoculars, the British the rubber. Problem solved. British forces would be able to see the Germans more clearly and be better able to kill them. The Germans would be somewhat harder to kill because they could move their army trucks around without having to use steel tires that chewed up the roads. And no doubt a few people made a little money out of the venture.[154]

The war was Canada's biggest business and a major player was Sam Hughes. Berton, in a nice burst of alliteration called him "the megalomaniac minister of militia.[155] Hughes became defence minister and presided over the war industry from 1914-1916, when he was forced to resign. A host of his friends made quick fortunes in the munitions business. They produced boots that came apart in heavy rain, wagons too big for European roads, bandoliers that would not hold modern ammunition, and provided spavined horses that had to be slaughtered.[156]

Hughes may be best remembered for his insistence on the Canadian-produced Ross rifle, which simply would not function in the conditions of this war, compared to the British Lee-Infield. Although he used his influence to mandate the use of the Ross, the troops hated it and one colonel wrote that it was nothing short of murder to send troops into battle with such a weapon. Hughes' successor, Joseph Flavell, improved this situation considerably, while also making a fortune selling bacon to the British. He was cleared of a charge of engaging in the familiar capitalist ploy of creating an artificial shortage to drive up the price, but from all his food enterprises he did manage to eke out an 80 percent profit.[157]

Ordinary soldiers were aware of the profiteering. Some of the Canadians who managed to speak to the press had a message not likely to appear on recruiting posters. One war correspondent reported that the soldiers wished the war profiteers death by poison gas, and that they prayed for God to send German Zeppelins to England so that people would know what war meant.[158] I doubt the Canadians really wanted anyone in England killed by Zeppelins, but their frustration is understandable.

Senseless Military Deaths: A Cruel Practice and a Humane Counterpoint

It was not only the inanity of the war itself and the poor leadership of Haig and others that produced senseless military deaths. To that list must be added the practice of executing prisoners and Britain's record of ritually executing her own soldiers, including Canadians. To these practices, however, one can find a humane counterpoint that lowered the tally of wasted lives---"Live and Let Live" arrangements among line soldiers and their designated enemies.

After the Somme, and certainly after Passchendaele, the folks at home might continue to build glorious myths but the ordinary soldier had had enough. Morale plummeted. Some French and Russian units mutinied or deserted. Some simply sat in the trenches and refused any more suicidal attacks.[159] British and Canadian troops did not mutiny at that time, but the zeal of those who had stormed the recruiting offices in search of adventure, glory, or patriotic fervor simply died. Young men worked to come to terms in their own way with the reality that their friends had died and would continue dying with no end in sight; that they would likely die as well.

Hochschild describes British troops shambling in silence toward the front with the expressions of men who knew they were going to their death.[160] In a remarkable little memoir, British veteran W. A. Tucker describes the experience of being ordered to the next objective: *We ordinary Tommies had not the slightest notion, neither did we care. These many months of trench and nomad existence had reduced our outlook to sheep-like vacuity. All destinations were alike.*[161] A returning Canadian spoke for many when he said that he felt like vomiting when friends asked for his war stories.[162]

The ordinary soldier did what ordinary soldiers do in all wars—curse the brass; do your best to look out for yourself and your buddies. Under these circumstances, the purported purpose of a particular war dims to irrelevance. Membership in a fraternity that civilians cannot understand is paramount. Much of current film and literary treatment of a "Band of Brothers" may be drivel, but the concept is grounded in reality.

And membership in the band is not always seen as confined to those on your side. Many more soldiers than their governments would have us acknowledge, came to realize not only that the sacrifice of their lives would be senseless, but also that the same just might be true of the enemy they were supposed to hate. Cook notes that snipers, like the one that killed private Price in the last moments of the war were the exception, but in the fraternity of No Man's Land troops did not buy the demonization of the enemy being pitched at home. Line troops saw little value in seeking danger just to kill those who also had families and were just as bad off as they were. He noted that often *a curious lack of animosity toward the enemy tended to prevail.*[163] Such an attitude understandably caused considerable consternation in high circles. Little wonder this reality is not emphasized as part of the official narrative.

The best-known example is, of course, the Christmas truce of the first December in the trenches near Ypres. German troops initiated it and it soon escalated from a mere ceasefire to a joint celebration. It lasted for hours and involved thousands of soldiers along most of the British sector. A Christmas tree was fashioned. Germans and British troops traded food items, cigarettes and souvenirs. They took photographs and even organized a soccer game with a sandbag. The event was so infectious that many officers participated. British Commanders at the time strongly disapproved, ordering that there should be no repetition. Nor did every German soldier approve. Adolph Hitler was there and rebuked his fellow soldiers.[164]

What is less well known, and certainly less appreciated, is the scope of what many ordinary soldiers came to realize about their relation to their enemies. Not only were there Christmas truces and other soccer games up and down the entire line every year, there were also numerous informal arrangements throughout the war. The adversaries met and exchanged gifts. They stopped shooting so that dead could be buried and wounded treated. They sang songs to one another and engaged in good-natured ribbing.[165] Informal rules developed. Tucker provides a curious example of some of the rules. Tommie and Fritz, he says, considered it bad form to fire on the trenches while orderlies were distributing breakfast, yet those on either side trying to make their way to the latrine trenches were fair game. Many troops on both sides were aware that senior officers were insisting on patrols outside the trenches, not for any legitimate reconnaissance purpose, but just to keep things active. Troops on both sides took to firing over one another's heads if they accidentally met during these ventures.[166] Canadians at Vimy were part of this phenomenon. One wrote: *One German prisoner, wounded in the leg, had his arm around the shoulders of a Canadian who himself was wounded in the arm.*[167] A German prisoner, walking back to the allied line to surrender, carried wounded Canadian Charles Dale on his back. Dale was so severely wounded he could not return to the war. He later remarked: *I was lucky. I never had to kill anybody.*[168]

Attitudes toward these gestures of understanding and solidarity with the enemy overlay precisely the three-tier British military system and its corresponding levels of experience with combat reality. Ordinary soldiers recognized their bond with those in trenches only a few yards away and participated in the activities. Junior officers, who were also dying at an alarming rate either joined in or looked the other way. Senior commanders, the most removed from reality had a different reaction.

Tucker arrived in the trenches in time for the second Christmas and recounts that the events of the first had lingered in the minds of the troops and this was troubling the high command: ...*it appeared that this kind of goings on was anathema and intolerable to British Headquarters. Such antics were unsafe for belligerency. These ideas could lead to a breakdown of war, even cause peace.*[169] The senior commanders had issued stern orders against any repetition. To make sure, the commanders ordered a Christmas artillery barrage. Reacting to the unexpected hostility marking the occasion, the Germans responded with a barrage of their own.[170] Everything went back to abnormal normal.

Tucker gives voice to many ordinary soldiers when he explains his decision to write the memoir: *In my opinion the most predominant feature of this lengthy hindsight is that the German soldier was no unspeakable Hun.*[171] Recounting how German medics ministered to the wounded in his unit immediately after his capture, he said *I began to wonder whether the main difference between British and German soldiers was one of uniform. How could it be that half an hour previously we were doing our best to dismember each other's bodies and now they were doing their utmost to patch them up?*[172]

Tucker was taken prisoner and what he learned about his enemies during that time was consistent with his experience in the trenches. His time as a prisoner did not change his realistic but compassionate outlook. He summed it up this way: *Not that our conditions were ever proper. On the contrary, they were always pretty barbarous. I blame the ruling command and seldom the ordinary German soldiers. Between the uniformed rank and file of Germans and British there was largely a bond of understanding and even respect; and the more each side had suffered actual fighting conditions, the greater that mutual sympathy.*[173] We will see Tucker's view of the enemy mirrored by that of Canadian survivors of Hong Kong in the next war, regarding an enemy demonized even more than were the Germans.

Soldiers, of course, are individuals. Nobody speaks for all of them. Heroes, however, are often accorded increased credibility, albeit often for propaganda purposes. Today the accolade is bestowed on almost everyone in uniform. But Tucker qualifies by virtually any definition. At the start of the war, at age 17, he lied about his age in repeated attempts to enlist until he was finally accepted as a member of the Royal Welsh Fusiliers. He served in the trenches, became a prisoner of war, and escaped. The final line in his book records that he was glad he did not miss the war. War propaganda employs heroes, real and constructed. But the message is not the message of William Tucker. Having survived the war, Tucker compared propaganda to reality, noting the falsity of images that appeared at home, always of British soldiers impeccably unformed, sometimes with head bandages but fighting bravely on. He adds that those at home should have been spared the lie of invading Germans holding Belgian babies aloft on their bayonets.[174]

This minor setback for war propaganda constitutes an eloquent statement about the war's senseless military deaths. A lone symbol of it was discovered after the war. In December 1999, a group of nine British called the "Khaki Chums" crossed to the Ypres area to commemorate that first Christmas truce. Before they left, they planted a timber cross in the mud. They learned months later that villagers had retrieved the cross, treated it, and set it in concrete.[175] It is probable though not certain that it became the memorial described by Hochschild, who reports that troops played one of the soccer games near the spot. A dozen smaller crosses now appear, each stamped in English with the words "In Remembrance" and containing a space to write a name. On one of them is written "All of You", and above that "Imagine".[176]

The muted wisdom of ordinary soldiers seeking to avoid senseless deaths stands as counterpoint to a tragic and avoidable example of such deaths---executions of prisoners and one's own comrades.

As was true in all of Canada's wars, her soldiers were not free of the crimes and inhumane conduct committed by some who endure the stress of battle and the influence of propaganda. From the beginning, some Canadian troops executed prisoners and those seeking to surrender. Ironically, in the Ypres salient they did so at a place that had been given the name Kitchener's Wood.[177] Later, Canadians even developed a reputation for shooting prisoners. A Canadian sergeant wrote home that rage at the loss of comrades produced a practice in his unit to take no prisoners before securing an objective. A 19-year-old Canadian at the Somme wrote in detail of a German prisoner shot as he desperately waved pictures of his family.[178] Cook opines that Canadians probably executed no greater number than other forces, just boasted about it more. He cites the impact of the story that the Germans had crucified a Canadian Sergeant. The story was widely believed and passed on to arriving reinforcements. A McGill university graduate was prompted by it to call for the extermination of all Germans.[179]

There is another seldom told story of senseless military deaths in the Great War. It is the story of British and Canadian soldiers executed by their own side. While some of the incidents of fraternization with the enemy we have seen were technically grounds for the death penalty,[180] a major factor in this story was ignorance about mental illness. Today, we recognize that our wars have produced several of the mental disorders suffered by soldiers in the Great War. We still search for the proper way to treat them, a task made more difficult by the continuing stigma attached to mental illness. Some of the conditions produced in the Great War we would today term PTSD. In that day, it might be called "battle fatigue" or "shell shock". Sometimes physicians recognized it as a psychological wound and treated it as humanely as their limited understanding would permit. Often they did not. One Canadian doctor concluded that it was a manifestation of childhood femininity and there was no cure.[181]

Tragically, sometimes shell shock was also called cowardice. Courts-marital sentenced 216 Canadians to death by firing squad. 25 were executed.[182] Some were victims of shell shock, some repeat offenders, some had exemplary battle records.

Private Harold G. Carter, 1st Canadian Infantry Division was executed after several incidents of unauthorized absence for the offence of avoiding dangerous duty--- the assault his unit made on Vimy Ridge. Private Carter had enlisted while underage and had seen action at the Somme. He was probably not aware that his country had agreed that Canadian troops would no longer be subject to the Canada Militia Act but to the 1897 British Army Act. He was one of 322 British and colonial soldiers executed pursuant to the act.[183] The Germans executed 48 of their own.[184]

We still don't fully understand PTSD and related conditions. We do not adequately fund the effort to understand, possibly because the victims do not fit the official profile of hero essential to support for other people's wars. Still, we no longer execute them. Unlike Private Carter, many of them appear able to handle the horror of war. Sadly, it is returning home they cannot handle.

All such executions followed an identical protocol but Carter's had a particularly cruel twist. Like all prisoners, he was blindfolded, placed in an ambulance and driven to the execution site. There he was seated on a box with hands cuffed to a post behind him. A white piece of paper was pinned on his chest by a doctor to guide the aim of the firing squad.[185]

After the firing squad had done its work, the protocol called for an officer to fire a pistol shot into the body. The post holes had been dug by other prisoners. After the shootings, they were required to carry the corpses back to the ambulance, take down the posts, and burn the blood soaked straw.[186]

The protocol also required that members of the condemned man's unit witness the execution. Members of the Black Watch of Montreal were summoned. The attendance of Carter's brother Ernie was required. Ernie was an ambulance driver. After his brother was shot, Ernie drove the remains to the Ville-au-Bois cemetery near Vimy for burial. Private Carter's family described him as an overeager teenager who enlisted *for the glory and fame of fighting for one's country, only to discover that he could not handle the horrors of war.*[187]

Among the Canadians who could not bear the slaughter at the Somme was William Alexander, from Alberta. Frederick Scott, chaplain of the First Canadian Division, witnessed his dawn execution. Scott sought mercy for Alexander even though his own son had recently been killed in combat. He wrote: *I have seen many ghastly sights in the war, and hideous forms of death....but nothing ever brought home to me so deeply...the hideous nature of war and the iron hand of discipline, as did that lonely death on the misty hillside in the early morning.*[188]

One of the executed British soldiers was Joseph Stones, who had distinguished himself on several occasions before a mental and physical breakdown. After his execution, his wife, who had been supporting herself and two children on a meagre dependents allowance, was informed that she would no longer receive it and would not be eligible for a widow's pension.[189] Citizen action decades later by an organization that included relatives of Stones and others who shared his fate, achieved some measure of redress for these injustices. The organization, Shot at Dawn, brought public attention to the executions. The group held Remembrance Day ceremonies in London wearing white badges on their chests. In 2006, the government granted a blanket pardon to all who had been shot.[190]

Most of the Canadians sentenced to death were pardoned. Why? What factors were employed to choose some to live and some to die? What part did the level of understanding of mental illness play? Were there improper factors? Canadian Private Eugene Perry was one of the unlucky ones who had fought well at the Somme but deserted before Vimy. He was shot because his British commanders thought the men in his unit needed their will stiffened.

Every death penalty scheme embodies these flaws. In all, as in the Great War, the threat of execution does not deter. Speaking of the widespread practice of self-inflicted wounds as an escape, Cook acknowledges this: *For men pushed to the limits of their endurance, the self inflicted wound was a way out of the line, and most neither thought nor cared about whatever form of punishment they might face.*[191]

Recognizing all these flaws, Cook defends the executions as necessary to the war effort: *If we condemn the practice...what was the alternative?* He writes that allowing men to leave the front would be a recipe for losing the war. As applied to this justification, however, he answers his own question. Of all the Commonwealth nations, only Australia refused to allow its soldiers to be executed. There is no evidence that this exemption was destructive of Australian combat capability.[192]

Execution of prisoners and one's own soldiers is part of the factor of horror and senseless military deaths. It is a cost of fighting in other people's wars. These ordinary soldiers did not get to fall into peaceful sleep on the battlefield. They did not even get to drown in the mud.

Reflection on costs and benefits

One reaches for some positive result of this war. Compared on the whole with the decades of damage to the lives of hundreds of millions of people that it inaugurated, there are none. The same propaganda themes and journalistic failures continue today to draw

Canada toward ill-conceived wars and military adventures. Their primary impact now is to promote indifference and resignation rather than enthusiastic jingoism--- a casual acceptance that when a more powerful patron calls, we must answer. The practical result is the same. Politicians continue to reprise the glorious Great War propaganda themes in their Remembrance Day pronouncements. Over the years, the public has developed a degree of awareness of the stupidity and horror of the war. Still absent, however, is any discussion of the proposition that we should have stayed out, and if not that we should have learned to stay out in the future.

Considered separately, however, there may be some positive aspects of Canada's bloody experience. First, while it is tragic and misguided to build the myth of Canada's coming of age on the world stage around this holocaust, it can be said that Canada's inevitable progression to political independence was likely speeded somewhat by the valour of its arms. Hochschild thought so, observing that horrendous Canadian and Australian losses from poor British leadership at Passchendaele and Gallipoli had that effect. That process was also advanced by the gradual dissolution of the British Empire, begun by its foolish decision to join the continental war.[193] The full value of that political independence, however, will be measureable only when Canada can determine her own international policy, free of the influence of all the world's big players.

Second, there were mixed results for that staple of imperialism---racism. On one hand, the continued oppression of people of colour during the war and as part of the peace helped ensure that Canadians would be drawn into conflicts in future decades. Civilian casualties from the war included two million African porters conscripted by the British. Without them, famine spread among their families. Hundreds of thousands died. Colonial troops of colour were segregated and overtly mistreated throughout the war. But they learned that they could fight equally well alongside whites in spite of that mistreatment and grave pay inequity. They saw established nation states in Europe and realized they could achieve the same. A month after the war ended, British West Indies troops mutinied when they were ordered to clean the latrines of white soldiers and were denied a pay increase given to the whites. Some of them were imprisoned and one was executed, but political meetings began. A troubled British official later wrote: *Nothing we can do will alter the fact that the black man has come to think and feel himself as good as the white.*[194]

Finally, our characteristic initial reluctance to enter wars, and concern for excessive casualties seems to have been enhanced by the experience of the Great War. Whether it was a product of the conscription crisis or other factors, Canada constructed a system of service that did not compel volunteers to fight outside the homeland.

As we will see in the next chapter, Canada was also part of the brief worldwide conversation about war that the sheer magnitude of losses in this one produced. For a moment in history, there were opportunities to do things a different way. Those opportunities passed, but the ideas and a remnant of the resources of those who articulated the case for peace remain today.

This then, was the war that Canada joined enthusiastically at its beginning, distinguished herself in on several occasions, and limped out of in turmoil. It remains the most important war Canada has ever fought. It was clearly someone else's war. Whether assessed by its human and emotional impact or by cold cost-benefit analysis, it represents a loss for Canada, and indeed for the world.

Chapter III

OPPORTUNITY LOST: HOW COULD THIS HAPPEN AGAIN?

At the end, the notion of 'just war' had faded into the reality of the disillusioned survivors.[1]

Canadian historian Ted Cook

The sheer horror of the Great War gave the world one shining moment to reconsider the destructive new trail it had blazed. Regrettably, the moment was lost. The next global conflict soon followed. It featured unimaginable numbers of civilian deaths, a final abandonment of any semblance of ethical or moral constraints, and a world appreciably less safe than it had been at the end of the Great War.

Why was the opportunity lost? How could this happen again? With the youth of entire nations virtually annihilated, with millions of soldiers and civilians maimed, with millions of grieving families on several continents, with the utter senselessness of the Great War and the stupidity of national leaders, how could there possibly be another war 20 years later? Why would Canadians be called upon again?

Significant parts of the answer may be found, but only by beginning with events that occurred well before the dates that mark the beginning of most people's recollection of World War II. The popular memory of World War II seems to start in 1938 with British prime minister Neville Chamberlain's "appeasement" of the monster

Adolph Hitler by meeting him in Munich and in effect ceding Czechoslovakia. Reference to that meeting has become a modern cliché that public figures invoke whenever they sense the possibility that a conflict might be resolved nonviolently. Canada's minister of foreign affairs, in a dazzling display of verbal irrelevance, called it up in 2013 to warn the United Nations General Assembly about upcoming talks with Iran.[2]

The popular narrative of Munich is straightforward and not widely questioned: Adolph Hitler was a madman bent on world domination, who massacred the Jews. Chamberlain triggered all this by letting Hitler have his way in 1938, which made it too late to draw the line at Poland a year later. Hitler's Japanese allies are remembered, though not often openly, as a version of the "yellow peril". The Italians, though militarily inept as usual, were seduced into Hitler's camp by a sort of junior Hitler, Benito Mussolini. Thanks to weakness and appeasement, there was nothing to be done but have another war, one that Canada had to join. Simple.

Ignoring everything before 1938 may indeed lead to the reasonable though not indisputable conclusion that by that point the war had to be fought and Canada had to help fight it. But we will see that there is much more to the story and it can be traced directly back to the Great War aftermath. 1938 is not the place to start. Failure to consider the two decades that followed the Great War blinds us to the reality that World War II was eminently preventable. That blindness, in turn, colours examination of World War II itself. It makes it more difficult to recognize and evaluate what we will see in the next chapter---the destructive war-promoting factors playing out again in that war.

So, how could this happen again? How was the opportunity for peace lost? What caused the next war? Was it necessary? Some of the answers may be gleaned from examination of the peace conference that followed the Great War armistice, and from the story of interwar peace movements.

Paris 1919: Old World Peacemaking with a Punitive Twist

At the end of the Great War, there was a real chance for the victors to rethink international relations in a way that would benefit the whole world. Tragically, they were not up to the task. In a 1918 speech to Congress, U.S. president Woodrow Wilson outlined a way to do that rethinking: the "Fourteen Points." Later that year, facing defeat, Germany asked Wilson to arrange an armistice. He agreed, on the condition that the Germans accept the Fourteen Points as the basis for a lasting peace. Germany accepted.

The Fourteen Points spoke of open diplomacy, freedom of the seas, disarmament, and consideration of the views of colonial populations. They also specifically addressed European borders, calling for example, for the return of portions of Alsace-Lorraine to France, adjustment of Italy's borders along clear lines of nationality, and a new Poland with access to the sea.[3]

Wilson's outline also revived long-held aspirations of the victims of colonialism. It was not lost on them that his progressive agenda called for an end to bartering lands and peoples through secret diplomacy; that it spoke of "self determination" in fashioning national borders, of mutual disarmament, and of an association of nations to guarantee independence to great and small nations alike. These peoples and the Germans might have cast their lot with Wilson's Fourteen Points. None of the other allies signed on, however, and even Wilson wavered at critical junctures. A peace treaty was signed, but the peace bore little resemblance to the Fourteen Points.

There are multiple reasons the plan the Germans accepted and assumed would be the basis of peace negotiations never materialized in the treaty imposed on them in June, 1919. Many of its terms helped bring on the next war. The victors were simply unable to recognize the dangers created by the Great War and equally unable to visualize a new and better way. They were trapped in the 19th century, but with a punitive twist. The important thing is not to condemn these failures but to recognize them. The treaty that formally ended the

Great War rejected Wilson's new vision, grossly miscrafted European borders, continued racist assumptions, ignored liberation movements, and reflected a destructively punitive approach that would return to haunt all the parties, and the world.

My principal source for evaluating the Paris treaty conference is *Paris 1919: Six Months That Changed The World*[4], the splendid work by Margaret MacMillan, great-grand-daughter of David Lloyd George. Canadians have been privileged to have her serve as a professor of history at the University of Toronto. The book is highly readable scholarship. There is no reason to question the accuracy of her account of the proceedings. Accepting it, I reach somewhat different conclusions about their significance. For me, her best selling account of the peace conference that produced the Treaty of Versailles overlooks or downplays some important matters and misses conclusions that she should have drawn.

In my respectful submission, MacMillan misses the point in particular on one important issue that propelled the world toward the next war. That is the matter of respect. In her book, and in a lecture based on it, MacMillan fails to appreciate this factor.[5] She is not alone. Many of us, once we are convinced that we are right, give no consideration at all to the impact of our words and actions on our adversaries. After all, the adversaries are wrong. If they are wrong, why should we concern ourselves with examining the matter from their perspective? This is an unfortunate approach in human relations. It is a catastrophic one in international relations.

Whether the product of the Paris Peace Conference was fair to Germany, which is reasonably debatable, the process was plainly unfair, as was the gratuitous contempt that characterized the imposition of peace terms. Instead of appreciating this point, MacMillan examined the treaty objectively and comparatively from a geopolitical and historical perspective and concluded that it was not all that bad. In a lecture following publication of the book she observed, probably correctly, that in some ways Germany was in a stronger strategic position in 1919 than she had been in 1914.[6] MacMillan downplays the qualitative difference between the disrespectful and punitive nature of the Paris treaty, and those that had ended earlier European wars: *No one who loses a war ever likes conditions of the peace settlements...In recent years, a number of historians, myself included, have come to the conclusion that the German treaty was not as bad as it has been portrayed...It [Germany] should have expected to pay something, just as France had paid after it lost the Franco-Prussian War.*[7]

In both the book and the lecture, MacMillan emphasizes the now accepted point that punitive reparations were not the cause of the next war. She is also dismissive of what came to be known as the "Guilt Clause", forcing Germany to accept responsibility for the war, pointing out quite correctly that it was really not a guilt clause in the strictest sense. She is plainly correct about the text of the "Guilt Clause" and the minimal practical impact of reparations. I do profoundly disagree, however, with equating the Paris treaty with the one that ended the Franco-Prussian War in 1871. I am not aware that France was required to forfeit all of her colonies, 13 percent of her territory and 10 percent of her population in that one. Much more importantly, what she and other historians miss is the impact of the massive disrespect visited on the loser of this war, especially when compared to earlier treatment of similarly situated losers, the Boers for example.

Perhaps MacMillan also fails to credit the full impact of propaganda. The fashioners of the Paris treaty, including even the French, at many points did not wish to be as punitive and disrespectful as they eventually were. But the public, consumers of the bayoneted Belgian babies stories, demanded blood. And the geopolitical correctness of MacMillan's observations about reparations, borders, and the actual wording of the "Guilt Clause" mattered not one whit to the German public, consumers of Hitler's later propaganda campaign.

Historians perform invaluable work in collecting facts and expressing what they see as the truths to be derived from them. Margaret MacMillan is one of the best. But in practical terms, when it comes to starting wars, keeping them going when they should end, and influencing outcomes so as to ensure more wars, the question of where the macro truth lies is comparatively unimportant. If that is at all correct, we should also examine the truth from the German point of view, beginning with some aspects of the Paris conference that shaped their viewpoint and arguably made some of Hitler's later demands quite understandable.

Setting Up for Failure: The Decision Makers

The failure of the Paris peace conference to get beyond the imperialist mindset and the harm caused by its treatment of Germany is particularly regrettable because those who gathered in Paris were essentially the government of the world in 1919. But they were a government with too many challenges, insufficient resources to meet them, and an unfortunate mix of leaders.

In addition to peace terms, they would have to draw new international borders. Further, the Fourteen Points had sparked hope for an end to secret deals dividing up countries.

They would also have to determine the role of a proposed new international body. In the end, abandoning imperialism and constructing a new and better world order was simply too much to ask.[8]

Four men, three really, bore responsibility for completing these enormous tasks. Committees and experts assisted them. Woodrow Wilson embodied almost all of the strengths and weaknesses of the process. He was the author of the new vision and representative of the most powerful victor, creditor nation to the others and a country with no territorial stake in the division of Europe.

Wilson, however, did not have a sufficient appreciation of terms like "self determination" and "open covenants." Though probably sincere, he did not even know what he meant by them. He was enough of a lingering imperialist himself to demand a Monroe Doctrine exception in the treaty to ensure U.S. dominance in the western hemisphere. Neither he nor any of the principals entertained the notion that self-determination applied to Africans.[9]

Wilson had not thought through the details and implementation of much of his vision. As the treaty took shape, he alternated between insisting and conceding. He probably could not have foreseen how the times he backed down produced many of the building blocks of World War II. His poor health and Republican opposition back home to anything remotely innovative did not help matters.

Instead of his first Secretary of State, reasonable peace advocate William Jennings Bryan, Wilson took to Paris war hawk Edward House. Worse, his closest confidant on all matters, including foreign affairs, was his beloved second wife Edith Bolling Wilson, who also accompanied him. She had been quite happy to see Bryan go.[10]

David Lloyd George of Britain supported Wilson's progressive positions on several occasions, but he saw his job simply as preserving as much of the Empire and its commercial ventures as possible. To that end, for example, he never had any intention of allowing Wilson's Point II — absolute freedom of navigation on the open seas.

Georges Clemenceau of France was the oldest. He had nursed his hatred of Germany at least since the Franco-Prussian War and the loss of Alsace-Lorraine. He said that he embraced a lifelong hatred of Germany because of what she had done to France. The Great War having been fought mainly on French soil, Clemenceau's pursuit of punitive measures could not be ignored. In addition to the physical devastation, France had lost a quarter of her male population between the ages of 18 and 30. Behind the scenes was also Marshall Ferdinand Foch, who took up the cudgel on the few occasions when Clemenceau was inclined to be conciliatory.[11]

Vittorio Orlando of Italy was the least influential of the big four but his presence was certainly an obstacle to any new way of thinking. He was a straight up imperialist whose mission was expansion of greater Italy, especially in the Adriatic. Italy, having chosen the right side in this war, though militarily insignificant as usual, was a loud and disruptive voice for doing things the old way.

And so, an ambivalent dreamer, a pragmatic rear guard imperialist, a revenge seeker, and an opportunistic land grabber would have responsibility for putting the world back together after the Great War.

Paris Failures: Exclusion of Germany and Russia

Wilson insisted on inclusion of a body called the League of Nations in the treaty in spite of absence of enthusiasm from the other victors. It was his panacea, to cover all flaws and justify concessions that violated the Fourteen Points. Germany was obliged to sign the treaty creating the League but barred from membership. Russia was excluded from the peace process altogether. It is not difficult to understand why both nations would be unenthusiastic about trying things Wilson's new way.

The capitalist allies were so terrified of the Russian revolution that even after the November 1918 armistice, Britain ordered its troops, including Canadian units, to keep on fighting — this time intervening against the Bolshevik side in a Russian civil war. By the end of 1918, the allies had 180,000 troops on Russian soil. They were supplying the White Russian forces with weapons and money.[12] To keep everyone motivated, Britain tried a propaganda campaign that mixed condemnation of the barbaric nature of Bolsheviks with a liberal dose of anti-Semitism.[13] This time the propaganda did not work. Troop morale plummeted. In the late winter of 1919, British, French, and Canadian units began refusing to obey orders. Still, the military intervention did not end until January 1921.[14]

Mistakes like this make the strange non-aggression pact between Germany and Russia in 1939 more understandable. Both countries were looking to regain territory lost in 1917 and they certainly were not going to achieve that through the League of Nations. There was little reason for the two outcasts not to keep playing the game the old way. In fact, Britain and France were negotiating for a similar agreement with Russia right up to the last moment. The union of capitalism and imperialism at the time prevented that.

Canada's independent signature on the Treaty of Versailles is cited as part of the Great War coming of age story. The exclusion of Russia

105

provides an interesting indication of the insignificance of Canada's actual role. With the military intervention failing, the four leaders, by then known as the Supreme Council, considered allowing Russia into the peace process. The options discussed were destruction, isolation, or invitation. Borden was given what he considered the great honour of contacting the Russians. He was unaware that Lloyd George could not find anyone else to take the job. The council was, however, too frightened of the Bolshevik message to allow a delegation to come to Paris. They eventually decided to invite the Russians to conduct discussions from an island located between the Mediterranean and the Black Sea!

The French undermined the idea, as did Churchill, who wanted to continue military intervention. The *London Times* joined in, terming the idea an "intrigue" and the work of international Jewish financiers and maybe the Germans also.

So prime minister Borden's moment did not come. The Bolsheviks, understandably, did not accept the precondition for the talks: a ceasefire in the civil war they were winning. So, Russia was out. Not for the last time had western nations intervened on the wrong side of a civil war. Not for the last time had they foolishly heeded the voices of those who opposed speaking to a perceived enemy.[15]

Paris Failures: The Old Way and the League of Nations

Leaving Germany out of Wilson's League of Nations, though she would later join and exit, was foolish and insulting. Practically, it did not matter, because the British, French, and Italians never had any intention of using the body for much beyond allocating the territory and colonies of Germany, Austria-Hungary, and the Ottoman Empire among themselves.

Wilson knew the conference would have to draw new borders in the defeated territories but believed the League would fix any errors. German colonies would be taken away but the League would see that they were run properly. Colonies in Africa and Asia would become League "mandates", nursed along humanely until they were in a better stage of political development. Periodic efforts, particularly by the Japanese, to have a racial equality clause in the league charter were rebuffed. The French were particularly concerned about League supervision interfering with use of their African "nigger armies."[16]

Overall, those who fashioned the treaty disregarded or downplayed the effect on parts of the world outside Europe. Price saw as particularly harmful the marginalization of Afro-Asian liberation movements, rejection of the racial equality clause, and gutting of similar clauses in the Charter of the new International Labour Organization (ILO) that would have ended the popular practice of reserving certain industries for whites. [17]

In the end, from Germany's perspective the League accomplished nothing. And Wilson was so happy to see it included in the treaty that he gave in on other matters important to Germany. The colonial powers simply sent yearly reports to the League and continued with business as usual.[18]

A good bit of the losers' territory in Europe as well as Africa was divided up the old way: the antithesis of Wilson's "open covenants, openly arrived at." For example, the framework for dividing some German and Ottoman holdings in Africa would turn out to be Sykes-Picot, a secret agreement in 1916 between Britain and France. When the Italians learned of it, they were furious and demanded a share. General haggling of this type was the norm for determining who would be given the "mandate" over German colonies in Southwest Africa and Cameroon in West Africa. Britain and France had already agreed in secret to a division of German colonies in Africa.[19] Another secret deal between the Japanese and British divided parts of Chinese and Pacific islands between them. The Paris powers allowed this over Chinese objections. Wilson went along because he feared that the Japanese, who had already lost on the racial equality clause, would not join the League.

The treatment of China at Paris was an indication of things to come. Japanese military power in the region resulted in years of this kind of exchange with the British on a larger scale. China was abandoned to her fate against the Japanese in the interwar years. At times it became necessary to construct a nuanced kind of racialization to accommodate this neglect. At Paris, Lloyd George told Wilson that Chinese "stagnation" justified, a great part of what foreigners had done there.[20]

In sum, the message to Germany was that a new day was certainly not dawning on the matter of controlling other people's lands. That message would get louder and more painful when the conference turned to dividing up Europe.

Paris Failures: Self Determination and "Tribes"

When it came to redrawing European borders, secret agreements also played a part. One was another Treaty of London, this one from 1915. In it the British, French, and Russians had promised Italy a large chunk of Slovenia and the northern Dalmatian coast. When the treaty clashed with the principle of self-determination, there was hell to pay at the conference. The Italians demanded what they had been promised, and more. The British and French were embarrassed. Wilson was furious. The Italians even walked out temporarily. They eventually backed down but in a separate deal they were given the Tyrol — and 250,000 Germans who did not want to be part of Italy.[21]

As damaging as secret agreements to future peace was the failure of the victors to understand the importance of tribes. Hannah Arendt states bluntly that the assumption that nation states could be established using the methods of the Paris council was preposterous.[22]

People define themselves in communities, and unfortunately define others as adversaries, based on a number of factors: ethnicity, religion, language, culture, history, and more. For want of an adequately inclusive term, call these communities tribes. To be fair, it was impossible to avoid altogether drawing borders that put hostile tribes together, with one dominant. In the Balkan region of Central Europe, for example, tribes defined themselves as Serbs, Croats, Slovenes, Bosnians, Montenegrins, Dalmatians, as well as Roman Catholics, Eastern Orthodox Christians, and Muslims. The tribes are still sorting that out today, sometimes violently. Add in Wilson's push for self-determination and you have a real morass, especially since Wilson did not know or say exactly what that meant. The Paris peacemakers made some gestures toward the notion of self-determination as they drew new borders. They just got it wrong.

It was clear, however, that the concept of self-determination was not to be applied outside Europe. In service of preserving the U.S. Monroe Doctrine, self-determination for Honduras was ignored. France also had little to fear. Restaurant worker Ho Chi Minh's plea on behalf of the people of Vietnam was ignored.[23] The reckoning would come 51 years later.

Important to the story of how World War II came about, and how it might have been avoided is that the self-determination principle apparently did not apply to the placement of tribes that defined themselves as Germanic.

While the task of grouping all tribes correctly was almost certainly impossible in any event, the peacemakers aggravated their shortcomings by considering at least three improper factors in addition to the secret agreements. The first was the issue of who had done what for the Allies during the war. The second was allocation of natural resources. The third was the "national security" concern about protection against Germany in the future and isolating the Bolsheviks. That is the consideration that gave Italy the German Tyrol. The demands for redrawing borders regardless of tribal factors in order to have a buffer against Germany betrayed at the outset the European victors' absolute lack of confidence in the League of Nations. Again, the message to Germany was—no change. When your adversary is up, you lose territory. When you are up, you take it back.

Both security and resource considerations trumped self determination on the matter of France's desire for that part of Germany lying on the west bank of the Rhine River, the Rhineland. Included were the coalmines of the Saar region. France pushed for everything from outright annexation, to an independent state, to permanent military occupation of the area: everything except self-determination. In the end, France got military occupation for up to 15 years, with an indefinite extension if Germany violated any provision of the peace treaty. The League of Nations was given administration of the Saar, but a plebiscite was to be held after 15 years. In it, 90 percent of the inhabitants voted to rejoin Germany.[24]

The failure that resulted from drawing borders and allocating resources based on improper factors rather than a dedicated effort to define tribes and keep them together was a significant causal factor in the coming of World War II.

Tribes: Austria, Czechoslovakia, Poland, and "Lebensraum"

Disrespect and failure to apply fair tribal criteria when deciding on borders and resource allocation raised legitimate post-war issues in Germany and provided her a propaganda bonanza. Germanic peoples and resources had indeed been unfairly allocated within the newly drawn boundaries of other nations, lending at least some credence to a demand for proper living space, or "lebensraum" in greater Germany. It was no coincidence that the run up to the next war not only involved the Rhineland, but also Austria, Czechoslovakia, and finally Poland.

Some for whom the World War II narrative begins in 1938 with Chamberlain and Munich also recall an earlier event that year, the Austrian "Anschluss." That term has always had a sinister ring, especially when accompanied by newsreel footage of Germans marching into Vienna. The term evokes an image of a sort of military avalanche. What it means, however, is unity. In this case that might not have been a bad idea. The soon to be defunct Austria-Hungary Empire sued for peace ahead of Germany in 1918. In its final months, its Emperor announced a new plan for territorial organization in which *every people would build its own political community in its own area of settlement.*[25] With much in common, including language and culture and for a variety of other reasons many Austrians called for unity with Germany. To be sure, not all Austrians were in favour and an honest early plebiscite on the question of Anschluss would have been desirable. Unfortunately, the Paris peace treaty effectively forbade it. Unity with Germany prevailed in a later, albeit suspect vote. By any measure, Germany enjoyed substantial support among Austrians. Whatever the geopolitics of the 1938 Anschluss, it can hardly be objectively viewed as an early step in a master plan to conquer the world.

Now we come to the famous Munich agreement so beloved by today's hawks. Was it the colossal mistake that should never be repeated? The matter was certainly not that simple and the flawed process of fairly drawing borders based on tribes was a major complication. Arendt cites with approval a comment by Mussolini made shortly after the agreement: *If Czechoslovakia finds herself today in what might be called a 'delicate situation,' it is because she was not just Czechoslovakia, but Czecho-Germano-Polono-Magyaro-Rutheno-Rumano-Slovakia.*[26]

At the Paris peace conference, Czechs and Slovaks papered over their very real divisions. Shortly before it opened, they were able to form and present a new nation and a united front. The delegation was well received. There was particular affection for President Tomas Mazarak, seen as a hero of the struggle against the Austrian Empire.[27] That superficial unity would come apart as a result of action by the Czechs, and would become a part of the appeasement story.

Mazarak's nation-building effort had included a tour of Czech and Slovak communities in the U.S. There he signed an agreement with Czech and Slovak organizations promising that in the new nation Slovaks would have their own courts, parliament, and language. As the Austrian empire was collapsing on the battlefield, there was much talk within it of independence, by Poles, Czechs, South Slavs — and German Czechs.

In September 1919 the U.S. recognized the new nation, but made no mention of where its borders lay. In fact, its borders were not settled. Earlier Czech/Slav unity had fallen apart. The Czech-dominated government began to resemble the Italians when it came to demanding territory, arguing for parts of other countries. The

Czech demand for territory from Hungary, for example, was denied, except that they were given the largely German town of Bratislava.[28]

More ominously, at the time of these demands the Czechs had already moved troops into German-speaking areas near the border of Austria and Germany. The Germans called this area the Sudetenland. There were at least 1.5 million people there who wanted to be in Germany, not under Czech rule. But the Czechs claimed their new nation could not survive without the area's industries, including textile mills, glassworks, and breweries. They prevailed, in spite of protests to the peace conference from the Sudeten Germans themselves.

Germans were the largest minority in Czechoslovakia, numbering three of fourteen million. Confident after the Munich agreement that the British would not intervene, German troops marched in to establish the new state of Slovakia in March 1939.[29] Decades later, the world would better understand the importance of tribes in drawing lines. Today Czechs and Slovaks each have their own country.

MacMillan contends that Hitler's embrace of the Slovak cause provided the excuse for him to destroy Czechoslovakia. Probably so. Perhaps, however, another excellent excuse was the treatment of Germany by the peacemakers drawing borders around tribes and resources.

Finally, it was no coincidence that World War II began with the German invasion of Poland. The Paris conference had also botched the question of her borders and resources, though somewhat understandably. Modern Poland did not exist in 1919. It had been gobbled up by several of its neighbours more than 200 years earlier. The Poles who wished to put it back together did not speak with one voice; the Paris peacemakers were presented with two governments. There was no hope of drawing workable borders according to any rational tribal criteria. Poland's former territory has been rightly termed an ethnic jumble. The peacemakers decided there should be a Poland and it should be independent. They were again, however, presented with a nation without borders.

In retrospect, the borders they fashioned left far too many Germans under Polish authority. Lloyd George saw this and warned his colleagues in vain of the future danger. The allocations most relevant to World War II related to Poland's western boundary. One of Wilson's Fourteen Points was that Poland should have access to a Baltic port. The solution was a corridor through Germany to Danzig, now Gdansk. The corridor split Germany and became a flashpoint for violence.

The matter of the southwest border of Poland raised the question of whether Germany would lose valuable mines and mills in Upper Silesia. She was already losing the Saar. That dispute was resolved after the conference by a committee of nations with no direct interest. German got most of the territory. Poland got most of the resources. During and after the peace conference, over the objections of Clemenceau, plebiscites were held in some of the contested areas. The preference in all of them was to be part of Germany.

In that fateful year of 1939, the Germans annexed Upper Silesia and sent troops to seize Danzig and the corridor.[30] The British responded and the avoidable war was on. Until that time, Hitler's position had resembled the reverse image of more than one claimant in Paris: He wanted the Treaty of Versailles abrogated — and more. We will never know the outcome if the Allies had, for example, negotiated about the question of returning most or all of her territory and resources to Germany, while at the same time issuing a stern warning that the "and more" part would not be acceptable.

Paris Failures: The Old Way and Disarmament

The treaty mandated significant German disarmament. For other nations, including the allies, reliance on the League of Nations to solve international disputes peaceably was supposed to lead to voluntary disarmament. That, of course, did not happen and it is not surprising that Germany, excluded from the League anyway, looked early on for ways around the restrictions of the treaty and ultimately repudiated them.

Paris Failures: Disrespect

Disrespect of Germany may be the most egregious failure. It bred hatred and it was avoidable without cost. Treating the German representatives to Paris as envoys of a defeated adversary in the traditional way would not in itself have required drawing a single border differently, or altering one figure in the reparations bill. Actually negotiating peace would not have required significant concessions. Regrettably, the scale and horror of the war likely prevented the victors from realizing that a focus on solutions rather than insulting an enemy bodes much better for any future relationship. We cannot know, of course, what the next 20 years would have brought had the conference on the whole acted fairly, thereby denying the Germans most of their grievances, both real and perceived. We can know that the personal slights were real and unnecessary. We know that disrespect played a part in bringing on the next war. As a practical matter, whether it was somehow justifiable seems quite irrelevant.

In 1919, the Germans thought the peace was going to be fashioned the old way. While the leaders at the Paris conference were constructing the treaty terms with input from experts and committees, the Germans were doing the same. Their work assumed the Fourteen Points would be the basis of the settlement. Their delegates arrived in early May with packing crates full of materials for negotiations they were never to have. There was understandable surprise when, after only a week in Paris, the delegation was handed the "take it or leave it" treaty.

The delegation was housed in an old hotel, surrounded by a stockade and guarded by sentries. In fairness, this virtual imprisonment was to some extent for their own protection against the French public, then being stirred to new heights of hatred by a rabid press. The same press referred to the location of the German delegation in the room where it was handed the treaty as the prisoners' box.[31]

The stunned German delegation was given two weeks to submit comments. In spite of now being aware of the nature of the process, its members prepared detailed and reasoned objections and counter proposals. There were those on the allied side, notably Lloyd George, who saw the future danger of the treaty and the need for modifications. A member of his delegation said, *We came to Paris confident that the new order was about to be established; we left convinced that the new order had merely fouled the old.* Herbert Hoover, the American administrator of relief for Europe, recognized *that the consequences of many parts of the proposed Treaty would ultimately bring destruction*[32]. These voices went unheeded. The German representative, Count Ulrich von Brockdorff-Ranzau, after being handed the peace terms spoke words that would reflect the opening being provided to the Nazis later: *The Fatherland has been dealt a heavy blow. There is work to be done. We are Germans. We will not forget. We will rise from this shame.*[33]

A new government was formed in Germany, with an American-style constitution. After the allies rejected its acceptance of the treaty save only a reservation about accepting complete responsibility for the war, Germany acquiesced and signed on June 28th. Hitler would condemn his government for this and later insist on Versailles as the place where Germany would accept the surrender of France in the next war.

From the same evidence, MacMillan and I come to somewhat different conclusions about the Treaty of Versailles and its importance as a cause of the next war that Canada would be asked to join, having done little or nothing to bring it about. I suspect that her position and that of other historians may be coloured by knowledge of what happened later. If ever anyone crossed the line from simply engaging in brutality to a greater *degree* than one's enemy and committed crimes that are more evil in *kind*, it was Adolph Hitler. Viewed only in light of his later actions, for example, the Austrians opposed to Anschluss were the good guys and the German Austrians were Nazi collaborators. The same vision is applicable to Czechoslovakia and Poland. But justifying Paris on the basis of later history is intellectually questionable at best. At the time the great opportunity to abandon imperialism and colonialism was presented, Hitler was not in power.

The failure of the Paris Peace Conference, understandable as it is, was a significant factor in the lost opportunity for peace in the interwar years. There was nothing Canada could have done about it, notwithstanding the symbolic value of her independent signature on the Treaty of Versailles.

How Could This Happen Again? Five Reasons for the Failure of Peace Movements

Canadians were part of a global conversation about war in the wake of Great War devastation. The propaganda screen could not conceal knowledge of the political blundering, stupidity, profiteering, and indescribable horror of the Great War. Never before had people talked so enthusiastically about a different way to resolve conflict. Such a conversation has not occurred since.

In the 1920s and 30s, many around the world believed that ending war was possible. The interwar years marked the high water mark of peace movements in many nations, including Canada and Great Britain. Peace seekers were never a majority during this time, but they were a force that was certainly noticed by governments. Without them, there would have been no conversation. Why then, did the peace movement fail? I suggest that there are at least five reasons, though I certainly do not contend that they constitute a complete answer. The factors we are examining were at play in all five, the overarching one being the union of capitalism and imperialism.

1. Multiple Cause Coalitions

First, there are inherent problems with inclusive coalitions. Peace seekers had before them a host of injustices in addition to war. The brutal legacy of the 19th century industrial revolution, xenophobia, and a patriarchal class system presented them with issues of women's rights, farming, immigration, and oppression of industrial workers and miners, among others. It is understandable that many of the same people opposed to war would also be committed in varying degrees to addressing other injustices, especially when causes were so interrelated.

Recall from the last chapter, for example, the execution of Private Stones. What part of the story of Lizzie Stones would move one to action? Lizzie was a young British mother of two, whose underpaid miner husband was sent off to a war she had no say about. Joseph, who had served with distinction, fled after suffering shell shock and was executed for cowardice. The government then withdrew Lizzie's meagre dependent allowance of 17 shillings a week and informed her that she would not be eligible for a widow's pension.[34] The senseless war would be the focus of some who knew her story. For others, it would be the powerlessness and poverty of Lizzie Stones and her children. Still others would be outraged at a callous government and the denial of her right to vote. Those moved by, say, the part played by capitalist oppression of miners in Lizzie's story would naturally be inclined to cooperate with those who were primarily outraged by the war itself. Coalitions that included advocates of peace, improvements in the status of women, and labour rights were a natural response.

This unity brought post war peace movements strength of numbers and the benefits of cooperation, but also major impediments. One of them was, as it always is, the question of priorities. And in an extreme situation, unity and cooperation are further threatened when it appears that advancing the cause about which one is most passionate means reducing or abandoning support for other causes one believes to be worthwhile. We will see examples of this in both Canada and Britain.

Coalitions of good causes have additional problems. One is diffusion of message; another is leadership and difficulty in decision making. Peace and justice people are by nature not authoritarian. Quite commendably, they want all voices to be heard. That can be cumbersome and lead to an inability to be decisive when the time is right.

2. Propaganda

In this period, government control of what people saw, read, and heard as well as failures of journalism continued. With the field left open to them, governments did all they could to preserve 19th century economic and class distinctions, including the implicit assumption that state violence is at the service of international business activity. Further, governments did not slow the aggressive campaign against peace movements. This is understandable. The aims of the peace movement were not compatible with the union of capitalism and imperialism, especially when the movement had a strong labour component.

3. Coercion

The third reason is the coercive power of the state. Governments engaged in violence and incitement to violence directed at peace seekers, conscientious objectors, workers, farmers, and virtually all members of the peace coalitions. Governments also passed repressive laws and imprisoned people. It required more than moral opposition to war and outrage about injustice to sustain peace seekers. It took more than the thick skin required to cope with insults and ostracism and the determination required to cope with being fired in hard times. For the unrecognized heroes of this time, it often took a willingness to suffer physical violence meted out by governments and those incited to violence by governments; to live with condemnation by family members and neighbours who had been incited by propaganda; to suffer raids on their homes and workplaces. In short, it simply took unrecognized, unappreciated bravery to oppose war and advocate for social justice in the years following the Great War.

4. Mainstream Organized Christianity

The fourth reason is organized Christianity and its historic fealty to government. Between wars, churches occasionally emphasized the nonviolent life and teaching of Jesus. When governments get themselves into an approaching war however, and call upon the

118

churches to put aside all that love and forgiveness stuff, churches comply. They readily join the campaign to vilify those who want to keep the message of peace alive. We will never know, and it is difficult to estimate what the effect would have been during this interwar period, when churches were still influential, had they stood fast for peace.

5. Hijacked Russian Revolution

The final reason is likely the most significant. At the end of the Great War, the Russian revolution had produced the only country offering the prospect that workers and farmers would be treated fairly. It was natural that labour in the West would see that development and want to be associated with it. Understandable as it was, inclusion of the labour movement was the corporate poison pill for peace coalitions.

We have already seen that western capitalist governments reacted to the Russian revolution with what bordered on terror from the moment of the overthrow of the Tsar. A *London Times* editorial headlined: *The Only Remedy for Bolshevism is Bullets.* Knightley writes: *It was bad enough for the landed gentry of Britain and France that the Bolsheviks had overthrown their betters in Russia; it was terrifying that they now spoke of spreading this appalling political dogma throughout Europe and perhaps the rest of the world.*[35]

The motivation of capitalist countries can scarcely be explained as revulsion at Bolshevik human rights abuses, since they had been perfectly content with the unmatched inhumanity of the Tsars. There was no reason to fear Russia militarily. The Russians were simply occupying or re-occupying their claimed share of parts of Central Europe. That is precisely what everyone else on the continent was doing. But Russia, remember, was unable to pursue these claims at the Paris conference. It is far more likely that western paranoia had its deepest root in the knowledge that the Bolsheviks, at least initially, represented a real threat to capitalist control of wages, hours, working conditions, and makeup of the work force.

Unfortunately for the peace and justice organizations, socialists and antiwar leaders were too slow to recognize the gradual betrayal of the aims of the Russian revolution, even after the vicious regime of Joseph Stalin came to power in 1926. An important reason for this blindness was their otherwise laudable focus on international solidarity and common bonds among peoples. Arendt writes: *The socialists kept implicitly intact the original concept of a 'nation among nations', all of which belong to the family of mankind, but they never found a device by which to transform this idea into a working concept in a world of sovereign states. Their internationalism, consequently, remained a personal conviction shared by everybody, and their healthy disinterest in national sovereignty turned into a quite unhealthy and unrealistic indifference to foreign politics.*[36]

This tragic shortsightedness gave capitalist governments not only a propaganda windfall, but also an excuse to ignore the merits of peace proposals and labour reforms and bring the hammer of government power down on the "reds." If laws got in the way, they were ignored or rewritten. Most significantly, the vigorous anti-communist campaign thoroughly convinced millions in the U.K., Canada, and the U.S. to act against their own interests, usually out of fear, or to turn away and not act at all.

Blind anti-communism may have been a disaster for all concerned in the field of international relations but it was a rousing economic success for capitalists. It delayed fundamental labour reforms, including those sought by women, for decades. It virtually destroyed interwar peace movements. It helped bring on World War II, with the added bonus that many would credit the war with ending the worldwide depression that capitalist greed had itself created.

Peace Movements in Canada and Britain: The Five Reasons in Play

Canada

The principal components of the Canadian peace coalition in the interwar years mirrored those of its British counterpart: peace, women's rights, economic and social justice. To varying degrees, the five reasons operated to obstruct both movements. In Canada, the relationship among advocates of the three causes, and the difficulties all three causes encountered can be glimpsed in the stories of a small number of prominent Canadians.

J.S. Woodsworth was a Methodist minister and one of the founders of the Co-Operative Commonwealth Federation (CCF), forerunner of the New Democratic Party (NDP). While others faltered, he never abandoned his faith-based commitment to peace and economic justice. The support of his wife, Lucy, helped him through the hardships he suffered as a result of his stands. Also keeping the faith, and being condemned for it, was a fellow clergyman, R. Edis Fairbairn. Another major figure was Agnes Macphail, the first woman elected to the House of Commons. Her career included activities in support of all three causes.

We will see an example of the "division within a division" in the peace movement in the life of Nelly McClung, widely read author and one of the "Famous Five" women who persuaded the Privy Council to reverse a decision of the Supreme Court of Canada that women were not to be recognized as persons under the British North America Act of 1867.[37]

Woodsworth's experience in his working class Winnipeg parish made him an advocate for basic labour rights. That is how he came to be involved in the 1919 Winnipeg General Strike and its violent suppression on "Bloody Saturday", June 21, 1919. Major factors in the dispute that led to the strike included conditions faced by returning Great War veterans, unemployment, housing shortages, exorbitant rents, long hours and low wages. Frightened employers called on government for help. As the strike date approached, solicitor general Arthur Meighen blamed the Bolsheviks. We will see Meighen again, doing a brief stint as prime minister, and demonstrating his unreconstructed support of imperialism.

One of the voices in opposition to Meighen and others in government before the strike was Woodsworth, a contributor to the *Western Labour News*, one of a very few papers to present the perspective of workers. In a response reminiscent of an issue that that remains divisive today, he wrote: *These men did their fair share. Now the rich should pay theirs!*[38]

The run up to the strike saw government officials at all levels turn on their constituents who were farmers, workers, and veterans. One weapon was legislation. As many strike leaders were immigrants, the federal government enacted laws permitting them to be deported without due process. Winnipeg passed ordinances restricting the right of assembly. It was a peaceful parade organized by veterans in defiance of those restrictions that came to a violent end.

In addition to legislation, government also knew how to use its monopoly on force. Reluctant police were fired and replaced by a militia whose members were paid more than the regular police. These "Specials" were given horses and baseball bats. Prime minister Borden ordered the Mounties to put down demonstrations with whatever force was necessary. On June 21st, some demonstrators tipped over a streetcar and set it on fire, an act identical to that of some who took to the streets of Vancouver in 2011 after the Canucks lost the Stanley Cup final. Many of the Vancouver rioters were prosecuted and a few even went to jail. In 1919, the Specials and the Mounties worked together to fashion a different response. They shot two demonstrators dead and wounded dozens more.

Woodsworth was arrested and charged with seditious conspiracy. One of the *Western Labour News* writers, Fred Dixon, who had urged the strikers to remain nonviolent, was similarly charged. Dixon was acquitted and the charges against Woodsworth were dropped, but the damage was done. This government outrage succeeded in breaking the strike, and delayed the right to bargain collectively and the eight-hour workday, for decades. Government force remained in the service of business.

Xenophobia played its usual effective role in the Winnipeg event. Some in the crowd held signs reading DOWN WITH BOLSHEVISM and DEPORT UNDESIRABLE ALIENS.[39]

Woodsworth also stood fast for peace in opposition to organized Christianity. He lost his position with the Methodist Church when he objected to churches being used as Great War recruiting centres. He left the church in opposition to the war, saying: *I thought as a Christian minister, I was a messenger of the Prince of Peace.*[40]

He kept the faith on the secular side as well, writing that the enemy of people was not just capitalism, but capitalism in league with militarism and imperialism — a deadly mixture that caused war.[41] His eloquent final statement on the subject was his opposition to Canada joining World War II. In September 1939, Woodsworth was leader of the CCF. In a speech to Parliament, he said: *I have sons of my own, and I hope they are not cowards. But if any of these boys, not through cowardice but through belief, is willing to take his stand on this matter and if necessary to face a concentration camp or a firing squad, I shall be more proud of that boy than if he had enlisted for the war.*[42]

Woodsworth was closely allied with R. Edis Fairbairn. The mainstream denomination with the greatest antiwar potential was the United Church of Canada (UCC). Biannually from 1932-1938, its General Council issued statements that *war is contrary to the mind of Christ.*[43] Following the declaration of war on Germany, however, the General Council and Presbyteries reversed course. Dissent came from 68 ministers who signed on to a document authored principally by Fairbairn, entitled *Witness Against War*, rebuking the church for abandoning its pre-war declarations. The Canadian press condemned the document and called for the church to take action against those who had signed it. The attorney general opened an investigation into possible violation of the War Measures Act.

Fairbairn lost his parish over the controversy and began to publish his own newsletter. In it he continued to explore the contradiction between the UCC statement about the mind of Christ and its support for the war. He also agreed with Woodsworth about the effect of the relation between capitalism and imperialism.[44]

The work of Lucy Woodsworth illustrates the link to the other component of the interwar peace coalition — the rights of women. Lucy was an active member of the Toronto chapter of the Women's International League for Peace and Freedom (WIL). This is one of the only major interwar peace organizations still active today. Suffragist women founded WIL at The Hague in 1915. A significant reason for seeking the vote was to bring an end to the Great War and prevent future wars. WIL came to Canada in 1920 and formed chapters in Vancouver, Edmonton, Winnipeg, and Toronto. In 1931, its members collected in Canada 491,000 signatures on an international disarmament petition.[45]

A more famous member of WIL, a woman who worked in all peace coalition causes, was Agnes Macphail. Another founder of CCF, her life reflected important work for all three components of the coalition. In Parliament, she worked on behalf of farmers, miners, immigrants, and prisoners. She was, of course, labeled a communist. A feminist, her efforts went beyond voting rights toward the goal of complete gender equity. She served as honorary president of WIL. She was the first woman member of the Canadian delegation to the League of Nations, serving on the disarmament committee.[46]

In the Depression years of the 1930's Canadian women, except in Quebec, had finally achieved voting rights and moved to address other important issues. Mainstream churches vacillated on the theology of peace. The desperate conditions of workers and farmers left the economic and social justice wing as the most significant component of the peace coalition. To address the perceived threat from that element, business once again called on government to use force.

One answer to the call was a 1935 replay of 1919's "Bloody Sunday". Unable to deal with the Depression, prime minister

R.B. Bennett blamed communists and railed against international conspiracies. Against the red tide, he led by example.

When more than 3,000 unemployed and hungry men approached Ottawa from the west to demand jobs, Bennett agreed to meet with their representatives. He responded to their demands by telling them they were communists seeking revolution, not work.

The main body of workers had remained in Regina. Some of them were meeting to discuss strategy on July 1st, when Mounties armed with baseball bats attacked them. The workers put up barricades and threw stones; the Mounties escalated to pistols. The encounter left one policeman dead, 40 workers and five bystanders wounded, and the city trashed. Some of the 130 men arrested probably learned for the first time about Section 98 of the Criminal Code, which required the *accused* to prove that the he was *not* associated with communists. The federal police force accomplished by force what the capitalists and the government desired. The march ended.[47]

During the first half of the 1930's, the Canadian peace movement continued its alignment with the movement for social change. Woodsworth and Fairbairn emphasized the relationship between war and capitalism. Agnes Macphail joined them.[48] The coalescence of peace and social justice advocates caused worried employers to ramp up the red scare and use the government monopoly on legislation to combat the threat of both. Government assisted actively, or looked the other way when they resorted to violence.

An example of the alliance is a 1931 event in Toronto. When government began to persecute advocates of economic justice, labeling them communists or "communist sympathizers," peace advocates spoke up for them. One peace group organized a free speech forum. It invited the police commissioner and a judge who was a member of the commission to participate. Instead, the Police Commission blocked the event, claiming that the organizers were "thinly-veiled communists."[49]

In addition to being subjected by association to the attacks on economic justice advocates and the government's paternal annoyance at those pursuing women's rights, leaders of the antiwar segment of the coalition faced a division within that division. There were absolute pacifists, not all of them religiously motivated. There were those who had not come to a complete pacifist position, but abhorred war and wanted the coalition to work primarily on disarmament, or support of the League of Nations, or on opposing the military curriculum in Canadian schools. And significantly, there were sincere opponents of war who came to believe that war against extreme evil might be acceptable as a means of cleansing the world of it. All in all, leaders of the Canadian peace movement faced serious internal obstacles in addition to those inherent in coalition membership.

Author, journalist, and feminist hero Nellie McClung represents the dilemma of that third group of war opponents. In a 1940 piece, she wrote: *War is not only a waste of things we can see or touch, but makes heavy inroads on the invisible and intangible things of the spirit...War is an ugly thing. No one tries to glorify it now.* Later, after lamenting what Germany had become: *War is waste, bitter waste, but not such a soul-destroying waste as government by violence and robbery...Our concern now is to win the war, dethrone the gods of violence and then make a just peace on the foundation of human brotherhood.*[50] She no doubt spoke for millions of Canadians, who would enter this war much less enthusiastically than had their parents.

Contrary to much public perception, it was not solely the rise of the Nazis in Germany that brought failure to peace movements. The potential for schism in the divisions I have described was aggravated by outside events that demonstrated a lack of international commitment to nonviolent dispute resolution. The world, including the West, was not very serious about peace, certainly not about creative nonviolence.

A barely remembered event known as the Riddell Incident illustrates Canada's attitude toward the League of Nations and nonviolent deterrent measures. The outcome was a blow to those in the peace coalition who had concentrated on the potential of the League of Nations. Some of those secret treaties from the Great War had promised Italy economic control of Abyssinia. Given the previous license the European powers enjoyed in Africa, Italy assumed it was free to dominate. The African nation, on the other hand, was a member of the League and assumed it could rely on that organization's guarantee of its territory. Abyssinian Emperor Haile Selassie was wrong. His early 1935 appeal to the League went unheeded and in October Italy invaded.[51]

Enter attempted Canadian diplomacy in the person of Walter Riddell, Canadian advisory officer to the League of Nations. When the question of Italian aggression came before the League, Riddell received from his superiors in Ottawa only vaguely worded bureaucratic doublespeak in response to his request for instructions about Canada's position. The government response, however, could reasonably be read as agreeing with the idea of economic sanctions against Italy. With encouragement from fellow diplomat Lester Pearson, he tabled in committee a proposal for oil sanctions. That would have been a hard blow to Italy.

Riddell's proposal received worldwide acclaim and enhanced Canada's international visibility. Mackenzie King, who had been preoccupied with an election campaign, however, was horrified. The Canadian government immediately and vehemently repudiated Riddell's proposal, saying it represented only his personal views. Riddell claims in his memoirs that implementation of his proposal would have caused Hitler to hesitate and could have prevented World War II. True or not, the hard blow was the one that fell on the young League of Nations. In any event, the proposal could not have succeeded. U.S. oil companies were not prepared to abide by sanctions. More importantly, Britain and France had already chosen appeasement over nonviolent deterrence by secretly promising Italian dictator Mussolini everything he wanted. Italy got Abyssinia. Shortly afterward, the Germans marched into the Rhineland.[52]

Interwar peace advocates who had put their energy into support of diplomacy also learned that only imperialist treaties carried any real weight. In 1928, 65 nations, including Canada as one of the first, signed the U.S. and French sponsored Kellogg-Briand Pact, renouncing war as an instrument for resolving international disputes. The treaty came to nothing, in part because the U.S. required an exception for its Monroe Doctrine domination of the Americas and the British made the same claim regarding security of the British Empire. There was also no enforcement mechanism. Signatories Japan, Germany, Austria, and Italy simply ignored the treaty. Today, the treaty is a minor historical footnote. Nevertheless, it remains legally binding, making most of the wars Canada has joined after 1945 violations of international law.[53]

Coalition members advocating for disarmament were also disappointed by the failure of treaties arising from the 1921 Washington Naval Conference, ostensibly convened to limit the deadly naval arms race. In truth, the conference was mainly about U.S., French, and British efforts to adjust Pacific zones of imperial interest with Japan. This détente continued until the later interwar years, with China the greatest loser. When it finally disintegrated, race was a factor. The British Imperial Defence Committee noted that the *most likely war for some time to come would be one between the white and yellow races whose interests lay in the Pacific.*[54]

Faith-based absolute opposition to war suffered greatly at a critical time. Influential American theologian Reinhold Niebuhr changed his mind. Niebuhr not only abandoned pacifism, he urged what he called a more realistic approach to international conflicts. This provided encouragement to those who could somehow see war as a means of ending war by defeating evil. But his Marxist take on social justice issues stoked government reluctance to confront fascism at all.[55] McClung, Macphail, Niebuhr, and many who came after them made the classic mistake of believing that making war could produce peace.

The first fascist to benefit from western appeasement in Europe was not Hitler or Mussolini. It was Francisco Franco, and the red scare played a major role. Closely following the capitulation to Italy in Africa was a conflict that deepened fissures in the coalition. The Spanish Civil War split off Canadians working to oppose war as a means of improving economic and social justice from their pacifist partners. Thousands who had been allied with pacifists went off to fight in Spain. The peace movement would never recover.[56] By the time Nellie McClung saw Nazi Germany as the evil that justified abandoning pacifism, by the time Agnes Macphail had done likewise and reluctantly voted in Parliament in support of joining World War II, many of their fellow antiwar Canadians had earlier perceived that level of evil in Francisco Franco's fascists.

In 1936, the democratically elected Republican government of Spain had no Socialist or Communist ministers, but often had the support of both of those parties. A junta of generals, led by Franco, revolted "to free Spain from communist domination." In a story to be tiresomely repeated in other contexts with other nations, they falsely claimed to have discovered secret orders to "Sovietize" Spain. The army started a war and by the end of the year controlled half the country.

One of the sad ironies of this prelude to World War II is that its future adversaries were *ad idem* on so many matters. Germany and Italy were as fiercely anticommunist as Britain and France. There was a clamour in all of these countries for government to deal harshly with labour unrest. The difference, at least in the popular narrative, is that the western nations were supporters of democracy. The Spanish Civil War revealed that they were considerably more opposed to communism than they were supportive of democracy. Aided by the direct military intervention of Germany and Italy, it was all over by the end of March 1939. The western powers watched. Even before the surrender of the Republicans, Britain and France gave final unconditional recognition to Franco. Spain had been saved from the communist menace. Commerce could continue.[57] Hitler had gained an appeasement by western inaction. And peace coalitions in Canada and elsewhere had lost many whose commitment to nonviolence was not as strong as their commitment to social justice and abhorrence of fascism.

These developments damaged a peace movement in Canada that began when the first organization, the Canadian Socialist League, opposed the Boer War. A proliferation of diverse groups followed, one even called the Imperial Order Daughters of the Empire. Together, the organizations enjoyed significant popular support late into the 1930s. When a Winnipeg newspaper criticized the 1938 Munich agreement, 12,000 readers cancelled their subscriptions.[58]

Government, however, was not interested in proposals from these groups. A grossly overlooked aspect of the period just before World War II is that the Chinese were left to fend for themselves. When Japan invaded China in 1937, peace groups lobbied for sanctions, for a boycott of Japanese goods and most importantly for Canada to cease sending war materials to Japan. Instead, Canada continued business as usual and in fact increased trade with Japan until 1939. Only when Japan signed the tripartite agreement with Germany and Italy in 1940 did Canada begin to give in on sanctions. Until then, Canadian policy reflected the racist view expressed by Mackenzie King: Japanese and Chinese were venting their animal instincts and whites should just let them fight it out. In spite of rhetoric about Japanese outrages in China, no assistance came from the West as long as Japan was willing to accommodate western colonial interests. The only country to help China during this time was the Soviet Union.[59]

Canadian peace advocates may have failed at preventing war, but they had some success. They succeeded against mandatory cadet training and physical education classes that were largely military drills. Canada was thereby spared a close counterpart to Nazi efforts to militarize youth. More importantly, pacifists worked to free interned Jews during World War II and prevent expulsion of Japanese Canadians following the war. The story of Japanese Canadians has received some notice. It is regrettable that there have not been equally prominent reminders of Canadian anti-Semitism, and the role of pacifists in opposing it.[60]

The fragile Canadian peace coalition played a small but important role in preserving and developing that peculiarly Canadian strain of caution first seen in Wilfrid Laurier.

Britain

Prospects for peace during the interwar years were, of course, much more dependent on developments in Europe than in Canada.

The British antiwar movement was the largest and most vocal in the world. Its fate affected Canada significantly. The peace coalition was made up of the same three principal players, suffered the same opposition from government and business interests, and failed for essentially the same reasons as its Canadian counterpart. The coalition experienced similar internal problems and had even greater difficulty recognizing and escaping the stigma of association with communism.

Typical of the state of free speech and debate was an antiwar rally at which Sylvia Pankhurst spoke in Trafalgar Square. Right wing thugs and soldiers from Australia and New Zealand broke it up. Police escorted her to safety in that one, and did not generally jail people for speech alone. The preferred method was to discourage participation by raiding offices, destroying files, pamphlets, and printing presses, as well as opening the mail of antiwar supporters.[61]

Investigative journalist Edmund Morel also angered the government. He founded an organization whose membership grew to 650,000 by the end of the war. Morel wrote, correctly as it turned out, that the worst outcome would be total victory by either side. He proposed a negotiated peace based on what would later resemble Wilsonian principles, including plebiscites to determine the future of disputed territories. The response was familiar, and involved more than outright rejection of this invitation to engage in rational debate. Newspapers condemned Morel as a German agent. Police raided his home and seized his private papers. He was imprisoned at hard labour for sending pacifist materials out of the country, an experience that broke him physically.[62]

The British government imprisoned all of the dissenters noted here, and thousands more. Some died there. Great War resisters, including conscientious objectors, were jailed at hard labour under conditions that included isolation in a 7x12 foot cell without a mattress and enforced silence when in the company of other prisoners. Remarkably, the resisters maintained their morale by creating surreptitious publications.

The imprisoned war resisters had a support group called the No Conscription Fellowship (NCF). Forgive a digression here, an anecdote from the activity of that group. The grim challenges facing social justice advocates always require the occasional resort to humour in order to preserve sanity.

Sir Archibald Bodkin, director of public prosecutions provided NCF with a much needed moment of comic relief. In agitated frustration about the peace movement, he complained: *war will become impossible if all men were to have the view that war is wrong.*[63] The NCF created a poster with these exact words, attributed to Bodkin. An NCF worker was arrested for putting up the posters. NCF lawyers then demanded the arrest of the author of the subversive statement. The NCF newspaper called for Bodkin to arrest and prosecute himself, but promised relief payments to his wife and children if he sent himself to jail.

In Britain, the extremes of oppression directed at all components of the coalition moderated somewhat as the interwar years wore on. By the end of the period, however, the formula of propaganda, defamation, imprisonment, destruction of civil liberties and incitement to violence had done much of its work to discourage public support for its peace wing. The public had been conditioned for years to hate all Germans. Internal divisions, typified by the Emmeline Pankhurst trade-off we have seen with Lloyd George as well as a partial victory for women's suffrage further weakened the coalition.

Most significantly, the economic justice component, and by association all of the coalition, had been shattered by the red scare. As noted, Europe's socialists and pacifists had understandably been elated by the Bolshevik revolution of 1917. They expected the emergence of a better society. But Russia in 1922 became the Union of Soviet Socialist Republics. In 1926, Joseph Stalin came to power. Although by that time, Sylvia Pankhurst and many others had become disenchanted, it was too late. Too many labour advocates were slow to appreciate the scope of the change in Russia. Stalin's ruthless murder and imprisonment of millions allowed governments and business to engulf the coalition in the red scare.[64]

It was not only the inattention of the left that gave the capitalist/ imperialist alliance this opening. Ironically, it was also the misdeeds of the capitalists themselves. After 1929, the attention of the world shifted to surviving the global depression. The disaster was brought on, as it would be again in 2008, by the greed of capitalist investors and financial institutions. For some reason, rather than creating a backlash, the Great Depression turned out to be capitalism's greatest gift. When the victims, ordinary workers and farmers, demanded answers they were tarred with the communist brush. Somehow, the depression enabled anti-communist paranoia to be used as a bludgeon against labour and peace advocates for decades. Tardy recognition by some peace activists of the betrayal of the Russian revolution undoubtedly helped, but it was not Stalin who threw much of the world into poverty. Nor was it Hitler, who was as anti-communist as they come.

There is a surviving link between the remnants of interwar peace organizations in Canada and Great Britain. The Peace Pledge Union (PPU) is the oldest secular pacifist organization in Britain. PPU is successor to a number of organizations whose history is entwined with the poppies that grow in Flanders fields. In the 1920s, the British Legion was using red poppies as a fundraising tool. Peace organizations suggested that the center of the poppies should read "No More War". Instead, until 1994, the Legion imprinted the poppies with "Haig Fund".

In 1933, the peace groups began to produce their own poppies--- white ones, with "Peace" in the centre. The following year, the PPU began widespread distribution of white poppies.[65] Many who distributed them had lost family members in wars. White poppies distributed in Canada number at present only a few thousand, but the numbers are increasing. That is happening because more people are coming to understand the message of the original distributors. White poppies are not intended as an insult to veterans. Rather, the poppies are a challenge to the continuing momentum toward war that has spanned generations.

Peace people are no closer to having the power to prevent war than they were in 1939. That is not surprising, considering the obstacles they have faced. It is remarkable that the framework for change still exists at all. But it is there.

If prospects for peace are to improve, several aspects of the surviving narrative from the interwar years must be challenged. One often heard is that western nations retreated into isolation when they should have been re-arming. Not heard is the practical question of the cost. Would the funds have come from the meagre resources available to the millions made homeless by the capitalist depression? This unanswered question resonates today.

The standard narrative for the interwar years begins at the earliest with Hitler's rise to power in 1933 and ignores a number of other questions. What if the Great War victors had seized the moment and followed something resembling the Fourteen Points? What if they had given authority and real support to the League of Nations? What if government policy had been directed toward strengthening international peace efforts rather than suppressing them? Such policies might also have failed, but they could scarcely have produced a more destructive result than did the path taken by western governments. World War II is about a lot more than the 1938 appeasement of the Nazis. The years 1919-1939 should be remembered as the time a great opportunity was lost.

Chapter IV

WORLD WAR II: THE NECESSARY UNNECESSARY WAR?

President Roosevelt once asked me what this war should be called. My answer was 'the unnecessary war'. Winston Churchill

Is there such a thing as a 'good war'? We in the Royal Canadian Navy think so. Harold Lawrence, Royal Canadian Navy

Let it be said then that I wrote this book in the absolute conviction that there never has been, nor ever can be a 'good' or worthwhile war. Mine was one of the better ones (as such calamities are measured), but still, a bloody awful thing. Farley Mowat, Canadian WWII Veteran

It has been called perhaps accurately, the last 'good war'…The 'good war epithet may be too self-congratulatory in the face of such trauma, villainy and violence. If that is the case, the war was without a doubt, a war of necessity. Tim Cook, Canadian historian

This is the war about which even many peace people were ambivalent. They believed it had to be fought and Canada had to a part of it. Even if this is true, we should see it as avoidable. It should have been unnecessary. It is a story about the world painting itself into a corner. It is hardly laudable to claim in the aftermath that the mess made of the floor in order to get out of the corner was not only justified, but was somehow a great achievement. At best, this was the necessary unnecessary war.

Once again, it was the Europeans who were initially in charge of painting. Once again, from Canada's perspective, the British and French were among the most inept of the painters. These are difficult truths, particularly because of the suffering and courage of British and French civilians. But they were not the only civilian victims of the fundamental shift in war making bequeathed by the Great War. This war killed many more in other lands.

The opportunity for peace and a new model of international relations having been lost, the destructive legacies of the Great War were free to operate, and the factors we are examining persisted. A group of American scholars writing a few years after World War II expressed consensus that the Great War was the decisive one in modern history.[66] Several essays see the human rights/civilian deaths factor as born of the war's turn to destruction of civilians and a public that became inured to slaughter on an unprecedented scale. Editor Jack Roth, noting that one of every two French males between the ages of 20 and 32 in 1914 had been killed: *If Europeans could accept casualties on such a scale, they could accept almost anything in the way of slaughter... Verdun and the Somme opened the way to Auschwitz and Hiroshima.*[67]

Stanford professor Gordon Craig saw this change as caused by the breakdown of the relationship between statecraft and war, a relationship where the ends and means had previously been determined by the requirements of policy, the results defined and legalized by negotiation. That separation continued and brought the escalation of civilian deaths to an unprecedented scale in World War II. Craig concludes that the Great War was *a Pandora's box of evils that the linkage of science with industry in the service of war was to mean.*[68] That linkage was accompanied by the abandonment of any semblance of ethics and morality in war making. Perhaps more than any other, it is important to examine the presence in World War II of the human rights/civilian deaths factor. Canadians were also a part of the mass killing of civilians, once again in furtherance of policies they did not make, and under the command of leaders they did not choose. Long after Vimy, Canada still had not sufficiently come of age to make an issue of this tragic aspect of fighting in other people's wars.

The Canadian factors of military skill and bravery despite poor leadership, longing for recognition, reluctant participation, and desire to minimize casualties are part of the story of this war.

Emerging from the Empire's Shadow?

The personalities and inclinations of prime ministers were highly important. They determined whether Canada would expand upon or retreat from Borden's notice to the British after Passchendaele that the days of Canada automatically rallying to mother's call were over.[69]

Borden's caution about Canada at war was part of the makeup of William Lyon Mackenzie King, the prime minister who would have to deal with the next war. King's personality complemented his caution. He did not succeed by charisma and inspired rhetoric, the attributes of so many war figures. Rather, he knew Canada and he knew the game of governing. Berton said of him that *he understood his country better than any senior statesman has before or since. In his often maddening circumspection, he did his best to save Canada from itself.*[70] One of King's heroes was Wilfrid Laurier. Laurier's example focused King on trying to keep the country together and keep it from being dominated by another.

The influence of the King approach in the interwar period was enhanced by the failures of imperialist Arthur Meighen, who was briefly prime minister twice. King bested Meighen in the 1921 election. That result was not surprising. Meighen had authored the divisive 1917 conscription bill, alienating most of Quebec. We have seen his alienation of labour in the Winnipeg strike. In 1922, he showed himself still out of touch by vigorously advocating for an expeditionary force to help the British in a minor dispute in Turkey. With fresh memories of the Great War, Canadians were having none of that.[71]

Meighen wanted to try again in 1925. He almost made it, and what is important to the World War II story is that Meighen was thwarted by growing support for Canadian independence and adroit manoeuvring by King of the kind that would serve him well in the war.

In part because of western discontent and the rise of the Progressive movement, Meighen's Tories won the greater number of seats. But the traditional two party system had been broken. King put together a shaky coalition of Liberals, Progressives, Labour, and Independents. That government, however, fell to a scandal and King lost a confidence vote.[72]

The governor general, none other than Vimy hero Byng, believed that he and King had agreed that if this happened, King would resign and Meighen would become prime minister. That was not how King remembered the agreement. Nevertheless, in the last assertion of colonial power by a governor general, Byng refused King's request to dissolve parliament, accepted his resignation, and called on Meighen to form a government.

King, as he later would in international affairs, manoeuvred brilliantly. Though Meighen was sworn in, King hamstrung Parliament procedurally. King was able to disqualify most of the Tory members and make it to the next election. From the affair, the fiction of the governor general ruling over a colony became an issue and King exploited it in the election. His stump speech always included the claim that *an English governor and a Tory minister were trying to reduce Canada to a colony.*[73] Given Meighen's now outdated raw imperialism, even Byng's hero status was not enough to blunt the impact of this line. King won, and the Liberals ruled for the next thirty years---except for a five-year period when King got lucky again.

This little bit of history, demonstrating the virtual end of blind public support for European imperialist struggles and the demand for international as well as domestic autonomy, was codified in the 1931 Statute of Westminster. Legality had caught up with reality. Whether to join World War II would be Canada's choice to make.

Politics, Propaganda, and The Great Capitalist Depression

Berton notes the similarity between uncritical public acceptance of Great War propaganda and blind acceptance of post war assurances by the captains of finance, whose paper profit empire collapsed and brought Canada and the world the Great Depression. *Canadians had been conditioned to accept the most unlikely fantasies and to swallow the most outrageous hogwash.*[74] The failure of the press played an important role in both disasters. During the war, newspapers dutifully passed on misinformation supplied by government. In the 1920's, they did the same with the economic pronouncements of bank presidents.

As with the war, it was not those who supplied the misinformation who suffered most. It is a mystery why the depression of the Dirty Thirties is still remembered by so many as some sort of natural disaster, like a mega version of a Winnipeg flood, rather than the greatest indictment of what was called capitalism that the world had ever known. Even more puzzling is the fact that the basic structure of this lottery capitalism continues today, largely free of reform or even criticism.[75]

Whatever its causes, two aspects of the Great Depression story were important to the nature of Canada's participation in the coming war. The first was that the anti-Bolshevik hysteria we have examined, fueled by companies and financiers, led to outrageous government measures and a significant backlash. The second was that cautious Mackenzie King would not be responsible for either.

King had the good fortune to lose the 1930 election badly and turn the country over to Richard Bedford Bennett, who would preside over the five blackest years in Canadian history. Although King probably did not know what was coming or how to deal with it either, he could hardly have done worse than Bennett. King's good political fortune, however, was not good for ordinary people. The Tory government response to their hardships was both callous and violent.

The callous component is highlighted by Bennett's own pronouncements that he would never "subsidize idleness" or commit the country to the "dole system".[76] Bennett probably had no real way to understand the life of most Canadians, much less promote policies to alleviate the economic crisis. He was a wealthy Calgary businessman and lawyer, former counsel to the Canadian Pacific Railway. Though he vowed to attack unemployment with his hardnosed business acumen, the symbol of his legacy came to be a multitude of trucks and automobiles that people could no longer afford to operate. They removed the engine and hitched the chassis to a team of horses, creating what was popularly known as the "Bennett Buggy"[77]

Bennett, of course, did not acknowledge the real cause of the crisis. He blamed the communists and Moscow's master plan to rule the world. Bennett was neither the first nor the last western leader to invoke this excuse. He was also neither the first nor last to employ oppression and state violence to fight the perceived threat.

The battle against the red bugaboo did not stop at propaganda and name-calling. The government turned to violence and oppression that had unintended consequences for Canada's wartime conduct. It ensured that it would be King and the Liberals, not the old guard imperialists who would guide Canada in the next war and for years after it. King and the Liberals not only did not have to wear the Great Depression, they could campaign against Bennett's iron fisted treatment of the suffering public.

The treatment of unemployed men was particularly egregious. The government established rural prisons, known officially as Unemployment Relief Camps. The camps were the idea of Bennett's military chief, general Andrew McNaughton, who would play an interesting role in the coming war. In 1932, McNaughton made a tour of military installations. He perceived an excess of idleness. He saw danger of a Marxist revolution and he had a solution. McNaughton persuaded the government that young unemployed men should be sent to rural labour camps. The camps were nominally voluntary but the reluctant could be arrested for vagrancy.[78]

When the men arrived, they found filthy conditions, subsistence level food, and make-work. The employment brought them twenty cents for an eight-hour day --- one tenth of the going wage for the same work. They were denied the right to vote or to organize. The Defence Department operated the camps and boasted that not a cent was spent on reading material or recreational equipment.

The camp inmates did not quietly abide their plight. They were the originators of the march we have already seen end so violently. In 1935, 4,000 in British Columbia left the camps. After a sojourn in Vancouver, they began a train trek to Ottawa to demand employment. Their numbers increased as they moved through Alberta into Saskatchewan. Though more unemployed men were waiting in Winnipeg to join, the trip came to a bloody end in Regina. A worried Bennett agreed to meet with a handful of the leaders who went ahead to Ottawa. In an absolutely stunning display of ignorance, all Bennett could manage to do at the meeting was to lecture the men about communism and accuse them of being revolutionaries. Back in Regina, the Mounties got out their baseball bats.[79]

No one knows, of course, how King would have handled the Great Depression, though his background and education portended a better understanding of the crisis.[80] He would undoubtedly not have been as blindly harsh as the blundering Bennett. In any event, King still had his luck. The year of the Regina debacle was an election year. King's Liberals won a solid majority. He closed the camps.[81]

A Distinctly Canadian War Policy

This unusual set of circumstances put Mackenzie King and not Richard Bennett in power during World War II. While we cannot know how Bennett would have led the country at war, it is almost certain that a greater number of Canadian lives would have been lost. The tenor of the times and King's personality produced a Canadian war policy devoid of eagerness for involvement in European conflicts. It is true that once the Europeans had painted themselves completely into the corner there was no way to keep Canada from being drawn into the effort to get them out. Nevertheless, the days of eager marching off to be "home by Christmas" were gone for good. Once Germany invaded Poland and Britain declared war, everyone knew Canada would have to join. But this time Canadian participation would be influenced by distinctly Canadian policy.[82]

Two of the most important differences between Bennett and King were the moral as well as political basis for King's opposition to war, and his vivid recollection of the conscription crisis near the end of the Great War. King came into office committed to keeping Canada independent of both Britain and the United States and narrowing the French/English divide.

Ironically, King adopted a component of Laurier's war statements — the unrealistic fear of invasion — to justify a focus on Canada, not Europe. Expressing fear of invasion by an enemy 3,000 thousand miles away that would ultimately be unable to negotiate 12 miles of English Channel made King's statements only slightly less "Pythonesque" than those of Laurier. But they furthered the purpose of commitment to limited overseas involvement and fewer casualties.[83]

The scheme for organizing the armed forces reflected King's cautious policy. The National Resources Mobilization Act of 1940 (NRMA) was a marvel. It differed significantly from the conscription regimes of other combatants. The NRMA scheme was that units made up of volunteers could serve in Europe and recruiting would continue. The necessity of defending Canadian shores, however, was said to require that no men be compelled to serve overseas. Thus, "conscription lite." Every able bodied man would be drafted for 30 days of training to defend the homeland, but was free to remain at home if he wished. The hybrid armies trained together and there was no objection to the real soldiers encouraging the others to volunteer for the whole show. The home guard trainees were tagged "zombies" in this "shaming lite" milder version of Great War recruiting practices.[84].

Even with this two-tiered opt-in system, it ultimately took a bit of the famous King luck to make the Canadian war one of comparatively limited liability. In 1942, a campaign by Meighen and the Conservatives for overseas conscription and a coalition government put pressure on King. His savvy response was to order a plebiscite, not on conscription but on whether to release the government from its promise not to impose it. The ploy avoided the worst features of the 1917 crisis, but reopened old wounds. The country voted yes. 73 percent of Quebec, joined by much of the west, voted no.[85]

What happened next, thankfully, was consistent with a revered feature of all government programs: implementation delay. Then and now, there is no chance that a public program will be implemented precipitously. Thanks to a reluctant prime minister, the need for a registration and administrative structure, and no small amount of resistance from the zombies themselves, the government did not act on its release from the earlier promise right away. The order for the first contingent of 17,000 troops did not come until 1944. Overseas conscription happened, but the European war ended before two thirds of the draftees arrived. In World War II, one Canadian soldier in 26 died, less than half the casualty rate in the Great War. The toll included only 79 draftees.[86]

This cautious approach was in tune with the general attitude of Canadians. Antiwar literature flourished in the period after the Great War, including accounts of the reality of the trenches. These stories of reality had some effect. But the Vimy myth also flourished and the antiwar authors faced the backlash of the "Flanders Field Syndrome" that McCrae had inadvertently created. One author, a wounded veteran, was denounced in the *Montreal Gazette* for doing a disservice to his fellow soldiers by emphasizing the evils of war and ignoring the good.[87] On balance, however, it appears that at least some of the truth of the Great War had overcome the propaganda machine and helped shape a distinctly Canadian policy in this one.

Two Disasters

World War II was yet another conflict that Canada had little to do with bringing about. It was yet another war where she was called to assist Great Britain, whose straits were considerably direr than last time around. It was another war where Canadian troops would be looked down upon by allies and often poorly led, sometimes even by their own commanders and politicians. It was another war that, in spite of bringing out the worst in some soldiers, would again demonstrate a degree of their skill and dedication that would be admired by others.

In examining the Great War, we looked somewhat closely at only the four battles that form the basis of the warrior nation narrative. In this chapter we examine in detail only two. These engagements gave rise to no nation-building myths, yet their stories capture every theme and factor we have seen from the first day of Britain's invitation to assist in subduing the Boers. Much of the true cautionary tale for Canada and other people's wars may be found in the stories of Hong Kong and Dieppe.

Hong Kong: A Call That Should Not Have Been Answered

Two years, three months and a day after Canada entered World War II the Winnipeg Grenadiers became the first Canadian unit to come under fire.[88] It was a bloody distinction that its members, and those of the Royal Rifles of Canada who soon joined them, would have preferred not to win.

The two units formed the Hong Kong Expedition of 1941. Hong Kong was Passchendaele writ small: a disaster that was a product of imperialism, arrogant racism, and poor military and political leadership. Like that senseless battle, it once again featured Canadian military bravery and skill, arguably even more remarkable this time because the soldiers were without essential arms and equipment and were largely untrained. All of them would either be killed on the battlefield, die in captivity, or survive years of imprisonment that would scar them for life.[89]

Act I of the tragedy began with a meeting between two good old boy imperial generals, Canadian-born British general Alan Grasett and Canadian chief of general staff Harry Crerar. The two had been classmates at the Royal Military College. In August1941, on his way home after commanding the garrison in the crown colony of Hong

Kong, Grasett stopped off in Ottawa to see his old friend Crerar. Grasett did not make a formal plea for assistance but suggested that one or two Canadian battalions in the colony could assist in its defence should there be war with Japan. The British saw such a war as a probability, but not an imminent one. Crerar made no formal commitment at the time, but Grasett kept the idea alive at a meeting of the War Office in London, submitting that the garrison should be strengthened and that Canada might supply troops.[90]

Why did political leaders in Canada, fail to kill the idea on the spot? This was supposed to be the era of our independence. No more running off to the corners of the world when the Empire called. There was no reason to do this. King was against the venture from the outset but was persuaded by minister of defence J.L. Ralston, Crerar and others in the army high command who were concerned that Canadian ships and planes were in action but the army was not. The Conservatives spurred the press to demand ground action. King did not want to appear timid compared to prime minister Winston Churchill. He reluctantly agreed.[91] It was not the last time senior military figures would override the better judgment of elected leaders. We will see a particular example 65 years later in Afghanistan.

There were other factors pushing Canada toward answering a call that echoed the Boer War invitation: "We don't really need you, but we will let you play". Canada at the time had no Far East intelligence capacity of its own and had to rely on the race-infected assessments of the British. Further, this would be a volunteer mission and King was mainly concerned at the time with avoiding another conscription crisis. There was also the matter of competition among the Dominions. In the request that eventually came to Canada, Churchill made specific mention of "the very great assistance, which is being furnished by the Dominions". He was plainly not speaking of Canada. Her troops were at the time marching up and down training fields in the English countryside. Australia, New Zealand, and South Africa, were actually fighting in the war.[92] So, once again Canada saluted with a final "Ready, Aye" and committed to send *two* battalions to a place they could not defend and from which they could not be evacuated.

What about the British? While it is never wise to underestimate British imperial hubris even at this late date, they had already recognized the folly of trying to defend Hong Kong. Less than a year before Grasett's proposal Churchill had rejected in the most emphatic terms a proposal from his Far East commander to increase the garrison to six battalions: *This is all wrong. If Japan goes to war with us there is not the slightest chance of holding Hong Kong or relieving it. It is most unwise to increase the loss we shall suffer there. Instead of increasing the garrison it ought to be reduced to a symbolical scale.* Churchill's General Staff had advised that Hong Kong was not a vital interest and could not be defended.[93]

It did not require a military genius to discern that these initial positions were correct. In addition to Japanese air and naval superiority, further evidence that Grasett's proposal was ill advised was the reality of 35-60,000 well-trained Japanese troops in the area, some as near as 20 miles away. Earlier Japanese campaigns in Manchuria and elsewhere in China had also provided the crown colony with 750,000 refugees to look after, more than a third of its population. Some of them would turn out to be very helpful informants for the Japanese commanders.[94]

To make matters worse, the same lingering imperial racism that had thwarted Japan's effort to have a racial equality provision included in the League of Nations Charter blinded the garrison commander to military reality. General Charles Maltby was convinced that Asians were an inferior race in every respect, including militarily. One of the disastrous elements of this nonsense was his belief that the eyesight of Japanese was so poor that they were unable to fly or fight at night. Another British officer was overheard describing them as "buck-toothed, slant-eyed, near sighted scrawny little people".[95] This attitude was typical of the times and was shared by most Canadians. White-led troops could easily prevail against little brown men.[96]

Even had all Canadians and Europeans shared Maltby's belief, it remains difficult to fathom why Churchill changed his mind about Grasett's idea. Perhaps he could not give it his full attention. It is true that he would have been more occupied with the imminent threat from Germany than with a remote outpost of the Empire. Though aware of the danger in Hong Kong, he ultimately may have decided that pulling out could not be done as a matter of honour, and cutting losses would lower morale.

A more cynical view is that he might have had greater concern for national pride than military reality because the reinforcements would, after all, be colonials. Though far from conclusive, there is some evidence for this assessment. All of Canada's wars at the behest of this patron featured British disdain and Canadian resentment of it. A Canadian at Hong Kong said the British saw Canadians as a bunch of "rowdy, cowardly colonists, not good for very much" and Canadians thought the British were condescending pigs.[97] In any event, Churchill did change his mind. After assurances about Japanese weakness from a newly constituted General Staff, Churchill authorized a fateful telegram asking Canada to consider providing *one* or *two* battalions to Hong Kong.[98]

Act II involved selecting the Canadian units and getting them to Hong Kong. The choice of units for the mission shared one characteristic with the Ypres campaign. It reflected the priority of politics over sound military judgment. Crerar and minister of defence Colonel J.L. Ralston made the fateful choice: The Royal Rifles of Canada and the Winnipeg Grenadiers. There were apparent political advantages, and military drawbacks. Ralston specified that the units be drawn from troops in Canada. The units in England were probably better trained, but the focus there was jostling for Canada's place in the main event invasion of Europe. Crerar was pleased with the choice of the Rifles and Grenadiers mainly because they represented both east and west and both languages. The Rifles, though officially an English-speaking unit, were headquartered in Quebec City.

Colonel J.K. Lawson, director of training, had been tasked with compiling a list of home standing infantry battalions in order of their combat readiness. Appearing at the *bottom* of the list were nine that he found insufficiently trained. Two of the nine were the Rifles and the Grenadiers. Lawson, ironically a decorated veteran of Passchendaele, would pay with his life for the errors of his superiors. He was promoted to command the expedition force. On December 19th, he would die firing his revolvers as Japanese troops overran his headquarters.[99]

Denominating the Rifles and Grenadiers as not combat ready was an understatement. Some had not yet been trained to use a rifle. In this mission, the Grenadiers bore a tragic misnomer. There were no mortars or grenades available for training. In Hong Kong, some troops would hurl grenades at the Japanese without pulling the pins.

Before the units left Canada, their readiness was further degraded by personnel shortages in the ranks of the Grenadiers. The Rifles were up to strength but the Grenadiers were considerably short of their authorized strength of 807. After the call to action came, medical and other reasons further reduced the total. In the end, half of the battalion's troops were hastily picked from other units in training. Many of them had not completed the most basic instruction. These emergency personnel levies always share two characteristics: The units required to supply people do not part with their best troops; the receiving units are pressed for time. Essentially, "any warm body" will suffice.[100]

Getting to Hong Kong became another offence against the soldiers of the two units. On October 27, 1941 most sailed from Vancouver on a New Zealand transport too small to carry all of them or any of their vehicles. The last minute roundup caused further confusion. Commanders found that 50 men had deserted and 23 who were on board had been deemed medically unfit. The vehicles and equipment were later loaded on a U.S. vessel, but it was diverted to the Philippines when war became imminent. [101]

And so, on November 16, 1941, the Royal Rifles and the Winnipeg Grenadiers arrived virtually untrained, without heavy weapons, and without transport to a place that their political leaders knew and their military leaders should have known was indefensible — under the overall command of another British General.

Act III, the fate of the Rifles and Grenadiers, is heartbreaking. It is a more than twice-told tale of courage and skill under good Canadian leaders and bad British ones. It is a story of many lives thrown away and many more permanently impaired.

The Canadians arrived at a colony the British had secured from the Chinese by typical imperial long-term leases. Initially ensconced on Hong Kong Island, the British had eventually secured a 26-mile buffer zone on the mainland, a few miles across the water. The principal mainland city was Kowloon, and that is where the Canadians were billeted. For some reason, they were housed in Sham Shui Po barracks there, but were to be deployed on the island. Many would soon return to Sham Shui Po as prisoners.

The rest of the colony's defenders were as underequipped as the Canadians. The two British and two Indian battalions had been training mainly with rifles. They had a handful of howitzers and mortars, and very little ammunition for them. Five obsolete airplanes complemented the 29 guns for coastal defence. A few hundred members of a land and naval militia rounded out the force.[102]

There is little point in dwelling on the tactical errors of the misguided General Maltby. He was no Haig; he was just not very good. Particularly costly to the Canadians was his decision to split his already inadequate force between the island and the mainland, and his assumption even after the mainland garrison fell that the main attack on the island would come from the sea. Like the minds of the politicians, the 29 guns were pointed the wrong way.[103]

December 8th, 1941, in Hong Kong was December 7th at Pearl Harbor on the other side of the International Date Line, the day that American president Franklin Roosevelt said would "live in infamy." It was the day Japan launched coordinated attacks on Hong Kong, Hawaii, and several other islands in the Pacific. The mainland Hong

Kong garrison fell in five days. It took another 13 to take the island from the Canadians and the remnants of the British and Indian force.

Nations seldom construct heroic myths from disastrous defeats. A temporary victory such as Vimy provides a much better story. But the Canadians at Hong Kong may well have surpassed even the performance of Currie's soldiers. Throughout the desperate struggle for the island, the Winnipeg Grenadiers were able numerous times to move and bring to bear effectively such firepower as they had. They engaged in small unit fire and manoeuvre much more complicated than that required of their Great War predecessors. At their level of training, this was truly remarkable.

The Royal Rifles of Canada fought with equal distinction. A counterattack is by definition an action carried out after a force has survived the losses and trauma of an assault. The Rifles conducted more counterattacks than all of the British and Indian battalions combined. Thus did two units who should not have been there, who had been trained in marching more than shooting, bring credit to themselves and their country.[104]

The final disservice to these men came when they were victims of the same pride and puffery that always sacrifices lives needlessly in the name of "honour" in wars. After the defeat of the mainland garrison, the final outcome should have been obvious to anyone. The Japanese made three separate demands for the surrender of the remaining forces on the island. On December 13th, a commander came across under a white flag and threatened an air and artillery attack if fighting continued. The demand was rejected. The attacks came. People died. On the 17th, the second demand came, this time with the threat of invasion. It was rejected. The invasion came. More people died. A final demand was rejected on Christmas day, as one writer put it, "preserving stiff upper lip pride and aplomb." The final assault lasted only three hours. More people died. The battle was over.[105]

During these exchanges, Churchill exhibited the same sort of willingness to spend lives senselessly for which we rightly condemn Hitler's "hold at all costs" orders when all was clearly lost. Churchill's first message to the garrison, on the day of the first surrender demand, claimed that he was following their stubborn defence day by day and hour by hour and every day of resistance was bringing victory nearer. As the situation deteriorated, Churchill wired again: *There must be no thought of surrender. Every part of the island must be fought and the enemy resisted with the utmost stubbornness.*[106]

Notwithstanding the understandable reaction of pride that most of us experience upon learning that a gallant beleaguered force on our side has refused to surrender, one of the surrender demands at Hong Kong should have been accepted.

The terrible stress inflicted on ordinary soldiers by high-sounding calls never to surrender is captured in the remarkable memoir of Hong Kong survivor George S. MacDonell. In the account,[107] MacDonell conveys the internal tension his men faced, men whose best years should have been ahead of them. They did not wish to surrender, but they were well aware of the futility of continuing.

As a result of casualties, MacDonell found himself a unit commander by the time of the final battle. His orders were to take a village lost the previous day — an objective of even less importance than Passchendaele Ridge. After writing of Japanese surprise at the rejection of the first two surrender offers, he described starkly the suicide mission that followed the final offer on Christmas day:

The sheer stupidity of the order to send us without artillery, mortar, or machine gun support into a village full of Japanese, in broad daylight, was not lost on me... My men would be attacking in the open and the Japanese defenders would have excellent cover from which to repel us. This was madness!... When I returned to my men, I told them to be prepared to attack the village at 1300. There was complete silence. Not one of them could believe such a preposterous order. They simply stared at me.[108]

Of the 120 men who reacted in silence to the preposterous order but did their best to carry it out, 26 died in the five hours between the attack and the final surrender order from the colonial governor. The wounded numbered 75. Their chances of surviving the harsh captivity that lay ahead were severely impaired.[109]

The order was one of several issued by British General Cedric Wallis. When the commander of the Rifles protested and argued that Wallis was committing exhausted Canadian troops instead of fresher British units, Wallis threatened to have him shot. After the war, Maltby and Wallis blamed the defeat on the troops, particularly the Canadians.[110]

Hong Kong and its aftermath also provide lessons in the impact of human rights violations and civilian deaths, propaganda and racism. Again, the wisdom of ordinary soldiers among the survivors of the battle aids us in understanding those lessons.

The final act of the tragedy remained to be played by the almost two thirds of the Canadian force that survived the battle. Examination of Hong Kong as a replay of much of what we have seen in earlier wars should also include a look at the relationships between enemies, particularly in the context of captor and captured. That story also features human rights violations and the death of noncombatants.

At Hong Kong, the Japanese committed unspeakable war crimes, killing prisoners, raping nurses in a hospital and bayoneting patients.[111] After the war, a Canadian medical officer concluded that the "full lust" of an ongoing battle carried the Japanese into St. Stephen's hospital on the final day. That is, of course, no excuse, only some explanation for the outrages. Even there, a Japanese officer who arrived in the aftermath saved Canadian prisoners from execution and found them food and water.[112] The propaganda value of atrocities like these was useful in painting all Japanese as sub-human brutes. Whether there was any net gain to the war effort from such propaganda is an open question, but it probably made it easier for the allies to decide to slaughter millions of Japanese civilians at war's end.

Did the popular image of Japanese perhaps make it easier for British Columbians to support rounding up their Japanese-Canadian neighbours the day after Hong Kong was attacked, confiscating their property and sending them to internment camps? Does it help to explain why four years after the war ended, Canadians of Japanese descent were still forbidden to live within 100 miles of the Pacific coast and those in British Columbia required a permit before they would be allowed to move more than 50 miles? Demonizing endangers more than the demonized.[113]

Yet what explains the terrible treatment to which the defenders were later subjected by the victors at Hong Kong? Any chance at an answer requires rejecting the notion that people of European descent are a more civilized "race". It also requires considering matters that help to explain wrongdoing without excusing it; not a common facility, but one that many Canadian survivors found a way to grasp. Japanese soldiers were also subjected to patriotic and religious propaganda. All volunteering to die for country were promised their names inscribed on a religious shrine.[114] The troops were not unmindful of the racism of Maltby and other westerners, or of the treatment of Japan, supposedly a victor, at the Paris conference. The story of the prison experience of Hong Kong survivors is in part another caution about propaganda and racism.

William Tucker gave us a lesson about the relationship between enemies in the context of captor and captured in the Great War. MacDonell recounts a similar experience as a prisoner of the Japanese. The conditions he endured were significantly harsher. Yet his story is also of a bond between ordinary soldiers on opposing sides enduring conditions that would make mutual hatred perfectly understandable. We see this relationship punctuated by acts of decency, small and large. In MacDonell's case, these acts were carried out by Japanese in the lower echelons of those responsible for the Canadians, sometimes at the risk of their own lives.

Although Tucker described barbarous conditions, the Great War veteran never observed the Germans physically abusing prisoners. Japanese prisoners did suffer such abuse and some were tortured, including some at camps where MacDonell was interned.[115] One example of that abuse says much about the unappreciated cost of racism.

British Columbians, safe at home, contributed indirectly but undoubtedly to the abuse of Canadian prisoners. Some of the abuse was inflicted by a particularly vicious interpreter for the Japanese named Inouye Kanao, better known by the place of his birth as the "Kamloops Kid." Kanao had been ridiculed as a child and often referred to by his neighbours as a "yellow bastard." He moved to Japan before the war, vowed revenge, and became a war criminal. After the war, he was hanged for his involvement in the torture and murder of prisoners.[116] Without doubt, neither those in Kamloops whose epithets helped forge Kanao's view of Canadians, nor those who may have stood by silently while others berated the "yellow bastard" would have wished ill of any Canadian soldier. They were simply thoughtless.

Long before the Kamloops Kid departed, a strain of racism worse than thoughtlessness had infected governments, especially in British Columbia. Price writes that the treatment of Japanese Canadians after Hong Kong was not a regrettable circumstance brought on by war but rather an expression of white racism expressed through elected leaders. Federal officials and the RCMP saw no threat. Registration requirements and denial of military service were already in place. Politicians wanted more. A Victoria representative said of his fellow Canadians that without internment *every little slant-eyed Jap will wave the flag of the Rising Sun if his countrymen invade.*[117]

There are hopeful signs of some learning. In 2013, Victoria MP Murray Rankin stood in the House of Commons to honour Tomohiko Hayashi, commandant of a Japanese prison camp, as "the Japanese Schindler" for his effort to save the lives of prisoners.[118]

MacDonell well knew that not all prisoners would be as fortunate as those saved by the Japanese officer at St. Stephen's. He had seen bound prisoners bayoneted. Before his company's final senseless attack, he had saved one bullet to end his own life.[119]

He nevertheless chose to write admiringly of the military skill and leadership of the enemy troops. He wrote dispassionately of joining them in that nondescript village the day after the final battle as each side collected its dead.[120] He would also spend several pages of his short memoir recounting acts of humanity by his captors. This connection between ordinary soldiers who have been through a maelstrom of violence trying to kill each other is a mystery. It would not have been unreasonable for MacDonell's book to be simply a chronicle of anger and outrage. Instead, about his captivity he wrote:

A great deal has been written about the cruelty of the Japanese toward their prisoners. For me, Japanese cruelty could not be exaggerated. I personally witnessed their behavior and they were savage in the extreme… However, I found in the private soldiers themselves, out of sight of their officers, little of this ferocity and cruelty…In fact, they sometimes turned a blind eye to prisoner's infractions…They said often, and I believed them, that they hated the war much as we did.[121]

MacDonell went on to tell of an interpreter at the Sham Sui Po camp who, at the risk and probably the later loss, of his own life smuggled a large amount of diphtheria serum to prisoners.[122] He wrote also of being treated well on the move to a camp near Yokohama. The prisoners were put to work in a shipyard where, incidentally, they sabotaged Japanese warships as eagerly as Tucker and his friends had sabotaged German trucks.[123]

In May 1945, when allied bombing had begun the destruction of Tokyo and Yokohama, the prisoners were moved to a camp to the north. They were put to work in an iron mine and there the foreman probably saved MacDonell's life. He writes of being so weakened by near starvation and forced labour that he could not have survived working in the mine. The foreman hid him away doing lighter work, first in the machine shop and later in the kitchen.[124]

The prisoners had a hidden radio. They knew of the aerial destruction of Japan, including the atomic bombing of Hiroshima and Nagasaki. They knew of the surrender before their guards did. Near the end of their ordeal, the prisoners came to know some of the ordinary people who lived near the camp. When the men were finally liberated, they went to thank them and the mine foreman. MacDonell wrote: *I developed no hatred for the people of Japan. Most of them were as kind to us as they could be under the harsh rules of their military dictatorship…as usual, it was the common people of Japan who paid the price for the military imperialism of their ruling elite.*[125]

Those in power learned little from Hong Kong. A politician with a separate agenda seized on public outrage and forced King to establish a public inquiry. King appointed Chief Justice Lyman Duff, a friend and supporter, to chair it. After a 22-day hearing, Duff dutifully reported no wrongdoing on the part of the government or the military.[126]

Hong Kong was a singularly egregious waste of lives. The next waste of good military lives would not involve the imperial racism that was so costly at Hong Kong. It would be caused in part by other factors we have been examining, among them, the longing for recognition--a desire to play with the big boys.

Dieppe: Failure, Fame, and Blame

The amphibious assault on the French port town of Dieppe on August 19, 1943 was Canada's greatest disaster. It has been rightly named the bloodiest nine hours in Canadian military history. [127] Aside from its larger scale and greater casualty numbers, there is little to choose between this bloodbath and Hong Kong.

There are certainly similarities between Dieppe and that final Hong Kong assault by the Royal Rifles on December 25, 1941. In both, good men did their best to carry out impossible orders. Without even a bare minimum of supporting fire, they attacked. In both, a substantial portion of the units involved were wiped out, their members killed or condemned to years of harsh imprisonment. That final Hong Kong attack achieved a delay of five hours before surrender. What the Dieppe raid achieved, if anything, has been a source of dispute for decades, with "nothing" being a legitimate position to take.

Like Hong Kong, the story of this minor engagement illuminates larger matters. It is a story about politics, including Canada's new and difficult status as an independent nation, a status still unrecognized by the British. It is further proof that relationships are more important than legalities. It is another story of skill and bravery under poor military and political leadership. Dieppe is also yet another story about the part a relatively small action played in the minds of ambitious generals who convinced themselves that something nobler than ambition underlay their willingness to sacrifice lives. It is about hundreds of dead young men whose courage was wasted by a process that never gave them a chance and proved again that in modern warfare bravery had become increasingly irrelevant to outcomes. Finally, like Hong Kong, acceptance of responsibility was not a characteristic of those responsible.

Questions live on about how and why 4,963 Canadians from Ontario, Saskatchewan, Alberta, and Quebec were ordered, without naval or air support, to land on heavily fortified beaches guarded by high cliffs; why 907 died and 1,946 were taken prisoner.[128] In addition to its record death toll, the raid resulted in more Canadian prisoners than were captured in the remainder of the European campaign. Legions of writers and historians have probed for reasons.

The principal questions are why this raid, why Canada, and why the disaster? The answers to all are affected in a major way by the Dieppe chain of command, or as one historian aptly called it, "the winding lane of command."[129] When most of the critical decisions about the Dieppe raid were made, there essentially was no chain of command. A basic military tenet is that a clearly constructed and understood chain of command is essential to the success of any operation. Its presence conserves lives. Its absence wastes them. A chain of command also ensures accountability. A commander is responsible for everything his unit does or fails to do, period. Without a chain of command, no one is responsible.

The Dieppe confusion descended directly from the ambiguity in Canada's international status. If Canada had won the right on Flanders fields to make her own decisions, the British were apparently unaware of that. In any event, in this operation Canada abandoned the right until there was only one all or nothing decision left to make: whether to send Canadians on yet another deadly mission planned and constructed largely by the British with little or no Canadian input.

When some semblance of a chain of command belatedly emerged, the decision whether to go forward ultimately fell to a Canadian general whose overriding ambition was to be the deputy commander of the whole European show and triumphantly lead Canadian troops into Berlin. This dream could hardly be realized as long as his troops were still marching up and down the English countryside. Father of Depression era work camps, General A.G.L. (Andy) McNaughton, commanded the Canadian Army Overseas. Some place most of the blame for Dieppe on McNaughton, claiming that he could have stopped the operation.[130] Cook observes that the defeat was multi-sired but faults McNaughton for accepting a flawed plan with little protest.[131] Whatever the truth, there is little doubt that McNaughton's ambition adversely affected his judgment.

Throughout the critical months when the operation, first named Rutter then Jubilee, was being put together, McNaughton was battling with general Sir Bernard Paget, commander-in-chief of British Home Forces, on the chain of command issue. Were his Canadian units a part of those British forces, or simply independent allies serving alongside them? Who would decide manpower, firepower, tactics, logistics and other critical matters? Given the quality of British leadership during the Great War, one can hardly quarrel with McNaughton seeking autonomy, whatever the motivation. The British military was still having trouble processing its colony's new status. The

Statute of Westminster did not decide this dispute. Relationships and personalities did. McNaughton's insistence eventually prevailed, on some issues.[132] During the haggling, however, critical parts of the plan were assembled, and not by Canadians.

Hong Kong enthusiast general Crerar was McNaughton's commander for the corps that would make the assault. With McNaughton's approval, Crerar relentlessly lobbied the British to let Canadians conduct this operation — indeed *any* operation that would give Canada a part in the show.[133]

General John Hamilton (Ham) Roberts was commander of the 2d Canadian Division. He would get much of the blame for Dieppe and be the only figure to accept it with grace, though excuses were available. Roberts was an artillery officer with little expertise in infantry assaults and none in amphibious operations. Further, for security reasons he was separated from his troops and squirreled away in a London hotel during much of the final planning. On May 8, 1943, he was summoned to get his first look at the plans that others had made. One writer observed: *He had not yet realized that in fact he had been plunged into a new form of warfare in which scientific planning of daringly novel schemes had replaced the old concept of a commander deciding his own destiny at the head of his men.*[134]

The plan Roberts and his troops were to attempt to execute might have been daringly novel, but it certainly had not been scientifically planned. Its British architects had their own problems with chain of command and ambitious officers with forceful personalities. One was Lord Louis Mountbatten, cousin to the king, who also had grand designs of a major role for himself in the coming invasion of Europe. Mountbatten was the first to suggest the raid to Churchill, who embraced the idea enthusiastically and named him head of something called Combined Operations. Churchill further muddled the chain of command by appointing him to several additional positions with ambiguous authority. Combined Operations was ostensibly a planning body but Mountbatten would more than once make operational decisions. The chain of command was never really sorted out.[135]

Another figure responsible for the Dieppe plan was the famous general Bernard (Monty) Montgomery. Ironically, he would be the one later living out McNaughton's dream. In 1942, however, he was commander of South Eastern Command, where the Canadians were located. Did that make him senior to McNaughton and Crerar? To Mountbatten? Matters certainly proceeded on that assumption until Rutter was scrubbed and Montgomery washed his hands of the project. Until then, he had not only been a major planner, but also apparently the officer responsible for having it carried out. As a planner, he had argued successfully for a frontal assault.

Agreeing with the lobbying by Crerar and McNaughton, it was Montgomery who offered Dieppe to the Canadians. Finally, it was Montgomery who summoned Roberts from his London hotel, gave him the outline of the plan, and told Roberts that as division commander, he had the right to turn down the assignment. By that time, Roberts was in no position to do so, though he had severe reservations. The real question is: who was in charge on the ground? Until a month before the Canadians sailed, it appeared to be Monty.[136]

The frontal assault, arguably the worst of Monty's decisions, survived his departure. Elements of the plan that were to mitigate the danger of such an assault did not. The original plan called for an amphibious frontal assault by a reinforced division on a rocky beach guarded by rocky cliffs and coastal guns. The obvious hazards of a frontal assault were to be mitigated by intense pre-assault bombardments from air and sea. In addition, a British paratroop and glider force would drop and neutralize two of the main coastal gun batteries. In the final version, the frontal assault remained, but the mitigators had disappeared one by one. The British navy decided it could not risk a battleship and supplied only destroyers, whose smaller four-inch guns could not destroy the coastal batteries. The aerial bombing turned into support by lighter planes. Paratroop support was dropped.

None of the planners had experience in large-scale amphibious landings. They finally concluded that this untried amphibious experiment would be executed on a precise time table and the element of surprise would make up for the disappearance of the original safeguards.[137]

When Rutter was cancelled at that last minute in July, Montgomery recommended that the entire mission be scrapped. Mountbatten managed to have it revived. He decided that there was not enough time to go back to the proverbial drawing board so only the name of the operation changed. It has been argued the Canadian commanders, even in the short time available to them, could have achieved changes in this suicide mission. Considering the plethora of individuals and groups that had a say in Rutter/Jubilee, including not only all of the generals mentioned here but also the British General Staff, the War Office, and even Churchill himself, that is doubtful. The only option was to refuse the mission as it was presented. The ambition of McNaughton and Crerar would certainly not permit that. Roberts was at first eager to have his troops see action. His reservations grew after Rutter was cancelled, but he was in no position to countermand McNaughton and Crerar, whatever Montgomery's strange view of the chain of command.[138]

Thus did the inability of Canada and Britain to sort out their relationship, combine with the rampant egos of their military leaders to seal the fate of 5,000 men. The Jubilee they created was no celebration.

The attack at Dieppe reprised many Great War failures. Canadians had not suffered such casualties since the Somme. Strategically, Dieppe was chosen mainly for political reasons. Tactically, there was once again the matter of the wire. The German guns that the downsized naval and air bombardment were unable to silence could be trained on it. Like the Somme, as men died on the wire, the assault on Dieppe failed soon after it began.

Basic military training includes a caution about the difference between cover and concealment. Failure to heed that caution helps to explain why the Canadians, who did their best, had no chance. Cover protects troops from fire. Concealment does not. The attackers laid down smoke at Dieppe. One of the reasons that the concealment it provided was useless is attributable to another basic instruction to defenders of territory — the Final Protective Line. The German gunners did not have to see through the smoke. They had much earlier sighted their weapons in on the places that attackers would have to be and had even planted distance markers to guide their mortar fire.[139]

Survivor John Mellor described assaults by three regiments. His description could have been lifted verbatim from 1916: *Frozen in grotesque positions with arms and legs in all directions, their bones shattered and pulverized by the rain of fire directed from the cliff top, they had died bravely but futilely—a pathetic monument to inflexible planning and inadequate intelligence reports.*[140] The commander of the Essex Scottish Regiment wrote of arms and legs amputated by shells and long ropes of entrails lying in clumps next to bodies.[141]

Dieppe also produced acts of bravery and sacrifice at the wire. Considering the usual role of religion in Canada's wars, it should be noted that one of the true heroes was a clergyman. Captain John Foote, chaplain of the Royal Hamilton Light Infantry finally gave Christianity a good name. He calmly moved through the rain of shells on the beach, comforting the dying and carrying the wounded to safety. When he brought a survivor to the last evacuation craft, he refused to board himself. He decided that he could do more good for the men if he remained with them as a prisoner of war. He did much good. Foote is the only Canadian chaplain to be awarded the Victoria Cross.[142]

Debate continues about whom to blame for the debacle: Montgomery for insisting on a frontal assault? Mountbatten for reviving Rutter and maybe launching Jubilee without authorization?

Churchill for giving in to political pressure from the Russians and Americans to do something? McNaughton for not refusing, and for misleading Ottawa? Crerar for incessant lobbying?

Interwoven with the search for accountability is the quest for a glorious reason for the disaster. After the fact justifications began to appear before the blood on the beaches had dried. The most popular is that Dieppe was an invaluable rehearsal for the coming invasion of Europe. Churchill and Mountbatten put that one out almost immediately. One historian offered the variation that the raid was "sadly necessary" as a measure of resources needed for the big invasion.[143]. But another argues that Mountbatten's claim that the D-Day landings would have failed without Dieppe, "... *was a hard sell because it was untrue*".[144]

There is a geopolitical explanation that has more supporting evidence. The war at that point was going badly. The Russians and Americans were putting tremendous pressure on Britain to open quickly a second front. Canada, as usual, was on the periphery. The Americans were pushing an even larger early operation, called Sledgehammer. That plan envisioned the sacrifice of an even greater number of Canadian troops. Dieppe might have been a compromise in lieu of a premature D-Day.[145] Yet another disputed theory is that the raid was necessary because all those Canadian troops who had been training in England were demanding to get in on the action and morale was plummeting.[146]

The latest justification emerged in 2013 from military historian David O'Keefe. In this one, the mission was to do no less than save the war in the Atlantic by stealing information that would enable Allied intelligence to decipher a German encoding machine without the enemy knowing it had been done.[147] Cook flatly rejects this theory, concluding that the tactical goals of Dieppe were almost trivial.[148]

It all mattered very little, however, to the families of the dead and captured. What understandably did matter to those families, and the Canadian public, was whether they would have to be told that their sons suffered and died in vain. Governments are never up to delivering that message. They must always seek noble justifications. Propaganda is always there to help. The Toronto Star reported Dieppe as a "decisive battle" that "smashed Nazi opposition".[149]

Whatever the justifications, they do not comfort some of the few remaining Dieppe survivors and their families. Vancouver Island resident Ken Kurry, 91, was a mortar crewmember with the Royal Hamilton Light Infantry. He very much wants the bravery of his comrades to be remembered. But about the operation, he said: *Over the years, it's been asked what did we do and what did we get? Well, we didn't get anything as far as I am concerned, except get killed.*[150]

After Hong Kong and Dieppe

Dieppe featured bravery under poor leadership, unnecessary military deaths, longing for recognition and, of course, propaganda to obscure all that. It did not enhance Canada's prominence or independence.

To be sure, after Dieppe the Canadian army was included in the big D-Day invasion of Europe on June 6, 1944. So were the Poles, the Free French, and everyone except the Northumberland Girl Guides. Every allied force had to have some role in the Big Show. The army fought well in the invasion and in Europe. Canadians earned gratitude for the liberation of the Dutch that endures brightly to this day. Fighting across France and Holland also produced 18,500 casualties, aggravating round two of the conscription crisis at home.[151] Canada was never considered for the push to Berlin.

The story of Canada in the Pacific after Hong Kong is even more of a footnote. Yet it has something to say about Mackenzie King as reluctant warrior and the transition of our military fealty. After Germany surrendered in May 1945, the Americans pressed for assistance against the Japanese. King, of course, wanted the least he could reasonably get away with. King faced the question of whether Canadian contingents would serve with the suspiciously imperialist British or the dangerously possessive Americans.[152]

Canada decided on planes to the Americans, and a few ships to the British. An air force squadron was assigned to join American general Curtis LeMay, who was doing to Japanese cities what allied bombers had done to Dresden and Hamburg. The naval component of King's attempt to satisfy both patrons resulted in an incident reminiscent of the reaction of Canadian troops to orders that they keep fighting after 1918 in the Russian Civil War. Similar to what their fathers had done on the ground in Russia, the crewmembers of the cruiser *Uganda* off the coast of Okinawa decided they had never volunteered to fight Japan and they were not going to do so now. The brass met their demands and the ship turned for home.

On that journey, the feisty Canucks heard of the atomic bombing of Hiroshima and Nagasaki. Thankfully, their airmen comrades were not directly involved in that unprecedented slaughter of civilians, though their government had supplied the uranium. Even the popular military justification for these crimes is not credible. Supreme allied commander Dwight Eisenhower, Pacific commander Douglas MacArthur, and even general LeMay, who authorized them, believed that the bombings had nothing to do with ending the war.[153]

Unfortunately, the horrific nuclear ending to the war differed not in nature but only in scale from air operations in which Canadians were required to participate.

Morality? Innocent Airmen and Innocent Civilians

In World War II, there were more volunteers for the navy and air force than for the army.[154] It appears that enough of the reality of the Great War had seeped through to create a significant aversion to anything with a potential for trench fighting. It is generally accepted that the Royal Canadian Navy (RCN), along with civilian seamen, provided Canada's greatest influence on the outcome of the war. They delivered critically needed supplies to Britain and Russia and helped keep German U-boats from severing this lifeline to both countries. That may well have saved the Allies from defeat.[155] Unfortunately, the civilian mariners did not receive the thanks of a grateful nation after the war.[156]

The service of those who chose to fight at sea was dangerous, but their work was free of a significant moral and ethical issue that faced those who chose the Royal Canadian Air Force, (RCAF). Some of them would have to participate in one of the most destructive legacies of the Great War: the now generally accepted practice of killing civilians. The decision of whether to do this would not be left to Canadian airmen or their commanders. The RCN and RCAF were left to be part of the ongoing transition from Canada's old patron to her new one.

Though the Americans were in overall charge of the sea campaign, Canada had a voice. The Americans consented to an arrangement that Britain and Canada would share responsibility for the North Atlantic.[157] But the British controlled all of Canada's part in the air war. Contrary to an agreement at the ministerial level, Canadian squadrons were directly integrated with the Royal Air Force (RAF). Canadian leaders could not decide air strategy.[158] When the British situation was uncertain in the early stages of the war, facilities to train aircrews of both countries were relocated to the safe haven of Canada. King hoped that this move, along with supplying war materiel could be Canada's major contribution to the war, in lieu of troops.[159] But it was the integration of Canadians into the British Bomber Command that brought about their participation in morally indefensible operations that would generate almost as many *post hoc* justifications as Dieppe.

Revenge is frowned upon by the world's great religions, including Christianity. "He started it" is a weak excuse even on a playground. But basic religious and parenting tenets are often casualties of war. After the Germans started it and killed 13,000 British in the Blitz, Churchill unleashed his air marshal Sir Arthur Harris to kill more than 500,000 German civilians, mostly women and children, and injure another 675,000.[160] Harris was clear about the purpose of Bomber Command missions: *They sowed the wind, now they will reap the whirlwind.*[161] Initially, civilians might have been unintended victims of the crude technology of early bombers. However, Harris soon made clear the intent of the campaign: *The destruction of German* *cities; the killing of German workers and the destruction of civilized life throughout Germany...the destruction of houses...and lives...These are the expected and **intended** aims of our bombing policy. **They are not byproducts of attempts to hit factories.**[162]* (Emphasis added)

I term the Canadians who flew these missions innocent airmen for several reasons. Although they made up a quarter to a third of the fliers[163], the RAF decided the targets. And the airmen killing civilians were themselves being killed at an alarming rate. In 1942, only one crew in three survived a 30 mission tour of duty. The British put Canadian squadrons last in line to receive new aircraft and technology. They died, and they saw their friends die, in circumstances every bit as horrible as their infantry predecessors in the Great War. They knew no more about what they were getting into than had those soldiers.[164]

Even more tragically, interviews with survivors suggest that they knew civilians were their victims, even before the missions officially changed from knowingly haphazard targeting of military and industrial facilities to a terror campaign of firebombing cities. Many accepted this, but many were troubled. One Canadian crewmember wrote: *Always in the back of my mind was the bombing of civilians... civilians were always killed...More than once I wondered 'how many people will those bombs kill?' But you couldn't dwell on it. That's the way war is.* He could have observed that *now* that's the way war is. The reflections of another Canadian pilot suggest a reason that killing from afar does produce the outrage evoked by directly perpetrated atrocities. He acknowledged that a moderating influence on guilt was the remote and impersonal form of warfare. *I never met an enemy in person, nor did he meet me. I never saw at close quarters the death and destruction delivered by a bombing attack.*[165]

The young airmen faced the very likely prospect of their own death. They should not have been required to bear the additional stress of killing civilians.

One Death, One Family

Anyone who writes about war is faced with the futility of trying to give some sort of life to casualty numbers, civilian or military. It is particularly difficult to convey the pain of family members of the dead on any side. Perhaps the story of one Bomber Command Canadian from Jasper, Alberta, can provide a glimpse. Let the story stand as symbolic of the thousands more that cannot be told here.

Doreen Ruddy is the wife of Dick Ruddy, who told of his father's survival of the Passchendaele triage death tent. She was 13 when her brother, Jim Maxwell 18, went off to Bomber Command. He was killed on a reconnaissance mission in 1942, soon after his posting to an RAF squadron and, mercifully, before he could be called upon to bomb civilians. The story of his enlistment, his death, and the process his family endured, however, is typical of all the 10,000 Canadians who died serving Bomber Command.[166]

The first to suffer was Jim's mother, Mae. He pleaded that she give permission for him to join up at 17. Mae had lost her first husband in the Great War and by fall of 1941 already had two brothers serving in the navy. The last thing she needed to face was the prospect of losing one of her two sons. Jim persisted, threatening to run away if she would not sign. Mae relented.

Why was Jim so eager to join the forces? "Pure ignorance" was Doreen's recollection. It would be an adventure. All of his friends were joining. None of them knew the first thing about war.

After returning home from training to celebrate his 18th birthday, Jim left to join an RAF bomber squadron in Cornwall, England. Jasper was a town of no more than 2,000 at the time. Everyone knew everyone. Townspeople came to the train station to see Jim off with gifts of cigarettes, gum, and chocolate. He stayed on the vestibule until the mountains he loved faded from view.

In Cornwall, Jim found that he was the only Canadian in his Whitley's six-man crew.[167] Still, he wrote home that he got along well with everyone, including the pilot, William Raffan.

Jim's life ended in October. A six-year ordeal for his family began. Doreen answered the door when the telegram arrived reporting her brother missing. She tried to comfort her hysterical mother, saying this did not mean Jim was dead. Very soon afterward, neighbours arrived and began the customary ritual of food and condolences. They had seen Mr. Pickering come to the door. Pickering was the manager of the telegraph office. For delivery of routine telegrams, Mr. Pickering employed a runner. The kind the Maxwells received, he delivered in person offering what comfort he could. When Doreen opened the door and saw Mr. Pickering, she knew the message.

The process that followed was replicated too often in too many families. After a period of time, Jim's personal effects were returned. Many months after that came news that he had in fact been killed. Periodic updates on efforts to locate his remains trickled in over time, and finally, news of his burial in France. Various official reminders of the loss would last until 1948.

The military bureaucracy unintentionally added to the family's pain. Correspondence to the Maxwells was lost but Raffan's widow provided her copies that were the same for all crewmembers. In those letters, we once again see the difference between those who share the bond of combat and bureaucrats, however well meaning the latter may be. The letter from the wing commander was personal and genuinely sympathetic. It acknowledged that the fateful telegram would already have arrived. In addition to providing information about the process, it detailed individual praise of Raffan. The tone of most correspondence from the Air Ministry was quite different. Each letter was impersonal. Each implied clearly that its author was following routine orders in writing. This 1943 letter is typical:

With reference to your letter of...... I am directed to inform you that action has been taken to presume, for official purposes, that your husband, Pilot Officer W.F. Raffan, lost his life on the 29th of October, 1942. I am to express the sympathy of the Department with your great loss.

Doreen's family members were more fortunate than many whose sons flew with Bomber Command. They learned of his burial and of acts of decency by both the villagers of Taule, France, and its German occupiers. In 1970, there were still living witnesses to the downing of the plane and the burial of the crew. Jim's brother learned that the Germans turned over the bodies to the townspeople, who conducted a funeral and burial in the community cemetery. The remains of this bomber crew do not lie among the endless rows of a military memorial cemetery. Rather, the six are side by side in a separately bordered plot. The French ensure that there are always fresh flowers at the grave. Each family was asked to compose a memorial message for its gravestone. Jim's is not about God, or service, or country. Fittingly, it reflects the impression the teenager left on his loved ones: *His charming ways, his smile, are a pleasure to recall. He died beloved by all.*

The children made sure that that Mae, like so many mothers before her, was shielded from the full reality of Jim's death. There is a gravestone for each crewmember in the cemetery at Taule, but there are two sets of remains in Jim's grave. His were so entangled with those of another crewmember that they could not be separated.

Doreen's account ended with this: *I don't know why the world can't live in peace. I just don't know.*

I also count the half million civilian victims of Bomber Command as innocent. I have no interest, as some have, in guessing the number of Germans who knew or should have known of the horrific crimes of the Nazis and are therefore thought to be somehow less deserving of sympathy. What a ghastly game it would be to try to allocate differences among the angry civilians who would have torn a downed Canadian airmen apart but were stopped by German soldiers; the fire bombing survivor who saw the burned corpses of his neighbours scattered in all forms of death, a man who opposed the Nazis but still felt some degree of responsibility; the woman who remembers as a small child being carefully instructed to lie down during the firebombing because if she sat up the concussion would cause her lungs to burst?[168] I have no use for the argument that "they started it" or that it shortened the war. For me, time would be better spent on efforts to get the evil genie released in the Great War back in the bottle. No killing civilians. Period.

British Bomber Command's killing of civilians was a military as well as moral failure. German industrial power survived to the end of the war. The Canadian death toll in Bomber Command exceeded that of the D-Day landings. The campaign left 600,000 Germans dead and 5 million homeless. If *Victory denies the victorious the necessity of reflection*,[169] so does censorship. A 2007 exhibit at the Canadian War Museum told the whole story of Bomber Command. Some misguided veterans groups successfully campaigned to water it down.[170]

The Italian Sideshow

In late 1943, Canadian politicians were worried about the war ending before those idle soldiers, still training, could bring Canada her share of glory. Newspapers taunted King for inaction and perception grew, in spite of statistics to the contrary, that the troops were bored and anxious for action. One even claimed that inaction was afflicting many troops with mental illness.[171] It was already too late to affect the outcome of the war. The Russians at Stalingrad and the British at El Alamein had determined that. So, while the D-Day wait continued, Canada's patrons sent troops to a bloody sideshow.

Not only did McNaughton not get to lead Canadians into Berlin, he was eventually not even able to keep his army together. It was split, with three divisions assigned to await D-Day in England and two joining the invasion of Sicily and Italy under the overall command of British field marshal Bernard Montgomery. Sicily went reasonably well, as wars go. After an easy landing, the troops were only gradually introduced to real warfare. The number of fatalities, 562, was considered reasonable. But neither the press nor politicians, other than King, were satisfied. Much more blood would have to be shed in Italy.[172]

Italy surrendered in September 1943. Her forces were replaced by battle-hardened German troops. What Churchill had termed the "soft underbelly of Europe," would prove far from soft. For the trip from Sicily up the boot, eager Canada once again offered more than she had been asked to give. Her two divisions were reinforced with the 5th Canadian Armoured Division.[173] Cook described what was in store for the Canadians: *With little imagination and less flair, the campaign had all the makings of a Great War battle of attrition.*[174]

Much that we have we have examined about war and Canada's part in other people's wars played out in the battle for a coastal town called Ortona. Once again, political considerations trumped good military judgment, with Canadians paying the price. The Canadian units under Montgomery were on the British side of a race with U.S. general Mark Clark's army for the glory of being the first to liberate Rome. Montgomery wanted to deliver a smashing blow at Ortona and then win the race west to the capital. He did not succeed, but he spent nearly 1,400 Canadian lives in the effort.[175]

Ortona could have been, and probably should have been, bypassed. That would almost certainly have made for a quicker journey to Rome. But here again, a thirsty press played a damaging role. Hungry for drama, war correspondents turned Ortona into the most important objective of the Italian effort—"a miniature Stalingrad." The propaganda was influential in bringing about deadly orders for each side: "Take Ortona at all costs," and "Defend Ortona at all costs."[176]

Montgomery was in a hurry. The principal terrain feature guarding the town was a heavily defended depression known as the Gully. Under continuous goading by Montgomery to get on with the job, Canadian Division Commander Christopher Vokes threw unit after unit into piecemeal frontal assaults, chewing up eight of nine regiments.

When the Gully was finally breached, many Canadian units were so depleted as to be ineffective. The question among commanders was whether they had sufficient strength left for Ortona. Here the tragic final verse of *In Flanders Field* decided the question. Vokes did not ask for relief. He decided that so many lives had already been sacrificed that Canadians had to take Ortona. Handing over the task to British units would harm morale and be a devastating blow to the reputation of the division.[177]

In the street by street, house by house fighting, well-trained German snipers and numerous booby traps made a deadly combination. On December 27, 1943, after a week of a kind of warfare for which nothing in their training had prepared them, the Canadians prevailed. It was the costliest fighting of the Italian campaign. It was also a campaign that would be forgotten two days after Rome fell to the Americans on June 4, 1944.[178] Today's tourists are taken to Juno or Omaha beach, not Ortona.

Farley Mowat provides a look from the perspective of the ordinary soldier. The later to be famous Canadian writer was a member of the Hastings and Prince Edward Regiment. He experienced Sicily and Ortona. From his memoir *And No Birds Sang*[179] we can see examples of much of what we have been examining.

Mowat believed that British and U.S. politicians had sold out to fascism and it was everyone's duty to take up arms against Germany. He tried to enlist in the RCAF, but was content when he eventually landed in his father's old unit, the "Hasty Pees".[180]

Near the end of the Sicily campaign, this initial fervor left him. Seeing the mangled bits and pieces of his comrades made war something quite different from what he had imagined. He writes that the urge for action that had driven him since his enlistment collapsed like a pricked balloon, and was replaced by a swelling sense of dread. That may explain why he understood what was happening when he later saw ambulances carrying casualties who had no visible wounds. He recognized, whatever the term then, the PTSD that continues to destroy lives today. Mowat recalled his father's warning that the most unfortunate in war were not those who lost limbs but those whose spirits were destroyed.[181] Cook described the 587 Canadians who experienced "battle exhaustion": *The advanced cases mumbled gibberish, exposed themselves dangerously to enemy fire, developed paralyzed limbs and slipped into a catatonic state.*[182]

Stanley Scislowski was a green infantry private in one of the units that followed the Hasty Pees into combat in Italy. In his own memoir, Scislowski attributed his enlistment primarily to ignorance: *I don't think there were many that looked to the fact that men die, often in droves, in the most brutal and gruesome ways. We had somehow been led to believe, perhaps through the movies, books on war, and our own government propaganda, that battle was the ultimate adventure.*[183]

Mowat's perspective gradually moved toward that of Scislowski. His experience, particularly at Ortona, prompted him thereafter to condemn the glorification of war in many Remembrance Day events, and insist that war should be remembered instead "as the abomination that it is".[184]

Facing his own fear and vulnerability enabled Mowat to empathize with others. He wrote of Italian civilians, involuntarily situated between the competing death machines, huddled like dumb and impassive beasts outside the blasted buildings. He described refugees walking barefoot in almost-frozen mud, plodding by expressionless, homeless and destitute. Seeing the dignity with which they endured all this got him beyond the stereotypes he had accepted about "greasy Italians".[185] Cook described stunned families taking shelter under rubble and pleading for safe passage. A Saskatoon soldier found a family of four holed up in a house with two children dead in their high chairs. Makeshift graves recorded the deaths of 1300 civilians killed in the fighting.[186]

One of Mowat's last experiences at Ortona was yet another example of the bond of humanity between ordinary soldiers assigned to kill one another. As the attack approached the town, a shell blast threw him through the doorway of a hut to land on the corpse of a German soldier. Another soldier was sitting upright in a corner and cried out to him in German for water. Mowat's rifle was still slung over his shoulder and he thought at first that the German would shoot him. When he looked more closely, he saw the reality of war: *His left arm was grasping the shattered stump of where his right arm had been severed just below the elbow...Most dreadful was a great gash in his side from which protruded a glistening dark mass which must have been his liver.* Mowat had no water. For his own sake, he had filled his canteen with rum. After first shaking his head and telling the German this, he saw that the man would die in any event. He sat down, and they shared the rum. *...and so the two of us got drunk together. And in a little while he died.* Mowat awoke from his stupor on December 23, 1943.[187]

Christmas at Ortona. The Christmas truce of 1915. Christmas at Hong Kong. "Home by Christmas." Embedded in the story of Canadians at war is something unfathomable; the celebration of the birth of the Prince of Peace.

Postscripts: Race, Demonizing, and Civilian Deaths

While arguably necessary, World War II was also someone else's war, at least a war of someone else's making. Once again, Canada's national security was not involved. Like Russia, we are not famous for our warm winters. Setting aside that debate, perhaps we can try to envision a better future role for Canadians. It may help to look a bit further at this war's dangerous refinements to the legacy of the Great War, particularly the factor of propaganda and its core requirement of demonizing, often ably assisted by racism.

We have seen that the process of racialization is flexible enough to accommodate even white versus white racism. The Boers and Germans were said to be less evolved than Anglo-Saxons. The Nazis touted the superiority of Aryans. Race-tinged propaganda against Jews is commonly referred to as Anti-Semitic, although both Jews and Arabs are Semites. Racializing Asians is relatively simple. Overall, the racialization process requires neither truth nor accuracy. Violence and civilian deaths are the product of its lethal mix.

Demonizing Hitler

When the horror unleashed by one person reaches the unimaginable level brought about by Adolph Hitler, it is difficult to discern any cost to demonizing him. But there is a significant cost, one that would likely bemuse war maker Hitler were he around today.

One of the principal obstacles to any reasoned consideration of World War II as avoidable, unnecessary, and in no case a justification for future wars is the perception of Hitler as the alpha and omega of evil---the cause of all that brought the devastation of war. There is thus no need to consider anything beyond his demonic persona and its consequences. But obsession with the view that he was a madman bent on conquering the world has elevated rhetoric about Munich to the status of foreign policy article of faith. Regrettably, the persistence of that view continues to impair international relationships today. Hitler and 1938 have been held out countless times over the years to justify the use of confrontation in lieu of intelligent efforts at conflict resolution. The result has been numerous ill-advised military adventures that certainly have not made the world any safer.

To invoke this "stand your ground", "don't talk to the enemy" position today, it is not even necessary to claim a threat that is the equivalent of Hitler's evil. Just having some person and some people to demonize is enough. The 2014 dispute over Russia's claim to parts of Ukraine prompted none other than England's Prince Charles to compare Vladimir Putin to Hitler during a visit to Canada.[188] Would the "no more Munich" mantra have achieved such force were Hitler not assumed to be sub-human in just the way he and Nazi leadership viewed others? It is not necessary to utter the slightest suggestion of a justification for the crimes of Hitler and his cohorts in order to challenge the destructive legacy of the myth of the madman as the sole cause of tragedy.

The myth of Hitler as history's insane uber-villain bent on conquering the world is not only a barrier to intelligent conflict resolution, it also works to absolve everyone else from any responsibility for causing the war. That, in turn, makes the next war easier to undertake. One historian who challenged the myth warned that, because of understandable revulsion to Nazi atrocities, some people automatically assign Hitler sole responsibility for the outbreak of the war.[189] But the crimes and the causes are not the same.

If we wish for Canada a different and better role in future world affairs, we should at least temporarily set aside outrage and examine other causes of war. It is the demonization element of propaganda that often prevents this. Looking past the madman/world domination characterization of Hitler is difficult but worthwhile.

Examining the necessity for World War II and Canada's participation without demonizing the eventual enemies provides much more useful guidance. The history of the run up contains more than a few relics of the Great War disaster. Imperialism, secret diplomacy, racism, a Machiavellian web of treaties and alliances all played a part. European powers had learned little.

A caution about separating legitimate moral outrage from the cause of the war was a theme of A.J.P. Taylor, a distinguished British historian. His 1961 book on the causes of the war made a stir in academic circles.[190] It prompted publication of a collection of essays by equally well-credentialed scholars later in that decade. Only one of the ten who address the issue concluded that Hitler was out to conquer the world. H.R. Trevor-Roper launched a vitriolic attack on Taylor, complete with the now familiar "aiding the forces of evil" charge.[191] What had him so upset?

Neither Taylor nor any other authority disputes that the German objective of reversing the Treaty of Versailles was a causal factor in bringing on the war. What so enraged Trevor-Roper was Taylor's assertion that Hitler acted the role of traditional German statesman, pursuing traditional German goals; that in the 1930's he had no real policy beyond waiting to exploit the ineptitude of his opponents. Taylor argued further that the Paris treaty made World War II inevitable. Taylor was no apologist for Hitler. He concluded that the inevitable consequence of a German desire for international equality and abrogation of Versailles would mean that Germany would become the dominant state in Europe. He did not endorse that outcome, noting it would put Germany in the same position as if she had won the Great War.[192] But Taylor's clear implication is that Hitler did not set out to conquer the world, but rather to dominate Europe by playing the imperial game better than his adversaries.

Taylor further enraged his critics by reminding them of the attitude of all Cold War leaders toward human life: *I cannot get out of my head that Hitler was an indescribably wicked man...but he was only a beginner. The rulers of the United States and Soviet Russia are now cheerfully contemplating a hideous death for seventy million or perhaps a hundred and fifty million people in the first week of the next war. What has Hitler to show in comparison with this?*[193] Whatever the validity of Taylor's position about Hitler, this comment is another reminder of human nature. People react with far more revulsion to millions being starved and led into gas chambers than to the same number being incinerated from above. But as we will see in the next chapter, Taylor was correct. Leaders from both sides were casually willing to destroy millions with atomic weapons.

The other essays contain reasoned attacks on Taylor's position, but none support Trevor-Roper. H.W. Koch flatly states that no evidence exists of Hitler's intention to conquer the world.[194] As new information emerges, historians continue this debate. The point for us is that much better guidance for Canada's future course is to be found in examining the causes of her wars than in the simplistic demonizing of any figure, in any war.

Setting aside the demonization of Hitler also reveals that the old practice of secret agreements affecting the fate of others once again played a part in causing a war. We have seen the consequences of an agreement to stand by while Italy took over Ethiopia.[195] A more important example was Britain's guarantee to Poland. Hitler knew of its existence, but did not know the secret details of the commitment. He also knew that as a practical matter the British would be unable to assist Poland militarily. He assumed that they knew this also, and concluded that they were unlikely to intervene.

Hitler had been seeking an agreement with Poland over Danzig and the Polish Corridor. When talks broke down, the British guarantee affected Hitler's options. Abandoning Danzig would be embarrassing. Resuming negotiations would strengthen the Polish position... His strange pact with Russia was the last option short of direct force. It was supposed to coerce Poland from both sides. When the Poles remained adamant, Hitler took what he saw as a reasonable risk, and invaded.[196] These tangled alliances and agreements bear a disturbing resemblance to the causes of the Great War.

Demonizing The German People

We would do well not to lump all Germans in with those who were willfully blind to the Nazi death camps. If we ignore propaganda stereotypes; if we do not demonize Germans, we find that their story is more complex. Indeed, the experience of ordinary Germans between world wars contains a caution for everyone about indifference and inattention to governments.

The first step in resisting propaganda and getting beyond demonizing is making an effort to imagine oneself in the position of one's adversary. Picture yourself as an ordinary German citizen in 1933. The Nazis were the National Socialist German Workers Party. After incidents such as French reoccupation of your industrial heartland on the pretext that your country had violated the peace treaty by not delivering telephone poles on time,[197] would fierce nationalism appeal to you? The party was socialist. You live in a country with six million unemployed, rife with bankruptcies and bank foreclosures. Your family and friends are leaving the country for opportunities elsewhere.[198] Would a party platform that gives priority to domestic needs and commits to common good before personal gain be attractive?

The first two items of the Nazi Party platform called for uniting Germans within a greater Germany and annulment of the Paris treaty. The document went on to demand confiscation of war profits and a requirement for profit sharing by large companies. It then demanded increases in old age pensions, maintenance of a healthy middle class, state educational support for poor children, bans on child labour, and improved maternal health programs. Reading all that, are you confident that you would have picked up on items later in the document that opened the door to press censorship, demanded unlimited authority for a central government, and condemned "the materialistic Jewish spirit"?[199] If you supported this party in the 1920s would you abandon it when it delivered on its promises, not just with highways and Volkswagens, but also with full employment, adequate nutrition and higher benefits for the old, sick, and poor?[200] In 1933, it was these matters, not international events that had the attention of ordinary Germans. They were not thinking of war.[201] But neither were they paying sufficient attention.

If you were unimpressed with the commitment to social programs, might you have had a favourable view of the party's stand on morality and social issues? The party agenda contained numerous positions loved today by right wing movements in the West. It promoted patriotism and glorified hard work by rugged individuals. It also provided an easy to loathe list of enemies. In addition to the Jews, those who were wrecking the morality of the country were said to be drug dealers, pornographers, and gay and lesbian perverts.[202] In post Great War Germany, would you have seen that it was wrong and dangerous to demonize members of these groups, especially the Jews?

To stand against all this would first have required a sense of community — of concern for those being vilified. How well are we all doing on that front today? Isn't acceptance of U.S. and Canadian "anti-terror" legislation and denial of civil liberties explained well by the maxim: "If you haven't done anything wrong, you have nothing to fear"?

As time went on, resistance to the Nazis became increasingly dangerous. In spite of this, there was real opposition, both from ordinary people and from some at higher levels, but opposition leaders received no outside support. As late as 1937, some of them sought help from Britain. Ironically, they were offering enough information to suggest strongly that if the British called Hitler's bluff on Czechoslovakia with a strongly worded bluff of their own, the matter might end right there. The British rejected offers of assistance and calls for help and tried to cover that up after the war.[203] Britons, Canadians, and others had by that time been thoroughly conditioned to have no truck with the Hun.

Finally, it would be grossly hypocritical to condemn Germans for not opposing Hitler once the war began. The assumption everywhere today, as it has been in every one of Canada's wars, is that those who oppose a war once it is underway have a patriotic duty to "support the troops." Nations have very little room for stone throwing at ordinary Germans.

Demonizing the Japanese

Canadian policy in the trans-pacific was no source of pride. Neither was Canadian complicity in the mass atomic slaughter of civilians. In that shameful episode, the demonizing of Japanese could not have reached the level it did by 1945 without the assistance of racism. Because of the pre-war situation in Asia, this required some creative racialization.

Canada and the western powers had left the Chinese to fend for themselves until Pearl Harbor, even assisting the attacking Japanese with trade and weapons. For most of the first half of the 20th Century, Great Britain and Japan enjoyed an imperialist détente in Asia. Japanese leaders did not set out to conquer the world either. They were simply playing the game of imperialism in what today would be called a "sphere of influence." They wanted to be the British of Asia.

Japanese foreign policy was conducted on the assumption that the country was as responsible an imperialist as her western counterparts. Before 1939, Japan sought to expand her empire cautiously so as not to infringe on the prerogatives of other empires, including the holdings of the British, French, Dutch, and Americans. Russia was her principal adversary. When the European imperial powers went to war against each other, Japan saw a new opportunity and went beyond the territorial wrestling match with the Soviet Union to seek mineral resources in Southeast Asia. This is what brought the conflict with western imperialists, including the French in Vietnam. This imperial jostling prompted the U.S. to send a fleet to Pearl Harbor in 1941 in an effort to deter Japan from upsetting the *status quo* in British, French, and Dutch colonies.[204]

While the sharing arrangement lasted, Canada's domestic policies, including immigration bars and employment law, reflected racism directed at all Asians. Once the war began, however, the racism inherent in imperialism had to be modified so that propaganda could distinguish between the "good Asians" and the "bad Asians". The Japanese, of course, then became the bad Asians. They were the slant-eyed, buck-toothed, night-blind, murderers and rapists of Hong Kong and Nanking. The Chinese became the good Asians, child-like victims to be led along.[205] This "paternal racialization" process was called into service often during the Cold War, particularly in Korea. There is no doubting the racial component of demonizing this World War II adversary. A bill in 1944 to allow overseas soldiers to vote denied that right to Canadians of Japanese descent while granting it to those of German and Italian extraction.[206]

Before the good/bad Asian racialization was reversed, there were periodic diplomatic efforts at imperial adjustments. One example was the Washington Conference of 1921-1922. The treaties it produced refused to recognize racial equality but acknowledged Japan as a full-fledged player in the imperial game. On balance, that was acceptable to Emperor Hirohito.[207] The Chinese did not fare as well. The American-dictated agreements granted equal opportunity to nine signatories to exploit China's resources and cheap labour.

Diplomacy eventually failed. The overstepping of Japanese leaders that ended power sharing with the British and began the war had horrific consequences for the Japanese people at its end. Racialized and demonized, they were set up to be the guinea pigs in an experiment equal in horror to the Nazi's "final solution", with arguably more dangerous lasting effects.

In the summer of 1945, the Japanese turned to their old enemy the Soviets for diplomatic help in beginning a surrender process. The Soviets were in no hurry. They wanted territory held by the Japanese and it was in their interest that the war continue long enough for them to get it. U.S. president Truman delayed engaging in surrender talks to allow testing of the atomic bomb. The U.S. Joint Chiefs of Staff finally recommended surrender terms that would allow the Japanese emperor to remain. The Allies at Potsdam, however, adopted the approach bequeathed by the Great War: not just defeat, destruction.[208]

And so came the atomic holocaust and the justifications. The bombs were dropped on Hiroshima and Nagasaki and 200,000 civilians were instantly obliterated. Hundreds of thousands more were poisoned. Japan surrendered unconditionally. The western world quickly embraced Churchill's unfounded justification that the bombs saved more than a million American and British lives. Today, at least eight nations have a total of more than 19,000 bombs that make those dropped on Japan look like toys.[209] The return on hundreds of thousands of dead and poisoned women and children was a world that would conduct its affairs thereafter in fear of the same fate.

The U.S. did not act alone. Canada and Great Britain knew in advance and were intent on becoming part of the "atomic action". Mackenzie King, speaking of what might have happened to the "British race" if the Germans had the bomb first, expressed relief that it was used on the Japanese rather than the "white races of Europe".[210]

Canada supplied most of the uranium for the bombs and was proud of it. Minister C.D. Howe praised Canadian scientists for their part in what he called a "great scientific development". Unremembered civilian casualties include First Nations Dene people who died mining the uranium and, like the Japanese, from radiation-related diseases in later years.[211]

Price's assessment provides a better lesson than the justifications and "collateral damage" crocodile tears that characterize our fleeting remembrances of Hiroshima and Nagasaki: *The pressures of war, technological imperatives, and disregard for civilians all contributed to decision makers not really caring about civilians. Racialized notions of Japanese as beasts, demonic savages…further exacerbated disregard for civilian lives in Japan.*[212]

It should not be necessary to caution against demonizing ordinary Japanese. They endured more than did British civilians during the Blitz. They had even less say than Germans about going to war. In defeat, they labored gracefully and stoically to reassemble a more peaceful society.

Demonizing Jews

European Jews, of course, were the greatest victims of propaganda. Today, Jews have little need for others to caution against demonizing them. They have numerous organizations that respond immediately to anything they perceive as remotely Anti-Semitic. Given the magnitude of the holocaust, that is understandable. But there are other lessons for Canada from this story.

Why was it Jews who were so easily demonized? Nazis began the persecution with communists and homosexuals. Hannah Arendt provides insights. She has impressive credentials. For researching the Nazis, she was interrogated by the Gestapo and briefly interned in a concentration camp in France. She alienated some on the left with her critiques the Soviet Union. After the war, she alienated some Jewish groups when she covered the trial of Adolph Eichmann, urging that it was important to try to understand evildoers even if one could not forgive them, she concluded that Eichmann's role in the holocaust was born more of thoughtless indifference than evil intent. She was also not popular for her view that victim groups sometimes unintentionally contribute to their own suffering.[213]

Arendt outlines several factors that resulted in the isolation of European Jews. One of them is the marriage of capitalism and imperialism and its accompanying violence----additional evidence of the overriding importance of changes in warfare and international relations spawned by the Great War.

Arendt outlines the history of European Jews as moneylenders to governments, a perfectly respectable enterprise that apparently keeps the world afloat today. Before the development of nation states, feudal rulers protected a class of "court Jews", whose lending was essential to financing wars.[214] A first step toward isolation.

Later, developing nation states also had need of capital and credit. Growing notions of equality made it more difficult to raise funds from the populace, especially for wars. The state need for financiers continued until the heyday of imperialism in the 19th and early 20th Century. There was no overt conspiracy to isolate European Jews further, but the marriage of capitalism and imperialism provided a new source of funding and caused the Jews to lose their exclusive position in state financing to imperialist businessmen.

The consequences of being replaced were dire. The Jewish financiers had already been separated by their special protections from their community at large. Their only relationship was with the state. States could not afford to have them assimilated into a general population that was resistant to financing state ventures. And many in this class, for their own reasons, guarded against assimilation. But not being part of the governing class either, their only relationships were based solely on their usefulness in finance. Further, the requirements of conducting international finance had meant that strong allegiances to any particular nation had to be avoided.[215]

International financing arrangements had also depended on the continuity of peace and war cycles that left warring parties intact. Once the Great War policies of completely destroying the enemy took hold, the old networks were destroyed and the usefulness of the financiers along with it. Individual financiers did for a time continue to play an important role. The best example is probably Benjamin Disraeli. You will recall that his struggle with Gladstone for the favour of Queen Victoria was assisted immeasurably by his ability to find financing for the purchase of the Suez Canal. Finally, came the new chaotic jumble of nations created by the Paris treaties.

Arendt sums it up: *As a group, Western Jewry disintegrated together with the nation-state during the decades preceding the First World War. The rapid decline of Europe after the war found them already deprived of their former power, atomized into a herd of wealthy individuals. In an imperialist age, Jewish wealth had become insignificant; to a Europe with no sense of a balance of power between its nations...the non-national, inter-European Jewish element became an object of universal hatred because of its wealth, and of contempt because of its lack of power.*[216]

Another ominous factor was that the Jews, like most financiers everywhere, were apolitical. This meant that they financed whatever governments requested. It did not matter whether the project was a canal or guns. Unfair as it may be, that made it easier in any country to portray them as war profiteers. Likewise, when government figures engage in corrupt ventures, as they are ever wont to do, and the losses fall on the poor and lower middle class, as they always do, it is easy to blame those who simply acted as middlemen. That factor can divide the powerless, and turn those who should be supportive into an anti-Semitic mob. *To the small shopkeeper, the banker appeared to be the same kind of exploiter as the owner of a big business enterprise was to the worker...Thus the leftist movement of the lower middle class and the entire propaganda against banking capital turned more or less anti-Semitic...*[217]

European Jews were also blindsided. In the two-decades before the Great War anti-Semitic movements had declined and there was general political, if not social equality. Most European Jews saw anti-Semitism as an ongoing political issue, not a threat to survival. There were anti-Semitic political parties all over Europe. The issue was a normal political one similar to the increasing angst of many in Europe today over immigration.

By the end of the Great War, the cluster of disadvantages outlined here coalesced. *Anti-Semitism, having lost ground in the special conditions that influenced its development during the nineteenth century, could be freely elaborated by charlatans and crackpots into that weird mixture of half-truths and wild superstitions which emerged in Europe after 1914, the ideology of all frustrated and resentful elements.*[218]

Fostering international indifference to Jews was relatively easy. The Nazi Ministry of Propaganda learned much from Britain's Great War operations about the art of managing news and demonizing enemies. Their social skills at co-opting the press made news management even easier. In the early days of the war, while Britain and France were continuing to make life difficult for correspondents, the Germans wined and dined writers and gave them easy access to officials.[219]

But neither the German propaganda advantage, nor uniquely isolating factors that beset European Jews, nor the extreme inhumanity of the Nazis fully explains the occurrence of a tragedy of the magnitude of the holocaust. When we go beyond demonizing

Hitler and his inner circle, we see that many nations, including Canada, had a part in that.

French Catholics and the French army in particular had provided the Nazis with an anti-semitic template, best illustrated by the well known story of the persecution of Albert Dreyfuss, first Jewish member of the French General Staff. During the years between his imprisonment in 1894 and ambiguous exoneration in 1906, the anti-Dreyfuss side produced techniques of propaganda and violence and revived old myths about Jewish conspiracies. Jewish shops were ransacked and Jews were attacked in the streets. Ironically, it was Clemenceau, the old Paris 1919 revenge seeker, who took up the cause of Jewish rights and defused the situation — until the collaborators of the Vichy government happily took it up again. By the time Nazis came to power, the recipe for persecution had been published.[220]

Western nations did their part by refusing to accept Jews fleeing persecution. Canada, with plenty of land and a relatively small population, was one of the worst actors. After the November 9, 1938, rampage against Jews in Berlin known as Kristal Nacht, Canada's Deputy Immigration Minister stood fast. *Pressure on the part of the Jewish people to get into Canada has never been greater than it is now, and I am glad to be able to add… that it has never been so well controlled.*[221] Nor were Canadians free of influence of the half-truths, superstitions, and stereotypes that are the stock in trade of propaganda: *If they would just divest themselves of certain of their habits I am sure they could be just as popular in Canada as our Scandinavians.*[222] King echoed the concern: *I am coming to feel that the democratic countries have allowed themselves to be too greatly controlled by Jews and Jewish influence.*[223]

The influential Catholic Church in Quebec echoed its French counterpart. As late as May 1939, when there was no excuse for ignorance of their plight, Canada turned back a ship with 937 Jews fleeing Germany. From 1933-1945, fewer than 5,000 Jews were allowed into Canada. Only eight thousand more were permitted from 1945-1948, when the holocaust was known.[224] Some Jews who died terribly in Auschwitz should have died peacefully years later in Red Deer.

The experience of German Jewry adds an important dimension to the hazards of demonizing. To adopt as a complete answer the notion that the reason people do evil is that they themselves are inherently evil is to take the easy way out.

Opportunity Lost---Or Deferred?

If the Great War did indeed foreordain this one, if World War II magnified terribly the destructive changes in warfare that the Great War introduced, there are at least two lessons that Canada should have learned by this point. One is that the Great War should never be glorified or celebrated. Identifying it as some pivotal event enhancing Canada's international status makes it difficult to learn that lesson. The second is that, even if other nations had erred so badly that Canada had to enter the next war, 1945 was the time for a fundamental rethinking of her role in the international community. It was time to build on the factors of reluctance and caution about wars that have been a part of Canadian history to a greater or lesser degree from the beginning. That may yet happen. It was not, however, to be the next chapter in the story of Canada and other people's wars.

CHAPTER V

THE COLD WAR, KOREA, AND VIETNAM: SERVING A NEW PATRON

A New Kind of War

By the end of World War II, there were indications that Canada had learned a bit from fighting in other people's wars. The importance of the uniquely Canadian factors had been enhanced and there seemed to be a good chance that the nation would not go blindly to remote parts of the globe at the behest of a powerful patron. Unfortunately, the first time that proposition was tested Canada decided to go to Korea, still as a minor player, this time under the direction of the Americans.

The new patron had come up with a new enemy in a new kind of war. The U.S. now called Canada to be engaged in a struggle against godless communism being spread by the Soviet Union. The call this time was not to join a war against that nation. Instead, an ephemeral enemy now provided opportunities for armed conflict anywhere in the world to combat the "worldwide communist conspiracy." Partly because of U.S. capacity to use atomic weapons again, a capacity soon matched by the Soviet Union, all-out global warfare was less likely — unless a madman or a miscalculation by either side put an end to everyone. We will see two examples of how close the world came to just such a catastrophe. World leaders generally knew that World War III would be the "war to end all wars" because nobody would survive to fight another. That did not stop them from risking the lives of most people on the planet.

Room remained for armed struggle over nations, regions and resources in what would now be called the Cold War. The western position was that not an inch of territory on earth could be ceded to the new menace. The timing of this development was unfortunate. Price writes that the U.S. began to implement policies of imperial anti-communism just as the decolonization movement got under way.[1] For the post-war powers, there was no such thing as a legitimate indigenous movement for independence or nationalist uprising against colonialism.

The paternal racism component of the wars in Korea and Vietnam was previewed at allied conferences in Cairo, Tehran, and Berlin during World War II. Roosevelt's call for the independence of Korea, Indochina and Thailand was rebuffed. The first draft of a communiqué had the conferees endorsing independence "at the earliest possible time". The language was watered down to "the proper time" and finally to "in due course".[2] The children were not ready to go out on their own. There was a dangerous red stranger out there.

Along with its paternal racism, propaganda followed a simple formula that went like this: "If we don't stop them in [insert any country], they'll be in [insert any local city].[3] This was the mantra recycled by the Americans when they, with Canada's help and to their regret, replayed Korea in Vietnam.

In sum, the world had to stay the way the World War I and II victors had carved it out or all would be lost. Keeping it that way required armed force. If heroic military action was really what defined Canada on the world stage, she would have to be a part of the colonial maintenance team.

True, there was a real adversary. Several factors had come together to produce a hostile Russia, led by brutal dictator Joseph Stalin. They included decades of capitalist paranoia about communists; unfortunate western decisions to isolate Russia, and the massive

Russian losses in World War II. The frenzied response of western nations, however, was grossly excessive.

Canada joined the panic at the moment World War II ended and a Russian defector showed up in Ottawa claiming a spy network was at work in the country. The groundwork for overreaction had already been laid by years of anti-communist propaganda orchestrated by business interests. A massive intrusion on the civil liberties of Canadians followed.

The *War Measures Act* was available and had already been used in earlier wars to target suspected communists more often than German agents.[4] Mackenzie King reluctantly invoked the act and then fretted about the similarity to Russia of the resulting interrogations, denial of counsel, and show trials. Some of those who were rounded up were convicted and imprisoned; some were acquitted. The fundamental unfairness of the investigations and trials precludes an accurate assessment of anyone's guilt. It is certain, however, that many lives were ruined.[5]

The early Cold War days also brought Canada yet another "bloody" day to mark in the calendar of labour relations. In 1949, asbestos workers in Quebec went on strike after the American company that employed them refused demands for a modest wage increase and some protection from asbestos dust. Premier Maurice Duplessis denounced the workers as communists, saboteurs, and subversive agents. The Quebec union called for a general strike and gained the support of unions across the country.

A familiar scenario played out, with the capitalists once again supplementing their own violence with help from government. "Bloody Thursday" was May 5th. Police armed with guns and batons arrested strikers, dragging some from churches. Some were beaten so badly during the ensuing interrogations that their appearance at trial might have provoked public outrage. Crown counsel dismissed the charges.

Unlike those of 1919 and 1935, this strike was not completely defeated. The workers did gain a wage increase. This result was due in part to support for the workers by the Catholic Church in Quebec and the efforts of a journalist, Gerard Pelletier, aided by a young lawyer, Pierre Elliott Trudeau. The American FBI promptly opened a file on Trudeau.[6]

Berton assessed the import of the Cold War hysteria: A *half century of witch hunts and blacklists, security clearances, charges of disloyalty and treason, careers wrecked by rumour… the spectre of suspicion stalking the nations, and worst of all, young men dying by the thousands in foreign climes in the service of a flawed ideal that we now realize had little substance.*[7]

Korea reflected the Euro-centric nature of the Cold War. Price writes: *The powerful term 'The East' was taking on a new meaning as the tattered portrait of the 'Yellow Peril' was overlaid with a new stain---this time with a reddish hue.*[8]

A particularly disheartening aspect of Canada's choice to be a part of the Korean War was the similarity to her experience in South Africa. Canadians were sent to fight in a far-off country where they understood neither the culture nor the language and the adversary fought by unconventional means. Casualty figures were also similar to those of the Boer War, including the predominance of death from disease rather than combat.

Louis St. Laurent succeeded Mackenzie King. The leader with the greatest impact on Canada's Korean adventure, however, was secretary of state for external affairs and future prime minister, Lester B. Pearson. In that office, and earlier as ambassador to Washington, it was he who was primarily responsible for dealing with Canada's new patron. With relatively minor variations, Pearson would play the role in the Korean War played by Laurier in the Boer War. Pearson was not entirely gullible, but like so many in his day, he saw the Soviets as a menace and viewed anything less than cooperation with the Americans as "isolationism".[9] Like Laurier, he was both fond and cautious of a powerful patron.

An important difference in this comparison is that Pearson believed Canada now had a way to participate responsibly in international affairs that had not been open to Laurier. Pearson believed that the end of World War II had brought Canada a way to do so without becoming the complete pawn of her new powerful patron. He had great hopes for the United Nations (UN), and for Canada's part in it. Pearson was also involved in the creation of the North Atlantic Treaty Organization (NATO), a body born out of fear of the Soviets. He believed that Canada could be a part of it without undermining the UN or compromising Canada's obligations to that organization.[10] Sadly, Pearson was wrong.

Koreans Trapped: "My Dictator is Better than Your Dictator"

It happened that neither Pearson, nor probably anyone else, could navigate the line that he hoped to walk. Once again, Canada would accede to the political will of her patron. Once again, her soldiers would fight well while serving under the patron's poor leadership. Once again, they would be confronted with their own racism. Once again, a combination of luck and caution would spare her the worst of the conflict. Korea was unambiguously someone else's war. That Canada participated is probably attributable more to the power of the Cold War mindset than to American coercion.

The most destructive factor at play in the Korean War was human rights violations and civilian deaths. Two million civilians were killed and more than 100,000 children orphaned. The land essential to an agrarian society was devastated. Our old friend and ally General LeMay firebombed villages as well as cities and boasted later that he killed more than a million civilians. Allied terror bombing in Korea left no building higher than one story standing in the north.[11] All this would have been tragic even if, like European nations in Canada's other wars, Koreans had chosen to be at war. But Koreans had no choice. Their lives were Cold War fodder.

Noted historian Max Hastings' penned an account of the war.[12] What is profoundly interesting about his work, and further testimony to the mood of the times, is that he sets out honestly and in detail many of the reasons that this war should not have been fought. He is clear that Korea was not part of any Soviet expansion plan. Yet he defends the war. Why? Just as the hindsight view of MacMillan and others about pre-war Germany may have been distorted by Hitler's later crimes, that of Hastings may have been affected by what North Korea later became. Hastings plainly buys into the Cold War position that the war was justified to save Korea from the communists. Ironically, he takes this position while candidly acknowledging that: *The local communists' credentials as fighters against the Japanese, their freedom from the embarrassment of landlordism and corruption, would almost certainly have enabled them to gain a popular mandate in 1945-46.*[13]

Because Canadians who fought and died in Korea did so with absolutely no knowledge of Korean history, culture, or language, it is worthwhile to examine some of the pre-war events in the country.

Koreans, including many communists, fought a guerrilla war against the Japanese in World War II. Russia entered the war against Japan late and began to drive the Japanese out of Manchuria and Korea. In the developing Cold War climate, the previously uninterested U.S. decided to be part of the post-war occupation of Korea. Two American officers drew an arbitrary line at the 38th parallel, designating the best agricultural land, industry, and more than half the population for occupation by their forces. One of the officers was future secretary of state Dean Rusk, who would later do greater damage to Vietnam.[14] As in 1919, a victorious power created a country that did not exist. Before the line, Korea was one country under the domination of another. The line did not quench the desire of the Koreans for unity and independence.

The advancing Soviets, of course, did not have to accept this division. Hastings concludes that had they continued and occupied all of Korea, the U.S. probably would not have made much of a fuss. But the Russians halted.[15] In contrast to their blunt takeover of much of Central Europe, it was the Russians who acted reasonably on several occasions.

The Americans went to work setting up a client government in the South, ordering their military to "create a government in harmony with U.S. policies".[16] Ultimately, Canadians would be asked to die for a regime that could match credentials with almost anyone for corruption and brutality. Once again, ordinary Koreans would be the losers. One of its features was U.S. employment of Japanese in the name of stability and administrative efficiency. The employees included war criminals and other Japanese against whom Koreans had waged a determined fight. The Americans left Japanese soldiers and police in charge of law and order.[17] This is not a recommended strategy for winning hearts and minds and it was not improved by the fact that Americans, as would Canadians later, viewed Koreans with disdain. Eventually, most Japanese were sent home. They warned the occupiers about the dangers of communist influence in Korea's newly forming political parties.

From this point, heeding the departing Japanese, the Americans were drawn further into the non-existent confrontation with the Soviets, who, as evidenced by their voluntary halt at the 38th parallel, had no interest in conquering the entire peninsula.

Canada's new patron, as it would do all over Asia, ignored the nationalist aspirations of the people and arguably chose the wrong side. The faction the Americans rejected, and indeed helped to suppress, included prominent members of the guerrilla forces that fought the Japanese. They were nationalists who wanted a unified Korea. But some were communists and all were vocal in their criticism of the U.S. occupation. The Americans chose instead an egotistical Harvard-educated dilettante. Syngman Rhee was not part of the resistance to the Japanese. He had been absent from Korea for decades. But he talked a great anti-communist game. Rhee met the only two requirements of the occupiers in the South: opposition to communism and a willingness to do business with the Americans.

He would become a brutal dictator, but a friendly one, at least for a while.

The Soviets, in the process of setting up their equally brutal dictatorship in the North, demonstrated that they did not see Korea as a proper Cold War battleground. At the end of 1945, they accepted a U.S. proposal that all of Korea be governed for five years by a four-power commission and then become a unified independent state. The Americans backed out in 1947. Despite objecting to the U.S. referral of the Korean matter to the UN, the Russians proposed the occupying powers simultaneously withdraw their forces and leave the fate of Korea to Koreans. Knowing that leftists would probably prevail, the Americans rejected this proposal. Instead, they convinced the General Assembly that a UN-supervised election should be held before withdrawal. Here was the first U.S. manipulation of the body on which Pearson had invested such hope.

All the countries dominated by the Soviets boycotted the vote and it was clear that they would reject any UN involvement. Going ahead with elections only in the South meant the end of prospects for a united Korea.

The body the UN designated to observe elections was called the United Nations Temporary Commission on Korea (UNTOK). The question of Canadian membership on the commission provoked a cabinet crisis in Ottawa. The Americans pressed for Canada to join. Without authority from still prime minister King, Louis St. Laurent agreed. King demanded Canada withdraw. He saw that without participation of the North, the vote would only aggravate tensions. He was further concerned about the U.S. assumption that Canada would back her in the UN no mater how unwise her proposals.

King and St. Laurent reached a compromise. Canada would appoint a member but withdraw if the Russians did not cooperate. The member was not to be involved in elections for South Korea only. The Canadian member was permitted to observe the election only after a statement from the Canadians that the resulting government was a creation of the occupying U.S. and not the UN.[18]

Rhee's faction, aided by the occupying Americans, conducted the election in an environment of repression. Police deputized what became known as "Rhee's goon squads" to terrorize anyone who opposed him. They detained 10,000 people in the run-up to the election and 589 people were killed. Rhee was elected and the American UN ambassador termed the election: *a magnificent demonstration of the capacity of the Korean people to establish a representative and responsible government.*[19]

Pearson went along with the phony election, but later concluded: *Rhee's government was just as dictatorial as the one in the north, just as totalitarian.*[20] In fact, Canadian diplomats had concluded at the time that the regime in the north was marginally better. It had instituted land reform, which Rhee constantly sabotaged. Democracy would not come to Korea until a revolution in 1987. The Rhee legacy was 40 years of corrupt juntas.[21]

In the next few months, Rhee solidified his reign of terror, arresting nearly 90,000 people. Cleverly, he fueled U.S. fear of the North. As the country was turned over to Rhee, allied commanding general Douglas MacArthur in Tokyo was already talking of invading the North and tearing down the "artificial barrier" that divided the country — the one the Americans erected. Meanwhile, the Soviet army was preparing to defuse the super power confrontation risk further by pulling out of North Korea. But the Soviets left behind their own dictator, installing Kim Il Sung, patriarch of today's despot.[22]

Koreans on both sides of the artificial barrier were already the losers in this senseless Cold War confrontation. The worst was yet to come. Propaganda was amped up. *The Globe and Mail* and the *Vancouver Sun* echoed the line about a Soviet conspiracy to take over the world. *Maclean's* was still buying that 50 years later.[23]

Rhee, Sung, and MacArthur had in common the absence of any intention to accept Rusk's line as an international border. Incursions by both sides across the 38th parallel continued into 1949. Kim Il Sung went to Russia and China seeking support for his plan to unify by force. The Soviets eventually acquiesced, with important caveats:

their forces would not participate and they would not bail him out if he failed. He must also get approval from China. The Chinese were surprised, but agreed. This was Kim Il Sung's war, not Moscow's or Bejing's.[24]

There were numerous miscalculations. Sung's argument that he could achieve a speedy victory assumed, like the misguided Americans decades later in Iraq, that his army would be greeted as liberators. China and Russia were unaware that the U.S. was spoiling to confront communism anywhere, even in a civil war in a place where none of the major powers had manifested interest. U.S miscalculations would come later. On June 25, 1950, Sungs' forces invaded and soon swept the peninsula save for an enclave around the port of Pusan. My father was part of the underequipped U.S. force in Japan thrown into its desperate defence. He was one of the few with combat experience.[25]

The Korean War was on.

The UN Charade and the Two Korean Wars

The U.S. needed two types of fig leaves. One was to provide international cover for her war. The other was for what would today be called "coalition partners". Canada helped out on both requirements.

While their troops were clinging to Pusan, the Americans went about constructing the charade that repulsing communist aggression in Korea would be a UN operation. Everyone, including the leadership of Canada, knew this was nonsense. The Americans were going to war in Korea regardless of the UN. President Truman had already made the war decision and given instructions on the matter by the time the UN took it up.

It must have been agonizing for Pearson. He kept up the rhetoric that Canada had to work to keep U.S. actions within the UN framework and not merely have the UN endorse unilateral American decisions, but he knew better. Still, he was generally pleased to see collective security put into practice, even in this imperfect manner. McKay and Swift write that he had hoped for a permanent UN peacekeeping force but instead got U.S. exceptionalism, unilateralism, and chosen-ness.[26]

The Americans got their UN fig leaf. Strangely enough, backing the wrong side in China helped them manage it. Permanent member of the Security Council Russia could veto any military force authorization. But at the time of the invasion, Russia was boycotting the council over China's seat. Communists had defeated China's corrupt former ruler, Chiang Kai Shek, who was holding out on the island of Formosa. The boycott was over western refusal to recognize the real China instead of Chiang's enclave.

With Russia not present to cast a veto, the Security Council approved an American resolution whose wording would become important to what would in effect be the second Korean War. It authorized members to *render such assistance to the Republic of Korea as may be necessary to **repel** the armed attack and **restore** international peace and security to the area* (Emphasis added).[27]

The U.S. began immediately pressuring nations to take part in the charade. Pearson's counterpart, U.S. secretary of state Dean Acheson, beat the bushes all over the non-communist world for support, including ground troops. He and UN Secretary General Trygve Lie persuaded Pearson, or persuaded him to persuade himself, that Canada would be acting to support the UN, not simply the U.S. Pearson and now prime minister St. Laurent acquiesced and Canada committed a brigade to serve one year.[28]

Propaganda continued to play its part. The Canadian press drew on both the developing Cold War fears and the fiction that Canada could enhance its position in the world by military action. The *Globe and Mail*, earlier quite critical of Canada's reluctance to join the Americans, expressed satisfaction at the commitment of ground forces. St. Laurent justified the decision by invoking the appeasement of Germany in the 1930's.[29]

Volunteers flooded recruiting offices. Canadians again signed up for time-honoured reasons: longing for adventure, hope of glory, boredom. Once again, "fighting for freedom" was far, far down the motivational list.[30]

Canada was able to insist on its own unit commanders, but the overall fate of contributors to the UN force would be in the hands of U.S. general Douglas MacArthur, the walking definition of megalomania. MacArthur ultimately wasted Canadian lives and brought the world dangerously close to a nuclear World War III.

MacArthur had retained Japanese emperor Hirohito as a figurehead, protected him from the consequences of his actions in the war, and ruled through him.[31] Whether this was a laudable strategy, it certainly did nothing to diminish MacArthur's self esteem. Pearson described MacArthur as the most imperial figure he had ever seen and wrote of a luncheon with him in Tokyo as involving more ceremony than he experienced at Buckingham Palace or the Vatican.[32]

As a military leader, MacArthur was sometimes a genius, sometimes a fool. In the prior war, he ignored good intelligence about the impending Japanese attack on the Philippines. When defeated, with his full retinue in tow, he abandoned his troops. He was slow to recognize that the North Korean invasion was more than a border incident, and even slower to realize that the South Korean forces could not repel it. However, once he got the picture he was ready to act on his belief that the greatest capitalist power on earth was destined for a decisive war with communism.[33]

MacArthur may well have survived his mistakes politically and achieved his regal stature in part because he lived the maxim "sometimes wrong, never uncertain". All his life MacArthur acted on the assumption that rules made for lesser men did not apply to him.

In Korea, that assumption played out at first in an act of military genius. MacArthur overcame the objections of his staff and many other experts and conducted an amphibious landing at Inchon on the western coast near Seoul on September 15, 1950. It was a complete success. The North Korean army had taken almost the entire country but its supply lines were stretched thin and its commanders were taken by surprise. The invaders quickly retreated north of the 38th parallel. The UN mandate had been fulfilled. The first Korean War was over.[34]

The first Korean War should have been the only one, if there were to be one at all. Had it been, Canada would have had the good fortune to miss it. Determined not repeat the experience of Hong Kong, and having only 20,000 soldiers in total when the U.S. call came, Canada insisted on training and equipping its volunteers this time and was in no hurry to join the fray.[35]

By the terms of the UN resolution, the armed attack had been repelled and international security restored. Even MacArthur, basking in the glow of Inchon, seemed mollified. He pronounced that the troops would be home by, you guessed it, Christmas. But the Canadians then heard from the Americans a now familiar tune: "We don't need you, but we will let you play". MacArthur offered Canada a chance to send a token force to "show the flag". The Canadian brigade was still in training, but Canada accepted and chose the Princess Patricia's Canadian Light Infantry (PPCLI). Berton wrote: *Once more, Canada, in the interests of international co-operation and hungering wistfully for international prestige, was preparing to send an expedition of untrained soldiers into a foreign war zone...*[36]

It soon became apparent that Canadian units, including the two battalions still training, would be required to show much more than a flag. It now appeared that when MacArthur said everything would be over by Christmas he meant that he would have conquered the entire peninsula. Ignoring opposition from his putative civilian superiors in Washington, he attacked north of the parallel and by November his forces reached the Yalu River, Korea's border with China. In the process, U.S. planes violated Chinese air space.[37] MacArthur contemptuously referred to any talk of leaving half the peninsula to the communists as 1938-style appeasement.[38] Mercifully, the PPCLI was still en route when disaster struck.

For months, MacArthur had ignored China's warnings that she would stand neither for an American-led army on her border nor a

Korea unified under the West's preferred dictator rather than theirs. The Chinese had 130,000 troops at the ready, some south of the Yalu. MacArthur's commanders knew this but ignored it.[39]

A cheeky Canadian warned the great man to his face that the Chinese were not bluffing. Captain Jeffry Brock was commander of the Canadian naval force at the Inchon landing. At a luncheon, Brock first suggested that perhaps UN forces, already starting to move north, should settle on the 38th parallel since the invaders had been driven from South Korea. When MacArthur told him not to worry because there was no chance of the Chinese intervening, Brock persisted. He said that he had personally observed Chinese forces assembling. MacArthur told him not worry, that he had them "in the palm of his hand".[40]

The Chinese attacked, and mauled the U.S. 1st Cavalry Division.[41] Their message sent, they broke off the attack. Three weeks later, MacArthur, unfazed, launched what he thought would be his final offensive. Instead, the Chinese army this time routed the entire U.S. 8th Army, sending it into headlong retreat, abandoning weapons, equipment, and wounded. The rout finally halted at the Hahn River, south of Seoul.[42]

The part of the rogue general's delusion of an apocalyptic struggle with communism that most endangered the world was his plan to employ atomic weapons. Worse, the entire military establishment, the American public, and many in the U.S. government approved. MacArthur prepared a list of targets for an invasion of China that would require 26 atomic bombs. At this moment, those who controlled Canada's future were in no mood to hear Pearson's plea to the UN that this was folly and negotiations for an honourable peace should begin.[43]

It was not restraint or sanity that took the world back from the brink. More likely, it was a tragic but fortunate change in U.S. leadership on the ground. The 8th Army commander, general Walton Walker, was accidentally killed. His replacement, Matthew

Ridgeway, managed to halt the U.S. retreat.[44] The defeats had ended American hopes of unifying the peninsula under their dictator. Had the Chinese advance continued, would they and their Korean supporters have been allowed to unify it under theirs, or would the U.S. have resorted to the ultimate weapon? Hastings, who remember, still thought the war was worthwhile, wrote: *The men who reversed the fortunes of the UN on the battlefield in Korea in the first weeks of 1951 may also have saved the world from the nightmare of a new Hiroshima in Asia.*[45]

In April 1951, Truman had had enough of MacArthur's contempt for civilian authority and dismissed him. It was the general's arrogance, not his nuclear plans that cost him his job. MacArthur's hubris meant that Truman could not rely on him to escalate the war gradually according to the government's schedule. Even after his dismissal, MacArthur's nuclear madness exhibited remarkable staying power with audiences.[46]

The blunder that brought on the Chinese intervention meant that the PPCLI, and later the two remaining battalions still training when the Chinese struck, would fight in a war that resembled the worst of the Great War. The conflict would dissolve into static warfare; two years of forays back and forth, taking and retaking nameless hills. Two years also of a reprise of the Great War's useless deadly patrols just to keep the troops on their toes.[47]

Upon arrival in Korea, the PPCLI commander found that the unit was now to be part of the effort to staunch an embarrassing retreat. He also found that, years after all that was supposed to have given Canada an independent place on the world stage, the matter of who was in charge remained unsettled. Canadians were to fight under their own battalion commander, but as part of a British Commonwealth Division that was in turn directed by the Americans.

Though the Americans, like the British before Dieppe, seemed not to have fully processed the news about Canadian independence, this time someone successfully stood up for it. An American 8th Army officer told PPCLI commander James Stone that not only would Stone's troops not be doing the quasi-ceremonial occupation duty they had expected, they would be thrown into the line in three days. Stone objected. Stone went directly to general Walker and produced an order from his superiors barring the unit from combat until he was satisfied that his troops were sufficiently trained. The PPCLI was far from sufficiently trained. Worse, the chaotic recruiting process had produced many in its ranks who were mentally or physically unfit. Walker reluctantly acquiesced. Stone put the unit through a rigorous training program, weeding out the unfit in the process, and saving lives that the new patron would casually have spent.[48]

The PPCLI played an important role in blunting the Chinese offensive while surrounded and cut off from other units.[49]

By the spring of 1951, the Chinese had been stopped and the war soon deteriorated, developing more characteristics of the Great War---rats, lice and stalemate. Negotiations for an armistice began in June. The armistice was not signed until July 1953. In the interim, the two sides did not have the sense to stop fighting. More people died while the combatants sought to gain a bit of territory here or there, taking and losing the same hills as the talks dragged on.[50]

A far greater number of soldiers, including Canadians, were killed during armistice talks than died during the active campaigns of the war. Perhaps the folly of Canada's participation in this war is not as much appreciated because the death toll was not astronomical. Combat deaths numbered 312 of the 516 fatalities. The remaining 204 died of disease.

The 3d Battalion, Royal Canadian Regiment (RCR) fought one of the bloodiest battles for those nameless hills only two months before the armistice was signed. Chief Warrant Officer Kenneth Himes was one of the survivors of the Battle of Hill 187. His friend Douglas Newell was one of 27 killed in action. Ken's widow Beverly shared his story. Its tragic details typify the fate of many veterans. The story encompasses much of what we are examining about the effect of war on ordinary soldiers and about public and government indifference.

The beginning is by now familiar. In 1950, Ken told his cousin there was a war on and they should join up. Beverly called it the "kind of bravado men have" and said Ken wanted to experience the glory of war. Ken joined the RCR. En route to Korea, he became fast friends with Newell. On one particularly brutal night in the senseless battle to defend the hill, Newell told Ken that he knew his time was up, that he would not be coming back. A short time later, he was killed. Ken was part of the detail tasked with negotiating a minefield and carrying bodies, including Newell's, off the hill for burial.

Officially, Ken came out unscathed and stayed with the RCR. Beverly knows better. She says that Ken never got over the experience. He was plagued with nightmares and drank heavily. He was awarded an honourable discharge after two suicide attempts in 1961. It does not take an expert to recognize PTSD in Ken's story. Yet he learned of entitlement to medical benefits only by chance. Another veteran happened to notice Ken wearing a jacket of the Korean Veterans Association commemorating the forgotten Battle of Hill 187 and pointed him to the application process for benefits. It says much that Ken learned of his entitlement from a fellow solider, not the Department of Veterans Affairs.

Until his death in January 2015, Ken and Beverly tried hard to get their fellow Canadians to remember Korea as the war that it was and the cost to soldiers. They did not have much success. I am able to include Ken's story only because of a chance encounter with Beverly in the summer of 2015. She was wearing the jacket.[51]

In this seldom remembered war, U.S. losses, and those of the Chinese and Koreans on both sides were staggering. The Americans lost 33,629. Korean and Chinese military deaths totaled well over a million.[52] Civilian deaths, of course, were only estimated. Price puts the total at three million. Berton writes: *We have no idea how many Korean civilians on both sides of the famous Parallel were killed, mutilated, or starved or uprooted and driven from their villages and homes...These were the real victims of an unwanted civil war that went on too long and solved very little.*[53]

Korea: A Primer on Propaganda, Racism, and Human Rights Violations

These factors appear with particular clarity in this war.

Overt racism was pervasive on the ground, and propaganda offered the benignly racist assumption that Koreans were "not ready" to decide their own fate. Integrating the usual racist elements into demonizing the enemy was more challenging. That would require claiming that the baby bayoneters resided on one side of the arbitrary line drawn by the U.S., while the freedom fighters were all on the other side. Ultimately, the pitch became that no matter where they were found, the demons were the communists, communist sympathizers, and fellow travelers. This naturally included the Russians and Chinese, but people were left to identify the "bad Koreans" on their own. For too many in the western forces, it was simpler just to lump all the "gooks" together.

Affirmative propaganda was similarly broad and not dependent upon nationality. Any government, no matter how brutal or corrupt, supporting the "free world" leaders in the global struggle against godless communism was a liberty-loving democracy, or could be easily made into one. Any war to defeat the threat was a titanic struggle of good against evil. The same formula operates today in the "global war on terrorism."

Cold War propaganda in general succeeded spectacularly, but with specific respect to Korea it could not generate the blind determination for compete victory that national leaders adopted in the world wars. The U.S. and Canadian public simply tired of Korea after things started to go less than well. This time, the leaders went along.

Patriotic propaganda failed even more miserably than in prior wars with the soldiers who fought in Korea. One reason was that there was little or no effort to explain to the troops who the enemy was or anything about the land, or the people they were fighting. One Canadian thought he was going to a tropical country. Another thought he was in Korea to fight Chiang Kai-Shek. Chinese soldiers were equally uninformed.[54]

And the reality before the eyes of the western troops belied the propaganda pitch. Obvious was the corruption and brutality of Syngman Rhee and his soldiers and police. The Japanese-trained police extorted people with threats to denounce them as communists. South Korean conscripts starved because their officers sold their food supplies. British troops witnessed, and in one case prevented, mass executions of women and children. The South Korean army shot prisoners, sometimes forcing them to dig their own graves while waiting their turn to die.[55]

Unfortunately, what the UN troops witnessed in Korea helped to bring out the worst in too many of them also. Abuse of civilians by UN soldiers was serious enough to prompt the U.S. 8th Army to issue a directive recounting incidents of abuse and ordering that they cease.[56] Little attempt was made to distinguish among Koreans. Said one Marine: *We probably shot some people who were innocent—but how could you know which side they were on?*[57]

Canadians participated in crimes against civilians. In September 1951 John Steeves of the Royal Canadian Engineers and two fellow soldiers took over the home of Shin Hyun Chan, so they could "party". That was the testimony of the two soldiers who accompanied Steeves. Shin's recollection was that the soldiers said they were looking for women and liquor. Steeves shot up the house and killed Shin's father. When found, Steeves was incoherent, complaining that a Korean had stolen his watch. While drunk earlier he had been muttering that unless he got his wife back, that night somebody was going to die.

Steeves was tried by court-martial, convicted of manslaughter and sentenced to 15 years in prison. Six months later he was freed when the judge advocate general ruled that the conviction was flawed by circumstantial evidence. Trust me as one experienced in both military and civilian criminal law: The testimony of two witnesses who were present at a shooting is not circumstantial evidence. Eyewitnesses may not be believable for a number of reasons, from mistake to bias, but their evidence is not circumstantial.[58]

Steeves and friends were model soldiers compared with Glen Bank, Alan Davis, and Donald Gibson of PPCLI. In April 1951 they invaded a farmhouse, beat and raped the women inside and then blew up the lot of them. They beat senseless a South Korean soldier who tried to intervene.

Bill Boss, a Canadian Press correspondent, followed up rumours of the atrocity. Later responsible reporting by Maclean's revealed that the story he filed and sent to the head office in Tokyo was censored. UN public relations officers attacked Boss as a subversive and tried to get him removed.

Thanks in part to Boss the three were court-martialed. Blank, who threw a grenade into the farmhouse, was convicted of manslaughter and received a life sentence. Gibson and Davis were convicted of attempted rape and sentenced to lesser prison terms. Eleven months later all were released. This was the pattern for 60 convictions of Canadians.

Eventually, a sufficient number of disturbing press reports reached Canada to get the attention of the government. A delegation of religious leaders was sent to Korea. Despite detailed referrals by reporters to specific incidents, the Archbishop of Quebec returned to intone that reports of mistreatment were wrong. The generals chimed in and the combination of God and guns leaders was enough to bury the issue.[59] After all, who wants to hear about such events?

The official response to atrocities by one's own side is predictable: (1) The other side is worse. (2) Perpetrators do not represent the vast majority of soldiers (3) War is hell. Often, Canadian troops did make efforts to mitigate the suffering of civilians. Price comments: *Such acts of benevolence need to be acknowledged. But they should not be counterposed to acts of criminal behavior, as if one offsets the other.*[60]

The manner in which thousands of other Korean civilians were killed again highlights questions arising from the difference between direct and indirect killing. Why does an account of rape and murder in a home produce a different reaction than stories of bombing the same home—or a refugee column? Does it matter that indirect perpetrators like the Bomber Command airmen, are following rules they did not make and cannot see the results?

Does the comparative body county affect the moral calculus? Steeves, Bank and comrades killed only a handful of civilians. The Korean air campaign killed thousands. When the Chinese intervened, hundreds of thousands of refugees streamed south. Jet fighters covering the retreat of the U.S. 7th Cavalry division massacred hundreds of them at a place called No Gun Ri south of Seoul. The bombing was not an aberration. It was part of an air and ground policy and it was not confined to No Gun Ri. More than 50 years later a memo surfaced directing that if refugees appear from the north of the U.S. line, *they will receive warning shots and if they persist in advancing, they will be shot.* "Persist in advancing"? Infantry units were also ordered to fire on refugees.[61]

As the war shifted up and down the peninsula (Seoul changed hands four times), massive columns of refugees were targeted. Pilots were assigned a stretch of road and instructed to shoot at anything that moved. Spotty intelligence about specific targets brought death from the air to civilians and friendly forces alike. Soldiers and civilians died horribly when the U.S. tried out the napalm it would later employ in Vietnam. A British correspondent wrote that the smell of napalmed human beings reminded him of Sunday dinners of roast pork back home. Censors quickly killed that story.[62]

All to what end? The bombing had no significant effect on the battlefield.[63]

Many Canadian troops could not get beyond ignorance and unvarnished racism. Berton went to Korea as a war correspondent in March 1951. He spent time with the PPCLI and sought to understand

and write about the condition and perspective of ordinary soldiers. He found an articulate source in corporal Kerry Dunphy. His platoon was the first Canadian unit to come under attack. Dunphy was originally a supporter of the war. He offered a $5 reward to the first person in his section to kill a Chinese. Dunphy's attitude, and that of virtually everyone else, soon changed.

To Dunphy and his men, all Koreans were "gooks" and the Chinese were "chinks." He spoke of them, and of propaganda, succinctly: *It seems that you've got to take somebody's word for it that the Korean people are 'liberty loving.' I haven't met a gook yet who was.*[64] Berton found that every solider he encountered shared Dunphy's assessment.

Berton saw such epithets as among the least of the harm done, though he well remembered the face of a Korean bus driver in Pusan listening to a soldier rant to his buddy about how he hated "gooks."

Some abuses went well beyond epithets. Troops rousted families from their homes at bayonet point. At the time Berton joined the PPCLI, three men were charged with the rape and murder of a Korean woman. Traveling with the unit, he experienced the medical officer's refusal to aid a young Korean whose feet were being eaten away by gangrene. The officer said he wasn't there to help Koreans.[65]

Official language about the enemy, in addition to concealing the poor performance of the Americans and South Koreans, carried its own racist tinge. Press officials could not acknowledge that they had been outfought. It was always "hordes" of Chinese who launched "human wave" attacks. These terms were used so frequently that one correspondent was prompted to inquire respectfully of the briefing officer: *Will you tell us how many Chinese battalions go to a horde, or vice-versa?*[66]

For Berton, the final reminders came near the end of his visit. Correspondents dined at the Pusan officers club. He invited three fully accredited South Korean newspapermen to dinner there. They were refused entry because they were Korean. They were "gooks." This incident was an example of how convoluted racism had become. Japanese correspondents were welcome.[67] Berton took the correspondents to dinner at a Chinese restaurant. One of them, assuming he was American, said: *You Americans are so stupid! You have made prostitutes of our women and beggars of our children. Surely you are not going to make the mistake of thinking Koreans love you?*[68]

In Seoul, Berton also witnessed the condition of those supposedly being liberated. *Here were thousands of wretched citizens, hungry and in rags, filthy, wounded, impoverished by war or orphaned by execution—a human panorama that would become increasingly familiar as the century moved on.*[69] Many lived in homes similar to that of Tak Sook Kyn, in Pusan. Her husband had disappeared. The infant she had carried down the peninsula was dead of exposure and hunger. She and eight members of her extended family were living in a 7x5x5 foot cardboard hovel made of C-ration cartons.[70]

Rhee, of course, did not abide in such primitive accommodation. After Chinese had looted his house it still boasted inlaid floors, a marble staircase, mosaics on the walls, and rare and expensive blue roof tiles.[71] Rhee may have planned to rebuild with some of the $90 million he billed the UN after the war for rent of land used by the forces that saved his beleaguered regime.[72]

Rhee criticized his benefactors for questioning South Korean outrages, and western diplomats backed him. After a meeting with Rhee, a British diplomat wrote, *The South Koreans--as is perhaps to be expected at their stage of national development—are going through one of the more acute stages of the 'awkward age'.*[73] The British have a way with words.

Censorship helped conceal the reality of Rhee's Korea. Correspondents were forbidden to criticize the war or anyone on the UN side. The few who defied censorship were harassed, barred from Korea, and in one case arrested.[74]

The Conversation Deferred--Again

This war revived questions for yet another conversation that Canada did not have. Just what does "coming of age" mean? This was the first war fought at the behest of a new patron. What was the degree of responsibility, if any at all, for the U.S. air war against civilians? It was not Canadian planes that bombed civilians and Canadian units were not ordered to fire on refugees. Does that absolve Canada? Did Canada's agreement to permit atomic weapons to be sited at Goose Bay, Labrador implicate Canada to any degree in MacArthur's dangerous plans?

Pearson eventually acknowledged that he and Canada gave in and always supported the Americans even when they knew better.[75] At various stages, Pearson sought to inject diplomacy, including a compromise proposal to stave off MacArthur's mad continuation of the war after Inchon. Yet he was an early and consistent supporter of sending Canadian ground forces. Perhaps isolation explains Pearson's inconsistency. The cautious Mackenzie King died at the start of the war, leaving few in government who shared Pearson's reluctance.[76]

Korea was simply by chance the place for a proxy Cold War battle; a war characterized by western arrogance and insensitivity. This is the assessment of *war supporter* historian Max Hastings. He concludes: *If the Americans behaved clumsily in South Korea, their conduct was understandable in the worldwide context of the period.*[77] "Clumsily"? "Understandable"? Hastings' apologia should be seen as evidence that Canadians finally should have had the conversation so long deferred. The new patron continues today to urge Canada to join its proxy wars, raising the same questions.

Hastings contrasted the later success of South Korea with what he saw as the disastrous fall of South Vietnam.[78] Of course, the fall of South Vietnam's equally corrupt and vicious regime later turned out not to be that great a disaster after all.

Canada and the Vietnam War

The U.S learned nothing from Korea and continued to fight imperialistic wars, including Vietnam. Of that war, Berton was relieved that Canada stayed out. Except that Canada did not. If only wars involving Canadians troops purposely sent into combat are counted, Korea might be seen as the last until Afghanistan. But

Vietnam should be counted as an example of Canada's involvement in other people's wars, alerting us also that several of the factors we are examining are still in play.

The common view in Canada is the same as Berton's. That is quite understandable. Vietnam was an absolute mirror of Korea, right down to the artificial division of a country, western support of a corrupt regime, a nationalist movement that developed into a communist state, and the power of Cold War propaganda to obscure those facts. Canada did not send the PPCLI this time, so surely she must have learned? Reluctant participation and desire to minimize casualties must have finally matured into real independence from more powerful sponsors? Not quite.

Canada's moral culpability in Vietnam is equal to that in other conflicts where she sent troops. If many of the earlier wars were mistakes, they were at least open and obvious mistakes. That was not the case in respect of Canada's duplicitous alliance with the U.S. in Vietnam.

Two complementary works tell of this regrettable relationship. Charles P. B. Taylor, a journalist with international experience, tells the story in *Snow Job: Canada, the United States and Vietnam [1954-1973]*.[79] Victor Levant, an academic, also tells the story and documents it more thoroughly in *Quiet Complicity: Canadian Involvement in the Vietnam War*.[80] Price, Engler, Mackay and Swift provide corroborating evidence.

Gwynne Dyer, both journalist and military historian, introduces Levant's work with this assertion: *We ran errands for the Americans; we lied for them; we spied for them—not once or twice but continuously for almost two decades*.[81] Canada engaged in these morally questionable acts primarily in two contexts. First, as a member of international commissions whose mandate was to be unbiased. Second, as arms merchant to the U.S. In both areas, successive governments headed by men who disliked one another, nevertheless consistently misled the public and echoed Cold War propaganda. A Conservative and two Liberals had learned very little from Korea.

The account of Canada's Vietnam involvement makes less exciting reading than stories of heroic battles like Vimy but is in many respects more instructive on Canada's current place in the world and her vision of it.

When the U.S. picked Vietnam as another Cold War battleground, the country had been resisting invaders, principally the Chinese, for centuries. In World War II, the invader was Japan. A force called the Viet Minh fought them. When the Japanese were defeated, Ho Chi Minh, the ignored supplicant of 1919 Paris, declared that the Democratic Republic of Vietnam was independent. France, with prior approval from major western powers, moved back in to recolonize and set up a satellite government in the southern region of the country, headquartered in Saigon. Vietnamese of all stripes took to the streets to condemn French colonialism and call for independence from Japan and France.[82]

The Viet Minh then fought the French, with no help from the Soviet Union or China. When Moscow rebuffed Ho, he offered concessions to U.S. businesses in return for recognition. The American rejection was couched in the Cold War rhetoric and a dollop of the benevolent racism we have seen in Korea. Not only were the Vietnamese not ready, they were not a loyal or industrious people and so were susceptible to Soviet manipulation. Even while admitting that the majority of Vietnamese supported the Viet Minh, the Americans refused to ask the French to negotiate.[83]

Canada played its usual role, again exemplified by Pearson's angst. He was content with U.S. dominance in Asia, but worried that developing nations would associate racism and imperialism and eliminate western influence in the non-aligned movement. Typically, Canada did not recognize emperor Bao Dai, a French puppet, but sent war materiel to the French.[84]

The war between the Viet Minh and French ended in 1954 with the complete defeat of the French at Dien Bien Phu. Prime minister St. Laurent saluted the heroic defenders.[85] The defenders were indeed heroic, though their cause was not.[86] In an earlier speech St. Laurent had argued that the role of Canadian universities was to educate people in the traditions that were the glory of *Christian* civilization that the *western* world had adapted from Greek and Hebrew civilization. Price summarized the message: *Hence the masses of Asia required benevolent assistance even if it killed them.*[87]

Next came the first phase of Canada's less than honourable involvement in Vietnam.

In 1954, a multi-national conference that included Canada convened to fashion a way for defeated France to withdraw gracefully from Vietnam.[88] The result was the Geneva Accords. The "accords" did not constitute a treaty. Neither the western-backed South Vietnamese faction nor the U.S. signed, but for the next decade the nations involved in Vietnam sometimes treated them as if they mattered. France did sign because the document provided badly needed cover for her withdrawal. Although the French satellite regime in South Vietnam did not sign, it was clearly the successor in interest to colonial France and bore the obligation to comply.[89]

The accords drew another partition line, this time, dividing North and South Vietnam at the 17th Parallel. As in Korea, the division was to be temporary until an election unified the country. The cease-fire and election were to be supervised by an international commission whose mandate was to act in an impartial manner, with the Cold War adversaries equally represented. Poland, under Soviet domination, filled one spot, non-aligned India another. At the behest of the U.S., Canada agreed to be the third member of the body, called the International Control Commission (ICC).[90]

The first major development was that the West and its regime again determined that they would lose the election. This time they refused to let it happen.[91] The U.S. backed a brutal Catholic nationalist, Ngo Din Diem. Together they made no secret of the fact that they would not permit unification of Vietnam by an election the Viet Minh could win. Instead, in a remarkable exercise in democracy Diem conducted a referendum where he garnered 650,000 votes from 405,000 registered voters. In 1955, he declared the Republic of South

Vietnam.[92] Ultimately, Diem lost both the geopolitical game and his life to a coup in which the U.S. knowingly acquiesced.

The war resumed, and although the accord barred introduction of military assets into the country, the U.S. immediately began to violate it in support of the Saigon government. All of this presented an early test for Canada. She failed.[93]

In the course of membership on the ICC, Canada engaged in all of the delicts that Dyer alleged. Canada surpassed Poland in bias. Using the access to North Vietnam provided by ICC membership, her representatives not only carried messages, including threats, for the Americans, they spied for them.[94] Canadian delegates assisted the U.S. Central Intelligence Agency (CIA) in determining bombing locations over Hanoi and Haiphong. They used their position on the commission to deny, minimize, or obscure every major South Vietnamese and U.S. violation of the Geneva Accords.[95]

This time, the UN was unavailable as cover. It was important, however, for the Americans not to appear to be making war in violation of the UN Charter. The Canadian ICC delegation helped with a bogus interpretation of the UN charter article on collective self-defence.[96] Canada supported a NATO statement that the French war in Vietnam was "in fullest harmony with the ideals of the Atlantic community".[97]

All this was more than an unfortunate diplomatic matter or a counter to Polish partiality.

Pearson instructed the Canadian appointee to the ICC to promote the anti-communist alliance while trying not to offend India.[98] Canadian ICC member Bruce Williams was even clearer: *Canada's main concern in Vietnam is not the fulfillment of the Geneva accords per se, but the maintenance of peace in southeast Asia as a means of thwarting communist ascendancy in the area.*[99]

Canada's conduct on the ICC added significantly to the death and destruction being wreaked upon civilians, including bombing and chemical warfare. The conduct was further aggravated by the fact that leaders lied about it and that it was not U.S. coercion or pressure that demanded it.[100]

Canadian ICC representatives also reported back to the U.S. on the state of the North Vietnamese economy and political situation. Worse, when the U.S. sought to bomb North Vietnam into submission Canadians reported military information, including troop movements. The Canadian government never told the truth about these activities.[101]

The U.S. use of napalm for the first time in bombings the Canadians facilitated was only part of the damage she inflicted on civilians, and even her own soldiers. In an earlier effort in 1962 to deny food supplies and concealment to the South Vietnamese insurgents, known as Viet Cong, the U.S. used its air power to spread chemical defoliants over the countryside. This chemical warfare included Agent Orange, a substance so toxic it ruined the health of many U.S. troops.

Gordon Cox, Canadian ICC commissioner at the time, assisted the American Agent Orange campaign. When Hanoi complained, he said that neither the herbicides dropped nor the aircraft used to spread them constituted war material introduced in violation of the Geneva Accords. Cox said the chemicals were the same stuff he used in his garden at home, with no worry about the safety of his children or pets.[102] This diplomatic complicity was not the limit of Canadian involvement in defoliation. The Americans tested chemical warfare agents in New Brunswick and U.S. bombers practiced over North Battleford, Saskatchewan, before going on to devastate North Vietnam.[103]

Vietnam was also good for Canadian war profiteers. Successive government leaders claimed adherence to long-standing policy that Canada would not ship arms to "sensitive areas." They knew this was false. Canadian firms supplied the U.S. war machine with a long list of war materials, including napalm and chemical defoliants, even the green berets worn by the celebrated U.S. Special Forces.[104]

The ICC eventually died a quiet death and was replaced by something called the International Commission of Control and Supervision. (ICCS) This body was the product of peace negotiations conducted in Paris between 1968 and 1973. The purpose this time was to supervise the graceful withdrawal of the defeated Americans. The Americans again assumed correctly that Canada would agree to serve. She did, but more reluctantly this time and with a view toward getting out when the inevitable failure came. Canada served even though the Americans ignored her 73 preconditions. The Trudeau government, however, only agreed to a 60-day term and only extended it once for 90 days. The conduct of Canada's delegates was less egregious than that of their ICC predecessors but the bias followed the same general pattern.[105] The U.S. continued its efforts to prop up the Saigon regime until the chaotic end came in May 1975.

Ironically, Canada's acquiescence to membership on the ICC may well have been the very thing that saved her from being badgered into sending troops. The American secretary of state implied as much. A Canadian official called the ICC Canada's "chastity belt".[106]

Why after Korea did Canada again join someone else's virtually identical war? Why did the governments of John Diefenbaker, Lester Pearson and Pierre Trudeau support a war that killed 1,724,562 people, created 13 million refugees, and cost hundreds of billions of dollars?[107]

Taylor concluded that Canadians' post-World War II self-image as good guys produced a policy myth that Canada could be a helpful fixer in international affairs and influence the U.S. with diplomacy. His criticism is of Canada's continued complicity when she should have known that diplomacy was ineffective in the face of the Americans image of themselves as exceptional. From the myth came a "snow job" Canada did on herself.[108]

Levant places much more responsibility on economic factors. He provides data in support of the position that Canada's actions were prompted by a desire to remain fully integrated into an international market system ruled by an internal elite that remained subordinate to U.S. financiers and oligarchs. Taylor's account is not inconsistent with this view. He notes that Canadian backers of the arms sales that contributed to the destruction of Vietnam justified them as vital to economic prosperity and job creation.[109] These answers suggest the continuing influence of the marriage of capitalism and imperialism. Worldwide business sometimes requires the service of military action, and vice-versa.

Another answer is that the most important factor driving this regrettable chapter in Canadian history was the continuing power of the propaganda. Three otherwise politically diverse prime ministers bought the notion that the outcome of civil strife in Vietnam was vital to a struggle against a global communist conspiracy.

At the time of the French defeat at Dien Bien Phu that should have marked the end of colonialism in the region, U.S. president Dwight Eisenhower laid out the "domino" theory. If the communists won Vietnam, that domino would fall over and in turn knock over Burma, which would knock over Thailand, and so on. Ike had this remarkable string of dominos going all the way through Japan to Australia and New Zealand. He said the consequences to the "free world" from the loss of Vietnam were incalculable.[110]

John Diefenbaker, a Canadian nationalist who was highly critical of the U.S., nevertheless spoke also in support of the dominos.[111] His successor Lester Pearson, firm supporter of the United Nations, was no different. In 1965 he gave a speech in the U.S. that supported the overall American line entirely, save in one small respect. He suggested that it might help the prospects of a negotiated settlement if the U.S. suspended its ongoing bombing campaign. He met shortly afterward with Lyndon Johnson and was chastised for the remark.[112]

Finally, there was Pearson's successor in 1968, Pierre Trudeau. This icon of Canadian nationalism did not give overt "domino" speeches and he ended Canada's ICCS membership. But he answered the U.S. call to serve on the commission and his representative conducted himself almost as poorly as had his predecessors.[113] And it should be noted that Trudeau's assistance to the Americans came at a time when they had lost their taste for the war. Like the French earlier, they only wanted help covering their retreat. Canadian refusal would have had few if any consequences.

Whatever the reasons, the fact that later history reveals most Cold War propaganda as false or grossly exaggerated is neither a complete explanation nor excuse for Canada's Vietnam complicity. Perhaps the best excuse is that the whole western world was buying it. A rational post-Korea evaluation in Canada, however, might have kept her out altogether.

The Cold War: The Most Dangerous Game

The Cold War should not be forgotten. It is a prime exhibit in the case for staying out of other people's wars. But since it ended in 1989 (U.S. Republicans have decided that Ronald Reagan won it single-handedly) Korea has been relegated to a footnote. Canada's role in it occupies barely more than a page of the 613-page *Canada, A People's History*.[114] Canada's Vietnam role, other than as a haven for U.S. war resisters, is a secret even better kept.

What should be remembered about the Cold War that brought us Korea and Vietnam is that choosing up sides and employing proxies in an ideological struggle is a very dangerous game. That lesson is just as important in the 21st century, as the only current superpower seeks to move nations like chess pieces in the Middle East, while Russia begins to to reassert herself there and in Europe. In the Cold War period, that game was very nearly fatal to millions of people who were well outside the proxy warfare battlegrounds. That danger is re-emerging.

We have seen that MacArthur came close in Korea to provoking an atomic weapons exchange that would have dwarfed the scale of destruction at Hiroshima and Nagasaki. In 1952, even more horrifying weapons came on the scene with the development of hydrogen bombs. Yet the Cold War continued. Leaders around the world continued their struggle with little realistic appreciation of the danger. Families constructed fallout shelters. Schools conducted "duck and cover" drills. Such measures in retrospect seem comical—until one considers the level of ignorance they reveal. "Better Dead Than Red" was a popular slogan during the period. Those who chanted it were doubtless unaware how close they came to getting their wish in October 1962.

The U.S./ Soviet Union standoff known as the Cuban Missile Crisis would in all probability have brought on World War III and the death of tens of millions, had it not been for the action of one Russian naval officer, Vasili Arkhipov. It is quite a story.

Cubans had overthrown Fulgencio Batista, an oppressive dictator who had ruled for 25 years after coming to power in a U.S.-backed coup. The new Cuban government, rebuffed by the U.S., turned to the Soviet Union and was welcomed into the Cold War. Both the U.S. and Russia had accumulated massive nuclear arsenals. The Soviets, lacking an intercontinental nuclear component, sought to put missiles in Cuba. A tense standoff occurred that was resolved when the Soviets withdrew their missiles and the Americans withdrew some from Turkey.

At the height of the tension, there was a Russian submarine off Cuba, armed with a 10-kiloton nuclear torpedo, a weapon only slightly less powerful than the bomb that wiped out Hiroshima. American ships bombarded it with depth charges. The U.S. later said that this was only to be a warning for the sub to surface. If so, the submarine commander did not get that message. He assumed that global war had broken out and ordered the torpedo prepared for firing, locked on a U.S. aircraft carrier. Had the torpedo been fired, it would have triggered the U.S. Single Integrated Operation Plan to launch 5500 nuclear weapons against targets around the globe.

Fortunately for the world, the Russian protocol required approval by all three senior officers aboard. Two assented. Second-in-command Arkhipov refused, perhaps influenced by the fact that he had been exposed to severe radiation in an earlier accident and thereby had an inkling of the dreadful consequences that might ensue. Whatever his motivation, Arkhipov probably saved millions of lives.[115]

The dangerous game continued throughout the Cold War. In 1983, a satellite signaled that the U.S. had launched missiles against Russian cities. Fortunately for the world, a soviet officer with authority to retaliate decided there was a 50/50 chance the signal was a computer error. For not starting World War III, Stanislav Petrov was later honoured by a body irrelevant to Cold War atomic decisions---the United Nations.[116]

Pearson, not Diefenbaker was on the wrong side of this issue. In secret negotiations in 1963, he agreed to bring U.S. nuclear warheads to Canada.

The risk continues. Nuclear powers today refuse to let go of their missiles. A major obstructionist is the U.S. In the West, the matter is ignored except when North Korea makes threats, or there is a development in the struggle to deprive Iran of nuclear weapons while justifying them for Israel.

Where then, had all this brought Canada on the world stage? Taylor concludes that by the mid 1970's Canadian governments had *so thoroughly entwined Canadian economic, military, and diplomatic interests with those of Washington that Ottawa virtually lost the habit—if not the possibility—of independent action.*[117] Perhaps not. Taylor's view that the image Canadians had of themselves as capable of a role in quiet diplomacy and international fixing may have failed during the Cold War but could it produce a new, independent role for Canada— as peacekeepers? Let us see.

Chapter VI

PEACEKEEPING---BUILDING ON A BETTER VISION

For 50 years—Korea to Afghanistan---Canada did not *directly* participate in someone else's war, though Canadians conducted armed operations and suffered casualties. During this period, the Cold War difficulties and ambiguities that marked Canada's unfortunate role in the Vietnam War continued. They have been magnified as the nature of warfare has changed. The most significant change is that wars are now seldom conducted by one nation against another. This and other developments have enhanced the importance of Canada's choices in matters of war and peace.

Internal tension over involvement in other people's wars has always undermined our sense of community, a significant loss to a diverse nation only recently cobbled together. In policy and resource terms, loss of personal connection with one another inevitably draws us further into the intrigues of our current patron. The choice of a better national vision on which to build policy is an important one and this is the time to make it.

The image of Canada as a warrior nation has a cadre of military historians to push it. One of the most enthusiastic supporters of Canadian militarism is Sean M. Maloney, who teaches at the Royal Military College of Canada. In *Canada and UN Peacekeeping, Cold War by Other Means 1945-1970,*[1] he sets out to denigrate early United Nations and Canadian peacekeeping missions and credits positive developments in the Cold War years to the North Atlantic Treaty Organization (NATO.

Maloney's thesis is that Canadian peacekeeping operations in the period were really conducted to project power in support of Canada's economic, military, and security interests. He sees peacekeeping as a dangerous impediment to future participation in military ventures. He fears that it *constrains us from acting in coalitions which enhance Canadian prestige and provide economic benefits.*[2]

Maloney's book was published just prior to the U.S. effort to assemble a coalition for its disastrous invasion of Iraq in 2003. Neither that campaign, nor any post-Cold War developments have affected his unwavering support for military action. His optimism continued even for the Canadian adventure in Afghanistan we examine in the next chapter.[3]

Maloney challenges what he terms "the great Canadian peacekeeping myth" by defining it in the form of a series of exaggerated claims and straw men he spends the remainder of the book knocking down. For example, the myth is said to include the notion that we are morally superior to others, especially the Americans; that we are not racist or xenophobic; that we have no serious economic ambitions outside North America. The implications of this myth are said to include the belief that the UN is a purely idealistic entity and Canada's military activity should be conducted only within its framework; that Canada's primary military activity since 1945 has been disarmament, which is and always has been the centrepiece of Canadian foreign policy. Such an overblown assessment is much easier to debunk than a more realistic description of who Canadians think they are. Maloney also denies the reluctant participation factor. In Maloney's view, *all* of Canada's wars have really been "power projection", part of a rich 100-year tradition of "forward security".[4]

Maloney admits that in the UN arena Canada was a biased Cold War champion for the West. The Vietnam story certainly confirms that. Interestingly, he concludes that in order to be effective in that role, Canadian governments had to conceal it from the public. This, unfortunately in his view, *produced a situation whereby Canadian cultural imperatives seized on UN peacekeeping as a prime component of a fragile but burgeoning Canadian identity...*[5] In sum, Canada had to conceal the details of her Cold War role from her people. The concealment allowed the "good guys" self-image and the implication that we were and should be peacekeepers to grow. Maloney contends that in reality peacekeeping operations were Cold War actions in support of NATO. For him there is a need to tell the truth and bury the myth now because it hinders an assessment of our proper role.[6]

Maloney's concern about the dangers of the competing vision is straightforward: *This view appeals to Canadians with an idealistic, altruistic view of man and his affairs, with a false moral superiority over those who must be prepared to deter and fight on behalf of Canada's interests in the real world.*[7] This statement raises interesting questions. How important to Maloney's view is the conclusion that idealists have a false sense of moral superiority over members of the military? Taylor and most other peacemakers also warn against the assumption of such moral superiority. What exactly are Canada's "interests" in the real world that are important enough to justify war? Is the notion of war as a last, or at least near last resort now subordinate to fighting for those interests? What are the implications for Canada and the world of abandoning idealism and altruism?

Maloney's contempt for the peacemaking vision is the official version being transmitted to members of the country's military, and to the public. But policies that flow from replacing what has been called the Coming of Age Myth carry the potential for a better role for Canada on the world stage, and this is a moment in history when there is a realistic opportunity to play that role. To contrast Maloney's characterization on his own terms, call it the Agent of Peace Myth. Peacekeeping is a part of what flows from this myth, part of a better vision upon which to build policy.

Peacekeeping is Much More Complex Than War Making

If the case is to be made that Canada's better role is as peacekeeper and peacemaker, it is necessary to deal with the reality that peacekeeping is more complex than war making. Making war, on any scale, is a relatively simple matter. Governments are able if necessary to convert whole economies to production of war materiel. Propaganda can usually produce a sufficient number of combatants. Permanent institutions exist to train them to kill. In all these areas, the only requirement is political will.

Political will is also required to adopt a different way of dealing with threats and conflicts. With respect to international peacekeeping operations, however, the process is significantly more complex. It produces much less exciting images than gallant men going "over the top". Challenges to peacekeeping operations that add to the complexity are outlined in a most comprehensive work on the subject, Alex Bellamy and Paul Williams' *Understanding Peacekeeping*.[8] Here are some of them:

- The structure of the United Nations. The UN is not the only body involved in peacekeeping, but it is the organization most of the world identifies as the principal actor. Its capacity for modern peacekeeping is weakened by the fact that it came into being when warfare was primarily a nation versus nation matter.

  UN mechanisms for preserving international peace are not geared toward the new face of warfare. In particular, the UN Charter is ambiguous on a subject that is critical to peacekeeping, as well as to an important factor we are examining—human rights violations and civilian deaths. The Preamble and Article 1(3) identify support for human rights as a purpose of the body's very existence, but Articles 2(4) and 2(7) reaffirm the principle that sovereign nations have full authority over their internal affairs. There is also the unfortunate World War II legacy of the Security Council. There is no reason that the United States, Russia, China, France, and Great Britain should have the power to frustrate UN action. The General Assembly reflects more accurately the wishes of most of the world's people. The composition of the permanent membership of the Security Council is an outdated anomaly, but there is little to be done about it at present. The UN has, however, sought to become more effective in regional peacekeeping despite this obstacle.[9]

• Soldiers are not necessarily the best peacekeepers. It is understandable that nations would turn first to soldiers in the transition from war to dealing with ongoing or potential conflicts through peacekeeping. In violent situations we traditionally rely on soldiers. But soldiers traditionally have not been recruited or trained with an eye toward some of the skills necessary to peacekeeping. As general Rick Hillier candidly stated, the Canadian military is not a public service agency. Its job is to kill people.[10] Hillier might well agree with Bellamy and Williams that: *unlike war fighting, peace-building often requires impartiality, sensitivity, and empathy, attributes that have been discouraged by military training.*[11] Unfortunately, soldiers as peacekeepers have been responsible for human rights violations, including abuses of women, which have severely set back support for peacekeeping operations. Yet we will also see that soldiers have often demonstrated not only compassion but also a real facility for mediation and defusing volatile situations. And they have often done so *ad hoc,* in the absence of instructions on how to handle such situations, or specific training. And importantly, we examine in the final chapter proposals from advocates of a stronger military who, while fiercely critical of government and the military hierarchy, are deeply committed to peacekeeping.

• With all these limitations, there remains a great potential role for the military in peacekeeping operations. Canadian peacekeepers in particular have done well, considering the many mission obstacles they have so far faced and the lack of recognition for those who have risked and suffered every bit as much as soldiers in conventional wars. During the Cold

War, Canada sent more troops on peacekeeping operations than any other country and suffered the highest number of fatalities.[12]

Finding the right nation to staff a mission. The idea of a permanent UN peacekeeping force has been around for a long time but has never gained traction. Instead, traditional UN peacekeeping has involved recruiting and authorizing action by member states. That mode of operation has been made more difficult by the evolution of imperialism. Imperialist countries began in earnest around 1960 to grant or cede independence to their colonies, possessions, and mandates. This process included retention of varying degrees of control over the subject areas, as well as varying degrees of assistance to them in preparation for nationhood. In all instances, the former masters sought to ensure that the policies of the newly liberated nations not stray too far from their own. This effort persisted through the Cold War and continues today as a driver of the "Global War on Terror".

Former possession have been understandably resistant, and wary of agreeing to peacekeeping forces from former colonial powers. The rub is that these powers have the greatest capacity to fund peacekeeping, as well as the best trained and equipped forces. A further complication is the fact that from 1919 on, colonial powers drew borders based much more on what they saw as advantageous political and economic factors than any regard for the mix of tribes they were throwing together. The result has been a bloody process of sorting out racial, ethnic, and religious mismatches that continues today and increases the need for effective peacekeepers. This situation is part of the reason that for a time Canadian peacekeepers were in demand.

Colonial powers have also undertaken peacekeeping activities unilaterally, with mixed results. Sometimes interventions have been for the purpose of protecting their economic and political influence, and sometimes for nobler motives.[13] Canada was once perceived as free of these mixed motives. That is no longer true.

- The missions themselves are varied and complex. Maloney correctly notes the erroneous tendency of the public to lump all UN activities involving blue helmets together as "peacekeeping". He identifies four distinct activities: conventional military operations; military formations interposed between parties to facilitate political negotiations; military observers deployed to observe and monitor compliance with international agreements such as ceasefires; and provision of humanitarian and disaster relief. Bellamy and Williams find no less than seven types of peacekeeping missions, including peace enforcement, and several aspects of the tricky business of what is currently short-handed as "nation-building". Further, the types of operations are not mutually exclusive and may shift within a particular mission.[14]
- Protecting the lives of peacekeepers and civilians in war zones challenges traditional notions of state sovereignty.

In terms of organization, personnel, training, and execution, the assault on Vimy Ridge was a simple matter compared with almost any peacekeeping mission.

Canada's Choices: <u>Comparative</u> is the operative word

Fairness requires that the determination of whether to support policies and actions that flow from an Agent of Peace Myth or the prevailing narrative must be the product of a *comparative* assessment, not an absolute or hypothetical one. Remembering this is essential when considering some fundamental questions. (1) Is the world *comparatively* better off now that the number, scale, and intensity of wars has diminished and the nature of warfare has changed than it was when wars were global and frequent? (2) If so, has peacekeeping played a positive part in that development? (3) Specifically, has peacekeeping, *when compared with wars and invasions,* been successful in furthering goals that Canadians would embrace?

In making this comparative assessment it is not unreasonable to assume that Canadians would be concerned with both military and civilian deaths as well as human rights abuses. If so, it should be noted that the centennial of the Great War finds the world comparatively better without widespread war and perhaps moving haltingly in the right direction. That is a revelation to many people, especially in light of the ongoing panic over a faction sometimes called the Islamic State in Syria (ISIS). News outlets draw many more readers and viewers with reports on death and violence than, say, by reporting that in the last 25 years two billion people gained access to clean drinking water and child mortality rates have fallen across the globe. As one expert put it: *Reporters are where the shells are exploding. Only when you look at the dogs that don't bark do you realize how much better off we are now than we used to be.*[15]

The wars we have examined so far killed about 100 million people. How much security has that loss of life provided? In contrast, the last decade has seen fewer war deaths than any decade in the previous century. Those who accept the inevitability of war often couch the question as Maloney did, as one of hard-nosed reality versus utopian dreaming. That is a false choice. The real one is whether to go for another 100 million or more deaths this century, or explore a new approach that appears to have some promise.

The number of lives saved is another example of a dog that does not bark. Since the end of state-to-state wars, properly organized, funded and executed peacekeeping missions and other UN initiatives have saved lives. Peacekeeping has helped armed conflicts end in negotiated settlements. There is a 77 to 85 percent reduction in the likelihood of a war resuming where peacekeepers are deployed, compared with areas where they are not. Even when peacekeeping missions are unable to prevent genocide and mass murder, they have been able to mitigate the slaughter and preserve lives.[16]

Canada and the challenge of assuming a different role

To defend against a charge of utopian altruism, a realistic comparison must also take note of the dark side. The peoples of the world are not at this point ready to walk hand in hand into the sunlight of peace. The major danger from the change in the nature of warfare is that civilians are even more vulnerable. The new wars target civilian populations and employ fear and coercion rather than any attempt to win hearts and minds. They not only kill civilians, they displace and starve them. A decentralized but global war economy permits the combatants to self-finance, removing that power from governments. It also creates an incentive for them to keep the wars going.

Part of that global war economy is the sale of the weapons. In modern war profiteering, the principal actors are a familiar group. Add Germany, delete Great Britain, and you find that the remainder of the leading arms merchants are the permanent members of the UN Security Council—the U.S., Russia, France, and China. Prying these profiteers from their money will not be easy. As the director of Project Ploughshares in Canada put it: *Do we really think that states engaged in a lucrative industry worth billions of dollars and inextricably linked to their own self-perceived economic and security interest (as perverse as those perceptions might frequently be) would awake one morning and sign a treaty that directly challenged all that?*[17]

The referenced treaty is the UN Arms Trade Treaty, passed by the General Assembly in 2013 on a vote of 156-3, with 22 abstentions. The negative votes were Iran, North Korea, and Syria. The treaty is but one example of how good is struggling to emerge from bad in the new world of warfare. The treaty is an imperfect document and bringing it into force will not be easy. Whether Canada will sign on remains to be seen.[18]

The U.S. signed but how sincere the Americans are remains a question. In the Middle East, they are still thrashing about trying to figure out which warring group in addition to Israel to weaponize. That is the bad news. But the existence of the treaty and its progress to date is one piece of evidence that the increased vulnerability of civilians in the new wars may also have the effect of focusing attention on protecting them. Denying weapons to all combatants, difficult as it may be, is a far more achievable goal in these conflicts than in conventional wars. The Arms Trade Treaty will not solve the problem, but it will be an aid to more responsible nations and shed some accusatory light on those whose reality differs from their rhetoric.

Unfortunately, there are indications that Canada will not choose to be one of those more responsible nations. We have recently vaulted into second place among those who profit from arms sales to the Middle East, and sixth place globally. On this shameful file, it appears the new Liberal government will be no help. What advanced Canada on the list was a massive $15 billion sale to notorious human rights violator, Saudi Arabia. The government intentionally passed up the opportunity ill the sale approved by its predecessor.[19]

The Arms Trade Treaty is but one of several international agreements that have saved lives in the altered climate of violence. The list also includes the Anti-Personnel Mine Ban Convention and Chemical Weapons Conventions of 1997, the latter having already resulted in significant reduction of chemical weapons stockpiles.[20] All of these agreements are internally flawed and imperfectly executed, but peacekeeping missions are far more likely to enhance their effectiveness than jet fighter missions.

The lesson for Canada arising from these halting steps gets even more pointed when we consider the most significant development to arise from a new focus on the factor of human rights violations and civilian deaths. That is the emergence of the doctrine of Responsibility to Protect (RTP). A great deal of credit for its introduction is due former Canadian foreign minister, Lloyd Axworthy.[21] The fate of this concept may be even more important to civilians than weapons control. Definitions of fundamental human rights abound, but there is agreement that they include at a minimum the right not to be murdered, starved, raped, or tortured. Sophisticated weapons are not required in order to violate these rights on a massive scale. A machete will do as well as a bomb. The new face of conflict includes human rights violations by one tribe seeking dominance over another, with governments sometimes turning a blind eye and sometimes joining in. This situation has created a severe challenge for those engaged in the new enterprise of peacemaking. It is a challenge that peacemakers, including Canadians, have sometimes failed to meet, but from which they are learning.

What happens in coming years to RTP is so important to civilians, and to Canada's choice of a future role in world affairs, that we will examine it a bit further after reviewing some of the Canadian experience in peacekeeping. The doctrine raises challenges that have had an effect on peacekeeping to date however, so it is useful to introduce it here.

The issue can be framed either as a question of defining the circumstances in which the international community may legitimately intervene to protect civilians, or as the scope of a nation's obligation to protect citizens from the worst human rights violations as a condition of retaining complete sovereignty. The latter is the language of the RTP doctrine, but the practical issues are the same.

In Europe, the notion of state sovereignty goes at least back to settlement of the Thirty Years War in 1648. That is why it is called the Westphalian order in academic circles. European wars, of course, have routinely violated sovereignty over the years, but the concept survived and evolved, always including the tenet that outsiders had no right to intervene in the internal affairs of a nation state. As decolonization took hold after World War II, the Westphalian order became a global norm. It is singularly unsurprising that former colonies sought all the prerogatives of sovereignty.[22]

Since the end of the Cold War, the disastrous consequences that the new intrastate conflicts visit on civilians have produced a challenge to Westphalian norms of sovereignty. In these conflicts, ethnic and religious differences are more important than political ones. Civilians are targeted. They are driven from their homes and murdered. National governments implode. Consequently, as Canadian minister of external affairs Barbara McDougall once put it: *The concept of sovereignty must respect higher principles, including the need to preserve human life from wanton destruction.*[23]

The post-Westphalian approach that states have full sovereignty only if they meet basic human rights obligations to their citizens faces obstacles from many sources. Developing nations do not want RTP to become an excuse for re-colonization. Competing major powers do not want it used as cover for modifying the geopolitical balance. Much of that wariness is justified. The marriage of imperialism and capitalism is no longer overtly manifested in conquest, colonization, or mandates but powerful nations continue to struggle for "spheres of influence" to protect their "vital interests". Those spheres and interests have economic and political components. Implementation of Responsibility to Protect is subject to abuse. Recently, the West in Libya abused it badly, but the doctrine also has potential for protecting the most basic human rights.[24]

The state of RTP at any time has important implications for peacekeeping because it requires abandoning what is known as the "holy trinity" of traditional peacekeeping operations: consent, impartiality, and minimal use of force. These operations, as we will see, often involve interposition of peacekeepers between belligerents after a ceasefire and can include a variety of activities designed to facilitate political dialogue. But if the nation where peacekeepers are deployed is unable or unwilling to protect its civilian population from human rights violations or is itself a perpetrator, the doctrine obviously requires peacekeepers to abandon the trinity. Intervention to protect cannot depend on consent and force may have to be more than minimal.[25]

Peacekeeping operations in which Canada has been involved to a greater or lesser degree are so numerous as to preclude mentioning them all, much less discussing them in detail. We will examine a few, including some that are widely held to have failed badly. We will see that such an assessment is seriously flawed and provides little justification for abandoning the enterprise. In any event, a fair *comparative* evaluation requires bearing in mind the recency and novelty of this fledgling approach to international conflict management. For centuries, nations have been studying methods of making war while only talking peace. They have only recently made serious attempts at collectively implementing peace.

Suez: The Template and the Trinity

While serving as secretary of external affairs in the government of Louis St. Laurent, Lester Pearson was a delegate to the UN General Assembly and chair of its Political Committee. If Canadians remember anything about peacekeeping, it is usually the story of how Pearson persuaded UN Secretary General Dag Hammarskjöld and most of the member nations to create the United Nations Emergency Force (UNEF) in 1956 and defuse an ongoing armed conflict over the Suez Canal.

Pearson was awarded the Nobel Peace Prize for his role. Berton called it Pearson's finest hour and for him it underlined the truth that Canadians are not a belligerent people and Canada is not a warlike nation.[26] Whether that is true remains to be seen. The UNEF story has much to say about the future of peacekeeping and whether Canadians will truly embrace it. The Suez mission served as a template for many that followed. It identified difficulties and by doing so presented future peacekeepers the opportunity to evaluate how the UN and UNEF addressed those difficulties.

If Pearson is seen by some as the father of UN peacekeeping, his later reflection on the child is worth bearing in mind as we examine the mission: *The birth of that force had been sudden and had been surgical. The arrangements for the reception of the infant were rudimentary, and the midwives had no precedents or genuine experience to guide them.*[27]

The crisis grew out of Cold War tension and the legacy of British and French imperialism. In 1947, Britain unceremoniously dumped its Palestine mandate in the lap of the young United Nations. With the horror of the Nazi holocaust still fresh, the UN decided to partition Palestine to make way for a Jewish state. There was to be economic union, freedom of transit, and UN administration of a demilitarized Jerusalem. Palestinians rejected partition and fighting broke out. This should not have been surprising. No one asked the Palestinians if they wanted to have most of their territory awarded to what at that time was a fourth of their population. Well-trained and armed militias of the new Israel defeated the Palestinians and the Arab forces that intervened later, displacing hundreds of thousands of Palestinians before a ceasefire in 1949. At the time of the Suez Crisis, Canadian general E.L.M. "Tommy" Burns was overseeing the armistice.[28] By 1956, when the militant David Ben-Gurion came to power in Israel with a policy of "ten teeth for a tooth", violence was widespread along the armistice lines.[29]

Two other players responsible for the crisis were Britain and France, the two nations that had effectively been exercising control over the canal since Disraeli secured it for Queen Victoria. The final player was Egypt, led by Gamal Abdel Nasser, who had overthrown the corrupt King Farouk four years earlier.

Nasser was a nationalist, not pleased about British military bases in the canal zone and hostile to Israel after Egyptian defeats in the intervention on behalf of Palestinians. Unfortunately, these developments took place in the middle of the Cold War. Britain, France, and later the U.S. were concerned about Soviet influence in the Middle East, especially the oil supplies that fueled much of Europe and provided significant profits to U.S. companies.

With U.S. encouragement, Britain withdrew its troops from the canal zone in June 1956, at the expiration of a treaty that had permitted their presence. Yet U.S. foreign policy, influenced by secretary of state John Foster Dulles, began to focus more on Egypt's place in the Cold War struggle than her efforts to gain complete freedom from British imperialism.[30]

The biggest American mistake was the scuttling of Nasser's major development, the Aswan Dam. Nasser looked to the U.S., Britain, and the World Bank for financing. A Soviet offer to help if the West refused overcame initial American reluctance. The U.S. and Britain made specific offers of financing, which Egypt formally accepted. Negotiations with the World Bank followed. Then Dulles, still in his Cold War mood, persuaded the U.S. to renege on the deal. Britain and the World Bank quickly followed suit. Nasser's response was to nationalize the largely French-owned canal company and freeze its assets, though he provided for compensation to stockholders based on the share price the day before the takeover. His plan was to finance the dam with tolls from the canal.[31] British prime minister Anthony Eden denounced Nasser as the "Hitler of the Nile". Chancellor of the exchequer Harold MacMillan chose "Asiatic Mussolini".[32]

Britain and France promptly acted out of the Great War secret agreements playbook. They entered a clandestine agreement with Israel that they hoped would permit them to invade without being seen as returning to raw imperialism. The ruse was that Israel would attack Egypt across the Sinai desert toward the canal. Britain and France would then demand a ceasefire and order the parties to retreat 10 miles from the canal. If they did not obey, Britain and France would send in troops to protect access to the canal. The plan was put into practice in October. Israel attacked. Britain and France issued their ultimatums. Egypt, of course, declined to comply as did Israel, citing Egypt's refusal.

Fortunately, the world discovered the collusion. The clumsy ultimatums came before the Israelis had even made it within 10 miles of the canal and the coordinated British/French military preparation was a bit too neatly done to escape suspicion. World public opinion turned against Britain and France. The U.S. strongly opposed any intervention. Nevertheless, within 48 hours the British and French commenced bombing Egypt.[33]

It was a violent, adolescent mess that challenged Pearson's effort to resolve a war in a different way. The situation created by Britain, France, and Israel threated a NATO split, with the U.S. on one side and Britain and France on the other. Britain kept Canada in the dark about its plans, and then arrogantly assumed Canadian support, thus threatening that relationship. Other Commonwealth nations were split over the British action. In addition to the propaganda victory being bestowed on the Soviet Union, Cold War dangers increased. The Soviets threatened their own intervention, even hinting that they were willing to use nuclear weapons. And, of course, there was the matter of a war in progress that was killing people.[34]

Pearson had supported the war in Korea, but remained troubled by the U.S. domination of the UN in that conflict. He wanted a more independent UN peacekeeping presence. In fact, when he came up with the idea of such a force to place itself between the Egyptians and Israelis and replace the British and French, the idea of a permanent UN force had been circulating. Pearson's proposal this time was for a temporary presence, but he had a difficult time selling even that to Hammarskjöld. After Pearson successfully lobbied his own government, as well as the Americans and the British, the secretary general came around.[35]

Now the problem was how to implement the proposal in a manner that all the players could live with. That would not be easy. While all this was in the works, Britain was blocking consideration of the matter by NATO and continuing its invasion. Israel took the opportunity to seize the Gaza Strip, killing more than 500 Palestinians, some by summary execution.[36] Yet the UN's first armed peacekeeping force came into being.

The Security Council deadlocked but the General Assembly was able to bring UNEF into existence through a 1950 resolution titled Uniting for Peace. In short, it provides that when a matter relating to international peace and security arises, the General Assembly may take it up without any referral by the Security Council and make recommendations to the secretary general for collective action to restore the peace. This procedure was followed, putting the onus on the combatants, including permanent Security Council members, to object. In the face of the ongoing mess they had created, and from which they needed to be extricated, none did. Indeed, all belligerents consented, satisfying the first requirement of the peacekeeping trinity. They acquiesced first in a renewed ceasefire resolution, followed by the Canadian resolution to create UNEF. The British and French, however, began landing troops in Egypt the same day.[37]

When the ceasefire finally went into effect, the task was to quickly assemble and deploy the UN force, as well as fashion its mandate. That operation highlighted many of the challenges that future missions would have to work out, but in many respects the Suez crisis was a perfect laboratory. There was a former colony at odds with colonizers who were trying to maintain there influence. There was an aggressive new nation involved in the violent sorting out of its tribes and expanding its territory. The situation also presented questions of the extent of consent given by belligerents. There was no user's manual for the mission.

The first problem in that context was the makeup of the force and its leadership.

Hammarskjöld chose general Burns to command the force, a widely approved appointment given his experience in supervising the 1949 Israel/Palestine ceasefire. Tommy Burns is in many respects a better figure after whom to model a better Canadian image than Pearson. He was a smart hard-nosed military man, veteran of Vimy, the Somme, Passchendaele and Italy. He once reminded veterans of the "stupid bloodletting" that characterized so many Great War battles. After Hiroshima he became convinced that no dispute was worth the risk of nuclear war. He had accepted the truce supervision job because he thought war was to be avoided at almost any cost. He would later become an arms control negotiator.[38]

Hammarskjöld conferred with Burns about the UN force and it was quickly agreed that no U.S., British, or French troops would participate. Canada, Colombia, Norway, Sweden, Finland and Denmark offered contingents ready to move immediately. The problem that arose next was indicative of Canada's evolving international role in wars, and of the difficulty of assuming a different role while identified with a powerful patron.

With a Canadian commander, everyone assumed Canadian ground troops would be part of UNEF. Everyone except the Egyptians. Nasser objected on the grounds that their presence in Egypt would increase the risk of violent confrontations with the public. Canadian forces at the time wore the same uniforms as the British. Worse, the Canadian government's choice for the mission was the Queen's Own Rifles. Pearson, although not famous for his wit, wrote of this aspect of the problem: *What we needed was the First East Kootenay Anti-Imperialistic Rifles.*[39] Abandoning the uniform, of course, would further strain relations with the British, who already saw a benign Canadian agreement to sell wheat to Egypt as a betrayal of the mother country, though Canada also sold fighter jets to Israel.[40] Dealing with problems like this one may be responsible for the distinctive blue helmets, now so clearly associated with UN peacekeeping. The helmets, and distinctive UN badges, were already planned for the entire force at Canada's suggestion. Still, this was not enough to assuage Nasser.

In the end, Canada provided logistical support only in the form of administration, communications, transport, engineers, and medical personnel. Having earlier witnessed numerous truce violations, mostly by Israel, Burns had wanted UNEF to be a force capable of fighting and too strong to be pushed aside or ignored. He assumed that he could call on the Queen's Own Rifles if needed, and indeed the unit remained on standby in Halifax, ready to deploy. The Rifles were not needed, however, and Burns later accepted the makeup of the force. He praised the performance of the Canadian logistical contingent, crediting it with making a huge difference in the success of the mission.[41]

The little drama about Canadians and uniforms, as well as Israel's initial refusal to allow UNEF in any area it controlled, highlights the importance of sorting out the question of consent in peacekeeping operations. Egypt and Israel had consented to the operation. But would Egypt or UNEF have the final world on the composition of the force? Would Israel or UNEF have the final word on how to deploy it effectively? What is the operational meaning of consent?

Establishing the mandate for UNEF without a user's manual was also a challenge. It is one thing for the parties to agree to a ceasefire and the insertion of some sort of international body between them, but how does that work on the ground? The UNEF mandate was 1) Secure and supervise the ceasefire and form a buffer zone. 2) Supervise withdrawal of foreign forces from Egypt. 3) Clear the canal. 4) Patrol border areas and deter incursions. 5) Secure adherence to the Egypt-Israel armistice agreements.

Burns was concerned about the generality of these instructions. He understood, however, that it was impossible for an international body to provide a military contingent with a detailed tactical order.[42] Burns recognized that fluid conditions would require improvisation, and his insight on this matter was likely a major factor in the success of UNEF. The lesson? Making every effort to select the right people and leaving specifics to them is preferable to attempting detailed control of discretion in advance.

Burns' insight manifested itself in incidents that were also instructive on the other prongs of the trinity, impartiality and minimal use of force. The withdrawing British were concerned that Egyptians would shoot their own citizens they considered collaborators. UNEF satisfied both sides by establishing UNEF-Egyptian patrols to prevent this. The first and second items of the mandate were not accomplished without gunfire, including defensive fire from the Swedes. But UNEF restraint and minimal use of force succeeded in gradually opening a buffer zone and securing the departure of the British and French.[43]

UNEF was not a complete success and not responsible for every positive result. It was a failed objective of Burns and Hammarskjöld, for example, that Israel not retain control of Gaza. It was intense diplomatic pressure from the U.S. that forced Israel to leave. The mission did not, of course, solve the larger Israel-Palestine conflict. It did, however, give the parties 10 years to work things out. Unfortunately, in 1967, Israel, eschewing diplomacy in a dispute with

Egypt that the Soviets fueled with misinformation, started another war, reclaiming Gaza and more. Israeli and Palestinian civilians would have fared better had Pearson's wish for the area to be under UN administration been realized.[44]

Maloney concedes the success of UNEF but sees it only in military and geopolitical terms: *It was, in sum, a team effort to prevent nuclear war and preserve NATO as an alliance.*[45] It was much more than that.

Pearson was also a supporter of NATO, but he recognized, as so many today do not, that it is ultimately not a body capable of providing peace: *It remained my conviction that there could never be more than a second-best substitute for the UN preserving the peace. Organizations such as NATO were necessary and desirable only because the UN was not effective as a security agency.*[46] In his Nobel acceptance speech, Pearson spoke in terms that present the choice for Canada today. He spoke of his experience in the Great War, the loss of most of his comrades, and the failure of nations since that war to establish peace. Significantly, he spoke of learning as a civilian in World War II of the demise of any distinction between soldiers and civilians.

Pearson's caution has gone unheeded. Expenditures for all of the 67 UN peacekeeping operations in the last 65 years total $90 billion—only about twice as much as Canada recently sought to spend on a handful of fighter jets to be at the service of NATO.[47]

Which approach is better? Like the March of Dimes after the eradication of polio, NATO after the Cold War had to reinvent itself and find a new *raison d'etre*. Part of that reinvention, one that we will examine closely in Afghanistan, includes forays into what it broadly terms peacekeeping. It will be particularly important for Canadians to evaluate how that worked out.

We will see that the difficult question of consent is always a delicate matter in traditional peacekeeping, as it was in the Suez crisis. Consent is a legitimate issue, and the difficulty of resolving it has sometimes been aggravated by the legacy of imperialism. Without the consent of their governments, expecting the people of formerly subjugated lands to view UN peacekeepers as something other than merely a different set of occupiers is unrealistic. As we will see, there is cause for the worry expressed by McKay and Swift that militarists in the 1990's managed to transform peacekeeping into something resembling imperial policing, with the UN either marginalized or quietly compliant.[48]

The issue is further complicated by the way imperial powers left their colonies. Some of the resulting governments are not representative. Some are themselves oppressive. The preferred choice for dealing with this problem at present is for powerful nations to continue competing for military alliances, arming this faction or that, and occasionally to invade or bomb without consent. As noted, the international community is groping toward a definition of occasions when consent should not be a requirement for intervention. Meanwhile, let us continue to examine examples of how the template established by UNEF played out, and Canada's contribution.

Cyprus: The Learning Continues

The story of what became Canada's longest peacekeeping mission provided lessons for the world about the application of all three prongs of the trinity. In Cyprus, the meaning and application of minimal use of force and its corresponding impact on perceptions of impartiality were particularly important to the developing methodology of peacekeeping. The state of the guidance provided to peacekeepers continued to affect these questions.

The Great War was a factor in the origin of this conflict on a Mediterranean island. The Cold War struggle complicated the attempt at resolution. Greece gained independence from the Ottoman Empire in the early 19th century and began to seek unity between the Mediterranean communities and the mainland. The foundation for a conflict between Greece and Turkey had thus been laid when Britain annexed the island during the Great War after defeating the Ottoman Turks. By the 1950's, after a migration of Greeks there were a half million Cypriots, 80 percent of Greek descent and 18 percent of Turkish descent.

Maloney views this story also in military and geopolitical terms. In *Tested Mettle, Canada's Peacekeepers at War*[49], veteran Scott Taylor and journalist Brian Nolan instead recount individual experiences of Canadian soldiers. Both accounts have value, but Taylor and Nolan's approach illuminates particularly well the challenges of adherence to minimal use of force under the authority of a vague mandate.

As in Suez, Britain had military bases on Cyprus and was loath to relinquish them. A Greek Cypriot guerilla campaign against the British and Turkish Cypriots prompted the British to reconsider the island's status. They began negotiating to get out, provided they could keep the bases, termed ironically as Sovereign Base Areas (SBAs). The result was a guarantee of the bases and an experiment in political and military unification of Greek and Turkish Cypriots. Many details were left unsettled but the formula provided for a Greek Cypriot president and a Turkish Cypriot vice president. Greeks were to have 70 percent of the seats in the legislative body, Turks 30 percent. The first president was Greek Archbishop Makarios III.

Cyprus gained independence in 1960 and joined the UN. Not having experienced Egypt's unpleasant history with Britain, the new nation soon joined the British Commonwealth. This development mitigated somewhat the consent issues that would arise when the political experiment fell apart in 1963. A war, with accompanying atrocities, broke out between Greek and Turkish Cypriots. The two mother countries, both members of NATO, exchanged threats to intervene.[50] A dangerous new mess arose, with similarities to Suez that included a split in the Cold War western alliance and a propaganda coup for the Soviets. As usual, it was a bad time for civilians.

There is little doubt that the Cold War nuclear danger was significant. Maloney saw the interest of NATO *and* Canada as maintenance of the SBAs, with the capability of doing an "end run" around Soviet air defences and making a *pre-emptive* strike to neutralize 700 Russian missiles in the region. The ranking Canadian diplomat confirmed the presence of nuclear weapons on Cyprus.[51]

A UN peacekeeping mission was not the first option. The British first raised the prospect of a NATO force, but asked in the meantime for UN observers. The NATO proposal included 1000 Canadian troops. The issue of consent arose when Makarios rejected the NATO option. He had agreed to a British, Turkish and Greek force under British control, but only if authorized by the UN. Although the West was suspicious of the Cold War leanings of Makarios, he prevailed. When the alternative of UN cover for a NATO mission could not be sold, the task finally fell to the UN and a very different force was formed.

In 1964, the Security Council authorized United Nations Peacekeeping Force in Cyprus (UNFICYP), with a general mandate to use its best efforts to prevent recurrence of fighting and contribute as necessary to the maintenance and restoration of law and order and a return to normality. It was not authorized to use coercive force or act to alter the political balance. Makarios agreed, provided the force included no Americans or Muslims.[52]

From the beginning, and on many fronts, Canada was the glue that held this mission together. Under the command of an Indian general, the force included troops from Australia, Canada, Denmark, Finland, Ireland, Sweden and significantly, Britain. Some of these nations, for various reasons were reluctant participants whom Canada had persuaded to join. Later, when things got tough, some would stay in only because Canada did.[53]

Pearson, now prime minister, drew attention to the critical matter of the terms of a peacekeeping mandate. He criticized the failure to include rules on combat operations and the use of force. Pearson's high commissioner to Cyprus gave the world an eloquent outline of challenges that would have to be addressed in the future: *UNFICYP must know what it is here to do… 'peacekeeping' and 'normalization' are not concepts that a soldier can be expected to interpret and carry out. The UNFICYP soldier must therefore be given a conception of peacekeeping that is intelligible, clear, and within his power to enforce… to give him more weapons or greater freedom in using them without first telling him to what achievable end the new power is to be used will merely increase the flow of blood, some of it Canadian, without helping the Cyprus situation.*[54] The plea also stated a position on the issue of consent. It asserted that the stronger and clearer mandate should be presented to the warring parties, not negotiated with them.

Like Suez, the Cyprus mission gave the parties 10 years of relative peace to work out their differences. The mission was more difficult because it initially required more than simply interposing a force between combatants along a well-defined line. That came about eventually, but before it did peacekeepers were required to establish multiple buffer zones, inserting themselves between hostile communities scattered across the island. All this was accomplished while the focus of the relevant powers remained Cold War geopolitics rather than the plight of civilians. The peacekeepers also worked in the face of continued invasion threats by Turkey and Greece.

Eventually, a clear demarcation of Greek and Turkish controlled areas called the "Green Line" came into being. Turkish and Greek invasion threats had been quieted by a message from NATO that if they did not behave and the Soviets attacked them, the alliance would not come to their aid. Ultimately, however, the invasion threat materialized. Turkey, always the most belligerent of the two, invaded in July 1974, days after a Greek-inspired coup by the Cypriot National Guard ousted Makarios. Turkey claimed a need to protect Turkish Cypriots and seized 40 percent of the island before a tenuous ceasefire was arranged.

UNFICYP was now in the middle of a hot war and peacekeepers were faced with new and greater challenges than those encountered in Suez. Their new mandate required policing a 180 mile buffer zone between Turkish Cypriots in the north and Greek Cypriots in the south, as well as humanitarian assistance to 200,000 displaced persons.[55]

Incidents involving interaction of Canadian forces, civilians, and combatants provided future peacekeepers with guidance on minimal use of force, impartiality, intelligent use of discretion in the absence of specific orders, and concern for civilians.

The invasion presented early examples of the need for quick decision-making in response to sudden turns of events. Canadian commander, Clayton Beattie, saw three options: 1) Withdraw to their UN bases and do nothing until UN headquarters decided on a response. 2) Withdraw from Cyprus altogether and let the parties fight it out. 3) Place his units between the combatants; attempt to negotiate ceasefires, and enforce Security Council resolutions calling for hostilities to cease. Beattie and the overall Cyprus force commander agreed to opt for the more complex and difficult third option. This set the stage for some of the peacekeeping lessons that Canada would help teach the world.

A decision to defend UN property resulted in the first Canadian use of force to protect the peacekeepers. An observation post was fired on and a Canadian soldier wounded. The Turks turned back the ambulance taking him to hospital. Greek National Guard troops later fired on the ambulance. Canadian troops returned fire and got the wounded man to hospital. The incident is an example of minimal use of force when necessary. The fact that the Canadians did not come out guns blazing initially, and that when turned back by the Turks sought an alternate means, is probably as important as the combat milestone.

The next incident required creativity and involved protection of civilians. Greek national guardsmen had taken over a hotel in Nicosia and came under heavy fire from Turkish Cypriots. The hotel had hundreds of frightened tourists and journalists who sought UN protection. The Canadian commander told both sides to stop firing while the civilians were evacuated. The first attempt failed and Canadian troops came under fire. Instead of joining the war, the Canadians tried again the next day. They organized a convoy of trucks and buses and got the hotel guests and their luggage out of danger. The commander then declared the contested hotel a UN position, deployed his troops to secure and patrol it, and raised a UN flag on the roof.

In these early examples of peacekeeping by confrontation, peacekeepers put their lives at risk in a humanitarian mission. The commander's *ad hoc* decisions also demonstrated minimal use of force and impartiality.

Another incident brought home the lesson that despite good faith adherence to the trinity, combat will sometimes be necessary. Blood will be shed. Lives will be lost. Both sides fired on the Canadian positions, which were right on the Nicosia Green Line. Canadians returned fire. As fighting continued, eight Turkish Cypriot soldiers fled to the Canadian encampment and asked for protection.

Impartiality would not permit the soldiers to remain. They were combatants and their presence would draw fire from the Greek side. The Canadian commander, with a UN flag and a bullhorn to announce his intention to both sides, undertook to return them to their side of a river dividing the two sides. This time, it did not work. Gunfire ripped into the commander and an aide and drove back another officer who attempted to rescue them. Two scout cars arrived and fired on the Greek positions, killing two Greek soldiers, and opening the way for evacuation of the wounded.

Finally, there was another example of Canadians protecting civilians while seeking to adhere to the trinity. The Greek side held the Nicosia airport but Turkish forces were advancing on it. Colonel Beattie, under direct fire from the Greeks, went to the Turkish position to remind them that both sides had agreed to a ceasefire at the airport. While there, he saw the Turks guarding a group of prisoners, including women, children, and an old man. He negotiated their release and put them under UN protection.

Then the Turks attacked anyway. Beattie persuaded both sides to withdraw. He then declared the airport a UN protected area. Facing a later threat of attack, he announced that the Canadian troops holding the airport would not surrender it to anyone. The on-the-spot decision to defend the airport forced the UN Cyprus command to go along.[56]

These incidents demonstrate that efforts at impartiality produce credibility with combatants and save lives. The declaration of UN protected areas was also a milestone in the operational scope of initial consent given by the parties to a mission. Well done, Canada.

Canadian casualties in Cyprus included three dead and seventeen wounded. Taylor and Nolan are understandably angry that the accomplishments of Canadian forces in Cyprus were ignored at home. Their work is a stinging critique of political leaders of all stripes and of the military hierarchy. They claim that combat deaths have been under-reported, over-classified, and sometimes reported as accidents; and that military awards and citations due peacekeepers have been withdrawn. They decry the absence of sufficient equipment and support, and condemn drastically reduced military expenditures. The two writers are pro-military in a way that Maloney and others are not. They report on Canadian peacekeeping missions, warts and all, and come out in support of realistic, intelligent peacekeeping. It is a military perspective that does not require the warrior nation image. Their first recommendation for change was the establishment of a permanent UN peacekeeping force of 2,000.[57]

Cyprus remains partitioned today, though diplomatic efforts to find a permanent solution continue, led by the UN. Turkey declared a republic in her 30 percent of the island—a nation that only Turkey recognizes. The UN mission has been criticized for being too successful. The argument is that absent an immediate threat of violence, the parties have little incentive to resolve the matter.[58] But ordinary Greek and Turkish Cypriots probably prefer the status quo to the killing that preceded it.

Canada withdrew the bulk of its force in 1993. By 2014, a lone Canadian officer remained to welcome Canadian troops from Afghanistan stopping over to enjoy the beaches before heading home.[59]

The Balkans: Straining the Trinity

Canadians were key members of the United Nations Protection Force (UNPROFOR), the peacekeeping mission to the former

Yugoslavia in the early 1990's. Bellamy and Williams refer to the mission as an example of "Wider Peacekeeping". They define that term somewhat euphemistically as an operation carried out with the consent of the parties, within states rather than between them, "but in an environment that may be volatile."[60]

For UNPROFOR, the specific meaning of wider peacekeeping turned out to be dealing with initial consent by the parties, including ceasefires, that were then continuously violated, renegotiated, and violated again. Peacekeeping involved a great number of tasks that the world expected the force to accomplish despite inadequate resources. It also involved numerous inadequate revisions of the mandate in an attempt to compensate for the fact that UNPROFOR found itself in the middle of a civil war.[61]

Bellamy and Williams, and most observers view UNPROFOR as a failure. If so, the failure was not attributable to the troops who served there, especially the Canadians. For Canada, UNPROFOR was another example of skill and bravery despite poor leadership, this time from the top—the Department of National Defence (DND) and the UN bureaucracy. On the ground, Canadians from master corporal to major general performed remarkably well, often under combat conditions equal to or worse than those of conventional war. For this, they were scarcely noticed by the Canadian public.

The Balkan mission put terrible strain on the traditional peacekeeping trinity. But those who served provided the world with valuable lessons about interpreting and applying consent, impartiality, and minimal use of force. More importantly, they provided a new template for applying the trinity if the goal of peacekeeping is redefined to give priority to humanitarian issues when traditional peacekeeping breaks down. Whatever the correct verdict on UNPROFOR, the mission provides no reason to abandon the ongoing enterprise of peacekeeping—one in which Canada can play a key role, particularly if protection of civilians becomes the dominant theme.

The Balkan war was another deadly land mine left by the Great War and the Paris peace conference. In its 1919 creation of the Kingdom of Yugoslavia, the conference outdid itself in drawing lines around a collection of hostile tribes and religions—Serbs, Muslims and Croats.[62] Detonation was delayed by German occupation in World War II, but intertribal hatred was later aggravated by disputes over who had fought for or against the Germans. Further delay in the inevitable violence came during the Cold War years of rule by Josip Tito, whose preoccupation was establishing an authoritarian communist state independent of the Soviet Union. Tito died in 1980, the Cold War ended in 1989. Two years later, Yugoslavia disintegrated.

Serbs and Croats declared their own nations. Bosnia, half Muslim, tried for a time to continue as a peaceful multicultural region but the Serbs managed to scuttle that effort. By the time 1,200 Canadian troops arrived in early 1992, there was no chance that the mission could replicate Suez and Cyprus. A civil war was in progress, and the sides were relatively well trained and quite well armed. Yugoslavia had been a major world arms merchant.[63] Most Serbs in the Yugoslav National Army (JNA) remained with it, while Croat and Muslim members left to fight for their tribes.

What put the Canadians in the middle of this war? In late 1991, Cyrus Vance, later U.S. secretary of state but then special representative of the UN secretary general, brokered a deal between Croatia and what was left of Yugoslavia, dominated by Serbs. Initially, it appeared to be a traditional peacekeeping mission. The agreement called for a ceasefire and insertion of 14,000 UN troops into United Nations Protected Areas (UNPA) in Croatia. Their primary mission would be protection of Serb civilians from the Croats. When the UN took over, JNA members were to leave for the state of their choice or disarm and remain in the UNPA as civilians. Apart from hope that this would produce a better climate for negotiations, that was about it. The details would have to be worked out on the ground.

Things began to go wrong early. One immediate problem was a harbinger of difficulties to come. Bureaucratic wrangling delayed deployment of the force. In the four months between the agreement and the deployment of UNPROFOR, the battle lines changed and that called for new and different UNPA locations. The Croats, already resentful at having troops on their soil, would not agree to any changes.

Canadians were initially tasked with manning Croatian UNPA. They would eventually become involved also in the Bosnian capital of Sarajevo, under the command of Canadian general Lewis MacKenzie, third ranking military officer in the UN effort. The experience of Canadians in both venues was a primer on refinements to the trinity that are required in furtherance of wider peacekeeping. Tactical diplomacy and the intelligent exercise of discretion are essential when traditional peacekeeping breaks down. Canadians provided both as they dealt with consent, impartiality, and minimal use of force in a hostile environment. What became clear is that a greater number of more heavily armed and better equipped troops would have helped in the application of all three prongs of the trinity.

The consent element of Vance's plan was essentially gone when the Canadians arrived in Croatia. Troops from the Royal 22nd and Royal Canadian Regiment came under fire from heavy weapons for the first time since Korea as they set up camp. At the same time, Bosnian Serbs increased their shelling of besieged Sarajevo, seeking to advance the vision of greater Serbia that had inflamed Gavrilo Princip. At the time, there were no Canadian troops in Sarajevo. General MacKenzie was there because, for some obscure political reason, the UN had decided that the Bosnian capital would be the headquarters for UNPROFOR to supervise the UNPAS in Croatia. The decision was made over MacKenzie's common sense objections.[64] Though there was then no UN mandate at all for Bosnia, Sarajevo would become the focal point of world attention and propaganda that would affect both the outcome and the assessment of the peacekeeping mission.

MacKenzie would eventually have to call upon the Canadians who were quietly going about their business in Croatia, clearing roads of mines and trying to demonstrate a military capacity for protection that in truth they did not have. That lack of military capacity was important to the question of consent when it came to movement of UN forces responding to the rapidly changing situation. A force that could not be ignored may not have been required for traditional peacekeeping, but it soon became apparent that it was badly needed for wider peacekeeping. When the parties give broad consent but deny ground level operational consent, underequipped peacekeepers are reduced to negotiating and bluffing. This is especially true when they are in enclaves surrounded by hostile forces and need to supply themselves, provide humanitarian relief, or simply move from A to B.

Canadian commanders at all levels, without special training, distinguished themselves in the art of negotiating and bluffing. In doing so, they saved lives and refined the relationship between consent and minimal use of force. In one of many examples, a superior force of Serb tanks held up a contingent of Canadians en route to relieve encircled Sarajevo despite the fact that Serbs, Croats and Muslims had all consented to UN presence in the city. The Canadian commander faced what would be a recurring problem in new wars: tactical units led by warlords, or militias who either did not receive or did not care about orders from superiors. The Canadians sat patiently for 18 hours and then decided to force the issue. The bluff worked. If it had not, there would have been deaths and the Serbs would have claimed that the Canadians had trespassed on impartiality. The besieged Muslims in Sarajevo, instead of welcoming the Canadian convoy would have lost faith in the UN mission.[65]

Canadian commanders who knew "when to hold 'em and when to fold 'em" were invaluable to what became the most important aspect of the UN mission: humanitarian relief. Units tasked with escorting aid convoys to encircled Muslim neighbourhoods near Sarajevo had to cross battle lines numerous times and negotiate their way through checkpoints in a 30 kilometre trek over a mountain pass. In one incident, general MacKenzie's successor declared another encircled town near Sarajevo, one with 50-60,000 Muslim refugees, to be a protected area, though he could not enforce such a decree. A Canadian platoon was ordered to make a symbolic delivery of food. The convoy was stopped several times by Serb forces demanding to search the vehicles as a condition of passage. The convoy commander knew when to fold 'em. He allowed the searches and the convoy got through. A few lives were saved and a UN presence was established. Such complex intrigue was the norm for Canadians serving in the Balkans.[66]

Since the UN and their own DND had placed their underequipped and shorthanded units in this kind of continuing danger, the Canadians made up their own common sense rules about minimal use of force. One commander, whose unit was issued a grossly insufficient amount of ammunition, decided it would be better to surrender immediately. The alternative was to engage in a firefight that would have to end in surrender and to endure the rage flowing from having killed some of his adversary's men. Another established the rule that if his unit were not heavily outnumbered, it would hold its ground and ignore the official rules that required a request for permission and warning shots.[67] None of this should have been necessary. It endangered lives and harmed the mission. In spite of their ingenuity, peacekeepers, including Canadians, did have to engage in combat. Every time they did, the adversary claimed that it was an example of UN partiality toward the other side.

It is worthwhile to remember that the need for an adequate number of well-armed and equipped peacekeepers does not stem from a purpose to make war. UNPROFOR peacekeepers engaged in combat. "Only" 167 died, 10 of them Canadians. But those lives were lost in a failed attempt to give belligerent tribes an opportunity to step back from violence, as well as to preserve the lives of civilians on all sides.

An essential component of the humanitarian mission in Bosnia was the opening of the Sarajevo airport. That required a Canadian battalion and a very skillful Canadian general. Before the Canadians arrived in force, Lewis MacKenzie had been instrumental in reviving an earlier ceasefire agreement and persuading the Serbs to give up their significant advantage in controlling the airport so that a humanitarian airlift could be resumed. The opportunity came after a courageous symbolic visit by French president Francois Mitterrand.[68] The only condition the Serbs required was that they be permitted to evacuate serious casualties across the runway to a field hospital, saving a much longer journey through the mountains. MacKenzie set up a procedure for inspecting the ambulances and agreed. The Muslim president of Bosnia was equivocal. Muslim snipers fired on the peacekeepers. With a combination of threats of bad public relations and military action, MacKenzie ultimately got them to back off. With the airport in UN hands, the UN high commissioner for refugees handled the subsequent delivery of hundreds of tons of food and medicine, some delivered by a Canadian C-130 aircraft. The deliveries were sometimes accomplished under fire in spite of the agreements, and there were casualties.[69]

Propaganda, as usual, was not helpful. Extensive media attention focused on besieged Muslims in Sarajevo. U.S.-inspired media soon made the Serbs the sole villains in the entire conflict. The UN imposed sanctions only on Serbia. The U.S. began to arm the Croats. The effect of this lack of impartiality, though not the doing of peacekeepers, often resulted in resentful Serb forces impeding UN access to critical areas.[70] It also laid the groundwork for intervention by the major western powers.

Another important humanitarian aspect of saving civilian lives in this chaos involved atrocities committed by all sides. The most highly publicized Serb war crime was the massacre of 7,000-8,000 men and boys and expulsion of thousands of civilians at Srebrenica in eastern Bosnia. Canada eventually designated a day of remembrance for it and a Dutch court held the Netherlands responsible for the conduct of some of its peacekeepers at Srebrenica.[71]

Much less noted or appreciated is that denial of essential resources to the peacekeeping mission probably aggravated the conditions that led to the crime. Canadians were present at Srebrenica before the Dutch. Once again, a UN commander had declared an enclave to be a UN-protected safe haven, without the resources to back up the declaration. This time, the bluff failed. The initial force left to protect 30,000 starving Muslim civilians surrounded by 6,000 Serb militiamen consisted of 18 Canadian soldiers, equipped with two armoured personnel carriers. A makeshift reinforcement force of 175 arrived 10 days later. Although defeated, some well-armed Muslim fighters were still active. An effort by the tiny peacekeeping force to effect compliance with a ceasefire provision by disarming the Muslim forces and demilitarizing the area went badly. The bitter reaction of the Serbs was that peacekeepers were partial to the Muslims.[72]

There is no day of remembrance for Croat war crimes at the Muslim village of Stupni-Do. Canadian peacekeepers witnessed the aftermath and saved civilian lives by preventing the perpetrators from committing further atrocities. When the Canadians arrived at the village they saw grim evidence that a Croat armoured brigade had raped and murdered, scalped victims and left children impaled on stakes. When word came down that the Croat unit was advancing on another village called Fornika, a Canadian commander took action on his own initiative. With a squadron of obsolete tank-trainer vehicles, his unit confronted the Croats, some of whom were still wearing scalps on their belts, and blocked their entry to the village.[73]

Canadian and French forces also witnessed atrocities carried out by a Croat force equipped and trained by the U.S. in the area of the town of Medak. The "Medak Pocket" saw Canadians engaged in outright combat on a scale not seen since Korea. They were in the middle of a battle between Serbs and Croats in which ceasefires and safe areas were largely ignored. They would take some comfort from the casualties they inflicted on the Croat troops.

Before retreating from a Serb counterattack, the Croat force began a campaign of ethnic cleansing. The Canadians could hear the screams of victims and requested permission from UN headquarters to intervene. Instead, they were ordered to remain in place and gather evidence for future use at a war crimes tribunal. Eventually, at great risk to themselves, they bluffed their way past the Croat force. They found corpses, burning homes, dead livestock. One officer found the corpses of two young women who had been raped, tied to chairs, and burned alive.[74] Politically ordered impotence produced a new strain of PTSD. Taylor and Nolan write: *these dead civilians were far more traumatizing to deal with because the Canadians had to stand by helplessly and listen to them die…many could not help but feel that they had somehow failed these brutally murdered people.*[75]

There is no point in trying to compare the frequency and scale of war crimes among Serbs, Croats, and Muslims. All would score points in that grisly contest. The lesson is that traditional peacekeeping resources and procedures cannot work in wider peacekeeping situations. The trinity has value, even in situations like Yugoslavia, but it has to be bent and peacekeepers need the capacity to bend it.

The perception of partiality sealed the fate of general MacKenzie, forced out of command in spite of heroic efforts to demonstrate impartiality to Serbs and Muslims. Every time he was forced to negotiate with the Serbs, plead for protection on behalf of his soldiers, or for humanitarian workers, the Bosnian Muslim leadership condemned him for bias and conducted a campaign of misinformation in the city. The goal of the Muslims, which they eventually reached, was to provoke outside intervention and escape integration into Serbia by partitioning similar to Cyprus. MacKenzie understood this and did not condemn them for it. However the absence of resources necessary to make his impartiality sufficient in fact, avoiding the necessity of constant bargaining with one side or the other, made him realize that he could not be effective if Bosnians did not perceive him as impartial. He resigned.[76]

Once propaganda had identified the Serbs alone as the enemy of peace, the NATO powers, led by the U.S. decided that rather than increase the effectiveness of peacekeepers they would settle the matter themselves. They were apparently unconcerned with the danger this would present to the lives of the peacekeepers. The Security Council, while denying requests for additional troops to protect civilians, approved a "no-fly" zone over Bosnia. NATO eagerly accepted the authorization to enforce it.

At Dayton, Ohio in 1995, the U.S. effectively imposed terms on the parties and sent in NATO troops, including Canadians who had left only six months earlier. NATO eventually persuaded 36 countries to deploy a total of 60,000 troops to enforce the settlement. Canadian fighter jets were part of a 78 day campaign that killed thousands, displaced 600,000 civilians and created a million refugees.[77]

In the years following, the western powers poured $14 billion in aid into Bosnia alone---$300 per year for each inhabitant. The UN, with a bloated bureaucracy and an inadequate communications system had tried to do peacekeeping on the cheap. The major powers did not scrimp on their war. They had no money for peacekeeping, but plenty for NATO. We should judge the comparative merits of peacekeeping and big power intervention with this reality in mind. MacKenzie concluded his memoir with this: *It would not take a major effort for the world body to improve significantly the command, control and logistical support of the people doing the dirty work for us. UN peacekeepers deserve nothing less.*[78]

Tension in the Balkans continues.[79] Western powers do not yet recognize that peacekeeping with a humanitarian priority is superior to unilateral military action. They are currently in the middle of complex ethnic, religious and political conflicts among tribes in the Middle East. The cost for civilians in death and displacement is many times that of the Balkans with little or no chance of achieving even the limited success there of NATO and its "coalition partners".

Rwanda: Racist Reluctance

If Yugoslavia represented some degree of concern about protection of civilians by some form of intervention, there was neither concern to protect the people of a small former Belgian colony from genocide. These civilians were the wrong colour.

The United Nations Assistance Mission in Rwanda (UNAMIR) in 1993-1994 is rightly regarded as a complete failure. The mission took place concurrently with UNPROFOR. A comparison of the two missions demonstrates again the double standard of human rights where black victims are involved. It is also an example of the folly of reliance on major powers, whether through NATO or any other alliance, to protect civilians.

Prevention of ethnic cleansing by Serbs against Muslims was a major justification for U.S.-led intervention in Bosnia. The upper estimate of murdered men and boys at Srebrenica is 8,000. As we have seen, the Dayton accords were enforced by 60,000 troops followed by $14 billion in aid. In Rwanda, the ethnic cleansing was the murder of 800,000 men, women and children. The U.S. and other permanent members of the Security Council not only did not intervene or commit resources; they did everything in their power to frustrate any UN effort to halt the slaughter.[80]

There are few better to tell the story of the western role in Rwanda than Samantha Power. In a remarkable article in *The Atlantic Magazine*,[81] Power, who recently served as U.S. ambassador to the UN, holds back nothing in her criticism of her country's conduct. Consistent with her account is the poignant memoir of Canadian general Romeo Dallaire, the commander of UNAMIR, whose life was shattered by his experience in Rwanda.[82]

Rwanda in the 20th century was under imperial/colonial rule until independence in 1962. Belgium took over from Germany in 1916. The two principal tribes in Rwanda were the Tutsi and Hutu. Belgian racism exacerbated moderate tension that existed between the tribes. Belgian colonial governments elevated the minority Tutsi because they had lighter skins. This racist choice was apparently influenced by 19th century Christianity. Noah, it was said had cursed his youngest son Ham and condemned him to be a slave to his brothers. An Englishman, John Speke, refined the myth with a completely fictional anthropology, holding that people who looked more like the Tutsi than the black Hutu had introduced all culture and civilization in Central Africa. [83]

When UNAMIR was formed, a civil war was in progress in Rwanda. A peace agreement in that conflict was the basis for what appeared at first to be a traditional peacekeeping mission. But almost immediately, the war became less important than a massive humanitarian crisis. The major powers nevertheless continued to focus on the war as a reason to ignore the developing genocide and limit UNAMIR to a traditional peacekeeping role---without even providing resources sufficient to accomplish that task.

After a 1973 coup, the majority Hutu took control and began to exact revenge on the previously favoured Tutsi. In 1990, an armed force of Tutsi, to be known as the Rwandan Patriotic Front (RPF) invaded from neighbouring Uganda. After negotiations in Arusha, Tanzania, the two sides, assisted by UN and other diplomats, came to a shaky, unrealistically ambitious peace agreement. It called for power sharing and a broad based transitional government, followed by multi-ethnic elections with free participation of all political parties, including the RPF, as well as demobilization of both armed forces and safe return of the Tutsi. Once civil institutions were rebuilt, the shattered country could call on the international community for financial aid. Rwanda was to accomplish all this in 22 months.[84]

Recall that the inadequate force assembled for UNPROFOR numbered 12,000-14,000. What would be required to implement the ambitious Arusha agreement in Rwanda? No one had bothered to brief Dallaire on the scope of dangers in the Rwandan conflict. Consequently, he saw it initially as a traditional mission. To avoid a Security Council veto, he reduced his initial assessment of the force needed from 8,000 to 5,500—three battalions. The U.S., France, and Russia thought 500 to 1,000 would do. His Canadian superiors refused to contribute. Dallaire's UN contact told him the Security Council would not approve anything that was not small and cheap. He eventually managed one Canadian deputy, Major Brent Beardsley, and about 2,500 troops.[85] The U.S. is the largest single contributor to the UN, which is a problem in itself. At the time of Dallaire's request, she was half a billion dollars in arrears on UN dues and peacekeeping costs.[86]

The fate of an earlier mission may have influenced U.S. obstructionism in Rwanda. After a humiliation in Somalia, the U.S. had lost her appetite for peacekeeping.

United Nations Operation in Somalia (UNOSOM) (1992-1995) had been given a Security Council mandate to disarm feuding warlords in a country where civil war and famine had killed 350,000 people and left most of the remainder malnourished. To assist, the UN sanctioned a concurrent presence by a U.S.-led Unified Task Force (UNITAF). The Americans contributed 25,000 of the 38,000 troops. For a time it appeared that black lives did matter. However, when one of the warlords managed to shoot down a helicopter, killing 18 U.S. soldiers, the Americans pulled out and were immediately followed by the other nations involved.[87] For the greatest military power in the world it appears the admonition not to "cut and run" was far less than absolute where black lives were involved.

Canada participated in UNITAF. The mission is remembered mainly for the racist war crimes of troops in the Airborne Regiment. The least of the crimes was gunning down two men who had breached the security perimeter after the Canadians put out food and water to attract them. The men were shot in the back with one finished off at close range.

The worst crime was the 1993 torture murder of 16-year-old Shidane Abutar Arone, caught going through abandoned junk. Some 80 members of the unit heard his screams for hours. One of them later remarked: *We haven't killed enough niggers yet.*[88]

The response at home is no source of pride. The government disbanded the Airborne Regiment and convened an inquiry, but quickly closed it down when the DND stonewalled. Historians Granatstein and Bercuson blamed the whole thing on the peacekeepers, with Bercuson somehow getting in a shot at the welfare state in the process.[89] The message of Rwanda and Somalia did not become: address racism. Instead, it became: don't do peacekeeping.

The tiny size of his Rwanda force was not Dallaire's only problem. Only 80 of his 300 vehicles were serviceable. The poorest contributor nations sent their troops with almost no personal gear. Dallaire's peacekeepers came from 26 different countries. English was the official language of the mission. In the military contingent, Dallaire's deputy was the only one who spoke it as a first language.[90]

The traditional peacekeeping mission ended before it began. Dallaire learned of Hutu extremist plans in the capital, Kigali, to murder Belgian peacekeepers in order to force their withdrawal and to register Tutsis for extermination. He asked his UN superiors for authority to raid Hutu arms caches. The request was denied and he was reminded that the U.S. would not support aggressive peacekeeping.

Tragedy followed. The Rwandan president was Hutu but had committed to Arusha, as had the prime minister. In April 1994, the president died when his plane was shot down under mysterious circumstances. A squad of peacekeepers from Ghana and Belgium was sent to the home of the prime minister, next in the government leadership order. She lived next door to the U.S. embassy. They were to escort her to a radio station to broadcast an appeal for calm. Hutu soldiers captured the peacekeepers. They released the Ghanaians then tortured and mutilated the Belgians. They hunted down and shot the prime minister, her husband and children. Soon they had eliminated all moderate Hutu leaders. The well-planned slaughter began. Hutu radio broadcasts included names, addresses, and even license plate numbers of targeted people.[91]

Given that we are all so inured to horror, graphic descriptions are of limited use in persuading people to abandon war. A lengthy graphic account of the Rwanda genocide alone would also likely be ineffective in making the case for the protection of civilians. I include only a brief account of how 800,000 civilians and 14 peacekeepers died while the world did nothing. It should at least be a reminder that the service of peacekeeping soldiers is no less worthy of respect than that of those in war.

This was Dallaire's reaction upon seeing the bodies of the Belgian soldiers:

... a heap of mangled and bloodied white flesh in tattered Belgian para-commando uniforms. The men were piled on top of each other and we couldn't tell how many were in the pile....it was hard to identify any of the faces or find specific markings. We counted them twice: eleven soldiers. In the end, it turned out to be ten.[92]

Power described the methodical massacre of civilians this way:

Killers often carried a machete in one hand and a transistor radio in the other. Tens of thousands of Tutsi fled their homes in panic and were snared and butchered at checkpoints. Little care was given to their disposal. Some were shoveled into landfills. Human flesh rotted in the sunshine... If the killers had taken time to tend to sanitation, it would have slowed their 'sanitization' program.[93]

The conduct of the U.S. respecting Rwanda is strong evidence that Canada should build policies on a better vision than Maloney's call that she be ready to play a supporting role in military interventions chosen by the western powers. In Rwanda, the Americans did not simply stand by. They consciously undermined the effort to save lives.

U.S. priorities were outlined in a secret presidential directive, issued days before the killing began. Excerpts leave no doubt that humanitarian considerations mattered little:

The United States remains committed to meeting such threats [post-Cold War threats] *through either unilateral or multilateral action, **as our interests dictate**.... The U.S. will not support in the Security Council proposals for UN involvement in situations where such involvement is not viable **or when it would interfere with U.S. interests**. Peace operations cannot and will not substitute for unilateral or coalition action when that is what **our national interest requires**. Multilateral peace operations must, therefore, be placed in proper perspective **among the instruments of U.S. foreign policy**.*[94] (Emphasis added).

That directive guided the Americans on Rwanda. It guides them today. In the Security Council, they pushed to reduce the already miniscule UNAMIR budget and did so rather crudely. UN ambassador Madeline Albright insisted that the Security Council consider ways to reduce the mission and "seek economies". Just before the killing began, the U.S. was arguing that Arusha implementation had been too slow and the whole mission should be scrapped.

The U.S. also refused Dallaire's request to jam the Hutu radio stream of hate broadcasts and human target information. The state department legal office even based part of its objection on the U.S. commitment to free speech! Legalisms were more important than lives. At a time when the death toll was between 200,000 and half a million, the Americans nitpicked the legal definition of genocide, fearing that if they used the term and were seen to do nothing it would damage both U.S. international credibility and the government's prospects in an upcoming election. U.S. media were complicit. The *Washington Post* editorialized that the U.S. had no national interest in acting. The American and Canadian public certainly had no interest. [95]

When revelations about the genocide continued to unfold, Dallaire appealed for reinforcements. The U.S. adamantly resisted, continued to demand withdrawal of UNAMIR, and refused to support a new UN mission. When the death toll reached 100,000, the Security Council voted to slash the force to 270.[96] However, when the shocked Belgians wanted to pull out but not be seen as doing so alone, they contacted the Americans for cover. They got it.

The Belgian evacuation was a clear example of western racism. Dallaire was ordered to make evacuation of foreigners his priority and told that he could abandon impartiality and his limited mandate on use of force if it was necessary to accomplish that mission. One thousand fresh, well-equipped French, Belgian, and Italian troops flew in to conduct the evacuation. Dallaire's rag-tag force watched enviously, knowing that integrating such a force into UNAMIR could have contained, if not halted the slaughter.[97]

The evacuation of whites had tragic consequences for blacks. A unit of Belgian soldiers had been protecting 2,000 Rwandans, including 400 children. When the troops were ordered to the airport to assist the departing foreigners, Hutu militiamen came in as soon as they left and murdered them.

In spite of all this, UNAMIR managed to save lives. Some 25-30,000 Rwandans gathered at positions staffed by the peacekeepers. The Hutu militias were not brave killers and it took very little effort to keep them away. A modestly increased UN force could have made a significant humanitarian difference.

In the humanitarian effort, there is a third Canadian who should be remembered. Canada reluctantly committed one C-130 aircraft to an airlift into Kigali from Uganda. At a time when no other nation would risk a flight, a crew led by Major J.E.R. Oliver flew four flights a day for weeks, in spite of being hit by ground fire.[98]

Power found it paradoxical yet natural that the failure affected most the person who tried hardest to save lives. Rwanda made Dallaire the most visible victim of the PTSD that governments continue to deal with inadequately in Canada and elsewhere. Dallaire remained an advocate of peacekeeping and protection of human rights, but was forced out of the army with a medical discharge in 2000. He later attempted suicide. He dedicated his memoir in part to his principal researcher, Sian Cansfield. She had immersed herself in everything about Rwanda for two years. She committed suicide before the book was published.[99]

Toward Canadian Leadership in the Transformation of Peacekeeping

For Canada, there is a better contribution to the world order than joining other people's wars. All of Canada's peacekeeping missions, including UNPROFOR and UNAMIR, provide lessons that can point the way toward a transformation in peacekeeping. And for once, Canada can lead rather than follow.

Respecting their military components, the lessons of the missions we have examined include the following:

1. Traditional peacekeeping within the trinity remains useful in true consent circumstances when for any reason the combatants see ending the conflict as in their interest.

2. When a mission begins with the general consent of the parties but becomes one requiring wider peacekeeping, the UN force must be capable of enforcing the consent as part of ground level decision making; the force must scrupulously demonstrate impartiality, and should have the media capability to demonstrate that to the world; the force must be robust enough, and operate under a mandate sufficient to permit it to protect itself, protect civilians, and deliver humanitarian relief.

3. While assistance in settlement of conflicts should remain part of both types of peacekeeping, first priority should be given to protection of civilians and humanitarian concerns.

4. The UN should develop criteria for fairly and impartially determining when massive human rights abuses are occurring on a scale that justifies intervention regardless of the consent of the political entity in power. Upon determining that the threshold has been reached, it must assemble a force sufficiently powerful to protect populations from such abuses.

Fortunately, many in the international community have been working on the details of a very practical framework that incorporates many of these components. There is much yet upon which to gain consensus and many issues remain. But those doing the work recognize that Canada can once again lead in the effort. It is exciting stuff and speaks to a far more prominent role for Canada on the 21st century world stage. Here is some of what has been achieved, and what could lie ahead.

In 2000, a UN panel of diplomats and soldiers prepared a report on all aspects of peacekeeping operations. A Canadian developed the blueprint for rapid assembly and deployment of a force. The report recommended that the military component of future peacekeeping missions be strong enough *to defend itself effectively,* 'confront the *lingering forces of war and violence' and protect civilians under its care.*[100] It also urged that peacekeepers who witness violence against civilians be presumed authorized to stop it, within their means. These recommendations face opposition from defenders of Westphalian peacekeeping who wish to limit the UN to traditional operations conducted only with the consent of governments. But the report tabled a more creative concept, and some guidance on implementing it.[101]

At the urging of Canada and Norway in 2002, the Security Council issued a memo on protection of civilians that included a range of specific measures.

Despite abuses such as those of the U.S. in Libya, RTP, a doctrine that was the product of an organization founded by Canadian Lloyd Axworthy, remains important. The 2005 UN World Summit endorsed it. A 2006 Security Council resolution did likewise, reiterating the demand that belligerents grant access to humanitarian agencies, and stating a willingness to act in the absence of state protection for deliberately targeted civilians.[102] The challenge remains to keep RTP from the hands of all who seek to use it only to further their "national interests" in futile geopolitical struggles like those in the Middle East today.

Peacekeeping with humanitarian priority faces enormous challenges. At the UN, there is corruption, inefficiency, and a bloated bureaucracy. These factors have always diminished the effectiveness of peacekeeping. And they have provided an excuse for the great powers to relegate peace to a back burner while they engage in the same failed 20th century geopolitical strategies. But corruption, inefficiency, and bureaucracy also characterize nation states, including those in the West. These obstacles are far from insurmountable.

Given Canada's contributions to date, her scholars and diplomats should be involved in the ongoing conversation about humanitarian peacekeeping and the trinity. An example is the Uniting for Peace (UFP) resolution that, in effect, permitted the secretary general and the General Assembly to authorize the Suez mission. Could that resolution be useful in a similar situation today to reduce the obstacles often presented by permanent members? In a scholarly exchange for the American Journal of International Law, Larry Johnson, a respected scholar, doubted the utility of UFP in current conflicts. Frederick Kirgis, an equally respected scholar, is not sure Johnson is correct.[103] These are just the kinds of exchanges that are useful and needed.

Such questions appear esoteric to most of us. Certainly they are less splashy than costumed Great War reenactments. But their resolution and the policies and public attitudes that result are far more important to the future of Canada, and the planet.

Canada should be part of the effort to prevent major powers from superficially embracing RTP in order to employ it for their own purposes. In the Middle East for example, unable to gain Security Council approval under RTP when the Syrian government began to murder its people in 2012, the western powers at this writing have been further frustrated by the emergence of ISIS. The group has joined the war against the Syrian government, while committing atrocious human rights abuses. The U.S. went from air strikes for the humanitarian purpose of saving some ISIS victims to intervening more broadly in the conflict. Canada is once again tagging along. The current venture against ISIS aligns Canada and the U.S. with countries they usually see as enemies, as well as countries with their own abominable human rights record. Choosing which side to attack is becoming an increasingly futile game. Canada does not have to continue playing it.

Postscript: Weaning Canada from the Arms Trade

If Canada chooses a better national vision, she will have to find a way to curb the nation's appetite for arms sales. This is particularly important because of some of her arms customers. An Ontario group called the Coalition to Oppose the Arms Trade details the rapidly rising volume of Canadian arms sales in the Middle East and North Africa, as well as the heavy investment of Canadian pension funds in the arms industry.[104] As noted, arms go to countries like Saudi Arabia that systematically violate basic human rights. If Canadians choose peacekeeping they will have to disavow the venerable capitalist practice of war profiteering. The Canadian arms industry was a major voice in a 2106 policy review by the DND. Predictably, the corporations called for more arms spending and touted jobs as the benefit to Canadians. It is time for Canadians to consider the moral implications such employment.

Instead of continuing to play a minor supporting role in a play that should close, Canada has the opportunity for a better part in a new production. She can stand on the shoulders of giants like Lester Pearson, Tommy Burns, Romeo Dallaire, Lewis MacKenzie, Clayton Beattie, and J.E. Oliver. But does Canada's most recent war in Afghanistan signal that she has already chosen the Maloney "forward security" approach? Or did her current patron lure her into Afghanistan on the pretext that the mission was mostly about peacekeeping? Let us examine that next.

Chapter VII

CANADA IN AFGHANISTAN: BAIT AND SWITCH OR BLIND BLUNDER?

There is no clearer illustration of the tension between the policies that issue from competing visions than the story of Canada's strange experience in Afghanistan. In it we can see that many of the factors we are examining play out much the same as in past conflicts. Still unclear is which vision will guide Canada now that the latest incidence of ground fighting in other people's wars has ended.

One might conclude that Afghanistan signaled the triumph of the coming of age---warrior nation narrative. After decades of at least blunting the demands of the U.S. patron, Canada sent troops into a war for the first time since Korea. But how those troops got into combat casts doubt on such a conclusion.

Journalist Linda McQuaig sees the story of Canada in Afghanistan as a classic example of bait and switch perpetrated primarily by the Canadian military establishment.[1] Perhaps so, or perhaps it was simply a blind blunder brought about by a host of diverse circumstances. Whatever the proper characterization, Canada was drawn into Afghanistan with the expectation of playing a quasi-peacekeeping and humanitarian role. Only later did the Americans persuade her to join in combat in the most dangerous part of the country--- areas where European nations wisely refused to send their forces. We will see that once again the federal leadership was initially hesitant and cautious. This time, however, Canada's senior military leaders augmented U.S. pressure significantly. They were motivated by a virtually seamless inter-relation with their U.S. counterparts. Once again, the Canadian people were kept largely in the dark, though it must be said that they did not demonstrate much interest in the parts of the truth that did emerge.

Canada's transition in Afghanistan from what the government wished and hoped would be something of a peacekeeping role to combat demonstrates now-familiar factors: longing for recognition, reluctant participation, desire to minimize casualties, eventual acquiescence to a powerful patron, exemplary performance by troops on the ground--- all in someone else's war.

The definitive guide through Canada's shifting experience in Afghanistan in the first seven years of the conflict is Janice Gross Stein and Eugene Lang's work, *The Unexpected War: Canada in Kandahar*[2]. Lang was chief of staff in the Ministry of Defence during the critical period of the war. The events that Stein and Lang take us through are the most significant ones because after 2007 Canada simply extended withdrawal deadlines and waited for the Americans to signal that it was permissible to join them and get out.

Graveyard for Foreign Intervention

The U.S. was the third major power to learn the futility of invading Afghanistan. A good summary of the fate of invaders is found in Peter Tomsen's, *The Wars of Afghanistan*.[3] Like Hastings on Korea, Tomsen, who was special envoy to Afghanistan for George H.W. Bush, supports the war while laying out most of the reasons it was a mistake.

The British conducted the first western invasion in 1838 as part of an imperial contest with Russia. It was again justified as a mission to civilize backward people. After initial success, the British were forced into a bloody withdrawal in the dead of winter.[4] They tried again in 1878. They gained some territorial and diplomatic concessions, but avoided another humiliating exit only by making concessions of their own and buying their way out.

A senior British diplomat summed up the results of the two invasions in a statement that could have been released today: ...*all that has been yet accomplished has been the disintegration of the state, ...the assumption of fresh and unwelcome liabilities in regards to one of its provinces, and a condition of anarchy throughout the rest of the country.*[5]

Before departing, the British persuaded the Afghan ruler to sign the Duran Line Accord, establishing what the West mistakenly assumes today is the border with Pakistan. The line was similar to mistakes the Paris treaty makers made after the Great War. It literally split tribes, clans and families. Britain and Russia decided, without any Afghan input, that Afghanistan would be a buffer state. Afghanistan reclaimed its right to an independent foreign policy in 1919 and in 1947 rejected the Duran line.[6]

Afghanistan is not a nation in any sense understood by the West. There is no border with Pakistan. Members of seven major ethnic groups, usually dominated by the Pashtuns, have been in the area for thousands of years. Today, as has always been the case, the writ of governments in the cities of Kabul and Kandahar barely runs at all in rural areas.[7]

Unfortunately for the Afghan people, the area was drawn into the Cold War, giving the Russians their chance in 1973 to demonstrate their overconfidence and ignorance of Afghan society. A series of coups, including a particularly brutal one, produced a resistance group called the Mujahedin. The West blindly supported the group with no attempt to examine its components or goals. Being against the Russians was enough.

Afghan tribes have a history of warring viciously with one another, but also of putting their differences aside in order to repel foreign invaders. Using the flexibility and decentralized tactical command and control that powerful nations never seem to understand, the Afghans humiliated the Russians and drove them out in 1989.[8] Tribal war resumed and the Taliban eventually emerged in 1996 to exert what authority is available to a government in Afghanistan. They brought brutal religious zealotry, but also order.[9]

A few years later, it was the turn of the U.S. invader to fail. In 2008, a Russian diplomat would say of that incursion: *They've already repeated all of our mistakes. Now they are making mistakes of their own, ones for which we do not own the copyright.*[10]

Tomsen concluded that the 1838 incursion established this pattern for all the future invasions: 1. Justifications. 2. Initial success. 3. Gradually widening resistance. 4. Stalemate. 5. Withdrawal.[11]

It was into this graveyard for foreign invasions that the U.S. persuaded Canada to spend a decade or so.

Canada's Slippery Slope Change of Mission

The intervening U.S. invasion of Iraq in 2003 played a part in in Canada's Afghanistan decisions. After U.S. president George W. Bush declared that "anyone who is not for us is against us", the government of Jean Chrétien retained just enough of Lester Pearson's respect for the UN to insist on its blessing for that war- -- something the U.S. could not obtain for a plainly illegal venture. Canada declined formal participation in Bush's "coalition of the willing". But resisting American pressure to send troops apparently required deceiving the Canadian public. While Chrétien was telling the House of Commons that Canada would not join "Operation Iraqi Freedom", Canadian diplomats were secretly telling the U.S. to disregard that statement and offering suggestions as to how Canada could "discreetly" aid the operation with air and naval forces, as well as with high level military assistance in planning the war. The U.S. asked Canada to destroy the documents containing these exchanges.

In fact, there was "discreet" naval and air force assistance. Canada granted air space and refueling operations in Newfoundland to support the Iraq invasion. Doing that alone qualified some nations to be listed in the "coalition of the willing". Canada also supplied surveillance aircraft to guide fighter jets.[12]

Further, hundreds of Canadian officers already embedded with U.S. remained with units deploying to Iraq. This intermingling of U.S. and Canadian military brass even resulted in a Canadian general serving as one of the high level planners of the Iraq invasion and becoming deputy commander of more than 35,000 troops. The general was Walter Natynczk. We will see him playing a part at several points in the government's lamentable treatment of Afghan veterans. For his command role, Governor General Michael Jean awarded him the Meritorious Service Cross.[13]

Canada's experience with the U.S. in Iraq reflects the contest between competing visions. Arrayed on one side, a cautious civil leadership and an uninformed public. On the other, military leaders spoiling for a fight anywhere and anytime the U.S. directed.

A significant factor in Canada opting out formally may have been that the Americans at the outset did not seem to care much.[14] Perhaps they remembered their easy success in the first Gulf War. Perhaps they believed U.S. defence secretary Donald Rumsfeld's laughable public pronouncement that Iraqis would greet the Americans as liberators. But Canada and Iraq affected Canada and Afghanistan. The U.S. illegally began the invasion of Afghanistan two years before it went illegally into Iraq, but the Iraq assault coincided with a critical decision-making time for Canada about Afghanistan. The governments of Chrétien, and later Paul Martin, feared that the Americans might not abide Canada repeating its Iraq resistance.

After the 9/11 attacks, the Americans demanded that the Taliban government in Afghanistan surrender the suspected mastermind of the event, Osama Bin Laden. Consistent with a long Afghan tradition of negotiating, the Taliban asked for evidence of Bin Laden's guilt. The U.S. responded that its demands were not negotiable and issued an ultimatum. The Taliban dropped its demand for evidence and suggested negotiation about a trial for Bin Laden in a country other than the U.S., perhaps even one like Saudi Arabia, Bin Laden's native country and a U.S ally that might even surrender him. Whether the Taliban were sincere, whether the negotiations would have gone anywhere became moot on October 7, 2001 when the U.S. began bombing a country that had not attacked her, bringing the first civilian deaths in a campaign that would kill tens of thousands.

McQuaig asks the legitimate question: By what logic or moral code are the lives of these people worth less than those who perished at the World Trade Center and the Pentagon?[15]

The U.S. attack plainly violated international law. In the outpouring of sympathy that followed the 9/11 attacks, the U.S. might well have secured Security Council approval to invade Afghanistan. The Americans did not bother. But a few weeks after the invasion, for the first time in its history NATO invoked article 5 of its founding document. The article provides that an attack on one member is an attack on all and all members must come to the aid of the victim. Canada was now in. But even though NATO would eventually take over most of the war and the UN would eventually approve, the U.S. would maintain forces in Afghanistan independent of both, as part of its quaintly named "Operation Enduring Freedom".

So much for legalities. What would Canada do in Afghanistan? At first, not much. In addition to deploying four warships in support of Operation Enduring Freedom, the Chretien government, unbeknownst to Canadians, did send part of the elite special forces Joint Task Force 2 (JTF2) to Afghanistan. Still, it appeared for a time that the hallmark caution of Laurier and King might prevail.

The emergence in late 2001 of a potential addition to Canada's participation did not appear to threaten that Canadian caution. The change would require sending some military personnel to Afghanistan, but not for combat. Instead, they were to be part of a UN-mandated quasi-peacekeeping effort known as the International Security Assistance Force (ISAF). Defence minister Art Eggleton described it as *a stabilization mission to assist in opening corridors for humanitarian assistance.*[16] It would be limited to the relatively safe area of Kabul. The military brass might not be happy but the government certainly would be content with a role that at once got the U.S. off its back and at the same time was consistent with Canadian public opinion. Chrétien observed:

*The principal role that we hope they [the Canadian forces] will have....
will be to make sure aid gets to the people who need it. Of course, we don't
want to have a big fight there.*[17]

ISAF thus began as a mission consistent with an agent of peace
vision. Kandahar would later become the symbol of its opposite.

How did Canada in Afghanistan slip from actions consistent
with one vision, to those of its opposite? Whatever the answer, it is
not because of any informed decision by Canadians. Neither was it
the result of any national security concerns or an assessment of the
risks, benefits, and costs of assuming a combat role.

Ironically, the first obstacle to Canadian participation in ISAF
came from the British who used to invite Canada *into* wars. ISAF was
shaping up as a European operation, led by the British, who made it
clear that Canada was not invited.

Shortly after this rebuff, acting through embedded Canadian
officers, the U.S. requested a Canadian presence in Kandahar
province. Canadian generals seized on this opportunity to send a
battle group of 800 troops. The government acquiesced but imposed
a six-month limit. The 2002 deployment became a step down a very
slippery slope. And it was the product of U.S. and Canadian military
officials making foreign policy. The Pentagon and the National
Defence Headquarters (NDHQ) called the shots. Stein and Lang
are candid about the part played by Canada's generals: *The occupants of
the South Tower of NDHQ have always been preoccupied, almost obsessed,
with their relationship with the U.S. Military...Indeed, Canada's generals
and admirals tend to be more concerned about their relationships with their
American counterparts than they are with their own political master in
Ottawa.*[18]

Still, the commitment looked minimal and low-risk. It was only
for six months and although the area was the most dangerous, the
Americans had already routed the Taliban and were just mopping
up. In fact, the first four Canadian deaths came from mistakenly
dropped U.S. bombs. In July 2002, new defence minister John
McCallum came to Afghanistan for a ceremony marking the end of
the Canadian mission. Except that it was not the end.

In the summer of 2002 the Canadian government had no further plans for Afghanistan, but NDHQ did. What did the Americans want, if anything?[19]

What the Pentagon wanted, it turned out, disappointed Canada's military establishment but proved a real temptation to the Canadian government. At a 2003 meeting Rumsfeld told McCallum that the U.S. wanted the ISAF in Kabul transferred from UN to NATO control, and wanted Canada to lead it. Europeans no longer objected. The Americans had decided to invade Iraq and wanted to free up their forces in Afghanistan. They also wanted nothing to do with the messy work of quasi-peacekeeping and humanitarian work in Kabul.

Rumsfeld mentioned one more thing. The U.S. might perhaps like a Canadian battle group to return to Kandahar, only because the focus was turning to humanitarian work and training the Afghan army now that the Taliban were defeated, and Canada was just the country to carry out such a mission. McCallum plainly told him that if Canada consented, there would be no capacity to do more later in Iraq.

Canada agreed to Kabul. It looked like a second chance to satisfy everyone. It would turn out instead to be the next step down the slope. If Canada was to return to Afghanistan, the generals wanted it to be for "real fighting". They even protested that Kandahar would be a safer place for the troops than Kabul. But the government, happy to be let off the hook in Iraq, signed on to Rumsfeld's plan for transferring the sticky work of constructing and maintaining stability in Afghanistan to Canada.

The commitment, however, was subject to pre-conditions. Before increasing the number of troops to 2,000, the largest in ISAF, Canada insisted on a partner nation that would supply the second largest number. Germany agreed to that role. More significant was the condition limiting the mission to one year and the geographical area to Kabul. Rumsfeld, still dictating policy, was reluctant about the last condition but agreed. He even offered a guarantee that the U.S. would extract the Canadians if the situation in Kabul deteriorated.[20]

At this point, the two military establishments had steered Canada from four warships and a handful of Special Forces troops, to six months of an 800-person battle group in Kandahar and a new 2,000 strong mixed purpose force in Kabul. The troops were not engaged in the heavy combat that the generals longed for so desperately. The mission was sufficiently ambiguous to satisfy the Canadian public. It was all now set to end in 2004.

It was not to be. Even as Canada took over ISAF, forces were at work that would move Canadians out of the relative safety of Kabul, out of primarily relief work and a partial peacekeeping role, and into an indefinite commitment to a full-scale war in the south. These forces grew from the actions of the Taliban, the Kabul government, the Afghan people themselves, the Canadian military—and, of course, the Americans.

As the Canadians arrived, the nature of the conflict was changing. The Taliban were not gone. Like the Boers, they had regrouped and changed to a mountain version of guerilla tactics. The easy part was over. The Americans had had their "home by Christmas" victory. Continuing the war would now require counterinsurgency fighting, not traditional combat. In the midst of this brewing maelstrom, the war-weary Afghan people wanted nothing more than peace and stability in their lives. The Kabul government could not provide it, and had little interest in trying. It was shot through with corruption, including the army and most especially the police. This should not have been surprising. An assembly of warlords from a group called the Northern Alliance had chosen the government's leader, Hamid Karzai. The warlords, who staffed Karzai's ministries, apparently knew where the money was. Karzai, who was a favourite of the West for a time, knew how to get it. He had been a consultant for a major U.S. oil company.

The human rights record of the Northern Alliance group is comparable to that of the Taliban. Little wonder that the Afghan people were at the time in favour of extending ISAF across the country.[21]

Another step down the slope came in early 2004, when Canada secured from NATO the right to name the commander of ISAF in Kabul. Named to the post was none other than the charismatic warrior and former deputy commanding general of the U.S. Army III Corps, Rick Hillier.[22] We have seen Hillier's candid reminder that the purpose of the Canadian military is to kill people. Hillier would later come to have an unwarranted say in Canadian policy making. He is not entirely to blame for that. He obtained his influence by default. Nevertheless, there was now on the ground in Afghanistan a leader who had no use for military involvement in humanitarian missions, or peacekeeping.

With the U.S. tiring of Afghanistan, Rumsfeld inserted one more idea into this volatile mix---another means of extricating the Americans. The proposal was for something called Provincial Reconstruction Teams (PRT) to be formed across the country. Participating coalition nations would be responsible for a particular area. This concept also appeared fairly benign. The teams would be made up of both soldiers and civilians who would *encourage peace and stability within the provinces/regions and monitor the supervision of developmental activities throughout Afghanistan.*[23] The Americans were so enthusiastic about having other countries tidy up for them that they put together a demonstration PRT, somewhat similar to a model home, and gave the Canadians a tour.[24] Unfortunately, the part about "stability" would require PRT members especially those assigned to the PRT in Kandahar, to be---certainly in the eyes of civilians---participants in a violent war that was disrupting their lives and killing too many of them. Canada signed on and committed another 200 people to the U.S. war.

At the time of the commitment, the location of the PRT had not been established. Eventually, the more cautious European nations set up PRT in the less dangerous areas, leaving few places other than Kandahar for Canada. In 2004, Defence successfully pushed Foreign Affairs for Kandahar. The argument was not that Kandahar was the best place for Canadians to further peace and stability and supervise development. The Defence position was that other proposed locations would not give Canada enough international recognition. The clearest voice for Kandahar was that of Hillier, who was completing his term as ISAF commander and could not have been happy about the planned reduction from 2,000 to 200 for the force in Kabul. Hillier outlined tactical problems with alternative locations for the PRT and added that there was no upside for the alternative being discussed because: *No one would have noticed that we were there.*[25] And so, as real war loomed, a Canadian PRT in Kandahar was added to the Canadian battle group assisting in the southern mop up work.

All these developments dovetailed nicely with U.S. plans for NATO forces to move out of Kabul, eventually expanding to the south to free up U.S. troops for Iraq.[26]

The final step in what Stein and Lang so aptly termed the unexpected war came primarily because of Paul Martin and Rick Hillier. Martin, Chrétien's finance minister and rival, took leadership of the Liberal party in 2003, and managed election of a minority government in 2004. The party platform supported a "peace and nation-building" role for the Canadian Forces. At this important juncture, a plurality of Canadian voters either chose against the warrior nation narrative or, more probably, had little interest in international issues.

Prime minister Martin had formed and chaired a committee on relations with the U.S., but Afghanistan was far down his list of priorities. It would have to move up. U.S./Canada tension worsened when, after much delay and some mixed signals, Martin became the one to inform the Americans that Canada would not participate in its Ballistic Missile Defense program (BMD).

Whether Martin was concerned, as were most Canadians, about the weaponization of space, or about practical politics is unknown, but it is most likely the latter. Martin's minority government depended on the NDP and Bloc Quebecois, both vocally opposed to BMD. The government had earlier indicated that Canada was likely to join. Martin had appointed David Pratt, a favourite of the military, as minister of defence, moving Bill Graham to Foreign Affairs. Pratt supported the U.S. on almost everything, including Iraq and BMD. It was he who contacted Rumsfeld with a signal that Canada was inclined to join BMD. Graham, who as defence minister had been opposed, changed sides with this later explanation: *Foreign Affairs view was that there is a limit to how much we can constantly say no to the political master in Washington. All we had was Afghanistan to wave. On every other file we were offside.*[27]

By the time Martin finally turned the Americans down, the prevailing view across government was that, after Iraq and BMD, Canada owed the U.S. one. That one was Afghanistan.[28] Enter Rick Hillier.

Although Martin began with little interest in Afghanistan, he did wish to revitalize the Canadian Forces. Hillier, completing his ISAF command was a rising star with a similar mission. Martin appointed him as chief of defence staff (CDC) in 2005 and from that point Hillier drove decisions about Afghanistan.

There was one last hurrah for the peacekeeping narrative. Martin began with more interest in the Darfur region of Sudan than in Afghanistan. In Darfur, a genocide was underway that would rival the scale of Rwanda. It is no surprise that Romeo Dallaire was championing the cause of replacing the ineffective UN force there with well-trained and equipped Canadians. He was mindful that the UN General Assembly had approved the doctrine of Responsibility to Protect. Martin agreed with Dallaire. He wanted Canadians to do what was necessary in Darfur.

The new CDC wanted none of this. Hillier was brilliant and persuasive. From a purely strategic perspective, he had some good ideas about transforming Canadian Forces. He opposed, for example, the continued procurement of big-ticket items like submarines and jet fighters in an attempt to form a junior version of American and British forces. But he had no use for peacekeeping and he ultimately persuaded the government to adopt a five-point plan for deep military involvement in Afghanistan.

Hillier was only able to outflank Martin on the matter of Darfur through duplicity. Before he would consider Hillier's plan for Afghanistan, Martin personally and directly demanded from Hillier a guarantee that Canadian Forces could perform both missions. Hillier gave it. Soon, however, Darfur disappeared from the agenda. Hillier eventually sent the peacekeepers there a few obsolete armored personnel carriers.

The plan that Hillier sold represents the last step in Canada's change of course in Afghanistan. Its provisions:

1. The PRT in Kandahar to remain from 2005-2007.
2. Deployment of Joint Task Force 2 back to Afghanistan.
3. Deployment of 350 troops and a general to assume leadership and command of the multinational forces headquarters in the Kandahar region.
4. Deployment to Kandahar of a combat infantry unit of up to 1,000 troops, initially as part of the U.S. Operation Enduring Freedom, and later under NATO. Hillier made it clear that the mission of the unit was *not* primarily to assist the PRT. Instead, it would be to conduct stabilization and combat operations throughout the province.
5. The final point was the only sop to the now moribund peacekeeping narrative. Hillier recommended a 15-person team to advise the Afghan government on public administration matters.

So in late 2005, just as things were about to go badly for the Americans in Iraq and Afghanistan, Canada went to war for real, although no one in government was permitted to use the word "war" or "counterinsurgency".[29]

Stephen Harper's minority government took over in 2006. The major shift in foreign policy was not a campaign issue. Harper ignored Afghanistan, except to state bravely that Canadians would not "cut and run". Canadians have yet to explicitly endorse the Hillier/ Rumsfeld view of international relations. Whether to do so is part of the conversation we do not have.

As the Tories took power, things started to go badly in Afghanistan. Canadian fatalities in the four *years* before February 2006 totaled eight. An equal number died in the following four *months*. By the end of the year, military casualties over 12 months in Afghanistan had exceeded the number suffered in any year since the Korean War.

One of the reasons that Canadians would die in increasing numbers beginning in 2006 was that fighting the war fell to a coalition of three---the U.S., Canada, and Britain. Defying NATO, the other European nations severely restricted where and how their forces would fight.[30]

Canadian TV began showing bodies coming home. The public, late as usual, began to carp. But, only three months into a minority government, Harper announced plans to extend the Afghanistan mission to 2009. He stated that he wanted Parliament to vote on the extension while simultaneously claiming the authority to extend it on his own, and announcing that he would do so even if the parliamentary measure failed. His government allowed only a few hours of debate on the subject.

It was not much of a debate. Other than following the wishes of the U.S., the government had no reason to stay in Afghanistan and it offered none. Still, Harper was able to secure enough Liberal votes to pass the extension in a close vote. Liberal assent was not surprising. The party leader was Michael Ignatieff, barely less an advocate of U.S. policies than Pratt.

In 2008, virtually all of the Liberals joined in to extend the venture to 2011. The official combat mission ended that year, but the Canadians, British, and Americans stayed on for another three years, joining the futile struggle to fashion some semblance of a government, a capable army and a police force. The last Canadian soldier to come home was Lt. Col. Eric Boucher, who arrived in Victoria on March 19th, 2014. Forty two per cent of Canadians were unaware that he and his comrades had still been in Afghanistan.[31]

Part of Canada's Afghanistan experience suggests that Canada may not accept Ignatieff's claim that peacekeeping died in Rwanda. It suggests that Canadian troops can be effective peacekeepers and do humanitarian work. It is the story of the Kandahar PRT.

Consistent with an approach termed 3D's---Defence, Development, and Diplomacy, Canada did invest significant sums intended to benefit the Afghan people. The investment was dwarfed by military expenditures, of course, but large enough that money could not be disbursed as it arrived.

Two thirds of the funds went to Kandahar, where the PRT had a civilian and military component. The Canadian International Development Agency (CIDA) at first focused on big projects like canals and dams. These well-meaning efforts faced several obstacles. One was skimming by the corrupt Kabul government. Another was that long-term projects do not impact the desperate day-to-day struggle of ordinary people. This, in turn, endangered both components of the PRT. People could not be expected to distinguish between civilian workers and combat troops. To villagers, they were all part of a foreign occupying force providing nothing but violence. The Taliban, on the other hand, were paying monthly salaries in the amount of Afghan yearly per capita income.

It was Canada's ground level military commanders who drew on her tradition of innovative peacekeeping to improve the situation by the time the PRT was turned over to the U.S. in 2010. Much of the tangible aid to people was fashioned by PRT civilians and soldiers working together on smaller projects. The military often used its own funds.

A Canadian general recalled: *When I was commanding our forces in the south, I was the biggest warlord in the south…When an Afghan wanted something done, I listened and got it done.*[32] A PRT military commander told of writing up a contract with a village council on a message pad and finding an Afghan contractor to repair and build police stations; of buying clothing made by war widows and distributing them in orphanages; and of hiring a local contractor who in turn hired 200 men of fighting age to clean streets and pick up garbage. These projects were activities directly between Canadians and Afghans, bypassing the Kabul government.

Even these exercises in common sense peacekeeping, however, did not succeed. McKay and Swift capture the main reason. For soldiers who were supposed to be diplomats providing humanitarian assistance: *There was also the bedeviling problem of having heavily armed soldiers looking very much like the forces of an alien empire...dressed as they were in bulky flak jackets and heavy boots and masses of high-tech kit... driving around a poverty-stricken country whose language they could not speak.*[33]

Local projects, including digging wells and repairing houses, building schools and clinics were a minor feature of the war---a feature that government propaganda grossly overstated. The DND took the lead, spending $15.5 million on military publicity, and employing 500 public relations officers to spin the war. DND ran familiarization courses for embedded journalists, expelled some for publishing what the generals did not like and generally made independent reporting difficult. There was even an effort to influence the academic community. A DND body paid some of the scholars who testified before Parliament about Afghanistan.[34]

Why Afghanistan?

Some of the factors we have been examining form part of the answer. An important one again is propaganda. The government could not package and sell the truth to even a mildly interested public that Canada had gone to Afghanistan because of the relentless urging of the military to follow the Americans, or from a general desire to be noticed on the international stage. Even a sophisticated propaganda campaign would have trouble marketing that. Instead, confident that it could rely once again on superficial and uncritical journalists, the government sold the war with two themes. Like the missions themselves, the official justifications shifted from time to time.

One reason urged was that Canadians would be in Afghanistan doing "good guy" work, helping the oppressed Afghans, especially women. This pitch dominated at the beginning and near the end of the war. This was relatively easy at the outset, when Canada took over ISAF in Kabul and the public was unaware of JTF2 in the south. But once the war began to go badly and the Americans wanted real combat help, the message, like the mission, began to oscillate. In 2005, while Bill Graham was on a speaking tour explaining that Canadians were rebuilding a troubled country and winning hearts and minds as "warrior diplomats", Hillier was touting the mission as killing the "detestable murderers and scumbags" in Kandahar who threatened western societies.[35]

Hillier's bombastic style drew more media coverage, a fact that became more significant as the war wound down. Participation in the phony war on terror to fight the "threat to western societies" became the only message going forward. But in his New Year video message for 2011, governor general David Johnston tried to revive the good guy theme one more time: *We should be inspired by the courage, determination and conviction of our men and women in the Canadian Forces. We think of them and the civilians working at their side to build a better society…Rebuilding schools and ensuring the peace that will permit boys and girls to have an education are the key to reconstructing family life in Afghanistan.*[36]

Individual Canadians and small groups of both soldiers and civilians did indeed try hard to make life better for ordinary Afghans. But to claim that this was why Canada joined the war is no more accurate than the U.S. *post-hoc* justification that invading Iraq was really not about weapons of mass destruction, or oil, but rather to save the Iraqi people from a brutal dictator.

The propaganda about concern for women in Afghanistan is particularly weak. As McQuaig and others point out, the position of women was better under the government that the U.S and the

Mujahedin "freedom fighters" (Osama Bin Laden among them) ousted. The Northern Alliance group of warlords supported by the West was already cancelling reforms and putting women back in burkas years before the Taliban gained power.[37] They continued the repression from posts within the American-backed regime of Hamid Karzai. Malalai Joya, the youngest female member of parliament detailed her experience with it. She was expelled from that body for "insulting the institution of parliament". She had criticized parliament for failing the Afghan people, saying that a stable or a zoo was better because at least there was a donkey that carried a load and a cow that provided milk. She continued to speak out, naming names of the warlords and drug lords who held government ministries. For her trouble, she was subjected to assassination attempts, assaults, threats of rape, and had her house blown up.[38] If Canadians thought they were fighting for the rights of women in Afghanistan, they were seriously misled.

Once again, the U.S. later joined by loyal Canada, backed the wrong side. It was the wrong side because there is no right side. As both Canadian and U.S. politicians finally came to say publicly, this is something that the Afghans will have to work out among themselves. That reality should have guided policy from the outset. Whatever the outcome of their latest invasion, it is now clear that western nations no longer care. The geopolitical choosing of sides has moved elsewhere in the Middle East.

Humanitarian justifications are only marginally useful to war makers. The "global war on terror" has an indefinite shelf life. The Harper government settled on it as the real reason Canada was fighting in Afghanistan and why she must remain vigilant, curtail her own people's liberty, and continue to follow the U.S. lead. Defence minister Gordon O'Connor even threw in the argument that the troops were in Afghanistan as retribution for 9/11. Retired general

O'Connor had earlier lobbied for a U.S. firm that planted a story about Iraqi soldiers throwing babies out of incubators in the first Gulf War---an updated version of bayoneted Belgian babies.[39]

The prime minister folded Afghanistan into the 90th anniversary of Vimy, remarking that the terrain of Kandahar must have looked as desolate as Flanders and eloquently claiming...*but those who wear the maple leaf on their uniform move forward against tyranny and fear with the same courage and determination that you did in your time and the heroes of Vimy Ridge did before you.*[40] And when Canadian forces finally ended their Afghanistan mission, Harper himself wrapped it all up with a gloriously ambiguous statement: *The end of the military mission and the lowering of the flag is a significant milestone in the fight against global terror.*[41]

Milestone indeed. Not, however, the end of the road for this valuable propaganda theme. At the time of the statement, the government was preparing to follow again the wishes of the U.S. and join a new bombing campaign in Syria and Iraq.

Afghanistan provides but one example of government expertise in information control. The Harper government mastered the art of censorship in many areas. The touchstone was a requirement that all statements by officials, or even publicly funded researchers, be routed through the Prime Minister's Office (PMO) for message laundering. In the Afghanistan war, the government permitted friendly journalists embedded with Canadian units and military officials to speak. Officials from Foreign Affairs and the CIDA were forbidden to speak publicly.[42]

With NDHQ and the government driving the message, and even the sporadically cautious views of Foreign Affairs silenced, the general failure of journalism has become even more damaging to prospects for a rational conversation about foreign interventions. Thankfully, there are notable exceptions. Dissenters may be heard here and there, but mainstream media still give excessive exposure to the voices of the warrior nation narrative. They include Rex Murphy,

Jack Granatstein, David Bercuson, Andrew Coyne, and others, along with right wing think tanks like the C.D. Howe institute.[43] There is nothing wrong *per se* with airing the government line in a fair debate, but that did not happen on Afghanistan.

Another factor is relevant to an explanation of Canada's decisions on Afghanistan. Notwithstanding the evolution of descriptive terminology, the union of capitalism and imperialism remains strong. The relationship has returned to the one that Arendt described before the advent of total war. The expectation is that the state's means of violence is to be available for the advancement and protection of business interests and national property.[44] The Harper government made no secret of the connection. It announced something called the Global Markets Action Plan (GMAP), which translates: Foreign policy is now trade policy.[45] Human rights are clearly on the back, back burner when Canada's two biggest trading partners are the U.S. and China.

The new economic/foreign policy was linked to the U.S., and included decisions about Afghanistan. As the real war there began, Sean Maloney opined that helping the Americans in Afghanistan could well help to resolve a dispute over softwood lumber exports and keep Canadian borders open to trade.[46]

The closest link between the reasons Canadians died in Afghanistan and the capitalism/imperialism factor, however, is a subject with which Canadians are becoming increasingly familiar—energy and pipelines. Afghanistan's neighbours hold a vast store of natural gas. American and Canadian companies want it. There is competition for it that implicates other geopolitical conflicts and "essential national interests" in the region. Afghanistan, an energy bridge, may well be the key to determining which countries prevail.

Here is an admittedly oversimplified outline of the competition. Turkmenistan, a former member of the Soviet Union, possesses a huge reserve. The only pipeline for it runs north to Russia. Pipelines running east to China and west to Europe are planned. U.S. and

Canadian companies plan a pipeline that runs south, through Afghanistan. The route would traverse the most contested provinces, Kandahar and Helmand, the area that was the responsibility of the Americans, Canadians, and British. Before the war the U.S. was negotiating with the Taliban government for this pipeline. Negotiations broke down two months before the invasion. Plans for the pipeline continue.

The project is now named TAPI for the involvement of four nations, Turkmenistan, Afghanistan, Pakistan, and India. U.S. oil giant UNOCAL, Karzai's former employer, and numerous smaller Canadian oil companies seek a part of the action. Unfortunately, there is a competing proposal from Iran, so Afghanistan is in danger of being embroiled in yet another geopolitical struggle. NATO officials have seriously discussed a role for the alliance in pipeline security. The options are to clear the Taliban from the pipeline route or negotiate a deal with the Afghan government, which might soon be the Taliban.

Only a dedicated conspiracy theorist would argue that the U.S. and Canada waged war in Afghanistan solely so that their energy companies could prevail in the pipeline competition. Yet it is not necessary to go that far to see that, whatever her real reasons, Canada was not in Afghanistan to rid the country of "detestable murderers and scumbags", or to build schools for girls.[47]

Costs: The Living and the Dead

In earlier wars, it was possible to discern benefits for Canada, though they were always outweighed by costs. Afghanistan yielded no benefits, only costs.

Among them, of course, was loss of life. Of the more than 40,000 Canadians who went to Afghanistan, 158 soldiers, a defence contractor, and a journalist died. A sample of the casualty list from 2010 reminds us of the lost potential. Andrew Miller was only 21; Steve Martin and Brian Collier were 24. And though war remains, as Emmeline Pankhurst said a century ago, primarily a male creation, women have always served and died. Their casualty numbers are rising in modern warfare, as we are reminded by the death of master corporal Kristal Giesenbrecht.[48]

Afghanistan does not fit well into the prevailing narrative. That may be one reason the government had trouble getting anything organized to honour those who served there. A Royal Proclamation designated May 9, 2014 as the day of commemoration. There was a brief mention of it on two government websites. The families of the 158 dead were notified by letter and encouraged to attend— at their own expense. Later, Harper personally scrapped a noon ceremony on Canada Day. Instead, Afghanistan is now to be lumped in and remembered in events over the next few years, with the 100th anniversary of the Great War, the 75th anniversary of World War II, and anything else that government officials might add on.[49]

In 2007, the government did name a portion of the highway between Canadian Forces Base Trenton and the coroner's office in Toronto as the "Highway of Heroes". That is about it for official recognition of the lives lost in the failed war in Afghanistan.

Survivors of service in Afghanistan and their families bear another cost---suicide and mental illness.

In every war, governments can sanitize deaths and designate all of the dead as heroes. But those who return with the most gruesomely broken bodies provide less inspiring images than the "fallen". Even more challenging to the warrior nation line are those who come home broken in mind. Over the years, whether from "shell shock", "battle fatigue" or PTSD, some of the heroes become dependent on drugs and alcohol; some lash out violently—and some commit suicide. These soldiers provide no help in selling the next war. All a responsible government can do is honour their service and make sure they are treated decently. That, the Canadian government, abetted by its senior military, has failed to do.

While the defence establishment pushed for the multi-billion dollar purchase of F-35 fighters, the government closed Veterans Affairs offices all over the country, increasing the caseloads of those that remain. How the government of Justin Trudeau will serve veterans remains to be seen. Veterans Affairs can hardly do worse than it did under Walter Natynczk, the Iraq invasion planner and commander whose disdain for veterans became a news story. Under the Harper government, returning soldiers apparently bore the onus of proving that their afflictions were caused by their service. Any lawyer will tell you that on an issue of causation, the question of who bears the onus is usually determinative. A sample case illustrates the point.

Fortunately, the suicide attempt of master corporal Kristian Wolowidnyk did not succeed. Had it, he would have been the fourth veteran to have died in a week. The Kandahar veteran tried to take his life when the army notified him that he would be separated from the force because his PTSD and depression made him unfit for duty. He was barred from a prolonged release program for injured soldiers. He would be 18 months short of 10 years service, the eligibility requirement for a permanent pension.

The story got out, including details of questionable military medical practices that led to the decision. The army backed off and promised Wolowidnyk participation in the extended release program. A few months later, when the Harper government was set to announce the May 9th Afghan war ceremony in Ottawa, and the corporal's story had faded from view, the army reneged and decided it would discharge him after all. This time the decision was based on a determination by the base surgeon in Edmonton that he was fit for civilian life --- a surgeon Wolowidnyk's wife says he never met. He remained short of pension qualification. The program promised Wolowidnyk was designed to prepare the injured either for transition to civilian life or return to duty. A former military ombudsman reports than 9 of 10 soldiers in the program are discharged, many of them, like Wolowidnyk, disqualified from pensions.

Veterans' advocates charge the military is treating PTSD like a disease to be eradicated from the ranks. Similarly situated veterans and their families claim that those who ask for help with mental injuries are stigmatized as losers and drunks, whose problems must have come from a source in civilian life. They say that seeking help also carries the risk of being discharged because of the universality of service rule that requires all Canadian Forces members to be fit for deployment at all times.[50]

The Harper government's defence and justice ministers publicly wished Wolowidnyk all the best. The good wishes were accompanied by a reduction of benefits for all modern veterans, compared with those for which their predecessors qualified. The government enacted in 2005 the New Veterans Charter. It changed the formula for benefits from a pension to a lump sum payment—from long-term support to a stipend to assist in the transition to civilian life. For those receiving military pensions, the government also decided to claw back the amount of any disability payments.

In response to these and other slights, veterans turned to one of the most remarkable institutions in Canadian society—the independent judiciary. In 2012, they won reversal of the disability claw backs. A class action over the disparate pension treatment of modern veterans has yet to be decided. That action has framed an issue that should be of interest to all Canadians: Does the government have a special obligation to soldiers? Government lawyers candidly argued that it does not; that promises made to earlier generations of veterans are mere political policy statements that do not bind current or future governments. Academics supporting this position note that this is a volunteer force and argue that its members knowingly accept the terms of service and agree to risk their lives without question.

A noted expert on military ethics makes a further argument. In doing so, he does not openly acknowledge the close analogy to a little known standard practice of military medicine on the battlefield. The argument is that once soldiers are too severely injured to perform duty, they lose any special entitlement to medical resources. That is the guide for "triage" in war. Priority of treatment for the wounded is determined not by medical criteria but by which patients have the best prospects for early return to combat.[51]

The important point is not the legal one of whether Canada has an enforceable special obligation to its veterans. It is that the only door open to many of the most broken of their number is the door to the courtroom.

It is difficult to determine if Canadians care about this matter, but at this writing Canadian veterans were continuing to fight---- with their government.

Costs: Moral Currency

A major cost of choosing to be in someone else's war this time was loss of Canada's hard won international reputation for supporting human rights. That has always been a risk when Canada has ceded to patrons the power to make decisions about the use of violence. It was the British and Americans in World War II who determined Canada's role in the firebombing of civilians. In some ways Canadian complicity with the U.S. in Afghanistan resulted in an even higher moral cost. There was no London blitz by the Taliban. Canada's current patron may display a positive balance in the weapons column but its moral account, and by association Canada's, is virtually bankrupt.

The moral cost to Canada was incurred by supporting the Americans as they compiled a considerable list of abuses. Canada and the U.S. killed civilians. Canada turned over prisoners to their Afghan allies to be tortured. The U.S. tortured prisoners and held them, including a Canadian child soldier, in illegal and inhumane detention. Canada cooperated and acquiesced. The U.S. shipped people to other countries to be tortured, including a Canadian citizen. Canada cooperated and acquiesced. All the while, Canadian soldiers were doing their best after being lured into regions in Afghanistan where they would suffer the most violent backlash to these actions.

Whether Canada was at specific times a direct participant in these abuses or, as McQuaig puts it, simply "holding the bully's coat", it is naïve to believe that the world has not noticed. The Canadian public was mildly interested for a while, and then went back to watching hockey as the country's leaders bartered her humanitarian birthright for a mess of commercial pottage. Before the public lost interest, however, many people became familiar with the names of Canadians Omar Khadr and Maher Arar.

Wherever Canada may have come of age, one her citizens came of age in an infamous U.S. gulag. In July 2002, Canada was beginning what her leaders thought would be mostly peacekeeping in Kabul. The U.S. was clearing out the remainder of the Taliban near the non-existent border with Pakistan. In a small village, a firefight was in progress. Omar Khadr, 15, was in a house surrounded by 100 U.S. troops who called in 500 pound bombs on the dwelling. Khadr was severely injured, but later was alleged to have thrown a grenade that killed a U.S. soldier. There began a story of disregard for the rule of law that would bring condemnation and shame on Canada.

Khadr would spend more than 12 years in the U.S. detention centre at Guantanamo Bay, Cuba. Cuba? The facility is a visible reminder of the days of unabashed American imperialism. In 1934, through its hand picked dictator Fulgencio Batista, the Americans secured a lease to 45 square miles of Cuba containing a provision that the lease could not be abrogated without the consent of both parties.[52] Despite U.S. barriers to access, a 2006 report authorized by the UN Commission on Human Rights found that practices at Guantanamo violated numerous international covenants, to two of which the U.S. is a signatory. Those documents, the International Covenant on Civil and Political Rights and the Convention Against Torture, forbid torture under any circumstances, though the U.S. essentially reserved the right to rely on its own interpretations of the term. There is little doubt that the U.S. acted at Guantanamo as an international outlaw.[53] The University of Toronto Faculty of Law maintains a database of all documents relevant to the ordeal of Omar Khadr.[54]

We will see that torture at Guantanamo was not the only instance of torture by the U.S. that involved Canadian complicity. But first there is the question of why Khadr was not treated as a prisoner of war and afforded rights guaranteed in the 3d and 4th Geneva Conventions, as well as the UN Convention on the Rights of the Child. The answer is another fanciful invention of the Americans in the face of international law. Since the forces opposing the western coalition invaders in Afghanistan did not wear uniforms or belong to a standard army, the U.S. declared that they were "enemy combatants". Those captured could be imprisoned indefinitely, denied the protections of international law, and treated as their captors saw fit.

Khadr, as part of a sham process also condemned in the UN Guantanamo report, pled guilty to murder and war crimes in violation of the "common law of war", a body of law whose very existence is doubtful.[55] As to Khadr's conduct, if he did kill the American soldier, something that has yet to be determined through any remotely fair process, he did so in combat with a highly trained professional force that had just bombed his location and wounded him severely. Khadr appealed his conviction on the grounds that the plea was involuntary. A "domestic common law" claim is about the only claim the U.S. has left. The government has already conceded that Khadr's offences were not international war crimes. A court has also rejected the charge of material support for terrorism. Consequently, it is becoming clear that the military tribunal at Guantanamo had no jurisdiction to try him.[56]

Canada did not just stand by while Khadr, who was not charged for three years, became the only western nation prisoner at Guantanamo. The Canadian Security Intelligence Service (CSIS) sent agents to assist the U.S. in interrogating him and shared information, all after publicly claiming that visits were only to check on his welfare. The International Red Cross, CSIS is not.

After Khadr pled guilty in 2010 and was sentenced to an additional eight years, the question of where he would serve the sentence remained. Once again, it fell to Canada's independent judiciary to shame the Harper government into following the law. A federal court ruled in 2009 that the Charter of Rights and Freedoms obliged the government to demand that Khadr be returned to Canada. The government appealed. It lost in the Federal Court of Appeal and appealed to the Supreme Court of Canada. The government lost there also, but unfortunately the court did not directly order it to seek Khadr's repatriation. This gave the government another two years to delay before he was placed in a maximum security Canadian facility in 2012. In 2015, Khadr was released on bail while his U.S. appeal is pending. The government fought that until the moment it was replaced in 2015. The new Liberal government announced that it would stop spending money to continue the injustice. Since his release, Khadr has been gracious and low key, saying of Harper's claims about him, "I am going to have to disappoint him".[57]

Much of the media still portray the story as a legitimate debate about whether he is a child soldier or, that omnibus term, a "terrorist" in whose case there were some unfortunate procedural missteps.[58] Anyone who cares enough to fight the tendency of their eyes to glaze over from reading the applicable law and compare it to uncontested facts will see that Canada joined the U.S. in flouting law, and did so in two areas that diminish her stature in the world community---children and torture.

Two months after Omar Khadr began his journey into oblivion at Guantanamo, another Canadian citizen was at JFK airport in New York, on his way home to his family in Montreal. Thanks to false information provided to U.S. authorities by the RCMP, he would never make it. Instead, he would become an involuntary participant in one of the more disgusting aspects of the U.S. "war on terror", the CIA extraordinary rendition program that scooped up people and sent them to cooperating countries to be tortured. The U.S. turned Maher Arar over to Syria, where he was confined in a cell about the size of coffin and beaten with electrical cables. Thanks to the comparative disinterest of the Canadian government, his ordeal would last for 10 months.

At the time, Arar was not under investigation for anything but his name came up in another investigation. Despite having no evidence against Arar, RCMP officers asked their U.S. counterparts to be on the lookout for him and for his wife. They added that the two were Islamic extremists suspected of having links to Al Qaeda. That is a reminder that we should be skeptical about government pronouncements that someone has "links to Al Qaeda", or "links" to anyone else. We all probably have "links to Al Qaeda".

When Arar was stopped at JFK, the RCMP officers had an opportunity to correct their earlier information. Instead, they complied with a request to submit a list of questions to be used in interrogating him. They added another falsehood, alleging that Arar had been in Washington, D.C. on September 11, 2001. In fact, if Arar had been any farther from Washington he would have been in the Pacific Ocean. On 9/11, he was in San Diego, California.

Instead of charging Arar or sending him to Canada for further investigation, U.S. authorities put him on a private jet bound for Syria. Arar later recalled that during the transfer a CIA agent, whom he named, told him: *If you want people to be well interrogated, you send them to Jordan. If you want people disappeared, you send them to Egypt. And if you want people to be tortured, you send them to Syria.*[59]

Not wishing to offend the Americans, the Canadian government response was *pro forma* at best. At one point, Canada's ambassador to Syria spoke optimistically about an upcoming meeting on the case as an opportunity to *rebut* charges of torture, not discover the truth. Apparently, it was only in 2011, when the U.S. State Department condemned the Syrian regime for murdering its own people and declared that it must be ousted, that Canada learn the shocking news that Syria tortured people. As McQuaig notes, Canada's foreign affairs minister could have learned about that eight years earlier, simply by clicking on a U.S. State Department website that even included a detailed list of Syrian torture techniques.

There is a hopeful side to this story. It suggests that Canadians are still concerned about basic human rights and not yet ready to cede all to the Americans. It suggests that there are yet responsible journalists. Word got out about Arar and the scandal forced the government to order an inquiry in 2004. Justice Dennis O'Connor of the Ontario Court of Appeal headed the commission of inquiry. Two years later, O'Connor's report definitively exonerated Arar and concluded that he was probably sent to Syria based on the RCMP misinformation. Among the conduct condemned in the report were leaks to Canadian news agencies falsely claiming Arar had admitted to training with Al Qaeda in Afghanistan, a country he has never seen. In the final chapter of the story, Canada's independent judiciary once again played a part. Arar sued the police service and other government officials. The government soon settled the case for $10 million. Arar also sued the U.S., where he was not so fortunate. A judge dismissed his action on "national security" grounds.[60]

The moral costs paid by Canada for joining the Afghan war were also multiplied on the battlefield. Canada's political and military leaders placed her troops in positions that led to their direct involvement in the human rights abuses that are the hallmarks of the Afghanistan war and the war on terror.

Canadians fighting in Kandahar had no facility of their own for interning prisoners of war. The options were to turn them over to either the Americans or the Afghan government. That was a serious problem. As we have seen, the Americans did not even recognize prisoners of war. Both countries were engaged in torture. International law forbids soldiers from knowingly handing over prisoners to authorities who torture.

At the outset, no one save defence minister Bill Graham paid much attention to the problem. In 2005, as Canadian units prepared to enter real combat in Kandahar, he dispatched Hillier to negotiate an agreement with the Afghan government about treatment of prisoners turned over to it by Canadian forces. Hillier, without authority, signed an agreement on behalf of Canada and Foreign Affairs retroactively approved it. Unfortunately, the agreement was done in ignorance and haste. Unbeknownst to Canada, Britain and Denmark had negotiated transfer agreements with important provisions absent from the Canadian document. Among them were a prohibition against the death penalty and a right to follow up with monitoring and visits by the military.

The Canadian military leadership vigourously opposed any requirement to monitor and visit until these omissions came back to bite the government---when a young reporter did his job. The Military Police Complaints Commission was asked to investigate allegations that Canadian soldiers had themselves abused three prisoners before handing them over to Afghan police. The investigation could go nowhere because the prisoners could not be found. Canada, with no way to follow up after surrendering prisoners, learned for the first time that the three had disappeared into the Afghan prison system. Things got worse for the government in 2006, when every reputable world human rights organization and even the U.S. State Department confirmed that the Afghan government routinely tortured prisoners. In Afghanistan, a reporter for the *Globe and Mail* found and interviewed 30 former detainees who claimed they had been tortured. The newspaper continued to follow the story, exposing the government's confusion and uncaring attitude toward the issue.

When Amnesty International sued to stop the transfers, the government, in effect settled the suit by hastily concluding a new agreement with Afghanistan.[61] This, of course, did not stop the torture and over the next three years more evidence came to light that the Canadian government had been warned.

The detainee scandal eventually died down, but it brought to light the methods employed by the Harper government propaganda machine. When the public outcry began to grow, Harper silenced Defence and Foreign Affairs and put his own communications people and cabinet members in charge of public statements.

Government spokespeople and Conservative MP's both played their part in the effort to make the issue go away without addressing its merits. One of the classic methods they employed was to attack the questioner rather than answer the question. Here are some examples of non-answers on the question of government knowledge about Afghan torture:

In 2009, diplomat Richard Colvin, testified before a House of Commons committee about his repeated reports warning the government that prisoners turned over by Canadian forces were being tortured in Afghan jails. Defence minister Peter McKay had promised to investigate how high up the reports had gone.

Instead of reporting on his investigation, McKay attacked Colvin's credibility in classic "deny without denying" style. He claimed that Colvin was getting his information from "people who throw acid in the eyes of schoolgirls". That, of course, was a lie. But it was another opportunity to demonize the enemy to justify atrocities and avoid revealing what the government knew.

Kory Teneycke, the PMO's minister of propaganda at the height of the scandal, and Hillier employed another equally evasive approach. Teneycke reminded the public that Afghan prisons were not the country clubs that the NDP and Liberals favoured in Canada. Hillier went further, comparing Afghan prisons favourably with a penitentiary in Ottawa and suggesting that, like the Taliban, Canadian prisoners would also claim mistreatment if they had the opportunity. Deny without denying. Attack the messenger and get a shot in at one's political opponents at the same time. Brilliant. Tory officials may have been uncaring, but they were not stupid.

The evasion worked. There is no question that the Afghans tortured prisoners they received from Canadian forces. There is no question that this fact was reported to Canadian government officials. But the public eventually lost interest in the question of exactly who knew of the torture and when.[62] That is particularly unfortunate. In 2014, the U.S. Senate issued an exhaustive condemnation of American torture activities, including the rendition program that snared Mahed Arar. A former senior intelligence officer with CSIS confirmed Canadian complicity.[63]

Canadian complicity in torture represents a massive cost of the Afghanistan war. It has inflicted still unrepaired damage to Canada's international reputation as a human rights leader. That reputation was earned by earlier generations of civilians and soldiers, including those who risked, and sometimes gave their lives to save lives as peacekeepers in Bosnia and elsewhere. It doomed to failure the efforts of many Canadians in Afghanistan who sought to win the war by improving the lives of ordinary people and acting as something other than one more in the procession of foreign invaders. For these soldiers and civilian workers, their own leaders poisoned the well of good will.

A particularly horrific event, long after Canadian forces left Afghanistan presents another aspect of the issue of complicity. On October 3d, 2015, the U.S. was also supposed to be gone. But, unable to resist continued intervention in the internal power struggle their 14-year war had aggravated, the Americans were bombing in support of the Kabul government against the Taliban. They bombed a trauma hospital operated by Medecins Sans Frontieres (MSF). They killed 19 people, including MSF staff and three children. MSF had repeatedly provided its location coordinates to all combatants. The attack continued for 30 minutes after MSF notified the Americans and the Kabul government that it was happening. These were not stray bombs. The main hospital structure was repeatedly hit with no damage to surrounding buildings. What has this to do with Canada? If there is a break and enter and one of the perpetrators leaves before the other kills a homeowner, is there any shared responsibility for the death?

The excuses for the hospital bombing are not worth repeating, save one. The Kabul government claimed that the Taliban were taking their wounded to the hospital. That could be true. MSF makes no secret of the fact that it treats all wounded. That is what allows it to function and in part explains the international esteem it has earned.[64]

Despite the fact that Afghanistan represents only costs and not benefits to Canada, the government relied on the collective indifference and amnesia of Canadians about it and once again joined the U.S. in a futile military campaign, this time in the Middle East. Yet indifference and a short memory do not equal endorsement. The warrior nation narrative and its policies have not yet prevailed. Perhaps exploring alternatives to it can yet help to keep Canada out of other people's wars.

CHAPTER VIII

STAYING OUT OF OTHER PEOPLE'S WARS

Until the nine year reign of Stephen Harper, ended in 2015, there was no chance for a conversation about staying out of other people's wars. The exchange is now possible, and it remains sorely needed. It appears that the government of Justin Trudeau will reverse many of the worst Tory policies but continue to follow the current patron. In response to the latest U.S. military adventure in the Middle East, Trudeau pledged to end Canadian bombing in the region. His government has already accepted 25,000 refugees and promised to increase humanitarian efforts. On the other hand, Canada is to increase front line training of those the U.S. has chosen as allies, and will otherwise provide support resembling Canada's role in Iraq.

The war to which Canada is currently invited will likely be as big a failure as Afghanistan. The conflict is even more confusing, if that is possible. The bombing of ISIS is an effort to assist a corrupt government in Iraq and also has the effect of assisting a brutal regime in Syria, the downfall of which the U.S. only recently demanded publicly. And on the U.S. side is Iran, anathema to Israel, the darling of the Harper government. For good measure, the Russians and Turks have joined in, bombing somebody; no one is exactly sure whom. Once again, the U.S. chose the wrong side because there is no right side.

So far, significant military casualties are unlikely. Civilians have not been as fortunate. They continue to be killed and dispossessed by all sides in record numbers.

War making and the popular will: defects in the structure of democracy

The government of Stephen Harper demonstrated how defects in the structure of Canadian democracy can virtually prevent the needed conversation from happening and in any event make the result irrelevant. Green Party leader Elizabeth May identifies the flaws from her experience within Parliament.[1] Award-winning journalist Michael Harris examines in detail how Harper exploited them.[2] The defects are few but significant:

- The "first past the post" system is anti-democratic. The last Conservative "majority" ruled with just under 40 per cent of the popular vote. Trudeau has promised to replace the system. Some doubt this, since he gained power with only marginally higher support. The difference is that Harper's 40 per cent was all he ever had. On many issues in 2015, including war and peace, strategic voters cast ballots believing that Harper's excesses required putting country ahead of their preferred party. They should not be put to that choice again. One hopes Trudeau will follow through.

- The current system is anti-democratic because of its excessive reliance on party loyalty. Having sent someone to Ottawa though they may have preferred someone else, constituents might yet expect to have their views represented, even when they vary from those of party leaders, especially the prime minister. A prime minister with a definite agenda, however, need not worry about independent thinkers. With rare exceptions, in the last government anyone opposing a significant policy was kicked out of caucus. That effectively ends a member's career. The flaw is aggravated by the demonstrated reluctance of parties to govern in coalition, as they could have done in 2008. Finally, opposition parties with many areas of agreement, instead attack one another.[3] For this phenomenon, all the Harper governments should be truly thankful.

- The current system is anti-democratic because, as Harper demonstrated, it allows the prime minister to assume dictatorial authority. The term is not too extreme. Harper himself in a 1997 speech described the government of Canada as a dictatorship run by the prime minister.[4] In the Harper years, there was little or no public enthusiasm for war,[5] but the prime minister went ahead anyway.

Included in a system that grants dictatorial powers is the ability of a prime minister who is so inclined to control the flow of information. Harper refined the propaganda function of the PMO, especially its censorship component. His governments exercised this power to a degree never seen in Canada in peacetime.

A system that allows dictatorship also allows the dictator to abuse the electoral process. Harris explains how Harper came to recognize the potential for manipulating Canada's parliamentary system in elections. Harper's connections with the extreme right wing in the U.S. were extensive. One of his early teachers was Arthur Finklestein, a pro-Israel, right wing U.S. political strategist in high demand. In addition to schooling Harper on the value of attack ads, Finklestein had the following counsel:

- Good politicians will first tell you things that are true and only later begin to mislead.
- Money is important because it determines who gets to hear what. Issues do not matter.

- Content has become the victim of speed of communication. People only skim the surface of events and do not want to know deep content.[6]

The axiom "power corrupts and absolute power corrupts absolutely" may also explain the abuse of the electoral process that characterized the election that moved the Conservatives from minority government to majority in 2011. Harris compiled a compelling circumstantial case that the Conservatives are responsible for the now barely remembered robocall scandal. As noted earlier, contrary to popular perception, circumstantial evidence can be very persuasive.

The focus of the scandal was a riding in Guelph, and later 18 or so others, but Elections Canada received thousands of complaints about pre-recorded phone calls made to voters in more than half of the ridings in the country, including several where Conservatives narrowly won. The phone numbers were selected from a Conservative Party of Canada database. The caller, often purporting to be from Elections Canada, falsely advised the voter of a change in polling station location. The recipients of these calls were chosen from a list of those unlikely to vote for the Conservatives. A smaller number of calls purported to be from opposition candidates. These calls were made at inconvenient times, sometimes late at night, in order to annoy the recipient.

The calls originated with a tech company in Edmonton called RackNine, with the capacity to make 200,000 calls per hour. RackNine worked only for Conservative Party clients, and a potential client needed an introduction from a former client or someone known to the former client. When the Tories could not completely contain the scandal, they selected one scapegoat and capped the well of information. Elections Canada investigated, but could do little. For good measure the government later ensured it could do even less be enacting the laughably titled "Fair Elections Act."[7]

The Conservatives were worried enough to pick a scapegoat, a low-level party figure. They protected everyone else, and the scandal became old news.

Preventing rational debate about fighting someone else's ill-advised war in Afghanistan was, of course, only one of the results of Harper's exploitation of the structural flaws in Canada's democracy. In a sense, the public is indebted to him for showing what could be done. With ups and downs, Canada's system worked reasonably well until Harper. But it did so not because of structural safeguards but primarily because prime ministers of all stripes exercised wide discretionary power responsibly. That Trudeau does not present at the outset as the extremist Harper was, does not mean that the potential abuse of power has gone away.

Alternatives are available. There are only three western countries still using first past the post. As Trudeau considers whether to go forward with reform, Canadians should perhaps make an effort to get their heads around some of the proportional representation systems that are working so well in other countries. There is a better fit for Canada in there somewhere. Virtually all alternatives would enhance our ability to debate and decide on the question of other people's wars.

Reconciliation should also be part of the way forward. The Conservative Party was not always the instrument of blind fealty to the American empire, sower of division at home and disdain for the community of nations that Harper brought about. There are conservatives who can remake the party into a responsible political player. Those who seek policies representing a better path beyond the warrior nation vision should encourage and assist them.

A New Paradigm: Rethinking "Heroes"

If we are to have a fair conversation about a different path, we will all have to do some serious rethinking on the subject of heroes. In *What We Talk About When We Talk About War*[8], Noah Richler emphasizes this need as part of his challenge to the warrior nation narrative. He notes the importance of heroes to the prevailing portrayal of the Great War as defining Canada's ascendance. It is not surprising that he concentrates extensively on the factor of propaganda and the failure of journalism as they relate to the concept of heroism.[9]

Richler specifically adds complicit journalists to the combination of extreme Tory politicians and generals who dominate the narrative. He offers some explanation of the complicity, noting that wars are more dramatic and exciting story subjects than strikes, plebiscites and public policy developments. Wars present career opportunities, and even give home bound reporters and academics a chance to comment on great matters.[10] And, of course, the simplistic appeal of war plays into the maxim that members of the public do no more than skim content.

We have seen the importance of heroes to the affirmative face of propaganda. The mother of every poor soul who was blown to bits on his way to the latrine in the Great War got a letter that mentioned his bravery. Whether they die from shells or disease, all who are slain are the "fallen". All are heroes.

Richler points out that a basic tenet of the warrior nation image is that all heroes wear military or law enforcement uniforms. There are no other heroes. These heroes "lay their life on the line" every day and sometimes make "the ultimate sacrifice" to preserve and protect our freedoms. He provides an example of a ceremony in Ottawa that added two policemen to a Police Memorial Wall of Honour. The premier lavished praise on them as heroes. The two died in garden-variety traffic collisions. Richler wonders if a single mother, bone tired after working the night shift, who died in a traffic accident the next morning while driving her children to school could qualify as a hero.[11]

The events of October 20th, 2014 provide an even more powerful commentary on the misuse of heroism. On that date, Martin Couture-Rouleau ran over and killed uniformed warrant officer Patrice Vincent in a Quebec parking lot. Two days later, Corporal Nathan Cirillo was standing ceremonial guard at the National War Memorial in Ottawa when Michael Zehaf-Bibeau shot him dead. Canadians were understandably shocked. The massive media coverage focused primarily on Cirillo. Thousands lined the Highway of Heroes for his funeral procession. The story was enhanced by the powerful imagery of the National War Memorial and the proximity of the crime to Remembrance Day.

But Patrice Vincent and Nathan Cirillo were not heroes. They were, by all accounts, thoroughly honourable men who were in the wrong place at the wrong time. Kevin Vickers, the parliamentary Sergeant at Arms, and Parliament security staff might be characterized as a hero. Zehaf-Bibeau, still armed, entered the parliament building after shooting Cirillo. There, security staff and Vickers cornered him. Vickers shot him. The symbolism of Vickers' position and his traditional garb played a part in the high level of publicity his acts earned. Much less coverage was afforded the heroism of Samearn Son, a security guard who slowed Zehaf-Bibeau with a tackle and was wounded in the struggle.

Making heroes of Cirillo and Vincent provided the opportunity to advance warrior nation policies in the never-ending "war on terror" against "Islamic extremists". To obtain maximum value from the event the government had to ignore the complexity of Zehaf-Bibeau's motivation. As Zehaf-Bibeau had some connection to the Muslim community in British Columbia, he was immediately called a terrorist. Only opposition leader Thomas Mulcair had the courage to challenge this label.[12] Another Muslim terrorist! The government immediately began preparing legislation to further erode those freedoms for which heroes have supposedly fought over the years.

If the government was truly interested in policies that would make Canadians a little safer from violence, it would have looked at important aspects of Zehaf-Bibeau's story that directly implicate policy. That might prompt officials to reevaluate the grossly inadequate mental health services available in the country and the futile war on drugs. Zehaf-Bibeau was a crack-addicted misfit who once committed a robbery for the purpose of getting *into* jail. He may have hit later upon religious extremism as an outlet, but it appears that any number of other perceived issues could have just as easily provided one. If even veterans cannot manage timely access to mental health services and some criminals have the idea that help is only available in prison, perhaps a second look is needed.

Equally important, an honest effort to learn from this incident rather than exploit it would lead to a sober reconsideration of the country's Middle East wars. What the government ignored in Zehaf-Bibeau's motivation was his violent misguided protest against Canadian military involvement there. An RCMP report cited this factor as one of the motives for his attack. Even more telling was the account of three witnesses who overheard a conversation between Zehaf-Bibeau and others as he waited in line to complete the purchase of a car. One of them heard him say, *If soldiers bombed your family, wouldn't you want to kill them?* Another heard him speaking of "airplanes, shooting, killing people".[13] Buried in the media avalanche the day after the Ottawa shooting was a Reuters report: The U.S. air campaign that Canada had recently joined in the Middle East had killed five women and six children.[14] Libya, where Canada joined the U.S. in exceeding the UN Responsibility to Protect mandate and ousting Gadhafi, killing a few civilians in the process, is home to Zehaf-Bibeau's father.[15]

The point, of course, is not that this disturbed individual or his deadly crime was a remotely acceptable means of protesting civilian deaths. In fact, revenge is more a part of the warrior nation image. But if the real question is the practical one of what measures might make Canadians at least marginally safer in the wake of this tragedy, a hard look at complicity in killing civilians is in order. On the day Zehaf-Bibeau died, the Canadian/U.S. bombing campaign in the Middle East probably produced 10 or 15 replacements, all with a better reason for revenge than he had. It is a challenge to seek and learn from actions for which there is no legitimate excuse. It is also better policy.

While the government sought to exploit the propaganda windfall that the attacks provided, it was refreshing to see signs that so many Canadians did not buy the official "terrorist" line. One survey found that only 36 percent would call them terrorist attacks, just over the number who blamed mental illness. Perhaps there were early fissures

311

in Finklestein's maxim. Perhaps some Canadians even consulted the University of Maryland global terrorism database and found that in a period of 45 years there have been only 102 incidents in Canada of terrorist attacks. Attackers have been motivated by a variety of grievances, everything from business disputes, private property grievances, to abortion.[16] These events may be cause for RCMP concern, but provide no justification for fear mongering about Muslim terrorists. In practical terms, the measure most likely to reduce somewhat the threat of a terrorist attack was Trudeau's notice to the U.S. that Canada would no longer be bombing in Iraq and Syria.

The art of manipulating heroism to advance a particular image has another nuance. The coming of age line requires that even some who serve in uniform are *not* to be treated as heroes. Like the first four Canadian troops who lost their lives in Afghanistan, Canadian major Paeta Hess-Von Kruedner was killed by "friendly fire". On July 25, 2006, precision-guided Israeli "bunker buster" bombs killed him and three other UN peacekeepers staffing an observation post in Lebanon. Like the Medecins Sans Frontieres hospital in Afghanistan, the location of the UN post was well known.

Israel refused to cooperate with a Canadian military board of inquiry. The board concluded that Israeli forces were intentionally killing non-combatants in Lebanon. The toll included seven Canadians. Predictably, Hillier termed the killings a tragic accident. The prime minister went further. Harper not only excused Israel, he blamed the victims, wondering aloud what the UN post was doing there anyway. Clearly, the major did not fit the government's hero category.[17]

In fact, none of the 114 peacekeepers who lost their lives was ever accorded a ceremony upon deployment or return. There was no procession of their coffins along anything like a Highway of Heroes. One who died in Bosnia was shipped home as air freight. When two RCMP officers serving as peacekeepers in Haiti after the devastating

2010 earthquake died, the deaths were largely ignored. The coffins were welcomed home only by a small contingent of their comrades.[18]

Before Cirillo and Vincent, the current generation of warrior nation advocates had been making do with the likes of John Babcock as hero. That posed some real problems.

Babcock was the last Canadian veteran of the Great War. He died in February 2010 at the age of 109. The government decided he was a hero who could advance the coming of age story. Harper called Babcock the last personal connection to a generation of heroes who had *asserted our independence on the world stage and established our international reputation as an unwavering champion of freedom, democracy, human rights, and the rule of law.*[19] Later in the year, the government decided there should be a joint celebration, remembering Babcock and the 93d anniversary of Vimy Ridge. There, Harper characterized Babcock as symbolic of the young people who risked their lives so that others could live in peace and freedom. Rick Hillier and Liberal Leader Michael Ignatieff chimed in with similar sentiments.[20]

Vimy Ridge Day was not the only attempt to exploit Babcock's passing. The government wanted to give him a state funeral. Another idea was to give the first Canadian gold medal won at the Vancouver 2010 Olympics to Babcock's family.[21] This bizarre idea to invent and exploit a hero in a spectacular setting, which Richler says Leni Riefenstahl could not top, reminds me instead of one of the most brilliantly funny anti-war films of the 20th century, *The Americanization of Emily.*[22] With the D-Day invasion of Europe approaching, an American admiral is concerned that naval heroes are underappreciated. Other services are getting the bulk of the glory ---and funding. He decrees, "The first dead man on Omaha beach must be a sailor!" See the film.

There were major problems with Babcock as a heroic symbol of the coming of age story. He enlisted at 15. He made it to England before his age was discovered, but never got into the war. The day it ended he was under house arrest after a brawl with British soldiers. Worse, Babcock definitely did not want a state funeral and he disliked war. Of war in general he said, *I think it would be nice if all the different people in the world could get along together so we weren't having wars.* About the war in Iraq, he opined, *I wish they'd get the hell out of there.*[23] In truth, Babcock is a hero in just the way virtually all ordinary soldiers are. But such heroes do little to advance the dominant myths about Canada and other people's wars.

Incidentally, the British could do no better at exploiting their last survivor of the Great War. At age 106, their veteran refused to attend a Remembrance Day celebration in Europe because he was against the glorification of war.[24]

What Now? Ideas for a new way forward

Notwithstanding that opponents of an alternative course enjoy an advantage in money and media, those with a better vision should not fear taking on the dominant story in the marketplace of ideas. The facts support an alternative.

Exposing and criticizing the staggering costs of being a part of other people's wars is not enough. Accordingly, I close with a sample of proposals that suggest how a new way forward might appear.

The life and work of American James O'Dea provides valuable guidance for implementing an alternative view of Canada's place in the world. O'Dea directed the Washington, D.C. office of Amnesty International. For years, he exposed human rights violations all over the globe and railed at the governments responsible, whatever their economic or political orientation. He spoke directly to government leaders, media, and anyone who would listen. He writes that he took comfort from occupying the moral high ground—until he began to realize that outrage was not enough.[25] He came to see that, while righteous anger is useful to focus attention on injustice, those who would be peacemakers must do more:

> *The emerging peace activist does not have the luxury of complaining about what is wrong with systems…unless he or she is committed to help*

solve the problems…we can neither be missionaries of a new self-righteous truth nor Pollyannas who passively affirm that everything is going to be just fine.[26]

So must it be if Canadians are to pursue policies arising from a better vision.

One of the realities that may require some adjustment in approach from the peace community is that it would be foolish to attempt to exclude Canada's military from the new vision. The splendid service of ill-trained, ill-equipped peacekeepers that we saw in Chapter VI makes that point emphatically. The old way has left us to live in a world where there is still far too much violence. Agreeing that it did not have to be that way is not a complete answer. There is a role for the military, albeit one that is trained, equipped, and deployed differently. Taylor and Nolan, as well as Richler, give us some ideas about how that transformation might work.

Putting themselves directly at odds with the generals, Taylor and Nolan offer specific proposals. The first resurrects and builds upon the idea of a permanent force available to the UN. They urge that Canada make such a contingent available for deployment anywhere in the world at any time. They would call the force the Canadian Legion. Their detailed proposals for alternating between training and deployment would have each member serving one year of every three on a UN peacekeeping mission. They would drastically reduce the regular forces and increase the reserve.

Urging a return to separate service branches, Taylor and Nolan envision a role for the air force and navy that is consistent with their new plan for ground forces. The only role of the air force would be support of the Legion. It would be equipped with tactical helicopters and be capable of airlift operations. The job of the navy would be protecting the environment and patrolling offshore fishing grounds.

These proposals, along with procurement reform proposals that, as they put it, "leave the arms lobby out in the cold", would likely save taxpayers billions. The legionnaires, recruited for skill and without regard to sex, religion or ethnicity, would have the appropriate weaponry that was denied the forces in 1990's operations.

But purchase of big-ticket items in their plan is scrapped. No F-35s. No jets at all. No submarines.[27]

Richler's ideas are similar and complement those of Taylor and Nolan. He offers three proposals. The first is creation of a peace operations regiment under the aegis of the DND and dedicated specifically to peace operations. The regiment would have regular tactical equipment, would cultivate the best possible intelligence, military strategies and physical resources in support of efforts to further peace, order, and good government *in ways that do not escalate tense or abiding conflicts.*

Richler's second proposal arises from the corresponding need of the new military and the public for an institution that is akin neither to a military college nor the now virtually destroyed Pearson Centre for Peacekeeping. The proposal is for a College of Peace Operations (CPO) with the degree requirement of at least a minor in peace operations. The CPO would be open to both foreign and domestic students and, importantly, to those who plan a military career as well as those with other aspirations. Students would study language, economics, finance, and engineering connected to peace operations. Opening this curriculum to military, civilians and foreign students alike is a brilliant suggestion that would increase cross-community understanding.

The third proposal complements Taylor and Nolan's focus on a military role that addresses Canada's domestic needs. It is a National Community Corps. Volunteers who seek to make a difference would make a two-year commitment and would be paid a modest stipend. They would serve both domestic and foreign hospitals, daycare centres, libraries, and social services agencies. Some would serve carefully vetted non-governmental organizations.[28]

These are but a few examples of how Canada might follow a better path. Consider the comparative advantages over continued subservience to great powers. A creative new path fashioned by proposals outlined here and others sure to come would likely prompt interest from other nations. The lessons learned from Canada's experiments, both successes and failures would provide a true example of leadership. The longing for international recognition would be satisfied to a degree that pursuit of policies derived from being in other people's wars can never approach.

A new path would save money. More importantly, it would promote a sense of community, a characteristic that has, until recently, been a source of pride for Canadians.

The threat of terrorism, such as it is, would be greatly diminished.

A new path would save civilian and military lives, here and abroad.

For more than a century, from South Africa to Syria, the current narrative has given us in the aggregate none of these benefits, only costs.

There is one more important planning matter to consider. If Canadians can ever get past the machismo propaganda and loaded terms like "hard" and "soft" power, they will appreciate the stark practical inefficiency of the warrior nation path. On the subject of the welfare, happiness, and safety of humans, it is war makers who are naïve. On all these matters it is war, not peacemaking, that has failed.

Before continuing to play the role of squire to the powerful knight of the day, Canada might also note the reality that great powers come and go. It has ever been so. The demise of the British Empire and the rise of the U.S. are only recent examples. And despite their incessant claims of exceptionalism, the era of American dominance will end. There are already signs. Where will Canada go when that happens?

Supporters of the current version of the link between capitalism and imperialism, claiming to be realists, often argue that economic ties to the U.S. prevent Canada from going her own way. But the current economic and military runner up in the world is China. If China emerges as the next great superpower, does the Royal Canadian Regiment go back to Hong Kong, this time to help the Chinese quell unrest? Absurd? Of course, but such is the lot of nations who cede sovereignty to the most powerful player of the day. Alternatively, Canada might shed blood in a futile effort to help the

U.S. maintain dominance as long as possible. These are the choices offered by violence for hire.

At the end of the day, the most powerful reason to seek a new way is that the current path does not reflect who we are as Canadians. Beyond the warrior nation story lies a better future for Canada.

The Trial The Verdict

Recall that in the Introduction I named you as trial jurors, and asked that you consider the case against Canada's involvement in other people's wars. Counsel made an opening statement outlining the evidence against the current path and what it has produced. The evidence has now been presented. At the conclusion of the trial, counsel have the opportunity to make a closing statement. I grant my closing statement to Canadian warrior, peacekeeper and diplomat, general E.L. "Tommy" Burns in the Cold War era:

... *the greatest threat to the survival of democracy is no longer the Russians or the Chinese or any other country professing anti-democratic ideologies, but rather war itself.*[29]

Members of the jury, you have heard the evidence and the arguments of counsel. It is now time for you to retire and say how you find.

Acknowledgements

A very modest staff of dedicated people produced this book. First among them is my in house editor, critic, cheerleader, fellow attorney, and beloved life partner, Elizabeth Ann Bennett. I am grateful also for administrative support from my former legal assistant, Gayle Hennon, and for research assistance from Alison Malis and Tanya Guven.

For spiritual guidance, I own much to my faith community, Unity of Victoria. For inspiration and the active hope that Canada can play a new role, I am thankful to Elizabeth May, and all the members of the peace community on Vancouver Island.

Notes

Introduction

1 Pierre Berton, *Marching As to War Canada's Turbulent Years 1899-1953*, (Toronto: Random House 2001), 585 (hereafter, Berton, Marching) Sadly, Berton concluded that after the Korean War, Canada had learned and Canadians now saved their aggressive emotions for hockey rinks.

2 Adam Hochschild, *To End All Wars: A Story of Loyalty and Rebellion, 1914-1918*, (Toronto: Houghton Mifflin Harcourt 2012), 4 (hereafter, Hochschild)

3 Hochschild, 17

4 Therese Delpech, *Savage Century: Back to Barbarism*, (trans. George Holoch) (Carnegie Endowment for International Peace 2007), xvii-xviii (hereafter, Delpech)

5 John Price, *Orienting Canada, Race, Empire and the Transpacific*, (Vancouver: University of British Columbia Press 2014), 7 (hereafter, Price)

6 *See, e.g.* Price, 257-268

7 Delpech, 11-12

8 Delpech, 83-92 In addition to focusing only on the wrongs of those she sees as enemies of the west, Delpech includes a fairly clear endorsement of war as a manner of dealing with these matters, lamenting only the loss of its "nobility" after the Great War. This seems a strange position to be taken by one who once chaired the United Nations Advisory Board on Disarmament in a work published by the Carnegie Endowment for International Peace.

9 *See, e.g.*, Canadian jets accused of causing civilian deaths in Iraq, Canadian Press, *Victoria Times-Colonist*, August 29, 2015

10 Price, 5

11 Thomas P. Socknat, *Witness Against War, Pacifism in Canada, 1900-1945*, (Toronto: University of Toronto Press 1987), 91 (hereafter, Socknat)

12 Socknat, 82

13 Pippa Norris, *Electoral Engineering: Voting Rules and Political Behavior* (Cambridge University Press 2004), 42

14 *See, e.g.* Gordon Gibson, "It's time to democratize our democracy", *Victoria Times-Colonist*, June 30, 2015

Chapter I

Boer War

1 Pierre Berton, *Flames Across the Border 1813-1814*, (Toronto: McLelland & Stewart Ltd. 1981) 424-425, (hereafter Berton, Flames)

2 Berton, Marching, 9

3 The account of the Disraeli/Gladstone contest for influence over Queen Victoria and the role of Cecil Rhodes draws extensively on the 2000 U.S. Public Broadcasting Corporation Documentary *Queen Victoria's Empire: The Moral Crusade* (Produced in association with Devillier Donegan Enterprises)

4 Don Gilmore, Achille Michaud, Pierre Turgeon (Eds.) *Canada, A People's History, Volume Two* (Toronto: McLelland & Stewart 2001), 57-59 (hereafter, People's History, Volume 2)

5 Hochschild, 10-13

6 Berton, Marching, 30-33

7 Carl Berger, *Studies in the Ideas of Canadian Imperialism 1867-1914*, (University of Toronto Press 1970), (hereafter, Berger)

8 Berger, 49-77, 169

9 Berger, 117-119, 130

10 Berger, 144-145

11 Berton, Marching, 20-26; Laurier's rhetoric on the occasion was, for him, unusually florid:...*let the bugles sound, let the fires be lit on the hills...whatever we can do shall be done by the colonies to help her.* People's History, Volume 2, 58-59

12 Paul Dukes, *A History of Europe 1648-1948, The Arrival, The Rise, The Fall*, (Macmillan Education Ltd. 1985), 288-289 (hereafter, Dukes)

13 Hochschild, 8

14 Hochschild, 16-17, 22-23; Dennis Judd, *The Boer War*, (Hart-Davis MacGibbon Ltd.), 33, (hereafter, Judd); Thomas Pakenham, *The Boer War*, (Random House, 1979), 295 (hereafter, Pakenham)

15 Hochschild, 16-19

16 Judd, 19

17 Hochschild, 4

18 Hochschild, 37

19 Pakenham, 612; *Queen Victoria's Empire: The Moral Crusade*, U.S. Public Broadcasting Corporation Documentary (2010)

20 Pakenham, xiii-xiv, 11-12; Hochschild, 19; Berton, Marching, 27-28

21 Berton, Marching, 27; Hochschild, 20; Judd, 14-17

22 Pakenham, xxv-xxix; Judd, 17-20

23 Judd, 20; Pakenham, 49-68

24 Judd, 25

25 Hochschild, 22-23; Pakenham, 90-91; Judd, 23

26 Berton, *Marching*, 31-32; Judd, 25; Hochschild, 23

27 Berton, Marching, *20*

28 Berton, Marching, *32-33*

29 Berton, Marching, *30-32*

30 Berton, Marching, *20, 30, 32-33*

31 Berton, Marching, 31

32 Pakenham, 12-13

33 Ian McKay and Jamie Swift, *Warrior Nation, Rebranding Canada in an Age of Anxiety,* (Toronto: Between the Lines 2012), 56-57 (hereafter, McKay and Swift)

34 Berger, 250

35 Berger, 251

36 Pakenham, 260; Phillip Knightley, *The First Casualty, From the Crimea to Vietnam: The War Correspondent as Hero, Propagandist, and Myth Maker,* (Harvest Books, Harcourt Brace Jovanovich, New York and London 1975), 75 (hereafter, Knightley)

37 Berton, *Marching, 28-29;* Knightley, 74-75

38 Knightley, 72-73

39 Hochschild, 22-23; Knightley, 72-73

40 In every war, we will see a version of one Canadian Boer veteran's explanation: *I thought it would do me some good. I was searching for adventure.* Berton, Marching, 35

41 See note 36

42 Knightley, 67-69; Hochschild, 17

43 Knightley, 74

44 Knightley, 74

45 Knightley, 73-74

46 Berton, Marching, 32-33

47 Berton, Marching, *37*-38; Pakenham, 105

48 Judd, 39

49 Berton, Marching, 44-45

50 Hochschild, 24; Pakenham, 189-192; Judd, 96-102

51 Judd, 89-90, 93, 98

52 Berton, Marching, 37-38; People's History Volume 2, 39

53 Jerrold M. Packard, *Farewell in Splendor, The Passing of Queen Victoria and Her Age,* (Penguin Books 1995), 1-2. Not all historians, however, have been completely uncritical of Roberts. *See, e.g.* Pakenham, 357-359

54 Berton, Marching, 43, 49-53; Pakenham, 345-357

55 Berton, Marching, 52-54; Pakenham, 356

56 Berton, Marching, 42-44,49; For the British, the figures were even worse. Fourteen of twenty-two thousand died from sickness. Knightley, 74

57 *Canadian Deaths in the Boer War,* http://www.rootsweb.ancestry.com/~abwcobit/LER/Boer/BoerWarDeath1.htm

58 Judd, 113

59 Knightley, 69-73

60 Judd, 105-106

61 Knightley, 71; Pakenham, 428-433

62 Judd, 110

63 Pakenham, 442

64 Knightley, 71-72

65 *See,* Lily Siewsan Chow, *Blood and Sweat over the Railway Tracks, Chinese Labourers Constructing the Canadian Pacific Railway,* (Chinese Canadian Historical Society of British Columbia 2014)

66 Judd, 26, 34; Hochschild, 5-6, 23-24

67 Berton, Marching, 60-61

68 Judd, 158

69 Judd, 159

70 Hochschild, 33

71 Judd, 156-157; Pakenham, 569-570, 574

72 Pakenham, 523-524, 549; Berton, Marching, 67; Judd's military history briefly mentions the camps and opines that: *There was, it must be assumed, no malevolent motive in the establishment of the concentration camps, despite the latter day emotive connotations of the term.* Judd, 161 Pakenham apparently agrees, concluding that Kitchener did not actively desire the deaths of women and children, but was simply focused on the war and had no interest in what happened in the camps. Pakenham, 524

73 Berton, Marching, 67; Knightley, 77-78

74 Pakenham, 523-524; Knightley, 76; Kitchener may have been technically correct, since most of their homes no longer existed.

75 Berton, Marching, 68; Pakenham, 531, 533

76 Knightley, 76

77 Pakenham, 538

78 Knightley, 76

79 Hochschild, 36

80 Judd, 161; Hochschild, 36

81 Meeting of the Women's South African Conciliation Committee, http://en.wikisource.org/wiki/Emily_Hobhouse:_Boer_War_Letters

82 Berton, Marching, 68; Pakenham, 546-549

83 The story of Emily Hobhouse and the South African concentration camps is detailed in documents and in commentary by her great-niece in Jennifer Hobhouse Balme, *To Love One's Enemies, The Work and Life of Emily Hobhouse,* (Stuttgart: ibidem-Verlag 2012) (hereafter, Balme, Love One's Enemies)

84 Balme, Love One's Enemies, 585-586

85 Balme, Love One's Enemies, 588

86 Berton, Marching, 75-77

87 Berger, 7, 41-42

88 People's History, Volume 2, 59

Chapter II

Great War

1 People's History, Volume 2, 91

2 Andrew Heard, *Canadian Independence (1990)* (Unpublished. On file with author)

3 Berton, Marching, 84-88

4 Berton, Marching, 91-96

5 Berton, Marching, 106

6 Berton, Marching, 108

7 Berton, Marching, 109

8 Berton, Marching, 112

9 Berton, Marching, 123; People's History, Volume 2, 83-88

10 Berton, Marching, 115

11 Berton, Marching, 118; People's History, Volume 2, 86

12 Berger, 49-77; 153-162; 239-245; 259-265

13 Hochschild, 75

14 Hochschild, 76

15 Hochschild, 70

16 Hochschild, 31

17 Hochschild, 61

18 Hochschild, 48

19 Hochschild, 74

20 Hochschild, 107

21 Dukes, 258-264; John Harris, *The Somme, Death of a Generation*, (Hodder and Stoughton, Ltd. 1966), 13-14 (hereafter, Harris)

22 Hochschild, 79-85

23 Dukes, 347-349

24 Hochschild, 88-94; The bulk of the treaty deals with land grants to nobility and boundary adjustments. Article VII, the key provision, reads: *Belgium, within the limits specified in Articles I, II, and IV, shall form an independent and perpetually neutral State. It shall be bound to observe such neutrality towards all other states.* www.firstworldwar.com/source/london 1839.htm

25 Tim Cook, *At the Sharp End, Canadians Fighting the Great War 1914-1916* (Viking Canada 2008) 15-19 (hereafter Cook, Sharp End)

26 Knightley, 81

27 Hochschild, 94

28 Berton, Marching, 132

29 Hochschild, 92

30 McKay and Swift, 34-48

31 Knightley, 82-85, 107; Berton, Marching, 128; Hochschild, 148-149

32 Knightley, 83

33 Berton, Marching, 166-167

34 Knightley, 106
35 People's History, Volume 2, 89; Cook, Sharp End, 28-31
36 Berton, Marching, 158-159; Socknat, 78-89. The situation was the same in the motherland, *see, e.g.* Hochschild, 188
37 Hochschild, 103
38 Cook, Sharp End, 65
39 Knightley, 85, 88
40 Hochschild, 139, 272
41 Hochschild, 103, 111
42 Hochschild, 162
43 Berton, Marching, 140-141
44 Cook, Sharp End, 109
45 Cook, Sharp End, 110
46 Berton, Marching, 145
47 Hochschild, 163; Berton, Marching, 177
48 Cook, Sharp End, 112
49 *Battle of Ypres*, Canadian Broadcasting Corporation (Accessed 15 December, 2010)
50 Hochschild, 140-142
51 Hochschild, 153, 320-321
52 Berton, Marching, 147
53 Berton, Marching, 146l
54 People's History, Volume 2, 59-60
55 People's History, Volume 2, 91-94; Berton, Marching, 165-166
56 People's History, Volume 2, 93
57 Berton, Marching, 166
58 Hochschild, 276
59 People's History, Volume 2, 94
60 Berton, Marching, 151; People's History, Volume 2, 98-99
61 Hochschild, 206
62 Berton, Marching, 153-154
63 Cook, Sharp End, 343-346, 379, 425, 485-495
64 Cook, Sharp End, 495
65 Cook, Sharp End, 498
66 Harris, 29-33, 37; People's History, Volume 2, 97-98
67 Cook, Sharp End, 419-422
68 Harris, 84
69 Harris, 86

70 Hochschild, 214

71 Harris, 86

72 Harris, 48

73 Hochschild, 207

74 Hochschild, 209

75 Berton, Marching, 151-152

76 Hochschild, 231; Berton, Marching, 152

77 Berton, Marching, 148

78 Harris, 110

79 Hochschild, 209-210

80 Hochschild, 181-182

81 Hochschild, 181

82 Knightley, 108

83 Cook, Sharp End, 523

84 Hochschild, 180

85 Hochschild, 181

86 W. A. Tucker, *The Lousier War,* (New English Library Books 1974), 20 (hereafter, Tucker)

87 *...he was prepared to use his forces to destroy Germans until not a single enemy was left, considering, like Joffre, that he would have won so long as there were still a few Englishmen on their feet. This kind of crude thinking can never be called strategy...*Harris, 122

88 Knightley, 109

89 Knightley, 109

90 Jennifer Hobhouse Balme, *Agent of Peace, Emily Hobouse and her Courageous Attempt to End the First World War,* (The History Press 2015), 97-122; Hochschild, 218-220

91 Hochschild, 166

92 Knightley, 108-109

93 Harris, 100

94 Harris, 100

95 Hochschild, 166

96 Hochschild, 166-167

97 Knightley, 110

98 Cook, Sharp End, 523

99 Hochschild, 222

100 Hochschild, 223

101 Hochschild, 148-149

102 Hochschild, 227

103 Hochschild, 151

104 Berton, Marching, 170

105 Socknat, 50

106 Socknat, 50

107 Berton, Marching, 163

108 Berton, Marching, 162

109 Berton, Marching, 163

110 Hochschild, 154

111 Berton, Marching, 158-160

112 Harris, 108, 118

113 Tim Cook, *Shock Troops, Canadians Fighting the Great War Volume 2* (Toronto: Penguin Canada 2014), 145 (hereafter, Cook, Shock Troops)

114 Ted Barris, *Victory at Vimy Canada Comes of Age:* April 9-12, 1917, (Thomas Allen Publishers, Division of Thomas Allen & Sons, Ltd. 2007) 121, 154-155, 223-224

115 Barris, 2-4

116 Barris, 41

117 Barris, 2

118 Berton, Marching, 177-178

119 Barris, 40-42, 69

120 Barris, 41

121 Yves Engler, *The Black Book of Canadian Foreign Policy*, (Red Publishing 2009), 257 (hereafter, Engler)

122 Berton, Marching, 178

123 Berton, Marching, 207

124 Edwin Tribble (Ed.) *President in Love The Courtship Letters of Woodrow Wilson & Edith Bolling Wilson* (Boston: Houghton Mifflin Co. 1981), 13-19, 26,32 (hereafter, Wilson Letters)

125 Alan Axelrod, *Selling the Great War: The Making of American Propaganda* (New York: Palgrave MacMillan 2009), 57

126 Hochschild, 286

127 Berton, Marching, 184

128 Berton, Marching, 184-186

129 Berton, Marching, 187

130 The account of the service of William Walter Ruddy (1895-1983) is taken from notes prepared in 2013 by his son Richard at the request of the author, on file with the author.

131 Harris sees the loss of a generation of the best people on both sides as a cause of the next war. Harris, 125

132 Knightley, 110

133 Hochschild, 341

134 Cook, Shock Troops, 569-579

135 Berton, Marching, 129

136 Hochschild, 348-349

137 Hochschild, 147-148

138 Hochschild, 148

139 Hochschild, 158

140 Berton, Marching, 159

141 http://archive.gg.ca/gg/fgg/bios/01/landsdowne_e.asp

142 Hochschild, 302

143 Hochschild, 302

144 Berton, Marching, 139; Hochschild, 275-276; Near the end of the war, Germany renewed its plea to Wilson, without success. Hochschild, 337

145 Hochschild, 303; Berton, Marching, 188

146 Hochschild, 357

147 People's History, Volume 2, 108-114; Berton, Marching, 194-196

148 Berton, Marching, 191-192; The Irish were similarly unenthusiastic about being compelled to die for someone else's country. Originally exempted in Britain's 1916 conscription act, Irishmen were later included but the government feared unrest and never implemented the act against them. Hochschild, 321, 329-330

149 People's History, Volume 2, 101-102

150 People's History, Volume 2, 111

151 People's History, Volume 2, 114-115

152 People's History, Volume 2, 116; Berton puts the figure at 24,132 and adds that *Canadians of both races were left with a bitter taste in their mouths that no amount of subsequent soothing syrup could ever expunge.* Berton, Marching, 201

153 Hannah Arendt, *The Origins of Totalitarianism*, (London: A Harvest Book, Harcourt, Inc. 1968), 126, (hereafter, Arendt)

154 Hochschild, 160-162

155 Berton, Marching, 134

156 Berton, Marching, 136-137

157 Berton, Marching, 138; People's History, Volume 2, 118

158 Berton, Marching, 161

159 Hochschild, 276

160 Hochschild, 292

161 Tucker, 36

162 Berton, Marching, 160-161

163 Cook, Sharp End, 267-269

164 Hochschild, 130-132

165 Stanley Weintraub, *Silent Night, The Story of the World War I Christmas Truce*, (The Free Press Division of Simon & Schuster, Inc. 2001), 47 (hereafter, Weintraub)

166 Tucker, 25

167 Barris, 149

168 Barris, 101

169 Tucker, 18

170 Tucker, 18

171 Tucker, 8

172 Tucker, 45

173 Tucker, 47-48

174 Tucker, 7-8

175 Weintraub, xvii-xviii

176 Hochschild, 375-376

177 Cook, Sharp End, 126-127

178 Cook, Sharp End, 450-451

179 Cook, Sharp End, 163, 308-309

180 Barris, 209

181 Cook, Shock Troops, 242

182 Cook, Shock Troops, 246

183 Barris, 208-209

184 Barris, 210; Hochschild, 242

185 Barris, 207-208

186 Hochschild, 243

187 Barris, 209-210

188 People's History, Volume 2, 100

189 Hochschild, 244

190 Hochschild, 371, Weintraub, 210

191 Cook, Shock Troops, 245

192 Cook, Shock Troops, 2246-254

193 Hochschild, 361

194 Hochschild, 352, 361-362

Chapter III

Opportunity Lost

1 Cook, Shock Troops, 634
2 Victoria *Times-Colonist,* October 1, 2013, A7
3 Dukes, 385-386
4 Margaret MacMillan, *Paris 1919: Six Months That Changed the World,* (New York: Random House, 2001), (hereafter, MacMillan, Paris 1919*)*
5 Margaret MacMillan, *Lessons from History? The Paris Peace Conference of 1919,* Department of Foreign Affairs and International Trade, O.D. Skelton Lectures (Ottawa: 2003). There is some irony in the forum for the lecture. O.D. Skelton was under-secretary for foreign affairs when Canada joined World War II. He noted the lack of pubic enthusiasm for doing so and doubted that a majority of Canadians would have supported it in a free plebiscite; Socknat, 193, (hereafter, MacMillan, Lessons from History?)
6 MacMillan, Lessons from History? 5
7 MacMillan, Lessons from History? 6-7
8 MacMillan, Paris 1919, 53, 57
9 MacMillan, Paris 1919, 9-19, 57, 97
10 Wilson Letters, 13-15, 26, 31-33, 48-55
11 MacMillan, Paris 1919, 27-28, 168-170
12 MacMillan, Paris 1919, 71, 74
13 Knightley, 165
14 Knightley, 138-139
15 MacMillan, Paris 1919, 45,74, 76, 80-82
16 MacMillan, Paris 1919, 99-101
17 Price, 26-28
18 MacMillan, Paris 1919, 99,100, 106
19 MacMillan, Paris 1919, 99-105,374
20 Price, 26-29
21 MacMillan, Paris 1919, 114, 290-291
22 Arendt, 270
23 MacMillan, Paris 1919, 59, 109-113
24 MacMillan, Paris 1919, 201
25 MacMillan, Paris 1919, 250-252
26 Arendt, 270

27 MacMillan, Paris 1919, 229-230

28 MacMillan, Paris 1919, 233-238

29 MacMillan, Paris 1919, 236, 241

30 MacMillan, Paris 1919, 215-221

31 MacMillan, Paris 1919, 463-464

32 MacMillan, Paris 1919, 467

33 Knightley, 134-135

34 Hochschild, 244

35 Knightley, 149

36 Arendt, 40-41

37 People's History Volume 2, 136

38 People's History Volume 2, 127

39 People's History Volume 2, 128-129

40 Socknat, 72

41 Socknat, 91

42 Berton, Marching, 322-323

43 Gordon L. Heath, "Irreconcilable Differences: Wartime Attitudes of George C. Pidgeon and R. Edis Fairbairn 1939-1945", in *Historical Papers of the Canadians Society of Church History* (1999), 30-31, 41-42, (hereafter, Heath)

44 Heath, 30-33

45 http:/thecanadianencyclopedia.com/articles/womens-international-league-for-peace-and-freedom.pdg.

46 http://.thecanadianencyclopedia.ca/en/article/agnes-macphail/

47 People's History, Volume 2, 145, 154

48 Socknat, 121-122

49 Socknat, 134

50 Nellie McClung, *Winning the war and dethroning the gods of violence,* Victoria *Times,* January 27th, 1940 (Reprinted Victoria *Times-Colonist, April 20th, 2104, D3)*

51 Knightley, 272; Dukes, 433

52 Berton, Marching, 311-313; Dukes, 433-434; Knightley, 187

53 Dukes, 400; http://history.state.gov/milestones/1921-1936/kellogg

54 Price, 29

55 Socknat, 170-175

56 Socknat, 163-163, 165, 169, 170

57 Dukes, 436-438

58 McKay and Swift, 108-110

59 Price, 50-60

60 Socknat, 175-176, 281-282

61 Hochschild, 186, 297-298

62 Hochschild, 187-189; 296-297

63 Hochschild, 191

64 Hochschild, 294, 315, 358-359

65 http://ppu.org.uk

Chapter IV

World War II

1 See, *World War I: A Turning Point in Modern History,* Jack J. Roth (Ed.), (New York: Alfred A. Knopf, Inc. 1967), (hereafter, Turning Point*)*

2 Jack J. Roth, "Introduction", in Turning Point, 5-6

3 Gordon A. Craig, "The Revolution in War and Diplomacy", in Turning Point, 9-11

4 Berton, Marching, 234

5 Berton, Marching, 243

6 Berton, Marching, 248-249

7 Berton, Marching, 245-265

8 Berton, Marching, 26

9 Berton, Marching, 272

10 An exception, probably not intended as the frightening indictment of the financiers who brought on the 2008 "financial crisis" that it is, was written by one of their own. *See* Andrew R. Sorkin, *Too Big to Fail* (New York: Viking Penguin Group 2009)

11 Berton, Marching, 286-288

12 People's History, Volume 2, 148

13 People's History, Volume 2, 145

14 People's History, Volume 2, 147-155; Berton, Marching, 293-294

15 King's Christianity and his Harvard education in progressive economic and social theory grounded him in concern for the less fortunate.; Cook, 163-165

16 People's History, Volume 2, 149, 155

17 Berton, Marching, 322; Cook reports that in fact King gave a speech using Laurier's exact words about Canada being at war when Britain

was, but added the major caveat that Canada would decide what that meant in terms of action; Cook, 208

18 Berton, Marching, 307, 330-331

19 Berton, Marching, 331, 360-361

20 Berton, Marching, 370

21 Berton, Marching, 328, 476

22 Berton, Marching, 302-305

23 Arthur Bishop, *True Canadian Battles that Forged the Nation*, (Toronto: Key Porter Books Ltd. 2003) (hereafter, Bishop)

24 Berton, Marching, 339; Bishop, 193

25 Berton, Marching, 3343; Bishop, 198-199

26 Tim Cook, *The Necessary War: Canadians Fighting the Second World War*, (Alan Land Canada 2014), 70 (hereafter Cook, Necessary War)

27 Bishop, 163-164, 198-199; Berton, Marching, 336

28 Bishop, 197

29 Charles G. Roland, *Long Night's Journey into Day: Prisoners of War in Hong Kong and Japan* (Waterloo: Wilfrid Laurier University Press 2001) 2-4 (hereafter, Roland); *True Canadian War Stories*, Jane Dewar, (Ed.), (Toronto: Key Porter Books Ltd. 1989), 165-167 (hereafter, Canadian War Stories)

30 Cook, Necessary War, 73

31 Berton, Marching, 335; Bishop, 196

32 Cook, Necessary War, 84

33 Bishop, 198-199

34 Canadian War Stories, 163-164; Bishop 200; Roland, 8-9; Berton, Marching, 352

35 Bishop, 200; Berton, Marching, 339, 341; Roland, 167

36 Berton, Marching, 337; Roland, 10-11

37 Roland, 2-4; Canadian War Stories, 165-166

38 Cook, Necessary War, 73

39 Canadian War Stories, 167, 170; Bishop, 205-218; Berton, Marching, 341

40 Bishop, 205-206, 217-218

41 Canadian War Stories, 167-168

42 George S. MacDonell, *One Soldier's Story: 1939-1945* (Toronto: Dundurn Press, 2002), (hereafter, MacDonell)

43 MacDonell, 30-31; 41

44 MacDonell, 44-45

45 Cook, Necessary War, 84, 90-91

46 Berton, Marching, 342; Bishop, 214; Roland, 29-30

47 Roland, 36-39

48 Berton, Marching, 356-357

49 Berton, Marching, 339

50 Roland, 255; MacDonell, 51

51 MacDonell, 51; Roland, 315

52 Price, 66-72

53 "Acts of honour in war, and after the fact," Victoria *Times-Colonist*, August 7, 2013, p. A2

54 MacDonell, 41

55 MacDonell, 45

56 MacDonell, 54

57 MacDonell, 54-57

58 MacDonell, 62

59 MacDonell, 65-66

60 MacDonell, 87

61 Berton, Marching, 345-347; Cook paints King as largely indifferent to Canadian losses. Cook, 92, 272-273

62 Bishop, 222

63 Desmond Morton, *A Military History of Canada* (Toronto: McClelland & Stewart Publishers Ltd. 1990), 203, (hereafter, Morton)

64 Terence Robertson, *Dieppe: The Shame and the Glory* (Toronto, ON: Little, Brown and Company 1962), 75-76 (hereafter, Robertson)

65 Berton, Marching, 381; Robertson concurs in the assessment of McNaughton's ambition. Robertson, 17

66 Cook, Necessary War, 283

67 Robertson, 59-60, 72, 139-140, 161

68 Berton, Marching, 375-378; Bishop, 223; Robertson, 39-40, 55

69 Robertson, 61

70 Berton, Marching, 380-381; Robertson, 18-19, 33-35; Cook, Necessary War, 253

71 Robertson, 39-40, 51-55, 60-63, 108; Berton, Marching, 377

72 Bishop, 224, 227; Robertson, 47-55, 62, 81, 91-96, 136, 75-76, 124; Berton, Marching, 378-379; Morton, 203

73 Robertson, 72, 131-134 141; Bishop, 228; Berton, Marching, 380-383

74 Cook, Necessary War, 278-279

75 John Mellor, *Forgotten Heroes: The Canadians at Dieppe,* (Toronto: Methuen Publications 1975), 66 (hereafter, Mellor)

76 Cook, Necessary War, 272-273

77 Mellor, 96; Robertson, 312, 366, 376-377

78 Berton, Marching, 373; Mellor, 193-194; Robertson, vii-viii; Morton, 203-204

79 Cook, Necessary War, 283

80 Robertson, 30, 36-37, 46, 113-114, 126-129, 156-157; Bishop, 221-222; Berton, Marching, 375

81 Morton, 204

82 David O'Keefe, *One Day in August: The Untold Story Behind Canada's Tragedy at Dieppe,* (Toronto: Knopf Canada 2013)

83 Cook, Necessary War, 259

84 Cook, Necessary War, 284

85 "A time of disaster and bravery," Victoria *Times-Colonist,* August 20, 2013, D1

86 Morton, 216-218

87 Morton, 223-224

88 People's History, Volume 2, 209-210

89 Berton, Marching, 402

90 Morton, 195-201; Berton, Marching, 416-420

91 Berton, Marching, 506-508

92 Morton, 200

93 Cook, Necessary War, 229

94 Morton, 181, 194-195; Cook, Necessary War, 161-162

95 Morton, 203

96 *Bomber Command—Hitting Back,* Canadian History Channel Documentary (2012), (hereafter, Bomber Command)

97 Cook, Necessary War, 152-159; Engler, 262 (Emphasis added)

98 Cook, Necessary War, 161

99 Morton, 204-206

100 Cook, Necessary War, 241

101 Jim Maxwell's story is drawn from an interview with Doreen Ruddy, 13 October 2013, and documents she provided which are on file with author.

102 Jim faced danger even before combat. The Whitley was known as the "flying coffin". At one training centre, nine crashed, killing 63 airmen. Cook, Necessary War, 169

103 Bomber Command

104 Morton, 207

105 Enger, 262

106 Cook, Necessary War, 331; Morton, 209-210

107 Morton, 209-212

108 Morton, 210

109 Cook, Necessary War, 379

110 Berton, Marching, 435-437; Morton, 211-213

111 Berton, Marching, 436

112 Cook, Necessary War, 405

113 Morton, 213; People's History, Volume 2, 200

114 Farley Mowat, *And No Birds Sang*, (Toronto: McClelland and Stewart 1979) (hereafter, Mowat)

115 Mowat, 3-4

116 Mowat, 107, 177-178

117 Cook, Necessary War, 416-417

118 Berton, *Marching*, 440

119 Richard Foot, "Blight of war turned writer to nature", Victoria *Times-Colonist*, May 4th, 2005, A2

120 Mowat, 157-160

121 Cook, Necessary War, 411-412

122 Mowat, 182-187

123 "Royal likens Putin to Hitler, report says," Victoria *Times-Colonist*, May 21, 2014, A9; "Hitler-Putin comparison inaccurate, historians say," Victoria *Times-Colonist*, May 22, 2014, A7; David Bly, "Playing the Nazi card is a lazy argument," Victoria *Times-Colonist*, May 25, 2014, A12

124 T. W. Mason, "Some Origins of the Second World War," in *The Origins of the Second World War*, *Historical Interpretations*, Esmonde M. Robertson (Ed.), (London: MacMillan and Co. Ltd. 1971), 105 (hereafter, Interpretations)

125 *See*, A.J.P. Taylor, "The Origins of the Second World War," (New York: Fawcett Books 1961)

126 H. R. Trevor-Roper, "A.J.P Taylor, Hitler and the War", in Interpretations, 83-104

127 A.J.P. Taylor, "War Origins Again", in Interpretations, 139-140

128 A.J.P. Taylor, "War Origins Again", in Interpretations, 138

129 H.W. Koch, "Hitler and the Origins of the Second World War", in Interpretations, 159-163

130 D.C. Watt, "The Secret Laval-Mussolini Agreement of 1935 on Ethiopia", in Interpretations, 225-234

131 H.W.Koch, "Hitler and the Origins of the Second World War", in Interpretations, 176-182

132 James Lucas, *World War Two Through German Eyes*, (London: Arms and Armour Press Ltd. 1987), 10 (hereafter, Lucas)

133 Lucas, 13

134 Lucas, 1-2

135 Lucas, 35

136 T.W. Mason, "Some Origins of the Second World War", in *Interpretations*, 107

137 Lucas, 11

138 Brian Martin, "The British Foreign Office and German Resistance to Hitler," in *Nonviolence Today*, No. 39, July/August 1994, 16-18. (Review of Patricia Meehan, *The Unnecessary War*, Better World Books Ltd. 1992)

139 Akira Irye, "Japanese Imperialism and Aggression", in *Interpretations*, 258-260; "Japan's Foreign Policies between World Wars," in *Interpretations*, 262-271; Herbert P. Bix, *Hirohito and the Making of Modern Japan*, (New York: Harper Collins 2000), 355 (hereafter, Bix)

140 Price, 62-66

141 Price, 113

142 Bix, 147-148

143 Price, 85-87

144 Price, 97-99; Theresa Wolfwood, 70 Years After the Bomb were dropped on Hiroshima and Nagasaki: Canada's gift to Japan, *Lower Island News*, August 20125 (hereafter, Wolfwood)

145 Price, 94, 105

146 Price, 92-93; Wolfwood

147 Price, 99

148 *The European Graduate School* http://www.egs.edu/library/hanna-arendt/biography/

149 Arendt, 11-12

150 Arendt, 5-28

151 Arendt, 14

152 Arendt, 37

153 Arendt, 53

154 Knightley, 220-223

155 Arendt, 89-120
156 People's History, Volume 2, 175
157 People's History, Volume 2, 176
158 Engler, 261
159 Cook, 283-284; Engler 261

Chapter V

Cold War, Korea, and Vietnam

1 Price, 173-174
2 Price, 85-86
3 Berton, Marching, 528-530
4 Cook, 213
5 Berton, Marching, 513; *People's History Volume 2*, 218-219
6 Berton, Marching, 520-522; *People's History Volume 2*, 217-218
7 Berton, Marching, 514-515
8 Price, 193
9 *Mike, the Memoirs of the Right Honourable Lester B. Pearson, Volume 2*, Alex I. Inglis and John A. Munro, (Eds.), (Toronto: University of Toronto Press 1973), 24-28, 31-33, (hereafter Pearson Memoirs Vol 2); *People's History Volume 2*, 223-224
10 *Pearson Memoirs Vol 2*, 35, 40-41, 120
11 Knightley, 356; Price, 269-272; McKay and Swift, 104
12 Max Hastings, *The Korean War* (London, UK, Michael Joseph Ltd. 1987), (hereafter Hastings, Korea*)*
13 Hastings, Korea 36-37
14 Price, 123
15 Hastings, Korea13-16
16 Hastings, Korea 16
17 Max Hastings, *Inferno: The World at War, 1939-1945* (New York: Alfred A. Knopf 2011), 648 (hereafter, Hastings, Inferno)
18 Hastings, Korea, 32; Pearson Memoirs Vol 2, 135-145
19 Hastings, Korea, 33
20 Price, 190
21 Price, 211, 257-264
22 Hastings, Korea, 33-36; Berton, Marching, 539
23 Price, 208-210

24 Price, 211-213

25 Hastings, Korea, 42-43

26 Berton, Marching, 531; Pearson Memoirs Vol 2, 147-148; McKay and Swift, 101-102

27 Hastings, Korea, 56

28 The three met in Washington. Acheson's pitch was laced with references to Korea as a phase of the 'free world' struggle against communism and predictions that victory in Korea would enhance preparation of the 'struggle ahead against world wide communism'. Lie also spoke of Soviet aggression and pleaded with Pearson not to undermine the position of the UN. Pearson Memoirs Vol 2, 149-157

29 Berton, Marching, 533

30 Berton, Marching, 534-535

31 Bix, 2, 544-545

32 Pearson Memoirs, Vol 2, 145-146

33 Hastings, Korea, 60-62

34 Berton, Marching, 540-541; Hastings, *Korea*, 116-133

35 Berton, Marching, 532-539

36 Berton, Marching, 541- 542

37 Price, 234

38 Hastings, Korea, 134-149

39 Berton, Marching, 544; South Korean forces captured prisoners whose uniforms and language plainly identified them as part of Chinese units. The U.S. Commanding General did not see this as significant, noting that there were a lot of Mexicans living in Texas. Hastings, *Korea*, 153

40 Berton, Marching, 543-544

41 Hastings, Korea, 154

42 Berton, Marching, 545-546; Hastings, Korea, 165-197

43 Berton, Marching, 554-555; Hastings, Korea, 221-226

44 Berton, Marching, *548*

45 Hastings, Korea, 226

46 Price, 231-235; Hastings, Korea, 237-244; Berton, Marching, 572

47 Berton, Marching, 558-573

48 Berton, Marching, 546-550

49 Hastings, Korea, 250

50 Hastings, Korea, 272-275; 352-356; *People's History Volume 2*, 225

51 Interview with Beverly Himes, October 2d 2015

52 Berton, Marching, 529, 562, 574; Hastings, *Korea*, 407

53 Berton, Marching, 574; Price, 235

54 Berton, Marching, 553-554

55 Knightley, 343-346; Hastings, Korea, 279-285

56 Hastings, Korea, 289

57 Hasting, Korea, 290

58 Price, 257-260

59 Price, 264-268

60 Price, 265

61 Price, 261-262

62 Knightley, 346-347

63 Hastings, Korea, 307-308; 326

64 Berton, Marching, 552

65 Pierre Berton, *My Times*, 69, 79

66 Knightley, 342

67 Berton, *My Times, Living With History* (Toronto: Doubleday Canada Ltd. 1995), 69, 79 (hereafter Berton, My Times); Berton, *Marching*, 576

68 Berton, My Times, 83; Berton, *Marching*, 575-576

69 Berton, My Times, 75

70 Berton, My Times, 83; Berton, *Marching*, 556-557

71 Berton, My Times, 76-77

72 Knightley, 355

73 Hastings, Korea, 282

74 Knightley, 344-349, 353-356

75 Price, 236-237

76 Pearson Memoirs Vol 2, 149-164

77 Hastings, Korea, 420-421

78 Hastings, Korea, 424

79 Charles Taylor, *Snow Job: Canada, the United States and Vietnam (1954-1973)*, (Toronto: House of Anansi Press, 1974) (hereafter, Taylor)

80 Victor Levant, *Quiet Complicity: Canadian Involvement in the Vietnam War*, (Toronto: Between the Lines, 1986) (hereafter, Levant)

81 Levant, i-ii

82 Price, 118-122

83 Price, 204

84 Price, 207-208

85 Levant, 41-46

86 For the definitive, and riveting account of the tragic fate of the French and colonial defenders, *See,* Bernard Fall, *Hell in a Very Small Place: The Siege of Dien Bien Phu* (Harper & Row 1967)

87 Price, 229

88 Russian and China were also represented. Pearson recalls that an American general reproached him for having any contact with the Chinese, ignoring the fact that the Russians were also brushing them off. Pearson failed to see this as an early sign that American propaganda about monolithic communism was a fantasy. Alex I. Inglis and John A. Munro (Eds.) *Mike, The Memoirs of the Right Honourable Lester B. Pearson Volume 3,* (Toronto: University of Toronto Press 1975), 120-121 (hereafter, Pearson Memoirs Vol 3)

89 Levant, 44-45

90 Taylor, 5-9

91 Levant, 45, 121-129

92 Price, 298

93 Levant, 41-46

94 Levant, 192-196

95 Levant, 4-6

96 Levant, 46-48

97 Engler, 124-125

98 McKay and Swift, 154-155

99 Engler, 125

100 Taylor, vii-viii

101 Levant, 177-181, 193-196; Taylor, 57, 80-85; Engler, 125

102 Levant, 174-177

103 Levant, 204-205

104 Levant, 54-61; Taylor, 120-124

105 Levant, 211-250

106 Taylor, 84

107 Levant, 46

108 Taylor, i-v

109 Levant, 2-12; Taylor, 122

110 Levant, 29

111 Levant, 15-16; Taylor, 25

112 Pearson Memoirs Vol 3, 138-141; Levant, 196-198; Taylor, 38-39

113 Levant, 231-25.

114 *People's History Vol 2,* 224-225

115 Edward Wilson, "Thank You Vasili Arkipov, the man who stopped nuclear war," *The Guardian*, October 27, 2012

116 http://www.msn.com/en-us/news/world/russian-who-saved-the-world-recalls-his-decision-as-50-50/ar-AAep6NJ

117 Taylor, 186

Chapter VI

Peacekeeping

1 Sean M. Maloney, *Canada and UN Peacekeeping: Cold War by Other Means 1945-1970,* (St. Catherines: Vanwell Publishing Ltd., 2002) (hereafter, Maloney)

2 Maloney, xi

3 Dr. Maloney spent time with Canadian forces in Afghanistan and placed himself at risk to write three books in support of the effort there. *See, Enduring the Freedom: A Rogue Historian in Afghanistan,* (Potomac Books Inc., 2005); *Confronting the Chaos: A Rogue Historian Returns to Afghanistan,* (U.S. Naval Institute Press, 2009); *Fighting for Afghanistan: A Rogue Historian at War,* (U.S. Naval Institute Press, 2011)

4 Maloney, 2-3

5 Maloney, xii

6 Maloney, ix-xiii

7 Maloney, 6

8 Alex J. Bellamy and Paul D. Williams, *Understanding Peacekeeping,* (Cambridge: Polity Press 2010) (hereafter, Bellamy and Williams)

9 Bellamy and Williams, 47-56

10 http://www.theglobeandmail.com/arts/books-and-media/review-a-soldier-first-by-rick-hillier/article1348130/

11 Bellamy and Williams, 363

12 McKay and Swift, 181

13 Bellamy and Williams, 32, 44-45

14 Maloney, 6; Bellamy and Williams, 8-9

15 Douglas Roche, *Peacemakers, How People Around the World are Building a World Free of War,* (Toronto: James Lorimer & Company Ltd. 2014), 28 (hereafter, Roche). The speaker was Harvard Professor Steven

Pinker, author of *The Better Angels of Our Nature: The Decline of Violence and its Causes*, (UK: Penguin Group 2011)

16 Bellamy and Williams, 1-3

17 Bellamy and Williams, 34-35; Roche, 19, 22

18 Lee Berthiaume, "Canada absent on illegal arms", *Vancouver Sun*, October 2d, 2015

19 Canada now the second biggest arms exporter to Middle East, data show, *The Globe and Mail*, July 12, 2016; The secret Saudi memo: Dissecting how the document contradicts what Ottawa has said, *The Globe and Mail*, April 18, 2016

20 Roche, 17-26

21 Roche, 29-30, 83

22 Bellamy and Williams, 29-32

23 Thor Frohn-Nielsen and Thomas Thorner, (Eds.), *A Country Nourished on Self-Doubt: Documents in Post-Confederation Canadian History* (Toronto: University of Toronto Press, 2010), 413

24 Bellamy and Williams, 36-41

25 Bellamy and Williams, 173-179

26 Berton, *Marching*, 583-585

27 *Pearson Memoirs, Vol 2*, 274

28 *Pearson Memoirs, Vol 2*, 212-217; For maps showing the continuous shrinkage of Palestine from 1947-2012, see the final unnumbered page of Miko Peled, *The General's Son Journey of an Israeli in Palestine*, (Charlottesville: Just World Publishing, LLC 2012) (hereafter, Peled)

29 Peled finds that Ben-Gurion wanted nothing but war from the start. Peled, 38. Current Israeli Prime Minister Benjamin Netanyahu is a firm subscriber to Ben-Gurion's "ten teeth for a tooth" approach. In 2014, his military killed nearly 2,000 civilians in the illegally controlled Gaza Strip in retaliation for the killing of three Israeli civilians. "Gaza conflict: Israel to pursue 'campaign' as truce ends, http://www.bbc.com/news/world-middle-east-28648242

30 *Pearson Memoirs, Vol 2*, 218-219

31 Bellamy and Williams, 179; *Pearson Memoirs, Vol 2*, 225-226; Berton, *Marching*, 581

32 McKay and Swift, 147

33 Bellamy and Williams, 180; *Pearson Memoirs, Vol 2*, 229-237; Maloney, 62

34 Maloney, 62; *Pearson Memoirs, Vol 2*, 228, 256

35 *Pearson Memoirs, Vol 2*, 247-251; Berton, *Marching*, 581-583; Maloney, 63

36 *Pearson Memoirs, Vol 2*, 229, 247; McKay and Swift, 148

37 Bellamy and Williams, 50-51, 180; *Pearson Memoirs, Vol 2*, 240, 253-254; Maloney, 63

38 McKay and Swift, 81-82, 140

39 *Pearson Memoirs, Vol 2*, 262

40 McKay and Swift, 147

41 *Pearson Memoirs, Vol 2*, 242, 257-271; Maloney, 67; McKay and Swift, 150

42 Bellamy and Williams, 182; Maloney, 70

43 Maloney, 71-72

44 Maloney, 66-67; Peled, 39-40, 43-45, 48; *Pearson Memoirs, Vol 2*, 272

45 Maloney, 76

46 *Pearson Memoirs, Vol 2, 274*

47 Roche, 76

48 McKay and Swift, 209

49 Scott Taylor and Brian Nolan, *Tested Mettle: Canada's Peacekeepers at War*, (Ottawa: Esprit De Corps Books, 1998), (hereafter, Taylor and Nolan)

50 Maloney, 188-198

51 Maloney, 191, 195

52 Maloney, 199-203; Bellamy and Williams, 183

53 Bellamy and Williams, 184; Maloney, 203-206

54 Maloney, 209-210

55 Bellamy and Williams, 184-185

56 Taylor and Nolan, 19-23

57 Taylor and Nolan, 248

58 Bellamy and Williams, 185

59 "Canadian peacekeeping mission in Cyprus", *Cypris Daily*, March 20, 2014, http://incyprus.philenews.com/en-gb/local-features/4409/40588/canadian-peacekeeping-mission-in-cyprus.

60 Bellamy and Williams, 193-194

61 Bellamy and Williams, 197-202

62 MacMillan, *Paris 1919*, 111-124

63 Taylor and Nolan, 41-44; Lewis MacKenzie, *Peacekeeper: The Road to Sarajevo*, (Madiera Park: Douglas & McIntyre 1993), 100-102, 118-119, (hereafter, MacKenzie)

64 Taylor and Nolan, 45-47; MacKenzie, 106-107

65 Taylor and Nolan, 54-55

66 Taylor and Nolan, 80, 96; This was dangerous business. An earlier convoy escorted by a French unit had failed when its vehicles hit land mines, which could have been remotely detonated. The blast injured the only medical officer assigned to the contingent in Sarajevo, the UN having declined to fund a casualty unit. MacKenzie, 205, 231, 247, 296-297, 311-316

67 Taylor and Nolan, 53, 86

68 MacKenzie, 248-264

69 MacKenzie, 265-287; Taylor and Nolan, 55-56

70 Taylor and Nolan, 60-61, 69-70

71 Canada, House of Commons, Bill C-533, 2010; Encyclopaedia Brittanica, *Srebrenica Massacre,* http://www.britannica.com/EBchecked/topic/1697253/Srebrenica-massacre.

72 Taylor and Nolan, 100-104: Bellamy and Williams, 201-202

73 Taylor and Nolan, 150-151

74 Taylor and Nolan, 123-140

75 Taylor and Nolan, 141

76 MacKenzie, 288-323

77 McKay and Swift, 220

78 MacKenzie, 334

79 Patrice McMahon and Jon Western, "The Death of Dayton: How to Stop Bosnia from Falling Apart, *Foreign Affairs,* September/October 2009; Jasmina Kuzmanovic, "Bosnia Federation Calls for Early Vote After Violent Clash, *Bloomberg News,* February 10, 2014

80 Bellamy and Williams, 202-206

81 Samantha Power, "Bystanders to Genocide," *Atlantic Magazine*, Sept 2001, (hereafter Power); For an authoritative account of life in Rwanda before, during and after the genocide, *See* Philip Gourevitch, *We wish to inform you that tomorrow we will be killed with our families,* Stories from Rwanda (NY Farrar, Strous and Giroux 1998)

82 Romeo Dallaire, *Shake Hands With the Devil The Failure of Humanity in Rwanda,* (Toronto: Random House Canada, 2003) (hereafter Dallaire)

83 Dallaire, 47; Philip Gourevitch, *We wish to inform you that tomorrow we will be killed with our families, Stories from Rwanda* (New York: Picador 1998), 47-53

84 Power, 4: Dallaire, 47-48, 53-54

85 Dallaire, 44-45, 56, 71-76, 87-88; Bellamy and Williams, 203

86 Power, 5

87 Bellamy and Williams, 223-226; Power, 9.

88 Engler, 198-199

89 McKay and Swift, 196-206; Taylor and Nolan, 81-83, 87-90, 93-98

90 Power, 5-6; Dallaire, 231; Bellamy and Williams, 204

91 Power, 6-8; Dallaire, 221-262

92 Dallaire, 255

93 Power, 8

94 Clinton Library, *Presidential Decision Directive/NSC-25*, May 3, 1994 (Emphasis added)

95 Bellamy and Williams, 204; Power, 13-17, 18, 21-23; Dallaire, 44, 272

96 Power, 20

97 Power, 11-13

98 Power, 20; Bellamy and Williams, 203;Taylor and Nolan, 185-186

99 Power, 32-33; Dallaire, xvi

100 Bellamy and Williams, 132 (Emphasis added)

101 Bellamy and Williams, 129-137, 340

102 Roche, 83-84; Bellamy and Williams, 338-344

103 Larry D. Johnson, weblog entry "Uniting for Peace": Does it Still Serve any Useful Purpose?"*American Society of International Law AJIL Unbound*, posted July 15, 2014, http://www.asil.org/blogs/percentE 2percent80percent9Cuniting-peacepercentE2percent80percent9D-does-it-still-serve-any-useful-purpose; Frederick L. Kirgis, weblog entry, "He Got it Almost Right," *American Society of International Law AJIL Unbound*, posted July 16, 2014, http://www.asil.org/blogs/he-got-it-almost-right.

104 Coalition to Oppose the Arms Trade, http://www.coat.ncf.ca ; *Sales of Canadian guns, ammunition surge overseas*, http://www.cbc.ca/news/world/sales-of-canadian-guns-ammunition-surge-overseas-1.2456022 ; Richard Sanders, "Pension funds force Canadians to invest in war industries,"Canadian Centre for Policy Alternatives (CCPA) *Monitor*, Vol. 19, No. 3, July/August 2012, 7

Chapter VII

Afghanistan

1 Linda McQuaig, *Holding the Bully's Coat, Canada and the U.S. Empire*, (Doubleday Canada 2007), 76 (hereafter, McQuaig)
2 Janice Gross Stein and Eugene Lang, *The Unexpected War Canada in Kandahar*, (Viking Canada 2007), (hereafter, Stein and Lang)
3 Peter Tomsen, *The Wars of Afghanistan, Messianic Terrorism, Tribal Conflicts and the Failures of Great Powers* (New York: Public Affairs 2011) (hereafter, Tomsen)
4 Tomsen, 38-39
5 Tomsen, 41
6 Tomsen, 41-44, 70-72
7 Stein and Lang, 21-24
8 Tomsen, 104-146, 159-178, 247
9 Stein and Lang, 24-32
10 Tomsen, 201
11 Tomsen, 38, 45-58
12 Engler, 43-44
13 Engler, 44
14 Greg Weston, Canada Offered to Aid Iraq Invasion: Wikileaks (CBC) http://www.cbc.ca/news/politics/weston-canada-offered-to-aid-iraq-invasion-wikileaks-1.1062501 May 15, 2011; Stein and Lang, 79-90
15 McQuaig, 91-95
16 Stein and Lang, 15
17 Stein and Lang, 1
18 Stein and Lang, 13-14
19 Stein and Lang, 18-20
20 Stein and Lang, 40-51, 65-72
21 Stein and Lang, 104-107; McQuaig, 96, 102
22 Stein and Lang, 100-102
23 Stein and Lang, 96
24 Stein and Lang, 106-108
25 Stein and Lang, 136
26 Stein and Lang, 97-98, 107, 134-138
27 Stein and Lang, 126
28 Stein and Lang, 117-129, 159-171

29 Stein and Lang, 147-148, 180-193, 196-198

30 Stein and Lang, 202; McKay and Swift, 225

31 Stein and Lang, 230-244; McQuaig, 41-42, 77, 106, 241-243; "Commons votes to extend Afghanistan mission to 2011", *Vancouver Sun*, March 14, 2008; "Canada marks end of Afghan mission", Victoria *Times-Colonist*, March 13, 2014; "Afghan forces prepare to fight alone as foreign troops leave", (Reuters), October 28, 2014; "Last soldier returns from Afghanistan", Victoria *Times*-Colonist, March 20, 2014

32 Stein and Lang, 274

33 McKay and Swift, 232

34 Engler, 155-156

35 Stein and Lang, 198-201

36 Tobi Cohen, "Troops inspire Governor General", Victoria *Times-Colonist*, December 29, 2010

37 McQuaig, 101-102; McKay and Swift, 223-224; Engler, 225

38 Asad Ismi, "An Interview with Afghan MP Malalai Joya: Karzai Government Treats Women as Brutally as Did the Taliban", in *Afghanistan and Canada Is There an Alternative to War?* Lucia Kowaluk and Steven Staples, (Eds.), (Black Rose Books 2009), 228-233 (hereafter, *Alternative to War*)

39 Stein and Lang, 201,239; McQuaig, 75

40 McKay and Swift, 258

41 "Canada marks end of Afghan mission", (Canadian Press), Victoria *Times-Colonist*, March 13, 2014

42 Stein and Lang, 282

43 McQuaig, 17-19, 46-56

44 Arendt, 126

45 Andrew Cohen, "Contradictory and incoherent foreign policy", Victoria *Times-Colonist*, December 4, 2013, A10

46 McQuaig, 104

47 48 John Foster, "What Our Leaders Won't Tell Us: Afghanistan Vital to U.S. as a Natural Gas Pipeline Route"; John Foster, "A Pipeline through a Troubled Land; Afghanistan, John Foster, "What Our Leaders Won't Tell Us: Afghanistan Vital to U.S. as a Natural Canada, and the New Great Energy Game", in *Alternative to War*, 241-272; Engler, 151-152; McKay and Swift, 273

48 Canadian Casualties in Afghanistan, http://www.ctv.ca.war January 14, 2011

49 "Families of Afghan war casualties may have travel covered to commemoration", Victoria *Times-Colonist,* April 4, 2014, A6; "Confusion surrounds Afghan commemoration", (Canadian Press), Victoria *Times-Colonist,* April 23, 2014, A10; "Afghan Tribute Rejected", (Canadian Press), Victoria *Times-Colonist,* March 18, 2014

50 Murray Brewster, "Soldier attempts suicide after being told PTSD will end military career", (Canadian Press), http://www.ctvnews. ca/canada/soldier-attempts-suicide-after-being-told-ptsd-will-end-military-career-1.1573087 December 3, 2013; "DND reverses decision on extended release for soldier with PTSD", (Canadian Press), http:// www.cbc.ca/news/canada/edmonton/dnd-reverses-decision-on-extended-release-for-soldier-with-ptsd-1.2631754 May 4, 2014; "Compassion sought for suicidal soldier", (Canadian Press) Victoria *Times-Colonist,* May 6, 2014; David Bitoni, "Cumbersome red tape creating care shortage for Canada's soldiers; watchdog", http://ctvnews. ca/politics/cumbersome-red-tape-creating-care-shortage-for-canada-s-soldiers-watchdog-1.1568891 (CTV News) December 1, 2013

51 "Legion presses for reversal of clawbacks Compensation for vets sought", (Canadian Press) Victoria *Times-Colonist,* January 25, 2014, B7; "Ottawa is failing veterans, advocates say", (Canadian Press) Victoria *Times,* April 9, 2014, A8; Michael Prince, "Restore the social contract with our veterans", Victoria *Times-Colonist,* August 9, 2013, A15; Paul Robinson, "There is no 'sacred duty' to Canada's veterans", Victoria *Times-Colonist,* August 7, 2013, A7

52 Alyssa Fetini, "A Brief History of Gitmo", *Time,* November 12, 2008

53 "United Nations Economic and Social Council, Report on Economic, Social and Political Rights—Situation of Detainees at Guantanamo Bay", February 15, 2006

54 University of Toronto Faculty of Law, Bora Laskin Law Library, *Khadr Case Resource Page,* http://library.law.utoronto.ca/ khadr-case-resources-page

55 Colin Perkel, "Secret memo pokes hole in Khadr case", (Canadian Press) *Vancouver Sun,* July 3, 2014, B2

56 Colin Perkel, "U.S. court ruling adds ammo to Omar Khadr appeal of war crimes convictions", (Canadian Press), *The Globe and Mail,* June 12, 2015

57 Colin Perkel, "Omar Khadr prison interview rejected by cabinet minister", www.*thestar.com* (Canadian Press), April 28, 2013;

Michelle Sheppard, "Khadr interview would require prison lockdown Corrections Canada says", www.*thestar.com* (Canadian Press), October 2, 2014; Colin Perkel, "Omar Khadr wins right to expand lawsuit against Ottawa", www.*thestar.com* (Canadian Press), October 23, 2014; Thomas Walkom, "Gracious, respectful Omar Khadr confounds Harper government stereotype", *The Star.com,* May 8, 2015

58 Michael Den Tandt, "Omar Khadr belongs in Canada, in prison", *Vancouver Sun,* October 1, 2012, B1

59 "Maher Arar, interviewed by Amy Goodman of *Democracy Now!*", June 13, 2011 http://www.democracynow.org/2011/6/13/maher_arar_my_rendition_torture_in

60 Government of Canada, Commission of Inquiry into the Actions of Canadian Officials in relation to Maher Arar, *Analysis and Reccommendations;*http://publications.gc.ca/site/eng/295791/publication.html ; McQuaig, 243-254; "Canadian Inquiry Finds Torture Survivor Maher Arar Completely Innocent, Criticizes U.S. for 'Rendition' to Syria", *Democracy Now!,* September 19, 2006; Jeff Sallot, "How Canada failed citizen Maher Arar", *The Globe and Mail,* September 19, 2006 http://www.democracynow.org/2006/9/19/canadian_inquiry_finds_torture_survivor_maher

61 Stein and Lang, 246-258

62 "Afghan detainees torture issue returns to Commons", (CTV News Staff) http://news.sympatico.ctv.ca/abc.home/contentposting.aspx?isfa=1&feedname=CTV-TO November 18, 2009; Juliet O'Neill, "Hillier 'trivializing' torture, lawyer says", Victoria *Times-Colonist,* December 29, 2009; "Afghan prisoner controversy fades", (Canadian Press) *Victoria Times-Colonist,* March 11, 2014

63 http://www.cbc.ca/news/cia-torture-report-why-canada-can-t-claim-innocence-1.2867716

64 http://www.msn.com/en-us/news/world/doctors-without-border-says-us-airstrike-hit-hospital-in-afghanistan-at-least-19-dead/ar-AFf4xa5

Chapter VIII

Staying Out

1 Elizabeth May, *Who We Are, Reflections on My Life and Canada,* (Vancouver: Greystone Books 2014) (hereafter, May)

2 Michael Harris, *Party of One, Stephen Harper and Canada's Radical Makeover* (Toronto: Penguin Canada Books 2014) (hereafter, Harris)

3 May, 86-88

4 Harris, 30

5 Promoting world peace is said by 90 percent of recently polled Canadians to be the country's most important objective. McKay and Swift, 294. Even allowing for a segment supporting bombing one's way to peace, the Harper government appetite for wars appears to have far exceeded that of the public.

6 Harris, 20-22

7 Harris, 76-103, 107

8 Noah Richler, *What We Talk About When We Talk About War* (Fredericton: Goose Lane Editions 2012) (hereafter, Richler)

9 Richler, 55-61

10 Richler, 91

11 Richler, 164-167

12 "Mulcair: Ottawa shooter was no terrorist", (Canadian Press) Victoria *Times-Colonist,* October 30, 2014, A9

13 "Ottawa shooter had religious, political motives", (Canadian Press) Victoria *Time-Colonist,* October 28, 2014, A10; Glen McGregor, "Exchange suggests ideological motive" (Postmedia News) *Vancouver Sun,* October 29, 2014, B2

14 "U.S.-led air strikes killed 521 fighters, 32 civilians in Syria: monitor", (Reuters) http://www.misn.com/en-us/news/other/us-led-air-strikes-killed-521-fighters-32-civilians-in-syria-monitor/ar-BBarGMoM

15 Peggy Mason, "Harper's war plan might make matters worse", Victoria *Times-Colonist,* October 9, 2014, A11

16 University of Maryland Global Terrorism Database, http://www.start.umd.edu/gtd/search/Results.aspx?chart=country&search=Canada

17 McKay and Swift, 217-220

18 Richler, 201-202, 283, 291-293

19 Ken Meaney, "Veteran's death at age 109 marks end of an era", Victoria *Times-Colonist*, February 19, 2010, A2

20 "Generations strive to emulate First World War vets: PM", (CTV News) April 24, 2010 http://ctv.ca/home/contentposting. aspx?feedname=CTV-TOPSTORIES V3

21 Richler, 170-174

22 Metro Goldwyn Mayer Studios, *The Americanization of Emily*, 1964

23 Benjamin Isitt, "Unlearned lessons from First World War", Victoria *Times-Colonist*, May 1, 2010

24 Richler, 173-174

25 James O'Dea, *Cultivating Peace Becoming a 21st-Century Peace Ambassador*, (Shift Books 2012) 25-26 (hereafter, O'Dea)

26 O'Dea, 29

27 Taylor and Nolan, 243-254

28 Richler, 348-357

29 McKay and Swift, 290

Printed in the United States
By Bookmasters